The Carolina Curriculum for Infants and Toddlers with Special Needs

Second Edition

by

Nancy M. Johnson-Martin, Ph.D.
Adjunct Professor
School of Education
University of North Carolina at Chapel Hill

Kenneth G. Jens, Ph.D.
Center for Development and Learning
and
School of Education
University of North Carolina at Chapel Hill

Susan M. Attermeier, M.A., P.T.
Center for Development and Learning
and
Division of Physical Therapy
University of North Carolina at Chapel Hill

and

Bonnie J. Hacker, M.H.S., O.T.R.
Developmental Consultants
Durham, North Carolina

·P·A·U·L·H·
BROOKES
PUBLISHING CO.

Baltimore • London • Toronto • Sydney

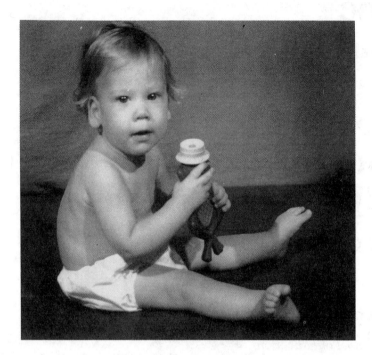

The Carolina Curriculum for Infants and Toddlers with Special Needs

Paul H. Brookes Publishing Co.
P.O. Box 10624
Baltimore, Maryland 21285-0624

Typeset by Brushwood Graphics, Inc., Baltimore, Maryland.
Manufactured in the United States of America by
Victor Graphics, Baltimore, Maryland.

Third printing, November 1994.

The Carolina Curriculum for Infants and Toddlers with Special Needs was produced under the auspices of the CHILD Project, a demonstration project located at Duke University Medical Center, Durham, North Carolina, and funded by the Handicapped Children's Early Education Program of the U.S. Office of Special Education and Rehabilitation Services. The content, however, does not necessarily reflect the position or policy of OSERS or Duke University and no official endorsement of these materials should be inferred.

The first edition of this book was titled *The Carolina Curriculum for Handicapped Infants and Infants At Risk.*

The Assessment Log and Developmental Progress charts found on pages 47–67 are also available for purchase in packages of 10. There is also an Assessment Log for the age range of 12 months to 3 years. These materials may be ordered from Paul H. Brookes Publishing Co., P.O. Box 10624, Baltimore, Maryland 21285-0624 (1-800-638-3775).

Also available as a companion volume is: *The Carolina Curriculum for Preschoolers with Special Needs,* by Nancy M. Johnson-Martin, Susan M. Attermeier, and Bonnie Hacker. It may be ordered from Paul H. Brookes Publishing Co., P.O. Box 10624, Baltimore, Maryland 21285-0624 (1-800-638-3775).

Library of Congress Cataloging-in-Publication Data
The Carolina curriculum for infants and toddlers with special needs /
  Nancy M. Johnson-Martin . . . [et al.].—2nd ed.
    p. cm.
  Rev. ed. of: The Carolina curriculum for handicapped infants and infants at risk / Nancy Johnson-Martin, Kenneth G. Jens, Susan Attermeier. c1986.
    Includes bibliographical references and index.
    ISBN 1-55766-074-3
    1. Handicapped children—Rehabilitation. 2. Handicapped children—Development. 3. Infants—Development. 4. Handicapped children—Education (Preschool)—United States—Curricula. I. Johnson-Martin, Nancy M., 1934– II. Johnson-Martin, Nancy M., 1934– Carolina curriculum for handicapped infants and infants at risk.
RJ138.C39 1991
618.92—dc20   91-13644
                                                                         CIP

Contents

Contents

Acknowledgments

WE ARE GRATEFUL to the staffs of the Clinical Center for the Study of Development and Learning, University of North Carolina at Chapel Hill, and the CHILD Project, Duke University, for their encouragement and support in the development of these materials. Susan Shier, M.S., made an important contribution to this curriculum by offering suggestions about adaptations for children with visual impairments. Sara Carter, CCC-Sp, provided major assistance in the development of the language section. Debra Watkins and Alfreida Stevens showed patience and persistence, as always, in typing the manuscript. We also owe a particular debt to Barbara Davis Goldman, Ph.D., whose enthusiasm about the conversations, learning, and capabilities of young children significantly affected our thinking as we developed the cognitive, language, and social sections of this curriculum.

We are also indebted to the children we serve and their parents; they have taught us most of what we know.

Finally, we would like to thank our various spouses and children for putting up with us as we completed this project.

chapter 1

Introduction

THE PAST TWO decades have witnessed rapid growth in the number of programs available to infants and toddlers with disabilities in the United States. Such growth has been fostered by the increasing evidence that proves that these infants and toddlers with disabilities are ready and able to learn. Furthermore, society is becoming aware that all children with disabilities need, and have the right to, an appropriate education made available through government supported early intervention programs, material development, and efficacy research. With the passage of Public Law 99-457 (Education of the Handicapped Act Amendments of 1986), Congress gave official recognition to the importance of intervention during infancy and the preschool years. By providing new incentives to states for the development of services to young children with disabilities and their families, this statute ensures that early intervention services will expand and prosper.

Historically, infant intervention programs have varied widely from community to community and from state to state. Many have been closely associated with university, medical, or rehabilitation centers and staffed by professionals from a variety of special areas, most commonly physical and occupational therapists, special educators, and communicative disorders specialists. Other intervention programs have been outgrowths of community-based day care programs for older individuals with disabilities and have primarily been staffed by volunteers, parents, or para-professionals who have relatively little formal training in special education or infant development. More recently, there has been a rapid growth in intervention programs staffed by "developmental specialists" or "early childhood special educators," who are responsible for individualized intervention programs with some consultation with other specialists, usually therapists. This situation created a need for comprehensive curricular materials that could be implemented by interventionists with widely differing training and skills. The first edition of this curriculum, *The Carolina Curriculum for Handicapped Infants and Infants at Risk* (CCHI) (Johnson-Martin, Jens, & Attermeier, 1986), was developed to serve this purpose.

As states move toward full implementation of Public Law 99-457, it is likely that intervention programs and staff training will become more uniform. It is also likely, however, that infants and toddlers with disabilities will continue to receive much of their intervention from caregivers, such as parents and day care providers, who will continue to bring a wide range of knowledge and skills to the task. Therefore, the need for a relatively simple, but comprehensive, curriculum will not diminish. Based on their experiences as early interventionists and trainers of both parents and other interventionists, the authors believe that, regardless of training, few interventionists or parents feel fully confident of their ability to provide appropriate and comprehensive intervention programs for the infants and toddlers who are entrusted to their care, given the extreme variability in these children's characteristics. Generally, these interventionists feel reasonably confident when dealing with children with mild to moderate disabilities whose development proceeds along a relatively normal course, but at a slower rate. These youngsters do not present major problems in either daily care or assessment and intervention. However, assuming responsibility for the intervention of children with severe and multiple disabilities who show markedly atypical patterns of development is another matter. Therefore, it is important that all interventionists have access to curricular materials that will not only enhance these children's development, but give the interventionists greater confidence in serving this group of children.

OBSERVATIONS ON CURRICULA

Curricula have been developed for use with children at risk for socioculturally related developmental delays, with specific etiological conditions, and, in some cases, with a broad range of disabilities. Although few curricula have been empirically tested and validated (Bailey & Wolery, 1984), procedures that are appropriate to the validation process are available (Wolery, 1983), and the value of the process to consumers is acknowledged. A review of curriculum materials available for use with infants and toddlers with disabilities has been provided by Bailey, Jens, and Johnson (1983).

Curricula that have been developed for children who are perceived as being at risk because of socioeconomic factors tend to be experiential in nature. They generally provide play and interactional activities that should be fostered at various developmental stages (e.g., Karnes, 1981; Sparling & Lewis, 1981) and emphasize the development of positive parenting behaviors (Bromwich, 1981). Materials of this nature, as well as some that have been developed for children with Down syndrome (e.g., Hanson, 1977), assume that development will follow a relatively normal course, with motor, language, cognitive, and social skills emerging relatively evenly—an assumption that is not generally true for young children with severe or multiple disabilities. As is generally acknowledged by their authors, these curricula would require extensive revision and expansion to be considered for use with a population of children with severe disabilities.

Materials developed for children with fairly specific developmental problems usually focus on those aspects of their development that are most obviously affected. For example, the materials for children with hearing impairments concentrate on the development of language (Northcott, 1977), autistic-like characteristics follow a specific mode of therapy (Bachrach, Mosley, Swindle, & Wood, 1978), motor disabilities discuss handling and positioning (Finnie, 1975), and visual impairments address sensory stimulation (Bortner, Jones, Simon, & Goldblatt, 1978).

A number of curricula, or assessment tools used as curricular sequences, have also been developed for use with children who have a broad range of disabilities. These curricula are essentially restructured lists of items that have been taken from existing assessment instruments, with items typically sequenced according to the mean ages at which normal children master these skills. Examples of curricular sequences developed in this manner are the *Hawaii Early Learning Profile* (Furuno et al., 1979), *Helping Your Exceptional Baby* (Cunningham & Sloper, 1980), and the *Portage Guide to Early Education* (Bluma, Shearer, Frohman, & Hillard, 1976). The atypical development of many youngsters with disabilities makes it unlikely that they will master skills in the sequences provided by these curricula. Therefore, it is frequently necessary to modify the sequences to fit the unique sensory and motor capabilities of each child. In addition, a significant number of children with severe and/or multiple disabilities will never develop certain desirable skills that are included in "normal" developmental sequences (e.g., talking, walking). Unless attention is directed to teaching skills that might provide alternative adaptive behaviors (e.g., shaping skills necessary for an augmentative communication system), these children are not adequately served by these curricula.

Some curricula (e.g., Meier & Malone, 1979; Schafer & Moersch, 1981) have attempted to deal with the problem of atypical development by identifying each item within a domain as belonging to one or more subgroups in that domain. But for the most part, the issue of teaching alternative adaptive behaviors to children with severe disabilities has generally been ignored in developmental curricula.

With the exception of a few Piagetian-based curricula, the theoretical orientation and underlying assumptions of curricula are rarely made explicit. In addition, there is a dearth of empirical information about the efficacy of these curricula for young children.

THE CCHI APPROACH

In reaction to the above observations, the following characteristics were incorporated into *The Carolina Curriculum for Handicapped Infants and Infants At Risk* (CCHI).

1. The curriculum was based on normal sequences of development, but did not assume that there would be relatively even development across domains (e.g., a child may exhibit normal cognitive development along with very delayed motor development). Thus, the curriculum was designed to be used with both the child who is developing slowly, but in a normal pattern, and the child with multiple disabilities whose patterns of development are markedly atypical.

2. The curriculum approached the problem of atypical development in two ways. First, the items in each developmental domain were subdivided into logical teaching sequences (i.e., a sequence in which item order is determined by how one skill builds on another, not by the mean age levels at which normal children learn the skills). Second, modifications of items were suggested in order to accommodate the child's particular sensory or motor limitations. Thus, a child with severely delayed motor abilities, but potentially average cognitive skills, is not "held up" in progressing through the cognitive domain because he or she cannot do items that require normal motor skills.

3. The curriculum was based on the recognition that most infants and toddlers with serious disabilities will never be "normal" in spite of intervention efforts. Thus, in treating these children, consideration must be given to teaching nonnormal, but highly adaptive, skills that temporarily or permanently replace normal skills,

when necessary. For example, should a child be unable to talk, it is appropriate to teach pointing or another indicator response that will allow him or her to make choices, communicate wishes, and so forth.

4. The curriculum made explicit the values and assumptions that the authors had chosen to emphasize when selecting the items for inclusion. Specifically, the curriculum was developmental, with many items being drawn from standard developmental assessment tools; the cognitive portions of the curriculum were based on Piagetian theory; behavioral theory and methodology were the foundation for item construction; and there was a strong emphasis on developing adaptive functional skills, even if these were not necessarily "normal" (e.g., moving by scooting on one's buttocks or using a scooter board when crawling or creeping is not functional).

5. The curriculum was field-tested in 22 intervention programs in North Carolina and in 10 national sites from Alaska to Maryland. Two different types of data were collected: questionnaire data on interventionists' perceptions of the usefulness of the curriculum, and data from progress charts that were used to measure the efficacy of the curriculum when implemented with children over a 6-month period. The data collected from the interventionists indicated that they could use the curriculum as intended and found it to be useful both for assessing infants with disabilities and for developing their intervention programs. The major reservations of interventionists dealt with the curriculum's limitations when used with children who have severe and profound disabilities. Efficacy was assessed by comparing the progress that was made in sequences that were the focus of the intervention with that made in sequences that were not of utmost priority for each child during two 3-month periods. Statistically significant differences were found for the sequences that were the focus of intervention in groups of children who were characterized as having mild, moderate, severe, and profound disabilities. However, the amount of progress made by the children in the group with severe and profound disabilities was not of practical significance. The authors suggested that a 3-month period of assessment for this group of children was probably too short a time period to accurately gauge the curriculum's effectiveness.

WHY HAS THE CCHI BEEN REVISED?

A new edition of the CCHI was prompted by several factors. In response to numerous requests for an extension of the CCHI to reach preschool children, the authors developed *The Carolina Curriculum for Preschoolers with Special Needs* (CCPSN) (Johnson-Martin, Attermeier, & Hacker, 1990). However, in the process of developing the CCPSN, the authors saw a need to change the CCHI's order of sequences in an attempt to make them more congruent with those sequences that are included in the CCPSN. In addition, the authors believed that the CCHI should include more adaptations to accommodate particular handicapping conditions, similar to those included in the CCPSN. Furthermore, information in the literature and greater exposure to working with children using augmentative communication systems prompted the authors to want significant changes in the communication section of the CCHI. Finally, based on feedback from interventionists using the CCHI in home-based programs and based on experiences working with infants with disabilities in group care settings, the authors felt that more attention should be paid to instructions for integrating intervention activities into the child's daily routines. Thus, a second edition of the CCHI was developed and retitled *The Carolina Curriculum for Infants and Toddlers with Special Needs* (CCITSN).

DIFFERENCES BETWEEN THE CCHI AND THE CCITSN

Although the philosophy, theoretical biases, assessment procedures, and basic content of the CCHI and the new CCITSN are essentially the same, there are changes throughout this volume. Some of the changes will have little effect on the curriculum's users, such as the revision of the introductory chapters to make them more current, a lack of new field-test data for the second edition, format changes, and differences in the way in which criteria for mastering items are stated. Other changes may require some adjustment by interventionists who were familiar with the first edition. These changes include the following:

1. Both the number of curriculum sequences in the five developmental domains (i.e., Cognition, Communication, Social Adaptation, Fine Motor Skills, and Gross Motor Skills) and their content have been restructured and expanded. In addition, some have been re-named to provide more congruency with the CCPSN.
2. Major changes have been made in the sequences in the communication domain. The number of sequences had been reduced from 5 to 4. Items that were in sequence 12., Vocal Imitation, and sequence 10., Gestural Imitation in the first edition have been combined into one sequence in this edition—sequence 11., Imitation: Sound and Gestures—in recognition of the interdependent ways in which these skills develop in most children. By modifying the items in the first edition in the communication domain, the second edition is now able to accommodate children who may develop one kind of imitation more rapidly than others. Similarly, the Vocal Communication (sequence 13.) and Gestural Communication (sequence 11.) of the first edition have been combined, expanded, and then divided again into two new sequences: sequence 10., Prevocabulary/Vocabulary, and sequence 13., Conversation Skills. The Prevocabulary/Vocabulary sequence essentially teaches the child to learn to say, or otherwise use, symbols that stand for objects or events. The Conversation Skills sequence emphasizes the interpersonal nature of communication development and the development of functional communication—the pragmatics of preverbal as well as verbal communication.
3. The CCITSN systematically provides specific information about adapting intervention strategies for children with motor, visual, and hearing limitations.
4. With each item in the CCITSN, suggestions are provided for integrating intervention activities into normal daily routines with the dual intention of making intervention a more natural part of the child's life and ensuring greater generalization of learning.

FOR WHOM IS THE CCITSN INTENDED?

Both the CCHI and the CCITSN were designed to provide curricular intervention strategies that would be appropriate for use with children with disabilities who are functioning in the birth to 24-month developmental range. They were designed to be used by both professionals and paraprofessionals. The first edition has been used successfully by educators, psychologists, day care workers, public health nurses, physical and occupational therapists, and speech-language specialists. There is every reason to believe that the CCITSN can also be used by a wide range of individuals. To encourage such usage, a major effort has been made to avoid professional jargon in the wording of the materials. There has also been an effort throughout this edition, as well as the first, to alert users to the child's characteristics or responses that require attention from professionals with particular skills (e.g., a physical, occupational, or speech-language therapist).

Although both the CCHI and the CCITSN are appropriate for use in center- and home-based intervention programs, it is anticipated that parents and day care providers will use these curricula only with professional consultation and guidance.

HOW WERE ITEMS CHOSEN FOR THE CCITSN?

Basic content for both editions of the curriculum was selected in the same manner that it has been selected for most other infant curricula. That is, the developmental skills listed on a variety of norm-referenced tests of development were reviewed and pertinent skills were incorporated into this curriculum (e.g., Bayley, 1969; Cattell, 1940; Folio & Dubose, 1979; Knobloch & Pasamanick, 1974). To these basic items were added skills defined by one of the better-known tests of development based on Jean Piaget's theory—The Ordinal Scales of Psychological Development (Uzgiris & Hunt, 1975), skills in the tactile integration area on The Callier-Azusa Scale (Stillman, 1977), skills that the authors judged to be alternatives to "normal" activities for children with specific handicaps, skills from The Communicative Intention Inventory (Coggins & Carpenter, 1981) to broaden the focus of the communication section, and a few other skills that were considered to be important by the authors for social development and motivation. Specialists in speech-language, occupational, and physical therapy; nursing; psychology; education; and nutrition reviewed the lists of skills and contributed to the final selection process.

REFERENCES

Bachrach, A., Mosley, A., Swindle, F., & Wood, M. (1978). *Developmental therapy for young children with autistic characteristics.* Baltimore: University Park Press.

Bailey, D.B., Jens, K.G., & Johnson, N.M. (1983). Curricula for handicapped infants. In S.G. Garwood & R.R. Fewell (Eds.), *Educating handicapped infants,* (pp. 387–415). Rockville, MD: Aspen Publishers, Inc.

Bailey, D.B., & Wolery, M.R. (1984). *Teaching infants and preschoolers with handicaps.* Columbus, OH: Charles E. Merrill.

Bayley, N. (1969). *Bayley Scales of Infant Development.* New York: Psychological Corporation.

Bluma, A., Shearer, M., Frohman, A., & Hillard, J. (1976). *Portage guide to early education.* Portage, WI: The Portage Project, CESA 12.

Bortner, S., Jones, M., Simon, S., & Goldblatt, S. (1978). *Sensory stimulation kit: A teacher's guidebook.* Louisville, KY: American Printing House for the Blind.

Bromwich, R. (1981). *Working with parents and infants: An interactional approach.* Baltimore: University Park Press.

Cattell, P. (1940). *The measurement of intelligence of infants and young children*. New York: Psychological Corporation.

Coggins, T.E., & Carpenter, R.L. (1981). The Communicative Intention Inventory: A system for observing and coding children's early intentional communication. *Applied Psycholinguistics, 2*, 235–251.

Cunningham, C., & Sloper, P. (1980). *Helping your exceptional baby*. New York: Pantheon Books.

Finnie, N.R. (1975). *Handling the young cerebral palsied child at home* (2nd ed.). New York: E.P. Dutton.

Folio, M.R., & Dubose, R.F. (1979). *Peabody Developmental Motor Scales and Programmed Activities* (rev. ed.). Seattle: University of Washington.

Furuno, S., O'Reilly, K.A., Hosake, C.M., Inatsuka, T.T., Allman, T.L., & Zeisloft, B. (1979). *Hawaii Early Learning Profile*. Palo Alto, CA: VORT Corporation.

Hanson, M.J. (1977). *Teaching your Down's syndrome infant*. Baltimore: University Park Press.

Johnson-Martin, N.M., Attermeier, S.M., & Hacker, B. (1990). *The Carolina curriculum for preschoolers with special needs*. Baltimore: Paul H. Brookes Publishing Co.

Johnson-Martin, N., Jens, K.G., & Attermeier, S.M. (1986). *The Carolina curriculum for handicapped infants and infants at risk*. Baltimore: Paul H. Brookes Publishing Co.

Karnes, M.B. (1981). *Small wonder*. Circle Pines, MN: American Guidance Service.

Knobloch, H., & Pasamanick, B. (1974). *Gesell and Amatruda's developmental diagnosis* (3rd ed.). New York: Harper & Row.

Meier, J.H., & Malone, P.J. (1979). *Facilitating children's development*. Baltimore: University Park Press.

Northcott, W.H. (1977). *Curriculum guide: Hearing-impaired children, birth to three years, and their parents*. Washington, DC: Alexander Graham Bell Association for the Deaf.

Schafer, D.S., & Moersch, M.S. (Eds.). (1981). *Developmental programming for infants and young children*. Ann Arbor: University of Michigan Press.

Sparling, J., & Lewis, I. (1981). *Learning Games for the first three years*. New York: Walker & Co.

Stillman, R. (Ed.). (1977). *The Callier-Azusa Scale*. Dallas: Callier Center for Communication Disorders, University of Texas.

Uzgiris, I.C., & Hunt, J.M. (1975). *Assessment in infancy: Ordinal Scales of Psychological Development*. Urbana: University of Illinois Press.

Wolery, M. (1983). Evaluating curricula: Purposes and strategies. *Topics in Early Childhood Special Education, 2*(4), 15–24.

chapter 2

Guiding Learning

Principles and Suggestions

THE GOAL OF *The Carolina Curriculum for Infants and Toddlers with Special Needs* (CCITSN) is to provide assistance to early intervention personnel, families of children with disabilities, and other caregivers as they strive to optimize children's interactions with their world and the people in it. As O'Donnell and Ogle noted in *The Carolina Curriculum for Handicapped Infants and Infants at Risk* (CCHI) (Johnson-Martin, Jens, & Attermeier, 1986), interventionists and caregivers "have the unique and exciting opportunity to arrange experiences that will allow children to know that what they do, indeed, makes a difference on their surroundings" (p. 7).

Each item included in this curriculum is based on basic principles that have been found to be effective in teaching young children. This chapter is an attempt to summarize those principles. It includes the teaching suggestions provided by O'Donnell and Ogle in the first edition, as well as a few additional ones emphasized more in this new edition of the curriculum. A Recommended Readings list is provided at the end of the chapter for readers who desire further elaboration.

FOLLOW THE CHILD'S LEAD

Everyone learns best when interested in the subject matter and when given opportunities for "hands on" experiences; this is especially true of young children. They are constantly experimenting to see what effect their actions have on their environment. Their motivation for learning is derived from their success in producing effects on their physical and social environments. One of the greatest dangers of providing a curriculum for infants and toddlers with disabilities is that adults will become too directive, always seeking to teach the child specific skills on the adult's timetable, thereby reducing the child's natural exploration and initiative, and often disrupting the joyful social interactions that are a critical aspect of early personal and emotional development.

Therefore, one of the most important principles to remember in developing intervention plans for infants and toddlers (or older children functioning at that developmental level) is to integrate intervention with the children's immediate interests and

9

ongoing activities. For instance, if a child is picking up blocks and mouthing them, this is a good time to demonstrate some other activities that can be done with the blocks (e.g., putting them into a container, stacking them, hiding one under a box). Try to choose an activity that can be incorporated into the intervention plan. The child's interests can be guided by the materials that are provided, but it remains important to carefully attend to what the child is doing and to blend intervention activities into those interests.

When a child has severe or multiple disabilities, ongoing activities may be few and identification of interests will be difficult. In these situations, the caregiver will have to take a more active and creative role in stimulating the child's attention and interest. Materials may need to be modified to provide more intense or varied stimulation (e.g., brighter colors, louder or more unusual sounds, more extreme textures or temperatures). It remains important, however, to wait for some sign of attention or interest in the material before trying to teach the child to do something with it.

PROVIDE CHOICES

In the normal course of development, children begin making choices soon after birth and continue to make choices throughout their lives. Early choices are simple (e.g., whether to look at a toy or at a person, whether to continue sucking or to stop). As the child becomes more capable and more mobile, the choices that are available to him or her increase dramatically. In addition, the child becomes both more consciously aware of making choices and more invested in the choices that were made. Being able to make choices is an important aspect of developing a sense of control and mastery. It is also an important foundation for communication, an action that usually begins as a desire to get or reject something.

The more severe a child's disabilities, the more the range of natural choices is apt to be reduced. Caregivers often fall into the trap of doing what they think is best for a child without offering him or her any options. This can result in a passive child who has little need or desire to communicate. Regardless of a child's disabilities, caregivers should make a conscious effort to provide many choices throughout the day *and* should respect the child's decisions. For example, at mealtime, hold up juice in one hand and a spoonful of eggs in the other. Give the child whichever one he or she looks at or reaches toward. Even if this is accidental and not a "real choice," it is teaching the child that actions make a difference, and will lay the foundation for deliberate choices at a later time.

> *Note:* It is vital that a caregiver accept the child's decision once a choice has been offered. Therefore, the caregiver must offer choices between acceptable alternatives and must not have a preconceived notion about what the "right" choice for the child is.

Many behavioral problems in the "terrible twos" phase can be avoided by providing choices. If a child is given a choice between doing one activity or another, it is highly unlikely that both will be rejected, even if neither is generally a preferred activity (e.g., "Would you like to brush your teeth now or put on your pajamas?"). This is especially important to remember when you are trying to help a child learn something that is particularly difficult. Present materials that are related to two or three different intervention activities. Let the child choose one, then the other(s) in turn. You are thereby following the child's lead, giving him or her a sense of control, "listening" to his or her communication, and indicating your respect for him or her.

CONSEQUENCES COUNT

One of the most fundamental precepts of teaching is that consequences are important in maintaining or changing an individual's behavior. A consequence is merely an act that follows another act as an effect or a result of the former. Consequences can be powerful in strengthening or weakening specific behaviors. Stated simply, this means that when a child does something that is followed by a desirable or interesting action, he or she will be more likely to repeat or continue that behavior. For example, if the child pulls a string on a mobile and the mobile moves, he or she will be more likely to pull the string again than if there had been no effect.

Likewise, a behavior that is followed by an unpleasant event or experience or one that appears to have no effect on the child's environment at all, will probably decrease the behavior's frequency. This is the principle underlying the fact that some behaviors are best changed by ignoring them, by providing a mild reprimand, or by removing the child from an interesting place for a very short period (e.g., time out). For instance, if a child is removed from the presence of other youngsters for 2 minutes each time he or she tries to bite another child, it is likely that the biting behavior will be reduced or eliminated.

MAKE YOUR CONSEQUENCES EFFECTIVE

Promoting learning through the use of consequences sounds simple—and it is. However, some crucial aspects must be remembered if your consequences are to be effectively used.

1. Naturally occurring consequences are the most effective in teaching a child about his or her ability to bring about change in the environment. This is especially true for the young, or developmentally young, child. Consider the difference between the child who can make a mobile move by pulling a string and another child who receives candy for stacking two blocks. Both children may repeat these activities and, thus, "learn" them. However, the first child has learned how to affect his or her physical environment (i.e., move the mobile) and will not only repeat this action, but will experiment with it during other activities throughout the day. The second child has learned to complete a task in order to receive a candy from an adult and may have no interest in the given activity or other objects unless an adult is around to provide a treat. The more serious a child's disability, the more a caregiver may have to "set up" learning situations for him or her, so that interesting and desirable events happen when he or she interacts with the environment. For example, if a child has severe physical limitations, it may be necessary to select toys that produce effects with minimal movement on the part of the child or to introduce electronic switches that activate toys with minimal action.

2. Social consequences are powerful. From birth, children need attention and will repeat activities that result in adult attention. The adult who learns to attend to the child's desirable actions and to ignore his or her undesirable ones will experience fewer behavioral problems. Genuine excitement over a child's accomplishments (e.g., hugging the child when he or she takes the first independent step) is a good supplement to the more intrinsic sense of accomplishment in the child. Clapping, hugging, and other signs of approval are effective consequences, but should be used judiciously, primarily to provide support for learning difficult tasks where the more natural consequences may initially be hard to achieve or appreciate.

3. Social consequences are a natural result when teaching communication skills. Learning to communicate depends on a responsive listener. This begins with attending to the child's eye gaze (e.g., returning a gaze, responding to an object at which the child is looking) and proceeds through turn-taking "games" to conversations.

4. The same consequences will not be effective with all children. Children enjoy many different types of stimulation. The child in the previous example may be more interested in a mobile, while another child may rather play with a musical toy. Some children will respond more readily and positively to interactions with toys, while others may prefer social exchanges. The first step in identifying which actions work best with a child to elicit a response will be to *test* the different consequences.

5. Effective positive consequences must be changed often. Like adults, children become bored, and previously desired events or experiences become less exciting. For example, the child with the mobile may only pull its string for so long to get one effect. However, he or she will become interested again when the mobile is changed.

6. For a particular consequence to work in promoting or reducing behaviors, it must immediately follow the target behavior. This helps the child to perceive the relationship between what he or she does and what happened in the environment.

7. Furthermore, if a child is to understand this relationship between what he or she does and what happens, the consequence must *consistently* occur. Consistency is particularly important when a child is learning something new and when the caregiver is providing "undesirable" consequences for a child's negative behaviors. When trying to get rid of a behavior, the consequence must be employed *every time* the behavior occurs. For example, a child may become confused if he or she was excluded from group activities only some of the times that he or she tried to bite others.

    When the nature of a task makes it necessary to support or replace natural consequences with social consequences, food, and so forth, it is best to begin to assure the child that the consequence will occur each time he or she exhibits the behavior. Studies have shown, however, that after initial learning has taken place, positive consequences can occur less often and a behavior will be maintained, usually then supported by the natural consequences.

8. When children begin to understand language, the effectiveness of consequences can be increased by verbally explaining them. In this way, the child receives an additional clue about the way in which he or she affects the environment (e.g., "Pull the knob . . . see the television come on," "Give me your hands and I will pick you up," "Eat lunch and then we will go outside").

BREAK A TASK INTO SMALLER STEPS WHEN NECESSARY

Each of the items within the sequences in the CCITSN is arranged in order of expected difficulty for most children. They are set up in a logical teaching order. While the procedures of each item will be sufficient for most children, there will be times when it is necessary to break the task down into smaller steps in order to facilitate learning. Breaking it down may involve changing materials and/or separately teaching parts of the task. For example, if a child has difficulty releasing blocks so that they balance on one another and the task is to build a three-block tower with small blocks, one might start with two bristle blocks that will stick together regardless of extra movement as the child releases it. The child can then work up to three bristle blocks. When this concept is learned, two large plain blocks can be used, then three large blocks, then two small blocks, and ultimately three small blocks. Many suggestions for modification are included in the items, but they will not be adequate for every child. Creativity will be necessary on the part of the curriculum user.

PROVIDE SAMENESS AND CHANGE

Although it sounds contradictory, children need both sameness and change in their surroundings. Sameness gives the child a sense of security. The interventionist and caregivers should provide order and routine in the child's life; this helps the child learn that the world is, in part, predictable. The child learns what to expect from specific people and in what order daily routines such as bathing, eating, and dressing occur. He or she also learns what to expect from particular toys and may take great pleasure in repeating an activity long after it has become uninteresting or even irritating to the adult. Of course, routines are altered sometimes, but a sense of sameness helps the child learn to feel safe in his or her world and to trust his or her caregivers. Within this secure world, the child is then able to recognize changes and be interested in bringing them about.

"SET UP" SUCCESS

To ensure a child's continued willingness to interact with the environment and to make events happen in it, it is vital that he or she have continued successes at each of the small steps you teach. For instance, if you are teaching a child to reach for an object, such as a ball, be sure to have the ball close enough for the child to grasp without any difficulty. As you move the ball further away to encourage an extended reach, make sure that the ball *can* be reached. Children can be discouraged by a task that is too difficult and may become bored with one that is too easy. The activity should be a challenge, but not an impossibility.

BUILD LEARNING EXPERIENCES INTO DAILY ROUTINES

A child learns in all domains of development, every day. Although development may be relatively advanced in some areas and more delayed in others, the child has a possibility of learning something new in a number of areas with each activity. Playing pat-a-cake, for instance, involves gross motor, fine motor, cognitive, and social skills.

Similarly, interventionists and caregivers have the opportunity to encourage learning in every interaction with the child, whether it be during a specific time that is set aside for particular activities or during routine caregiving activities. In fact, there is ample evidence that shows that experiences that take place as a part of daily routines are more effective for teaching than those that are isolated in a specific teaching activity. For instance, a child who is learning to improve his or her grasp has many opportunities to practice this skill during the day (e.g., during dressing, eating, bathing, play).

ALLOW QUIET TIME

Like adults, all children need time to themselves (i.e., time to play by themselves or time to play with adults without the adults making any demands). The adult can teach a great deal by simply being responsive to the child and showing interest and enthusiasm for the child's interests. Use curricular materials, such as those provided in this book, consistently and regularly, but keep in mind that the activities featured in this edition constitute only a few of the important routines that the child will do on a daily basis.

REFERENCE

Johnson-Martin, N., Jens, K.G., & Attermeier, S.M. (1986). *The Carolina curriculum for handicapped infants and infants at risk.* Baltimore: Paul H. Brookes Publishing Co.

RECOMMENDED READINGS

Bartt, K., & Kalkstein, K. (1981). *Smart toys for babies.* New York: Harper & Row.
Biber, B.E., Shapiro, E., & Wickens, D. (1971). *Promoting cognitive growth: A developmental interaction point of view.* Washington, DC: National Association for the Education of Young Children.
Bower, E., Bersamin, K., Fine, A., & Carlson, J. (1974). *Learning to play, playing to learn.* New York: Human Sciences Press.
Caplan, F. (1982). *The first twelve months of life.* New York: Perigee Books, Putnam Publishing Group.
Caplan, F., & Caplan, T. (1977). *The second twelve months of life.* New York: Bantam Books.
Kabau, B. (1979). *Choosing toys for children from birth to age five.* New York: Schocken Books.
Leach, P. (1982). *Babyhood* (2nd ed.). New York: Alfred A. Knopf.
McLean, L.K.S. (1990). Communication development in the first two years of life: A transactional process. *Zero to Three, 11*(1), 13–19.
Stern, D.N. (1990). *Diary of a baby.* New York: Basic Books.

chapter **3**

Sensorimotor Development

THE MOTOR SECTIONS found in the CCITSN present sequences of skills to be used as guidelines for gross and fine motor intervention program planning. These sequences are based on the work of Lois Bly (1980), Berta Bobath (as interpreted by Finnie [1975]), Emmi Pikler (1971), and Margaret Rood (as interpreted by Stockmeyer [1972]), along with the clinical experience of the authors. Each sequence reflects a typical pattern of development, and, thus, can be considered a reasonable model to follow.

The Motor Development chapter from *The Carolina Curriculum for Handicapped Infants and Infants at Risk* (CCHI) (Johnson-Martin, Jens, & Attermeier, 1986) has been retitled, expanded, and updated in this second edition to reflect current theories of motor control. This new chapter now presents more information on fine motor and sensory development.

The curriculum items in the gross motor skills section are divided into three separate sequences—Gross Motor Skills: Prone (On Stomach), Gross Motor Skills: Supine (On Back), and Gross Motor Skills: Upright. In order to maintain appropriate sequencing of skill development, attention should be paid not only to the horizontal order of the items in each sequence, but also to their vertical clustering (e.g., see CCITSN Developmental Progress Chart, p. 65).

The Fine Motor Skills section of the Fine Motor Skills domain is divided into four sequences, primarily for ease in assessment and intervention. These skills do not develop independently of each other, so, therefore, generally more than one item at a time from varying sequences can be assessed while observing a child at play. These sequences encompass topics from tactile integration to bilateral skills development. The final sequence within the Fine Motor Skills domain—Visual-Motor Skills: Pencil Control and Copying—describes skills that only begin to emerge in the second year of life, building on the aforementioned fine motor skills.

This chapter includes information on the tactile and visual sensory systems, as well as the vestibular (inner ear) and proprioceptive (body sensation) systems, in order to assist interventionists in understanding the impact of these areas on development.

Since children with disabilities generally show deficits in their performance of skills as compared to normal children, the services of physical and occupational therapists should be enlisted in order to develop an individualized intervention program for each child. The therapists will demonstrate appropriate techniques for working on the items in this curriculum. If an item seems too difficult, the therapists can break it down into smaller steps, or present an alternate method for working on that particular motor skill. For example, item 24g. in the sequence, Gross Motor Skills: Prone (On Stomach), requires the child to support him- or herself on the hands with the arms extended and the head lifted to a 90° angle. A child with cerebral palsy may be supporting on his or her extended arms, but at the same time, may display the undesired patterns of pulling forward at the shoulders and flexing his or her hips. In such a case, the therapist would demonstrate the proper techniques for keeping the child's shoulders and hips well-positioned throughout the activity as well as add other exercises to the child's daily activities in an attempt to improve his or her shoulder stability.

The sequence of skill acquisition that is presented in this curriculum is that which is typically seen in normally developing children; however, children with disabilities frequently gain skills in a different order. Furthermore, many children with disabilities may never achieve "criterion" level on some items. Physical and occupational therapists can assist parents and interventionists in deciding which skills should be developed and how to state the goals. In this chapter, the term "therapist" refers to either an occupational or physical therapist. Although their roles are not interchangeable, both professions have some similar training in promoting sensory-motor development.

CHARACTERISTICS OF NORMAL MOTOR DEVELOPMENT

Motor skills emerge in similar patterns in all normally developing children. There are variations in the rate at which children acquire these skills, with some children reaching their goals at earlier ages than others. There are also variations in the order in which these skills are acquired (e.g., some children learn to walk before creeping).

Motor functions emerge because of the interaction of several factors, which include:

Motivation: Infants move either to express some internal idea or sensation or to obtain an external goal. Normal infants and toddlers work very hard at mastering motor skills and enjoy challenging themselves.

Strength: Newborns have almost no ability to function against gravity. During the first 6 months of life, the extensor muscles gain in strength so that the baby can lift his or her head and limbs off the ground in prone (on stomach) position. These skills can be tested by the use of the curriculum's items 24a.–24c. of the Gross Motor Skills: Prone (On Stomach) sequence (pp. 328–329). Between 6 and 9 months, infants learn to push up with their arms, rise onto their knees, and hold a straight trunk in a sitting position, and then learn to pull themselves to a standing position.

Balance: Balance can be thought of as the ability to keep one's body mass centered over one's base of support. In each successive developmental position (e.g., supported on extended arms, sitting, standing), the child learns to stay centered, then to move off center and use his or her trunk movements to prevent loss of balance. Vision, proprioception, and vestibular senses interact to help the child develop his or her sense of balance by use of stable postures and movement.

Motor patterns: Infants are born with a set of motor patterns that are relatively stereotypic in nature (e.g., sucking, hand-grasping, kicking). Throughout time, these patterns become more variable, and the child is able to use a very wide range of movement combinations to achieve his or her goals. There is a group of movement patterns that has been known as "primitive reflexes" (e.g., asymmetric tonic neck reflex, symmetric tonic neck reflex, primitive stepping, Moro reflex). Current theory on motor control treats these not strictly as "reflexes," but rather as motor patterns that can be generated either by the child or by an outside stimulus. In the CCITSN, the term "pattern," rather than "reflex," is used.

Fine Motor Skills

From birth to 6 months of life, the infant discovers his or her hands and establishes the foundation for more mature fine motor skills. Development of eye-hand coordination depends on the child's integration of visual skills, with information received through tactile and proprioceptive input. The development of adequate fine motor coordination is essential, not only for play, but also for independence in self-care and daily living activities.

During the first month of life, the infant's hands are generally fisted. "Reaching" is done with his or her eyes, making face-to-face contact between the child and the primary caregiver very important. Gradually, an infant begins to open and close his or her hands. He or she then discovers the hands, and brings them together in play at midline. Early play emerges as the child moves the toys that are placed in his or her hands (e.g., shaking rattles). As the child starts to reach out to swat at objects, he or she learns to judge the distances between him- or herself and other objects. By 6 months of age, the child is able to look at a toy and directly reach for and grasp it. He or she discovers that the hands are a part of his or her body, and that he or she can use them to manipulate the environment. Between 6 and 12 months, the child refines his or her hand skills, moving from whole-hand grasp to picking up objects between the thumb and first two fingers, and then to using a fine pincer grasp (i.e., grasping an object between the thumb and index finger). The child also begins to develop control of his or her individual finger movements, allowing for use of the index finger for pointing. Toward the end of the first year, the child learns to easily release objects. Development beyond 12 months primarily consists of the child refining the skills that have emerged during the first year of life.

Gross Motor Skills Development

Gross motor skills development in the first 12–15 months of life basically consists of learning to counter the forces of gravity by rising from a horizontal to a vertical position, staying upright, and moving through space without falling. The terms that therapists use to describe these specific movements are illustrated in the following display:

Newborn infants are incapable of effectively resisting the pull of gravity. Their postures and movements are characterized by *flexion,* with varying degrees of *abduction* and *adduction,* depending on their position.

Abduction = Moving the arms or legs away from the body

Adduction = Moving the arms or legs toward the body

Flexion = Bending of the joints

The development of *extension* in the spine and extremities allows the child to pull up against gravity and move into upright positions.

Extension = Straightening of the joints

The ability for *rotation* appears gradually in lying, sitting, standing, and walking, and is crucial for developing smooth, skilled transition from one position to another.

Rotation = Twisting

In the first month of life an infant has almost no ability to work against gravity or to change his or her position. Between 2 and 4 months, he or she gains enough head and trunk extension to push him- or herself up onto his or her elbows and to roll from the stomach to the back. By 6 months, the child can usually pull him- or herself around on the stomach and stay in a sitting position. And between 6 and 9 months of life, the child finally becomes mobile, learning to creep on his or her hands and knees, to get into and out of a sitting position alone, and to pull him- or herself into a standing position next to a support (e.g., furniture). This is followed by the child taking sideways steps next to the support, using his or her chest to support the body as he or she moves, and ultimately utilizing his or her feet. Finally, the child learns to stand alone and to take his or her first steps, usually between 11 and 13 months. From this point on, the child refines his or her recently acquired balance and speed abilities, becoming safe and adept at walking, stooping, and climbing onto furniture.

CHARACTERISTICS OF ABNORMAL MOTOR DEVELOPMENT

Abnormal motor development can result from a wide variety of conditions, including prenatal problems, birth trauma, chromosomal disorders, accidents, and severe illness. Many of these conditions can be given specific labels, such as cerebral palsy, Down syndrome, and spina bifida. These labels, however, do not describe the specific motor function that is the result of the condition. Children with dissimilar labels can show similar motor patterns. For the purposes of assessment and treatment, it is more useful to characterize children with abnormal motor development as being delayed in the development of motor skills, exhibiting abnormal performance of motor patterns, or having abnormal muscle tone.

Delay in Development of Motor Skills

Slow acquisition of motor milestones is very common among children with developmental problems. Depending on the severity of the condition, the delays can range from a lag of a few months behind normal motor development to complete absence of motor skills.

Abnormal Performance of Motor Patterns

When the motor portions of the brain are damaged, the resulting condition is called cerebral palsy. There are several distinct types of cerebral palsy, which are described in Table 1. The hallmark of cerebral palsy is motor patterns that have an abnormal appearance, being stereotypic, too wide-ranging, poorly directed, or absent. Motor pattern disorders range from mildly to severely abnormal. As severity increases, one often sees dominance of early motor patterns that have failed to be replaced by more mature ones. Patterns of posture or movement that are never seen in normal development may also be seen.

The most common atypical motor patterns are:

1. *Persistent Asymmetric Tonic Neck Pattern:* With a persistent asymmetric tonic neck pattern, the child's head is turned to one side, his or her arm is extended in front of the face, and the other arm is flexed. The child's legs assume a similar position. This makes it difficult to bring objects close to the child's face for him or her to look at or place in the mouth. Rolling over is also difficult if the child cannot move out of this position.

2. *Retracted Arms Pattern:* With the retracted arms pattern, the child's shoulders are pulled back and his or her arms are flexed, with the hands held near the shoulders. This pattern often interferes with toy manipulation and the child's discovery of his or her hands.

3. *Persistent Grasp Pattern:* With a persistent grasp pattern, the child will show a strong tendency to keep his or her hands tightly closed. This will interfere with his or her development of functional grasp patterns. Even as some voluntary control develops, the child will have difficulty with more refined use of his or her hands and fingers, limiting his or her ability to manipulate objects. Controlled release of an object requires significant command of the hands and fingers. Such control is often a problem for children with cerebral palsy.

4. *Associated Movements Pattern:*   A child who has better control over one side of his or her body often shows associated movements or reactions on the other side. When a child performs a task with one hand, his or her other hand will mirror the same action. This pattern interferes with the child's development of a higher level of bilateral skills. Extraneous mouth movement, accompanying the arm movement, is also common.

5. *Hyperextension of Neck, Trunk, and Legs Pattern:*   When the child hyperextends his or her neck, trunk, and legs, the resulting action is a strong backward arching movement of the body. This arching makes it difficult for the child to be placed in a sitting position. This pattern is often seen when the child is lying on his or her back or stomach, and often makes it difficult for the child to change his or her position or assume more complex postures.

6. *Scissoring Pattern:*   In the scissoring pattern, the child's legs are pulled together tightly, sometimes crossing over one another when he or she is held in the air or lying down. This pattern interferes with the child's ability to take steps, even with assistance.

7. *Bunny Hopping Pattern:*   If a young child wants to get around on his or her hands and knees, but cannot move the legs separately from each other, he or she will use a bunny hopping pattern. With this pattern, the child will first move both arms forward, then pull both of his or her knees forward, at the same time. If you see this pattern, consult a therapist. There are some children who can be taught to switch to reciprocal creeping, and others for whom bunny hopping is the only option.

8. *W-Sitting Pattern:*   In the W-sitting pattern, the child bends his or her knees and places the heels next to the hips while sitting on the floor. In this position, the trunk is often curved forward as well. W-sitting is a stable position that is often used by children with weak muscles and poor balance. Children without developmental problems or atypical motor patterns will use this position at times; however, they will also employ a variety of other sitting positions. If a child can only sit by using the W-sitting position, consult a therapist.

Table 1. Characteristics of the most common types of cerebral palsy

TYPE:	Spastic	Athetoid	Hypotonic	Ataxic
MUSCLE TONE:	Increased	Fluctuating between low and high	Decreased	Normal or slightly decreased
DISTRIBUTION:	1. *Hemiplegia:* Only one side is involved (right arm and leg or left arm and leg), but the arm is more involved. 2. *Quadriplegia:* All four extremities and trunk are involved. 3. *Diplegia:* All four extremities are involved, but the legs are more involved.	Whole body is involved.	Generally the whole body is involved, but there may be differences between arms and legs, trunk and extremities.	Whole body is involved.
CHARACTERISTICS:	Movements are carried out in stereotypic patterns; freedom of movement is restricted; child is "stiff."	Movements are large and difficult to control. Head control is a major problem, as are speech and feeding. Some athetoid children are very tense ("tension athetosis"); others are very hypotonic. When reaching for objects, the fingers overextend.	Movements themselves are fairly normal but lack holding power. Child is "floppy." Hypotonic infants frequently develop spasticity or athetosis.	Child may have good movements in prone, but will look "wobbly" in sitting and standing. Reaching patterns show poor directionality.

Abnormal Muscle Tone

Normal muscle tone can be felt by bending and straightening the arm of a person without a disability and feeling the amount of resistance that is encountered. The muscles of a person without disabilities can be easily lengthened and will have the same feel throughout the body. Contrarily, most children with cerebral palsy and other such conditions will have muscle tone that is either too high or too low. The terms used for muscle tone that is too high are *hypertonia* and *spasticity*. Hypertonic muscles resist being moved and feel stiff. The term used for muscle tone that is too low is *hypotonia*. Hypotonic muscles offer too little resistance to being moved and feel floppy. Some children have muscle tone that fluctuates between hypertonia and hypotonia.

Abnormal motor patterns and abnormal muscle tone are generally seen together in children with cerebral palsy. These two conditions result from lesions in the central nervous system, but are not causally related to each other.

DEVELOPING MOTOR SKILLS

General Guidelines

It is helpful to periodically spend time with children without disabilities in order to become re-acquainted with their motor capabilities. This will offer a basis of comparison and assist in preventing overestimation of capabilities when working with children with disabilities.

When working with children who have motor delays, it is helpful to keep in mind the following principles:

1. Motor development is not strictly a stepwise process. At any given time a child will have some skills at a proficient level of development and others at lower stages. Every child's motor development program should include a variety of activities in different positions.
2. Both developmental level and chronological age should be taken into account when planning the overall motor program. In general, exercises will be geared toward improving deficit areas and increasing the child's developmental level. At the same time, some children want to participate in activities that are more appropriate to their chronological age, even though their performance is not normal. They should not necessarily be prevented from doing so. A therapist can help determine appropriate activities for the child. Ultimately, function is more important than the manner in which a skill is performed, and there are many children whose movement patterns will never be normal. The overall prognosis for motor skills acquisition is tied to the severity of the child's motor disorder.
3. As much as possible, let movement be its own reward. Avoid excessive use of social praise or tangible reinforcers for performance of motor skills. The child's motor skills should be used primarily for exploration and play, rather than to gain the caregiver's approval.
4. Children do not "think" about moving; rather, their actions fall into place around a particular goal. It will be more successful to give commands that relate to a goal, such as, "Hit the balloon," rather than to say, "Straighten your arm." Likewise, it won't be of much value to repeatedly tell a child to sit up straight or hold his or her head up. If posture is poor, the child's muscles must be strengthened and his or her positioning should be improved.
5. If a child's motor dysfunction prevents a normal level of activity, he or she is at risk for becoming even weaker just because of the inactivity. Yet these children are typically passive, placing few demands on caregivers to be moved. It is important, therefore, that caregivers encourage frequent practice of movements and postures.

Improving Specific Motor Skills

For best results, the child's sensorimotor development program should consist of two major components: a specific exercise program, and a general routine of handling and positioning the child throughout the day.

Exercise Program An exercise program should be developed for each child on the basis of assessment of each item in both the Fine Motor Skills and the Gross Motor Skills domain sequences. Therapists may add, delete, or modify the items within these sequences, based on each child's abilities. Once the assessment is completed, the general procedure for training is:

1. Choose the activity in which the child will participate.
2. Prepare the child for the activity, if necessary, through relaxation, stimulation, or positioning.
3. Have the child perform and repeat the activity.
4. Gradually make the activity more challenging by changing the child's position, placing objects further away from him or her, and so forth.

Handling The other component of the child's sensorimotor development program is the way in which he or she is handled and positioned throughout the day, at home, and at school. By incorporating motor skills goals into daily routines, motor development progress is sped up and the onset of deformities can be slowed down. Along with providing appropriate procedures for activities in which the child may participate, each item in the CCITSN also offers suggestions for ways in which to use those activities as part of the child's daily routines. This requires extra attention on the part of parents and interventionists at first, but with practice, incorporating these important activities into daily routines will become second nature.

Implementing a sensorimotor development program involves skill in physically handling the child. The most important points to consider when implementing such a program are:

1. Always give the child the opportunity to perform as much of the movement as possible. This usually means doing the routines more slowly, so that the child has an opportunity to organize the movement. For example, when bringing a child from a back-lying to a sitting position, roll him or her slowly to the side and give him or her time to push up with one arm, even if all the weight is not borne on the arm.
2. When carrying the child, allow for as much independent head and trunk control as possible. Carrying a child over a shoulder or hip, rather than nestled in your arm, helps build strength while allowing the child to more readily visually inspect his or her environment.
3. Never pull against the tightness of a child's stiff muscles. Instead, relaxation can be achieved by gently moving the child's shoulders and hips back and forth, then slowly extending his or her arms and legs.
4. A child with severe impairments, especially one with athetoid features, will show hypersensitivity to touch, sound, and visual input. He or she will startle easily and withdraw from touch on the mouth, hands, and feet. Such a child should be approached slowly and quietly. Encourage him or her to keep head, hands, and visual focus at midline.
5. A child with hypotonia (i.e., weak, floppy muscles) will need a more vigorous sensorimotor development program. However, he or she is likely to require more frequent rest periods.

Body Mechanics With the increase in lifting and carrying that is done by many parents, interventionists, and therapists throughout the day, there is a danger of

injuring your back. In an effort to reduce such risks, a few simple rules of body mechanics should be routinely used when lifting and carrying:

1. When lifting a child or piece of equipment, bend your knees and get a firm grasp
    on the child or item. Never lean over, with your legs straight to lift or put down a
    child or item.

2. During lifting and carrying, hold the load close to your body. The closer you hold
    something to your center of gravity, the less muscle power you need to carry it.

3. If the child or item is very large or difficult to manage, use a two-stage lift. That
    is, begin by sitting on a low surface, then bring the child to your lap. Then hold
    the child close to your trunk as you stand.

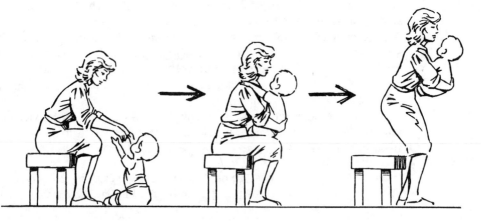

Positioning and Adaptive Equipment   The primary purpose of positioning is to appropriately place a child for optimum *functioning* in a given activity. A second, and important, purpose is to prevent or delay the onset of *contractures* (i.e., permanent shortening) of muscles in children with spasticity. The muscles most prone to contracture are:

Ankle downward flexors (gastrocnemius)
Knee flexors (hamstrings)
Hip flexors (iliopsoas)
Elbow flexors (biceps)
Wrist and finger flexors

When a child is involved in a task that requires hand use, such as playing or feeding, be sure to provide adequate trunk support. This may mean giving more support than is needed during other activities. If a child can only remain in a sitting position if his or her hands are propped on the knees, provide additional trunk support so that the hands can be freed for play. For a child with severe impairments, the side-lying position may work best. Ultimately, though, some type of adapted seating or positioning should be provided to each child.

Back-lying (supine) is a position that is preferred by many children with developmental problems because it allows them to see what is going on without exerting muscular effort. While there are obvious benefits to this, there are also drawbacks. Some children get so used to the back-lying position that they refuse to work in stomach-lying (prone) positions, which promote development of back muscles. Many children also assume undesirable postures, such as arm retraction and trunk hyperextension when on their backs. These tendencies should be countered by routinely placing the children in a variety of positions, including stomach-lying, and using semi-reclining postures as an alternative to back-lying. Make sure that the arms and legs are as relaxed and normally aligned as possible.

There are many ways to provide positioning support, and each child needs to be individually evaluated to see what works best. Therapists know how to evaluate and obtain the needed equipment. Some of the support devices that could be used are illustrated in Figure 1.

Safety Precautions   One result of securing children into pieces of adaptive equipment is that it takes time to get them freed. Caregivers are strongly encouraged to practice emergency procedures, so that if a fire occurs, or if a child chokes, proper measures can be taken. Caregivers should practice taking children out of equipment quickly, and removing them from the building while still in the equipment. There should always be at least one person available who is trained in basic first-aid procedures, including cardiopulmonary resuscitation (CPR).

USING TOYS TO PROMOTE DEVELOPMENT

Toys are valuable for children, not only for their intrinsic play value, but also because they can help promote cognitive and motor development. In selecting toys for a child with a motor impairment, keep in mind the child's need for cognitive and motor development. The result may be the selection of several different types of toys. Children also need toys that are within their motoric ability to manipulate and ones that will challenge them to develop and refine motor control. Hence, the 2-year-old who continues to have difficulty reaching for toys still needs, and will probably enjoy, sus-

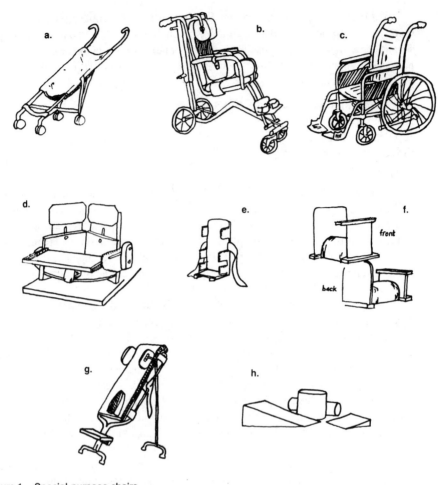

Figure 1. Special-purpose chairs.

a. *Folding strollers* are inexpensive, lightweight, collapsible, and convenient for transportation.

b. *Upholstered wheeled chairs* provide good support at the head, trunk, hips, and feet. Trays can be attached for mealtime and play. The back wheels retract so that the chair can be placed into an automobile without moving the child. These chairs are suitable for children with poor control of head and trunk. They cannot be propelled by the child, however, and are intended only for children with severe handicaps. When used in cars or schoolbuses, additional safety restraints *must* be used.

c. *Standard wheelchairs* come in a variety of sizes and can be used with trays and head supports. A child who has use of the upper extremities can independently propel the chair. These chairs are more cumbersome in terms of automobile transportation because the child has to be removed and the chair folded.

d. *Corner chairs* provide some support at the shoulders and hips. An extension to the back portion can provide support at the head, and wedges on the seat control hip position. A tray can be attached. This type of seating places children who are spastic with low-trunk tone in a functional position with shoulders forward and hips apart. Children with hypotonic muscles also make good use of corner chairs.

e. *Seat inserts* can be used to support small children in chairs that would otherwise be too large or would not offer enough support.

f. *Bolster chairs,* to which a tray can be attached, require some head and trunk control on the part of the child. The straddle seat ensures good separation of the legs for a child who is spastic.

g. *Prone-standers* can be adjusted to accommodate virtually any child, and are used to provide activity in upright positions, while maintaining good body alignment. Arm use, head/trunk control, and social interaction are all facilitated in this position. Care should be taken in placement to make sure that the feet are flat and the entire body is properly aligned.

h. *Bolsters and wedges* of various sizes allow play in prone position for children with poor control of head, trunk, and arms. Care should be taken to make sure that the child's legs are not thrusting stiffly. If necessary, place a towel between the knees or keep them turned slightly outward.

pended toys that can be activated by a swat. At the same time, if that child's cognitive abilities are at the 2-year-old level, age-appropriate toys should be chosen, even if assistance or modification is required to use them. For children who are experiencing significant motor difficulties, introduce electronic toys that operate by switches. These type of toys can be a useful addition during the second year of life. The child's ability to control his or her environment in spite of motor limitations is an important aspect of cognitive and emotional development. This control also provides a foundation for future augmentative communication devices, should they be necessary.

CHARACTERISTICS OF NORMAL SENSORY DEVELOPMENT

The development of motor skills is closely linked to reception and interpretation of sensory input. Of primary importance to the development of motor skill is the information that is received through the visual, tactile, vestibular, and proprioceptive systems. As a child interprets this basic sensory information, he or she learns about his or her body and how it moves.

Vision: Vision provides the child with an enormous amount of information about the environment. It has been estimated that in children with no visual impairments, 80%–90% of learning occurs through visual input. Motor development both contributes to and is aided by visual development. The emergence of head and eye control provides needed stability for focusing and tracking. In turn, visual input, along with proprioceptive and vestibular input, contributes to the development of balance and mobility. At birth, the child is able to focus best at 8–10 inches. Complex patterns and faces are preferred over simple designs at this age. By 6 months of age, a child can focus on far away as well as near objects, and vision has become integrated with motor skills, allowing the child to direct his or her reaching.

Tactile: The sense of touch is extremely important to infants. It helps them establish attachment to persons or objects in their environment, provides a primary means of comfort, and enables them to learn about their bodies. Touch is an integral part of a child's earliest motor activities. For instance, when stroked on the cheek, an infant will turn toward the touch. This ability helps him or her locate a nipple or bottle to obtain nourishment. Likewise, when the child's palm of the hand is touched, his or her fingers will close, grasping whatever is in the palm.

At first, infants cannot tell where they have been touched, but can feel the sensation. Touch provides comfort, and, as is well known, infants enjoy being cuddled. By 3–4 months, infants start to use their mouths to explore their hands and toys. And at approximately 7 months, they become interested in exploring textures with their fingers, enabling them to refine their fine motor skills. By the second year of life, children can generally tell where they have been touched. At this age they enjoy playing with a wide variety of messy materials.

Vestibular: Information regarding gravity and movement is received through the vestibular (i.e., inner ear) system. Integration of vestibular input contributes to the development of balance and postural control. Even newborns are aware of movement, and will react to sudden changes in position by extending their arms and legs. Slow, regular vestibular input is used to comfort infants (e.g., rocking). By 6 months of age, the infant enjoys activities involving increased vestibular input, such as being gently swung through the air or being cautiously turned upside down. Enjoyment of such input continues to grow, and when children reach their second year of life, they find much pleasure in rough play, twirling, and swinging. For example, at this age, children will often pursue intense vestibular input by spinning around in circles until they become dizzy and fall to the ground.

Proprioception: Proprioception refers to the sense of position and movement that is received through the muscles and joints. Along with tactile and vestibular input, proprioceptive input helps children establish a good sense of their bodies, determine where their limbs begin and end, and discover how they move. Weight-bearing on the arms and legs and antigravity extension provide important proprioceptive input. For instance, as infants rock on their hands and knees, and later creep, they are making continual motor adaptations based on sensory input.

SENSORY DYSFUNCTION

Children may have specific losses or impairments of vision or hearing that disrupt development. Further information regarding these difficulties, as well as intervention approaches, can be found in *The Carolina Curriculum for Preschoolers with Special Needs* (Johnson-Martin, Attermeier, & Hacker, 1990). Within this curriculum, adaptations for visual and hearing impairments are provided, as necessary, in individual items. In addition to specific sensory losses, children may experience differences in the interpretation of tactile and vestibular input; adaptations for these differences are described in the section, "Intervention with Sensory Dysfunction." Perceptual hearing and vision disorders are typically not evident in children until they are nearly 6 years of age.

   If a child has difficulty interpreting and integrating sensory input, this can be identified early in the child's life, whether or not he or she has specific motor impairments. Children who demonstrate either of these difficulties may later have subtle problems with motor skills and coordination. Early intervention, with the help of a therapist who is trained to deal with these problems, is important, not only for motor development, but also for the child's emotional stability.

   Tactile Defensiveness   Tactile defensiveness refers to discomfort or a negative emotional response to light or unexpected tactile input. The nervous system provides for two options for dealing with tactile input. One is a protective response, which leads us to avoid the input or pull away from it. The other is a discriminatory response, which leads us to identify the characteristics of the input (e.g., Is it rough or smooth? Is it hot or cold?). Children with tactile defensiveness are using the protective mode rather than the discriminatory one. Infants with tactile defensiveness can be difficult for parents to handle. They cry often and are not easily comforted. They often seem happiest when left alone in a crib. They may also cry or pull away when adults try to cuddle them. Diaper changing, dressing, and bathing may be particularly stressful. These infants may be slow to accept solid foods, and may accept only a narrow range of foods.

   Gravitational Insecurity   Gravitational insecurity consists of discomfort with or fear of sudden movement or heights. It is probably related to the child's difficulty in integrating vestibular and proprioceptive input. Children with gravitational insecurity are often described as "earthbound," as they are uncomfortable with activities in which their feet are not on the ground. Infants with gravitational insecurity dislike being moved quickly or suddenly. They often show fear with typical adult-infant play, such as being bounced on a knee or swung in the air. Having a diaper changed on a table may be frightening as well. Gains in gross motor skills may be slower than normal due to reluctance to move and fear of falling. During the second year of life, these children do not engage in the "daredevil" climbing that is common to most children. They may also be slow to accept riding toys. Furthermore, as the time for toilet training approaches, they may be fearful of sitting on the toilet.

Intervention with Sensory Dysfunction

Sensory input is an integral component of developing motor skills as well as emotional well being. Be aware of the impact of sensory input as you work with the infant and young child. Enrichment of sensory input should be incorporated into the child's daily routine, and not confined to isolated activities. Specific sensory input can also be used to prepare a child for activities. For example, if the child is irritable, you can use sensory input to calm him or her by dimming the lights, lowering the noise level, providing firm pressure (e.g., holding securely, swaddling, placing in a beanbag chair), or rocking the child slowly. Similarly, if the child is sluggish, you can use sensory input to make him or her more alert by brightening the room, playing lively music, rubbing his or her arms and legs with terrycloth, or bouncing him or her on your knee or on a ball.

Helping a Child Who Demonstrates Tactile Defensiveness In general, a child who demonstrates tactile defensiveness will tolerate firm pressure better than light touch; therefore, hold him or her securely. Massage may also be a helpful calming procedure. Other alternatives include: swaddling the young infant to provide constant pressure, hanging a small hammock in the crib to cuddle the infant, or carrying the infant in a front or back pack that snuggles him or her close to your body. Above all, don't interpret the infant's withdrawal as a personal dislike, and do not give in to the infant's desire to be left alone. Infants with tactile defensiveness need more personal interaction and touch input than other infants. It is strongly recommended that you consult with a therapist who is trained to work with this type of infant to provide advice and support to the parent or interventionist.

Helping a Child Who Is Gravitationally Insecure Move a child who is gravitationally insecure slowly, providing firm support. Do not engage the child in rough play if he or she is clearly frightened by it. Being picked up in the air or turned upside down may be particularly frightening for a child with this dysfunction. Look for ways to provide sensory input that are not threatening to the child and are under his or her control as much as possible. For instance, a child who is fearful on a changing table may feel more secure having his or her diapers and clothes changed on the floor or in a crib. Likewise, a child who might be frightened when placed in an infant swing may tolerate and begin to explore movement better in an infant bouncer seat that is located on the floor. Similarly, a toddler with gravitational insecurity could be provided with small riding toys, so that his or her feet touch the ground, rather than being placed on a rocking horse, which is generally elevated. For toilet training a child with this dysfunction, try providing a low potty seat. It is strongly recommended that a therapist who is trained to work with this type of child be consulted to provide treatment and support.

REFERENCES

Bly, L. (1980). The components of movement during the first year of life. In D. Slaton (Ed.), *Development of movement in infancy.* (pp. 85–135). Chapel Hill: University of North Carolina, Division of Physical Therapy.

Finnie, N. (1975). *Handling the young cerebral palsied child at home.* New York: E.P. Dutton.

Johnson-Martin, N.M., Attermeier, S.M., & Hacker B. (1990). *The Carolina curriculum for preschoolers with special needs.* Baltimore: Paul H. Brookes Publishing Co.

Johnson-Martin, N., Jens, K.G., & Attermeier, S.M. (1986). *The Carolina curriculum for handicapped infants and infants at risk.* Baltimore: Paul H. Brookes Publishng Co.

Pikler, E. (1971). Learning of motor skills on the basis of self-induced movements. In J. Helmuth (Ed.), *Exceptional infant: Vol. 2. Studies in abnormalities* (pp. 54–87). New York: Brunner/Mazel.

Stockmeyer, S. (1972). A sensorimotor approach to treatment. In P. Pearson & C. Williams (Eds.), *Physical therapy in the developmental disabilities* (pp. 186–222). Springfield, IL: Charles C Thomas.

RECOMMENDED READINGS

Ayres, A.J. (1979). *Sensory integration and the child.* Los Angeles: Western Psychological Services.

Connolly, B., & Montgomery, P. (1987). *Therapeutic exercise in the developmental disabilities.* Chattanooga: Chattanooga Corporation.

Geralis, E. (Ed.). (1991). *Children with cerebral palsy: A parents' guide.* Rockville, MD: Woodbine House.

Hanson, M., & Harris, S. (1986). *Teaching the young child with motor delays: A guide for parents and professionals.* Austin, TX: PRO-ED.

Leach, P. (1982). *Your baby and child.* New York: Alfred A. Knopf.

Levy, J. (1975). *The baby exercise book.* New York: Pantheon Books.

chapter *4*

Using the Curriculum

TRADITIONALLY CURRICULA FOR young children with disabilities have been divided into six developmental domains: Cognition, Communication/Language, Social Skills/Adaptation, Self-Help, Fine Motor Skills, and Gross Motor Skills. Within each domain, however, the items usually have not been arranged in a logical teaching sequence. Rather, the sequence of items has been based upon the mean ages at which normal children master the skills. This procedure creates some major problems in planning intervention programs for children whose development is atypical.

In an attempt to deal with this problem, *The Carolina Curriculum for Handicapped Infants and Infants At Risk* (CCHI) (Johnson-Martin, Jens, & Attermeier, 1986) identified 24 areas of development within the above mentioned developmental domains, as well as logical sequences for teaching the skills within each. *The Carolina Curriculum for Infants and Toddlers with Special Needs* (CCITSN) maintains the basic structure of the CCHI, but has regrouped and re-named some of the sequences and their items in order to provide an easier transition between the CCITSN and *The Carolina Curriculum for Preschoolers with Special Needs* (CCPSN) (Johnson-Martin, Attermeier, & Hacker, 1990). Table 2 lists the content overlap of the CCHI and CCITSN, along with the traditional developmental domains under which the sequences fall.

In selecting the 26 areas (sequences) of development and the itemized list of skills within each curriculum, the authors have assumed the following:

1. The ability of a child to exert some control over his or her physical and social environment is crucial for the development and maintenance of a motivation for learning. One primary goal of the curriculum must be to enhance the child's potential for bringing about changes in his or her environment. Working toward that goal often means changing both the social and physical environments to make them more responsive to the child.
2. Communication should also be a major focus of an infant curriculum. Communication is the most effective way to bring about changes in the child's social environment. In addition, for children with the most severe physical limitations, it is often the primary means of influencing the physical environment, by causing other people to make changes for them. Communication can and does take place without speech—through facial expressions, gestures, signs, and augmentative

Table 2.   Content overlap in the sequences of the original curriculum and the CCITSN

CCITSN domain and sequence	Source of items from original curriculum (Sequence numbers in parentheses)
Cognition	
1. Visual Pursuit and Object Permanence	Visual Pursuit and Object Permanence (3.)
2. Object Permanence: Motor and Visual	Object Permanence (Visual-Motor) (4.)
3. Auditory Localization and Object Permanence	Auditory Localization and Object Permanence (2.)
4. Attention and Memory	
5. Concept Development	
6. Understanding Space	Spatial Concepts (5.)
7. Functional Use of Objects and Symbolic Play	Functional Use of Objects and Symbolic Play (6.)
8. Problem Solving	Control over Physical Environment (7.)
9. Visual Perception	"Readiness" Concepts (8.)
	Object Manipulation: Form manipulation (20–1.)
Communication	
10. Prevocabulary/Vocabulary	Gestural Communication (11.)
	Vocal Communication (13.)
11. Imitation: Sound and Gestures	Gestural Imitation (10.)
	Vocal Imitation (12.)
12. Responses to Communication from Others	Responses to Communication from Others (9.)
13. Conversation Skills	Gestural Communication (11.)
	Vocal Communication (13.)
Social/Adaptation	
14. Self-Direction	Self-Direction (15.)
15. Social Skills	Social Skills (14.)
16. Self-Help Skills: Eating	Feeding (16.)
17. Self-Help Skills: Dressing	Dressing (18.)
18. Self-Help Skills: Grooming	Grooming (19.)
Fine Motor Skills	
19. Fine Motor Skills: Tactile Integration	Tactile Integration and Manipuluation (1.)
20. Fine Motor Skills: Reaching, Grasping, and Releasing	Reaching and Grasping (19.)
21. Fine Motor Skills: Manipulation	Object Manipulation (20.)
22. Fine Motor Skills: Bilateral Skills	Bilateral Hand Activity (21.)
23. Visual-Motor Skills: Pencil Control and Copying	Object Manipulation: Placing pegs (20–IV.)
	Object Manipulation: Putting in and taking out (20–V.)
	Object Manipulation: Drawing (20–III.)
	Object Manipulation: Block patterns (20–II.)
Gross Motor Skills	
24. Gross Motor Skills: Prone (On Stomach)	Gross Motor Activities: Prone (On Stomach) (22.)
25. Gross Motor Skills: Supine (On Back)	Gross Motor Activities: (On Back) (23.)
26. Gross Motor Skills: Upright	Gross Motor Activities: Upright (24.)
26–I. Posture and locomotion	Posture and Locomotion (24–IV.)
26–II. Stairs	Stairs (24–I.)
26–III. Jumping	Jumping (24–III.)
26–IV. Balance	Balance (24–II.)

communication systems. At the early developmental levels, the curriculum items within the communication domain are more directed toward increasing the caregivers' sensitivity to the child's communicative cues than toward "teaching" the child particular skills.

3.   An infant curriculum should be as complete as possible, with every effort made

to enhance the child's strengths and remedy his or her weaknesses. The child should be allowed and encouraged to develop rapidly in areas where he or she has strengths, even if this increases the gap between the strengths and weaknesses. It is particularly important not to neglect cognitive and communication skills in children with severe motor impairment, even though physical therapy for motor functions may seem to be the most pressing need.

4. The sequences of cognitive development described by Jean Piaget (1952) have been substantiated by a sizable volume of literature and can, therefore, logically form the basis of the cognitive portions of an infant curriculum. However, it is important to also include in the curriculum information that may arise from more recent research on memory and communication.

5. It is important that anyone who is educating children is familiar with the methods of teaching that are contributed by behaviorism. For young children with developmental disabilities, however, it is important that this methodology be integrated with a good understanding of developmental abilities and needs.

ASSESSING A CHILD FOR CURRICULUM ENTRY

The first step in planning any intervention program is to carefully assess the child's current developmental abilities. For this purpose, the items from this curriculum's 26 sequences have been incorporated into an "Assessment Log" (pp. 48–64), with space for scoring several weeks' assessments. (Additional copies of the Assessment Log, available as a 24-page pamphlet, in packages of 10, may be obtained from Paul H. Brookes Publishing Co., P.O. Box 10624, Baltimore, MD 21285-0624.) The numbers assigned to the curriculum sequences are not related in any way to the importance of a given sequence. Each of the sequences represents a significant area of development. Thus, it is important that each child using this curriculum be evaluated in all 26 sequences except when this is precluded by a particular handicapping condition (e.g., children with total blindness will not be evaluated on items requiring vision).

Before evaluating a child, assemble the materials described in Table 3. Assessment proceeds more smoothly if most of it is done in the context of parent-child interaction, rather than being clinically structured. Begin by having a parent (or another caregiver who is very familiar with the child) play with the child as he or she normally would, using the toys or objects that they would generally use in such interactions (or the materials you have assembled, if the assessment is not taking place in the child's home or other usual care environment). This time allows the interventionist to determine what activities the child and parent enjoy doing together and how the parent elicits the child's attention and responses. It also enables the interventionist to get a "fix" on the child's developmental status. After the interventionist familiarizes him- or herself with the curriculum sequences, he or she will find that the brief (15–20 minute), informal observation period will allow time to score many of the items in the sequences without further assessment, as well as to establish a comfortable relationship with the child and his or her parent.

To complete the assessment, the interventionist should either instruct the parent to try particular activities with the child or to attempt to assess the child him- or herself. When a child fails an item, the interventionist should ask the parent if she or he has ever seen the child do a similar activity under other circumstances. Items that

Table 3. Assessment materials

The following materials have been found to be useful when assessing a child with the CCITSN. Feel free to modify the materials as appropriate for the child's disabilities or the customs of the family, provided you maintain the intent of the item.

Toys with different textures or scraps of fabric

Box of sand, beans, rice, macaroni, or other textured materials

Bells, rattles, and other noisemaking toys

A variety of small, brightly colored toys, including some that produce interesting sights or sounds with minimal action on the part of the child (e.g., chime ball, soft squeeze toy)

Several small cloths (i.e., handkerchief size)

Spoon, cup, bottle, and a variety of foods

Mirror

Crayons

Large (approximately ¾"–1") and small (approximately ¼") pegboards and pegs

Tub of water

Finger paints, pudding, or whipped cream

Play-doh or clay

A variety of containers, some with holes in the lids

A selection of "everyday" objects (e.g., eating utensils, toothbrush, hairbrush, shoe, ball)

Small broom, dustpan, dustcloth, purse (i.e., items that a child would use to imitate adult activities)

Dolls, doll furniture, stuffed animals, toy cars, and trucks

Square blocks of various sizes

Simple form boards with circles, squares, and triangles

Several short dowels of different diameters

Gum or candy in wrappers

Pop beads

Beads for stringing (approximately ¾"–1")

Small jars with lids

Several picture books and magazines

---

the child has passed during other recent evaluations (e.g., the Bayley Scales of Infant Development) should also be recorded.

The items within each curriculum sequence are listed in the order of their expected development. That is, item a. is generally expected to be learned before item b., item b. before c., and so forth. Ideally, if a child is observed to have mastered item c. of a sequence, and failed item d., it could be assumed that he or she had also mastered the preceeding items a. and b., and would fail the following items e. and f. However, general expectations may not match the development of some children. Even among children without disabilities there are frequent developmental irregularities. Often a child practices several related skills at once. For example, a child practices coming to sit and sitting when placed during the same time period, but there is little consistency as to which skill will emerge first.

Handicapping conditions may increase the likelihood of irregular development. Therefore, it is important that a sufficient number of items be assessed in each sequence to be certain whether skills have or have not been mastered. There is no set number of items that must be tested; the decision should, however, be based on the judgment of the person doing the assessment. As a general rule, three items beyond the first failure and three items below the first success in each sequence will give a reasonably complete picture of the child's skills.

Note: There are some developmental skills that children "outgrow." That is, once they demonstrate a more mature skill in a sequence, they will no longer demonstrate the less mature skill. Obviously, these early "failures" should be ignored.

In a few instances, the same item is listed in two sequences. This was done since particular skills appeared to be important building blocks for subsequent skills in both of the sequences in which they were listed. When this occurs, a notation is made by the item (e.g., [same as item 6a.]), both in the Assessment Log and on the curriculum items.

Most of the items that are listed in the sequences in the Assessment Log are self-explanatory. However, if it is unclear as to how a given skill should be assessed or scored, simply turn to the corresponding curriculum item and read the instructions for teaching it; then, hopefully, the assessment will become clearer. When it is difficult or impossible to assess a skill in the assessment setting, ask the parent or primary caregiver if the child has mastered the skill. Be sure to make all questions as clear as possible. Items may be credited on the basis of parental report, but every attempt should be made to carefully check these assessments during the intervention process since misunderstandings about the criteria for accomplishment of items may occur. For the gross motor skills sections of the assessment, it may be helpful to have Figure 2, Motor Milestones in Infant Development (pp. 36–37) (discussed in detail below) readily available. This chart illustrates the normal motor pattern of an infant from birth to 12 months, since development in this period is more apt to be misunderstood in assessment by parents than the developmental period between 12–24 months. If a motor item can be functionally performed, but in an abnormal manner, score it as emerging (see scoring section below) and make a notation on the Assessment Log.

SCORING THE ASSESSMENT LOG AND CHARTING THE RESULTS

Items in the Assessment Log should be scored as passed (+), failed (−), or emerging (±). Emerging items include: 1) those that the child passed, but only after it had been tried repeatedly; 2) those representing behaviors that a parent reports that the child exhibits only at home (i.e., behaviors that are clearly not generalized); 3) those representing skills that clearly need more practice; and 4) motor items that are functionally present, but are not performed normally (i.e., items may or may not ever be performed normally). If you find that simply recording a skill as passed, failed, or emerging does not satisfy your record-keeping needs, supplement that system with more complex scoring codes to suit your particular purposes.

Once the Assessment Log has been filled in, the CCITSN Developmental Progress Chart (p. 65) should be completed to reveal a profile of the child's skills. (Additional copies of the CCITSN Developmental Progress Chart, available with the Assessment Log, may be obtained from Paul H. Brookes Publishing Co., P.O. Box 10624, Baltimore, MD 21285-0624.) Each item that appears on the Assessment Log is represented by a blank on the CCITSN Developmental Progress Chart. If an item is passed, the corresponding space should be colored in completely. If the skill appears to be inconsistent or emerging, the space should be colored in only partially (e.g., ▰▭). If this charting procedure is employed regularly, using different colors to complete the charting with each new assessment, a visual display is provided of the youngster's progress through the curriculum sequences.

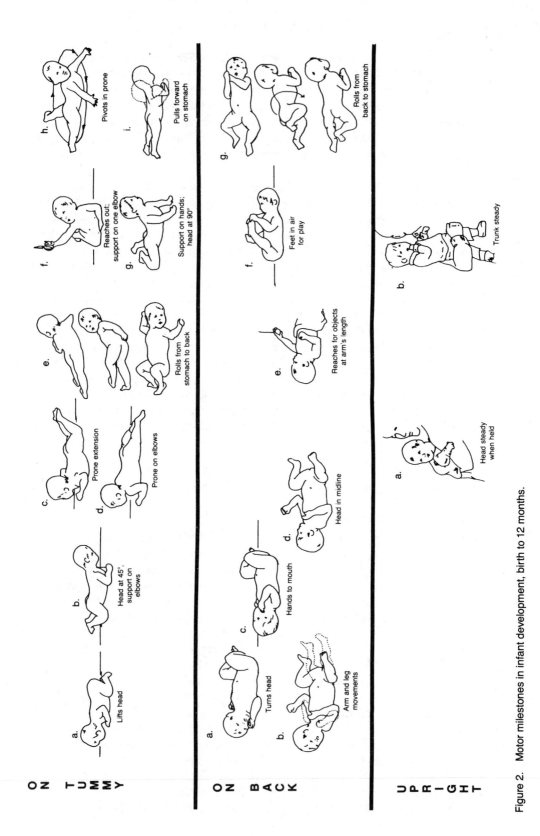

Figure 2. Motor milestones in infant development, birth to 12 months.

36

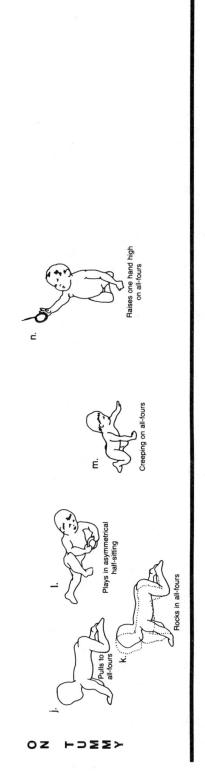

ON TUMMY

j. Pulls to all-fours

k. Rocks in all-fours

l. Plays in asymmetrical half-sitting

m. Creeping on all-fours

n. Raises one hand high on all-fours

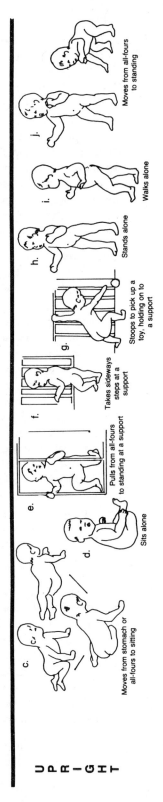

UPRIGHT

c. Moves from stomach or all-fours to sitting

d. Sits alone

e. Pulls from all-fours to standing at a support

f. Takes sideways steps at a support

g. Stoops to pick up a toy, holding on to a support

h. Stands alone

i. Walks alone

j. Moves from all-fours to standing

Figure 2. *(continued)*

37

SELECTING CURRICULUM ITEMS
FOR EACH CHILD'S INTERVENTION PROGRAM

Within the Curriculum Sequences section, there are teaching activities (indicated by a lower-cased letter) that correspond to each item in a sequence, as depicted in the CCITSN Developmental Progress Chart. Interventionists should select activities for a given child by either choosing the first item that the child failed, or the item that was judged to be just emerging in each sequence, unless a particular handicapping condition makes this strategy inappropriate. However, using this procedure could produce an intervention plan that includes up to 26 items. If that is translated into 26 different intervention activities, the plan will be unwieldy for many families and intervention programs. There are several strategies for reducing the number of items and developing a comprehensive intervention program.

Strategy #1:   Combining two or more intervention goals in one activity. Young children rarely learn one skill in isolation from others. For example, at the same time a child is learning to pull to a standing position next to a support, he or she is reaching for an object that is on top of the support. When the object falls off the support and rolls out of view, the child encounters the problem of getting around the barriers, and so forth. If the interventionist makes a list of all the skills that a child should be learning, it is generally easy to determine how two or more intervention goals can be integrated into one activity. It is often very effective to combine motor and cognitive tasks, such as working on grasp and release patterns while also working on combining objects or object function.

Strategy #2:   Incorporating several items in a routine care activity. Young children learn best through play and exploration in a responsive environment, not through artificial "sit down" teaching sessions. Each curriculum item includes a section entitled "Use in Daily Routines," that describes how learning a skill can be incorporated into everyday experiences. Many of the items suggest learning activities that can take place during bathing, diapering, feeding, and other daily care routines. Including two or more activities in each of these care routines insignificantly adds to the time spent in the care routines but greatly increases the child's opportunities for systematic intervention. Furthermore, it is in just these kinds of situations that caregivers have traditionally provided the stimulation that promotes development. For infants and children functioning at the infant level, intervention in daily care activities is "education in the least restrictive environment."

Strategy #3:   Alternating the sequences that are the focus of intervention. It is reasonable to choose to work through part of some sequences for a given time period (e.g., 3 months) and then to switch to those sequences that have not yet been attempted. If this strategy is selected, it must be re-emphasized that all 26 sequences represent important areas of development and that it is essential to promote development in areas in which children show strengths, as well as in areas in which they show weaknesses. In fact, it is by enhancing strengths that most people compensate for their weaknesses.

The following guidelines may be helpful in selecting particular sequences and items for a given child's intervention program when using strategy #3:

1.   Since motor behaviors provide such a vital link between the child and his or her world, items should be selected from all of the appropriate motor sequences

(19.–26.) for every intervention period. Figure 2 shows sequential development of a child's motor milestones in "on tummy," "on back," and "upright" positions, skills that correspond to the Gross Motor Skills sequences, 24.–26. It is important, however, to observe the vertical clustering of items in these three Gross Motor Skills sequences. It should be noted that particular skills in the upright position cannot be expected to be achieved before skills in the other positions.

2. The other curriculum sequences should be ranked, thereafter, according to the level of skills that the child demonstrated in the Gross Motor Skills domain. It is recommended that you choose half of the nonmotor sequences to work on for the first treatment period, so that equal areas of strengths and weaknesses will be represented. The choice of which "strong" and "weak" sequences to include in the first intervention plan should be guided by parental concerns, as well as the assisting professionals' interests.

3. As you develop the first intervention plan, decide how much time to allot to a treatment period before re-evaluation. When children are developing rapidly, the treatment period may be as short as 2 months; for slowly developing children, it may be as long as 6 months.

4. For the second treatment period, the nonmotor sequences that were initially omitted in the first treatment should form the basis of the second half of the program. This will provide ongoing documentation of the effectiveness of the intervention program (see the field-testing information in Chapter 1 under "The CCITSN Approach," pp. 3–4).

USING THE CURRICULUM ITEMS

Each curriculum item indicates at the top which materials will be necessary for the activities to teach the item. Most materials that are needed are toys that are common in homes or can be readily made from simple, inexpensive materials. For many items, particularly those in the Communication domain, no special materials are needed. The materials are described simply as "A normal home or group care environment."

Each item is divided into four major parts: Procedures, Use in Daily Routines, Adaptations, and Criterion. The "Procedures" section describes the way to teach the skill in a one-on-one situation. It often includes two or more activities that may be used to teach the skill, and describes ways in which to prompt and reinforce the child's learning.

The second section, "Use in Daily Routines," describes ways that teaching the skill can be integrated into daily care activities. In some cases, this means doing the activities described under "Procedures" at particular times of the day (e.g., when diapering or feeding the child). In other cases, it means providing the child with particular materials when he or she is playing alone, or suggesting ways that the caregiver can use the activities to entertain the child while doing household chores or other adult activities. The authors have two goals in including this section in the curriculum items: 1) to ensure that intervention naturally takes place throughout the day, rather than in particular times that are set aside for such intervention; and 2) to maximize the likelihood that the skill that is learned by the child will be "generalized" (i.e., the child will be able to demonstrate the skill in a variety of settings).

"Adaptations" for visually, hearing, and motor impaired children are included in the third section, as appropriate. It is not practical to try to list adaptations for the endless variety of handicaps, or their possible combinations, ranging from mild to severe disabilities. Rather, the intention is to make suggestions for modifications (or, in some cases, for alternate items) that will be adequate for some children and help curriculum users to think about additional modifications that would be appropriate for other children.

The last section describes the "Criterion" for skill mastery. In a departure from the first edition of the curriculum, the criteria are no longer described in terms of a particular number of successes out of a specific number of trials. The authors made this change because few curriculum users keep such detailed records that would make this approach useful, and because such an approach is likely to lead to "set-aside intervention times" in which data are readily collected, rather than to an integration of intervention into the child's daily routines. In the final analysis, the interventionist must use his or her judgment about whether a skill has been sufficiently mastered so that the child can move on to the next skill in the sequence. "Sufficiently mastered" should refer to skill generalization; the behavior should be observed on more than one occasion and in a variety of different circumstances. In some cases, the interventionist will feel it is appropriate to begin work on the next item in a sequence, even though an item is not yet mastered. It is quite acceptable to work on two items in the same sequence at the same time if the activities involved are congruent. In fact, there are several places in the curriculum where the authors suggest that two items be worked on simultaneously. There are also sequences in which more advanced items are simply extensions of early items. For example, in sequence 10., Prevocabulary/Vocabulary (pp. 171–180), essentially the same activities are used to facilitate the production of 2, 3, 7, and 15 words, although these represent different curriculum items.

INDIVIDUALIZED FAMILY SERVICE PLAN

Public Law 94-142 (Education for All Handicapped Children Act of 1975) required that Individualized Education Programs (IEPs) be developed for each child who is receiving special education services, and that the IEP be approved by his or her parents. In Public Law 99-457 (Education of the Handicapped Act Amendments of 1986), there is a greater acknowledgment of the roles that parents play in intervention for their preschool child with special needs. Part H of Public Law 99-457 sets forth the requirements for services for infants and toddlers with special needs. These requirements include multidisciplinary assessments of the needs and strengths of both the infant or toddler and the family. Rather than an IEP, an Individualized Family Service Plan (IFSP) is to be developed for each child who is receiving special education/early intervention services. This requires not only an assessment of the child, but an assessment of the family's strengths and needs.

It is beyond the scope of this curriculum to suggest particular strategies for family assessment or formats for their IFSP. The authors refer the readers to the articles and books listed in the Recommended Readings section at the end of this chapter. The authors feel that it is important, however, to make a statement about the role of the CCITSN in the development of the IFSP.

The CCITSN is not a complete multidisciplinary assessment, although it does cover the domains that are generally evaluated in such programs. Likewise, it is not a standardized assessment, since the age levels that are attributed to the items are, at best, rough approximations based on other tests and the developmental literature that the authors have read. Standardized assessments are essential for determining eligibility in many states. Furthermore, individual professionals should assess attributes of the child not covered in this curriculum. For example, the physical or occupational therapist will need to look at motor patterns, range of motion, and other characteristics that are not part of a developmental curriculum. Therefore, the CCITSN is not a short-cut to a multidisciplinary assessment. What the CCITSN does provide, though, is a guide for selecting the developmental attainment goals for the child.

There has been some discussion in the literature about the extent to which parents should be involved in selecting the developmental attainment goals for the IFSP. On one hand, it is argued that no goal should be included in the IFSP that does not originate with the parent(s). On the other hand, it is argued that professionals have done their assessments, have the best knowledge of a child's developmental needs, and should select the developmental attainment goals to present to the parents for approval. Most interventionists typically choose a middle ground. Parents and other major caregivers provide most of the care and intervention for an infant or toddler. If intervention is to be successful, it is critical that caregivers be committed to the developmental goals. Such commitment comes from understanding the goals and agreeing to their relative importance. The selection of developmental attainment goals should, therefore, be a process that involves: 1) the interventionist's getting to know what the caregivers' concerns are, what they want for the child, and why; 2) the interventionist's thinking carefully about how the developmental attainment goals suggested by the CCITSN fit into the caregiver's concerns and desires for the child; 3) a dialogue between the interventionist and caregivers regarding the developmental attainment goals and how they relate to the caregiver's concerns; and 4) a joint agreement as to the nature and number of initial goals for the child.

There will be instances in which an interventionist is frustrated because a family has very different goals for a child than those that the interventionist believes are appropriate. For example, it may be quite clear that a 20-month-old child with severe athetoid cerebral palsy does not have either the breath control or the oral motor control to develop speech as a primary mode of communication in the near future. The professional may feel it is urgent to begin developing the skills that would facilitate the use of an augmentative communication system. Yet, the family may be opposed to any intervention that could be construed as using something other than speech for communication. In such a situation, it is essential that the sense of partnership between parent and interventionist not be disrupted. The interventionist should seek ways in which to help the family diligently work on their primary concerns (e.g., obtaining speech therapy), while remaining ready to explore other options when (and if) they become ready to do so. In the meantime, the interventionist may find that many of the skills that would be helpful in converting to an augmentative system are being developed as part of other developmental attainment goals with which the parents are in full agreement (e.g., shaping up an indicator response to do matching tasks as part of improving cognitive skills).

When developmental attainment goals are chosen for the IFSP it is important to recognize that these are *only initial goals*. The intent of the CCITSN is that the child work through the sequences, not just on particular items. Thus, as soon as any item is mastered, the interventionist moves on to the next item in that sequence without waiting for a new IFSP to be developed.

IMPLEMENTING THE INTERVENTION PROGRAM

When assessment and item selection have been completed, the intervention process can begin. There is an expanded curriculum item, found in the Curriculum Sequences section (pp. 69–366), for each item in the Assessment Log. Included in the expanded item is a description of the "materials" that will be needed; a "Procedures" section, for encouraging the child to learn the skill; suggestions on how to integrate the learning of the skill into the child's "daily routines"; "adaptations" for visually, hearing, and motor impaired children; and the "criterion" of mastery. These items are basically very simple and can be condensed into a few words of reminder for whoever is implementing the intervention in a particular setting. These reminders might be written on record keeping forms (see discussion and example below) or may simply be given to a caregiver as one list or several lists to be posted in locations where the intervention procedures should take place. For example, there might be a list of activities to incorporate into the child's diaper changing time and other routines taking place at the diaper changing table; a list for mealtime activities; a list for outdoor activities; and so forth.

In order to maintain continuity and to measure progress and make program modifications, it is essential that careful records be kept for each child. However, the kinds of records that need to be kept will vary tremendously depending on the setting, the involved caregivers, and the assisting professionals.

At the simplest level, record keeping will consist of entering the date when an item was mastered in the Assessment Log, in the column to the right of the last assessment. When the next full assessment takes place, these items will, of course, not have to be assessed again.

In center-based intervention programs and with certain families in home-based programs, more extensive records will be possible and will provide a clearer picture of a child's progress. One approach is to have a form made up that will detail the child's weekly activities. On this form, the caregiver or interventionist will have to check whether the child had an opportunity to practice the skill and whether he or she was successful. Figure 3 is an example of such a form.

Another approach is to have each item written on an individual activity sheet. Figure 4 is an example of a form that has proved helpful. Figure 5 gives instructions for Figure 4's use. By using this form, a trial-by-trial account is provided of the child's opportunities to practice a particular skill. This form may be a particularly helpful record of the skills of a child who is progressing very slowly or whose performance is especially erratic.

USING THE CCITSN IN CONJUNCTION WITH THE CCPSN

Many children with special needs have skills that fall between the 1- and 4-year-old levels. Neither the CCITSN nor the CCPSN has an adequate range to provide a good assessment of these children's developmental capabilities. The CCITSN dovetails directly with the CCPSN so that a child can be working in both curricula simultaneously. The Developmental Progress Chart: CCITSN and CCPSN (pp. 66–67), combines both curricula and shows the relationships between the sequences in each. (Additional copies of the combined progress chart and an assessment log for the age range of 12 months to 3 years are available from Paul H. Brookes Publishing Co., P.O. Box 10624, Baltimore, MD 21285-0624.)

Name: _____   Week: _____
Location: _____

Situation for activities	Opportunity to observe					Mastered (date)
	M	T	W	Th	F	
Child on back (e.g., diapering, playing) Visually tracks in circle						
Turns head to search for sound						
Feet in air for play						
Child on back or sitting supported Glance from toy to toy when one in each hand						
Plays with toys placed in hand(s)						
Places both hands on toy at midline						
Looks or reaches for ojbect that touches body out of sight						
Reacts to tactile stimulation with movement						
Repeats activities that get interesting results						
Social interactions, including meals Anticipates frequently occurring events in familiar games						
Responds differently to stranger and family members						
Laughs						
Repeats sounds when imitated						
Turns to name being called						
Repeats vocalizations that get reactions						
Smiles reciprocally						
Mealtime Munches food						
Vocalizes 5 or more consonant-vowel combinations						
Bathing and dressing Holds trunk steady when held at hips						

Figure 3.   Sample weekly record for child learning objectives of the IFSP.

USING THE CCITSN WITH OLDER CHILDREN

Although the CCITSN has been designed primarily for use with infants and young children, the original field-testing population did include some older individuals with severe and multiple disabilities. Caregivers who want to use the CCITSN with these groups will need to make appropriate adaptations in the items and materials that are used. Generally, the sequences can be maintained, but the over-riding concern should be to teach behaviors that are adaptive for the individual. For example, it is appropriate to use blocks when teaching matching to a young child. With a teenager or pre-teen, however, more benefit would be derived by constructing a prevocational task using tableware or different-sized envelopes.

Individual Activity Sheet

Student _____ Date begun _____

Teacher _____ Curriculum number _____

Target behavior (goal)

Training method (description of positioning, materials, and toys needed, etc.)

Steps

Step 1 _____

Step 2 _____

Step 3 _____

Criterion

| State of the child | | | | | | | | | | | | | | | | | | | | | | | | |

Trials	5 5 5 5 5		5 5 5 5 5		5 5 5 5 5		5 5 5 5 5
	4 4 4 4 4		4 4 4 4 4		4 4 4 4 4		4 4 4 4 4
	3 3 3 3 3		3 3 3 3 3		3 3 3 3 3		3 3 3 3 3
	2 2 2 2 2		2 2 2 2 2		2 2 2 2 2		2 2 2 2 2
	1 1 1 1 1		1 1 1 1 1		1 1 1 1 1		1 1 1 1 1

Step

Date

| State of the child | | | | | | | | | | | | | | | | | | | | | | | | |

Trials	5 5 5 5 5		5 5 5 5 5		5 5 5 5 5		5 5 5 5 5
	4 4 4 4 4		4 4 4 4 4		4 4 4 4 4		4 4 4 4 4
	3 3 3 3 3		3 3 3 3 3		3 3 3 3 3		3 3 3 3 3
	2 2 2 2 2		2 2 2 2 2		2 2 2 2 2		2 2 2 2 2
	1 1 1 1 1		1 1 1 1 1		1 1 1 1 1		1 1 1 1 1

Step

Date

Comments:

Figure 4. Example of an individual activity sheet.

Using the Individual Activity Sheet

(Student)	Record the student's name.
(Date begun)	Record the date the curriculum item is started.
(Teacher)	Record the person who will be teaching the item.
(Curriculum number)	Record the number and letter of the item (e.g., 20a.).
(Target behavior [goal])	State the item goal (i.e., the Behavior found centered above each curriculum item).
(Training method)	Generally describe the item procedures (e.g., arrangement of materials, toys needed) in simple terms, so as to avoid constant referral to the curriculum book.
(Steps)	List the steps in the curriculum item. Additional steps may be derived through task analysis if necessary.
(Criterion)	State the standard on which the decision is made to progress to the next step.

(State of the child)	Describe the state of the child during the programming (e.g., drowsy, fussy, alert).
(Trials)	Five trials should be run on each item, if at all possible. Starting with 1 and moving vertically, mark each trial using a slash (/) for a correct response or a cross (X) for an incorrect response. After 5 trials have been run, circle the number out of a total of 5 that the child got correct. If no correct responses are obtained, add a zero below the column and circle it. After 5 sets of 5 trials have been run, connect the circled numbers. This will give a visual trend of the child's progress and the program's effectiveness (see example of data below).
(Example of data)	On the 1st set of trials (1st column), the child got 1 correct—circle the 1; 2nd set (2nd column), 3 correct—circle the 3; 3rd set (3rd column), 3 correct—circle the 3; 4th set (4th column), 4 correct—circle the 4; 5th set (5th column), 5 correct—circle the 5.
(Date)	Under each set of 5 trials, record the Date that the trials were run. (Please note that 5 or 40 trials can be done on one day; while data is collected in sets of five, more than 5 trials may be done at one time.)
(Comments)	Add information that enhances the program, such as suggested toys for variety, or the time of day the child is most alert.

Figure 5. Instructions for using individual activity sheet (see Figure 4).

REFERENCES

Johnson-Martin, N.M., Attermeier, S.M., & Hacker, B. (1990). *The Carolina curriculum for preschoolers with special needs.* Baltimore: Paul H. Brookes Publishing Co.

Johnson-Martin, N., Jens, K.G., & Attermeier, S.M. (1986). *The Carolina curriculum for handicapped infants and infants at risk.* Baltimore: Paul H. Brookes Publishing Co.

Piaget, J. (1952). *The origins of intelligence in children.* New York: International Universities Press.

RECOMMENDED READINGS

Bernheimer, L.P., Gallimore, R., & Weisner, T.S. (1990). Ecocultural theory as a context for the individual family service plan. *Journal of Early Intervention, 14*(3), 219–233.

Deal, A., Dunst, C.J., & Trivette, C.M. (1989). A flexible and functional approach to developing individualized family support plans. *Infants and Young Children, 1*(4), 32–43.

Gowen, J.W., & Johnson-Martin, N.M. (1989, April). *Infant assessment and the individualized family service plan.* Paper presented at the 67th annual convention of the Council for Exceptional Children, San Francisco. (Available from J.W. Gowen, Western Carolina Center, 300 Enola Road, Morganton, NC 28655.)

Johnson, B.H., McGonigel, M.J., & Kaufmann, R.K. (Eds.). (1989). *Guidelines and recommended practices for the individualized family service plan.* Chapel Hill: NEC*TAS. (Available from CB# 8040, Suite 500, NCNB Plaza, Chapel Hill, NC 27599.)

Assessment Log
and
Developmental Progress Charts

The Assessment Log and Developmental Progress charts found on pages 47–67 are also available for purchase in packages of 10. There is also an Assessment Log for the age range of 12 months to 3 years. These materials may be ordered from Paul H. Brookes Publishing Co., P.O. Box 10624, Baltimore, Maryland 21285-0624 (1-800-638-3775).

ASSESSMENT LOG

Insert the date of your assessment at the top of the column and insert a + in the box for each mastered item.

Age (Months)		Curriculum Sequences	Date: ___	Date: ___	Date: ___	Date: ___
	1.	**Visual Pursuit and Object Permanence**				
	a.	Visually fixates for at least 3 seconds				
	b.	Visually tracks object from side to side				
	c.	Visually tracks object from forehead to chest				
	d.	Visually tracks object moving in a circle				
(3)	e.	Gaze lingers where object or person disappears				
(6)	f.	Continues to look at caregiver when caregiver's face is covered with a cloth				

Omit the following for children physically able to do sequence 2.

Age (Months)		Curriculum Sequences				
(9)	g.	Looks at cover under which object has disappeared after a momentary distraction				
(12)	h.	Looks to the correct place when object is hidden in 1 of 2 places				
(15)	i.	Looks to the correct place when object is hidden in 1 of 3 places				
(18)	j.	Looks at correct place for an object after seeing it covered in 3 places successively				
	k.	Looks successively at 2 different covers until an object is found that was hidden from the child's view (i.e., visual displacement)				
	l.	Looks systematically at 3 different covers until an object is uncovered that was hidden from the child's view.				
	2.	**Object Permanence: Motor and Visual**				
	a.	Pulls cloth from face				
	b.	Pulls cloth from caregiver's face				
(6)	c.	Uncovers partially hidden toy				
	d.	Uncovers fully hidden toy				
	e.	Finds toy hidden under a cover, when 2 covers are present				
	f.	Finds toy when it is hidden under 1 of 2 covers, alternately				
(9)	g.	Removes cover when object is hidden under 1 of 3 covers				

Age (Months)	Curriculum Sequences	Date:	Date:	Date:	Date:
(12)	h. Finds toy hidden under 3 superimposed covers				
	i. Finds toy after seeing it covered in 3 places, successively (i.e., visible displacement)				
(15)	j. Finds object after it is covered in 2 places, successively (i.e., invisible placement)				
(18)	k. Finds object under 1 of 3 covers after a systematic search (i.e., invisible displacement)				
	3. Auditory Localization and Object Permanence				
	a. Quiets when noise is presented				
	b. Visually searches for sound				
(3)	c. Turns head and searches for or reaches toward ear-level sound while lying down				
	d. Turns head or reaches toward source of ear-level sound while sitting level				
(6)	e. Turns head toward sound and looks or reaches directly at noisemaker when noise is presented at shoulder level				
	f. Looks directly at (or reaches for) noisemaker when sound is presented to the side at waist level				
(9)	g. Turns head and looks back and forth to 2 sounds (or reaches to either side as sounds are presented)				
(15)	h. Reaches for an object after it no longer makes noise (for children with visual impairments)				
(18)	i. Reaches for an object that no longer makes noise, at midline and both sides, above and below shoulder level (for children with visual impairments)				
(21)	j. Reaches in the correct direction for an object that has made noise in several places (for children with visual impairments)				
	4. Attention and Memory				
(3)	a. Shows anticipation of regularly occurring events in everyday care				
(6)	b. Anticipates frequently occurring events in familiar "games" (e.g., nursery rhymes) after 2 or 3 trials				
(9)	c. Anticipates frequently occuring events in familiar "games" on first trial				
(12)	d. Remembers location of objects that are put down for a few minutes				
(15)	e. Reacts to a change in a familiar game or routine				

Age (Months)	Curriculum Sequences	Date:	Date:	Date:	Date:
	f. Recognizes familiar toys, people, and places				
(18)	g. Imitates adult actions with novel objects several hours after observing actions				
	h. Retrieves own toys from usual locations				
	i. Imitates novel action involving a combination of objects several hours after observing the action				
(21)	j. Recognizes own and others' clothing, toys, and personal belongings				
	k. Retrieves household objects from usual locations on request (i.e., signed, spoken)				
	l. Puts objects away in correct place				
	m. Says or acts out parts of rhymes or songs independently				
(24)	n. Repeats a 2-word or 2-number sequence				
	5. Concept Development				
(3)	a. Responds differently to warm/cold, rough/smooth (same as item 19a.)				
(6)	b. Responds differently to family members and strangers (same as item 15h.)				
(9)	c. Responds differently to adults and children (either familiar or unfamiliar)				
	d. Reacts to a "different" object in a group of similar objects				
(12)	e. Laughs or smiles at adults who are engaging in "baby" or other unexpected behaviors				
(15)	f. Is puzzled or surprised when objects "vanish" or cease to function in usual ways				
(18)	g. Points to objects or pictures by simple category names (e.g., dog, cat, house)				
	h. Sorts objects into categories				
(21)	i. Sorts by color				
	j. Sorts "big" and "little"				
	k. Points to or otherwise identifies "round" and "square"				
(24)	l. Points to or otherwise identifies "big" and "little"				
	6. Understanding Space				
	a. Shifts attention (i.e., visual fixation, body orientation) from one object to another				

Age (Months)		Curriculum Sequences	Date:	Date:	Date:	Date:
(3)	b.	Looks for or reaches toward objects in sight that touch the body (omit for children with visual impairments)				
	c.	Looks for or reaches toward objects out of sight that touch the body				
(6)	d.	Looks for or reaches toward objects that fall from view while making a noise				
	e.	Looks for or reaches toward objects that fall quietly from view				
(9)	f.	Looks or moves in the right direction for objects that fall and roll or bounce to a new location				
(12)	g.	Searches for objects moved out of visual field or away from midline				
	h.	Retrieves toys from a container when they have been dropped through a hole in the top				
(15)	i.	Pulls string to get object from behind a barrier				
	j.	Reaches object from behind a barrier				
(18)	k.	Moves self around a barrier to get an object				
	l.	Retrieves familiar objects from usual locations in another room, upon request				
(21)	m.	Puts objects away in correct places				
(24)	n.	Uses "tools" to deal with spatial problems (e.g., extends reach with a stick, extends height with a stool) (same as item 8k.)				
	7.	**Functional Use of Objects and Symbolic Play**				
	a.	Moves hand to mouth				
(3)	b.	Explores objects with mouth				
	c.	Plays with (e.g., shakes, bangs) toys placed in hand				
	d.	Commonly performs 4 or more activities with objects				
(6)	e.	Explores objects and responds to their differences				
	f.	Demonstrates appropriate activities with toys that have obviously different properties				
(9)	g.	Combines 2 objects in a functional manner				
(12)	h.	Imitates activites related to the function of objects				
(15)	i.	Plays spontaneously with a variety of objects, demonstrating their functions				

51

Age (Months)		Curriculum Sequences	Date: ___	Date: ___	Date: ___	Date: ___
(18)	j.	Imitates adult behavior with props				
(21)	k.	Spontaneously engages in adult activities with props				
(24)	l.	"Talks" to dolls or animals and/or makes them interact with one another				
	8.	**Problem Solving**				
(3)	a.	Repeats activity that produces an interesting result				
	b.	Persists in effort to obtain an object or make an effect				
	c.	Pulls string to obtain an object or make an effect				
(6)	d.	Repeats an activity that elicits an interesting reaction from others				
	e.	Overcomes obstacles to get toys				
(9)	f.	Plays with a variety of toys to produce effects				
(12)	g.	Increases rate of usual activity with a toy when it stops working or tries another activity to make the toy work (work on items 8h. and 8i. simultaneously)				
(15)	h.	Uses adults to solve problems (work on items 8g. and 8i. simultaneously)				
(18)	i.	Imitates an adult action to solve a problem (work on items 8g., 8h., and 8i. simultaneously)				
(21)	j.	Solves simple problems without adult assistance				
(24)	k.	Uses "tools" to solve problems (same as item 6n.)				
	9.	**Visual Perception**				
(15)	a.	Places large round form in a form board				
	b.	Places square form in a form board				
	c.	Imitates building a "chair" with blocks				
(18)	d.	Places round and square forms in a form board when they are simultaneously presented				
	e.	Places triangular form in a form board with a triangular hole				
	f.	Places round, square, and triangular forms in a form board when they are simultaneously presented				
	g.	Completes simple puzzles				
(21)	h.	Places correct forms in a form ball				
(24)	i.	Imitates a block train				

Age (Months)		Curriculum Sequences	Date: ___	Date: ___	Date: ___	Date: ___
	10.	**Prevocabulary/Vocabulary**				
	a.	Provides consistent signals for states of hunger, distress, and pleasure				
(3)	b.	Vocalizes 5 or more consonant and vowel sounds				
	c.	Laughs				
(6)	d.	Vocalizes 3 or more feelings				
(9)	e.	Vocalizes repetitive consonant-vowel combinations				
	f.	Uses 2 or more gestures associated with verbal concepts (e.g., "all gone," "so big," "more," "bye-bye")				
(12)	g.	Uses 2 or more words or signs to label objects or to name people				
	h.	Uses 3 or more words or signs to label objects or to name people				
(15)	i.	Uses one or more exclamations or signs that stand for an exclamation				
(18)	j.	Uses 7 or more words or signs				
	k.	Meaningfully says or signs "no"				
(21)	l.	Appropriately uses 15 words or signs				
(24)	m.	Names or makes appropriate signs for 3 or more pictures of familiar objects				
	11.	**Imitation: Sound and Gestures**				
	a.	Quiets to voice				
(3)	b.	Looks at person who is talking and gesturing				
	c.	Repeats sounds just made when imitated by a caregiver				
	d.	Continues a movement if it is imitated by a caregiver				
	e.	Shifts sounds—imitates sounds in repertoire when made by a caregiver				
	f.	Imitates an activity in repertoire after observing the caregiver doing that activity				
(6)	g.	Imitates inflection (i.e., pitch)				
	h.	Attempts to match new sounds				
	i.	Imitates unfamiliar movements				

Age (Months)	Curriculum Sequences	Date:	Date:	Date:	Date:
	j. Imitates familiar 2-syllable words (e.g., baba, dada, mama)				
(9)	k. Experiments with making own mouth move like that of the adult				
(12)	l. Imitates familiar 2-syllable words with syllable changes (e.g., baby, uh-oh, all gone) or Imitates 2 signs that stand for words (e.g., Daddy, all gone, more, eat, drink)				
	m. Imitates most new one-syllable words or Imitates most simple signs that stand for words				
(15)	n. Imitates familiar words overheard in conversation or Imitates signs observed in others' conversations				
(18)	o. Imitates environmental sounds during play				
(21)	p. Imitates 2-word sentences or Imitates sequences of 2 signs				
(24)	q. Imitates 3-syllable words				
	12. Responses to Communication from Others				
(3)	a. Appropriately reacts to tone of voice and/or some facial expressions				
	b. Turns to the direction from which name is being called				
	c. Stops activity when name is called				
(6)	d. Does previously learned task on verbal or gestural cue				
	e. Responds with correct gesture to "up" and "bye-bye"				
(9)	f. Responds to "no" (i.e., briefly stops activity)				
	g. Identifies 3 objects or people that are spoken or signed				
(12)	h. Responds to "give me" (spoken and/or signed) (same as 15l.)				
	i. Follows simple commands (spoken and/or signed)				
(15)	j. Identifies most common objects when they are named and/or signed				
	k. Appropriately indicates "yes" or "no" in response to questions				
	l. Identifies 2 body parts when they are named or signed				

Age (Months)		Curriculum Sequences	Date:	Date:	Date:	Date:
(18)	m.	Retrieves objects from the same room on verbal or signed request				
	n.	Identifies at least 4 animals in pictures when they are named or signed				
(21)	o.	Identifies 15 or more pictures of common objects when they are named or signed				
	p.	Understands 2 or more category words (e.g., animals)				
	q.	Identifies 5 body parts				
	r.	Correctly follows 3 different 2-part commands involving one object				
(24)	s.	Follows 3 different 3-part commands				
	13.	**Conversation Skills**				
	a.	Smiles to person who is talking and/or gesturing				
(3)	b.	Protests by vocalizing disapproval of actions and/or events				
	c.	Repeats vocalizations and/or gestures that elicit reactions				
	d.	Indicates interest in a toy or object through eye gaze, reaching, or vocalization				
	e.	"Requests" continued action of familiar toy, song, or activity by starting body movements, eye contact, and/or vocalization				
	f.	Waits for adult to take his or her "turn"				
	g.	Begins to listen—coordinates looking with listening				
(6)	h.	Makes requests by directing caregiver's attention				
	i.	Indicates "no more" and "I don't like this" by turning or pushing away				
	j.	Notices and vocalizes when primary caregiver prepares to leave				
	k.	Uses eye gaze to select other person as partner in communication exchange				
(9)	l.	Changes pitch/volume to signify intensity of desires				
	m.	Raises arms to be picked up				
	n.	Indicates desire to "get down" or "get out" in some consistent fashion other than fussing or crying				

Age (Months)		Curriculum Sequences	Date: ___	Date: ___	Date: ___	Date: ___
(12)	o.	Plays reciprocal games (e.g., taking turns making sounds, playing the Peek-a-boo game, clapping your hands)				
	p.	Uses words or signs to express wants				
(15)	q.	Seeks adult's assistance in exploring the environment through vocalizations, pointing, or other communicative signals				
	r.	Uses inflection pattern(s) when vocalizing (or uses gestures as if signing)				
	s.	Greets familiar people with an appropriate vocalization or sign				
(18)	t.	Directs caregiver to provide information through questioning look, vocal inflection, and or words				
	u.	Uses inflection patterns in a sentence with 1 or 2 understandable words (or mixes recognizable signs in with other gestures)				
(21)	v.	Experiments with 2-word utterances or 2-sign gestures to achieve specific goals (e.g., "Me go," "Doggie up," "Daddy sit")				
	w.	Spontaneously says (or signs) familiar greetings and farewells at appropriate times				
	x.	Says (or signs) "no" to protest when something is taken away				
	y.	Spontaneously uses words (or signs) in pretend play				
	z.	Uses word (or sign) combinations to describe remote events				
	aa.	Uses word(s) (or sign[s]) to request action				
(24)	bb.	Answers simple questions with a verbal response, gesture, or sign				
	14.	**Self-Direction**				
(12)	a.	Moves away from primary caregiver who is in same room				
	b.	Moves partially out of primary caregiver's sight for short periods of play				
(15)	c.	Makes choices (e.g., has preferred toys, foods, clothes, storybooks)				
	d.	Gets toys with which to play from a box or shelf of toys				
(18)	e.	Plays alone with toys for 15 minutes				

Age (Months)		Curriculum Sequences	Date: ___	Date: ___	Date: ___	Date: ___
	f.	Approaches peer or adult to initiate play				
(21)	g.	Explores				
	h.	Resists attempts from others to assist with feeding				
(24)	i.	"Asks" for snacks or drinks				
	15.	**Social Skills**				
	a.	Stops crying when sees (or touches) bottle or breast				
	b.	Can be comforted by talking to, holding, or rocking				
(3)	c.	Smiles to auditory and tactile stimulation				
	d.	Smiles reciprocally				
	e.	Smiles at familiar person				
	f.	Smiles at mirror image (omit for children with significant visual impairments)				
	g.	Tries to attract attention by making sounds, smiling, eye contact, or body language				
(6)	h.	Responds differently to family members and strangers (same as item 5b.)				
	i.	Participates in simple games				
(9)	j.	Repeats activity that elicits laughter from observer(s)				
	k.	Initiates game-playing				
(12)	l.	"Gives" items to others upon request (same as item 12h.)				
	m.	Spontaneously shares with adults				
(15)	n.	Shows affection (e.g., hugs, kisses)				
	o.	Tries to please others				
(18)	p.	Plays alongside other children—some exchange of toys				
	q.	Provides "help" in simple household tasks— imitates adults				
(21)	r.	"Performs" for others				
	s.	Tries to comfort others in distress				
(24)	t.	Spontaneously shares with peers				
	16.	**Self-Help Skills: Eating**				
	a.	Sucks from nipple smoothly				

Age (Months)	Curriculum Sequences	Date: ___	Date: ___	Date: ___	Date: ___
(3)	b. "Roots" toward food or objects infrequently				
	c. Bites down on spoon infrequently				
	d. Gags infrequently—only when appropriate				
	e. Munches food—chewing up and down				
	f. Uses purposeful tongue movements				
(6)	g. Pulls food off spoon with lips				
	h. Holds own bottle (omit for breast-fed infants)				
	i. Assists in drinking from cup that is held by an adult				
	j. Eats junior or mashed table food without gagging				
	k. Cleans lower lip with teeth				
(9)	l. Chews with a rotary/side-to-side action				
(12)	m. Feeds self with fingers				
	n. Holds and drinks from cup				
(15)	o. Brings spoon to mouth and eats food off of it				
	p. Scoops food from dish with spoon				
(18)	q. Chews well				
	r. No longer uses bottle or breast				
(21)	s. Feeds self without spilling—almost no help				
	t. Feeds self a meal with spoon and cup as main utensils				
(24)	u. Distinguishes between edible and nonedible substances				
	17. Self-Help Skills: Dressing				
	a. Cooperates in dressing and undressing (e.g., holds arms out for sleeve, foot out for shoe)				
(12)	b. Removes socks and partially pulls shirt over head				
	c. Indicates need for change of soiled diaper or pants				
(15)	d. Removes loose clothing (e.g., socks, mittens, hat, untied shoes)				
(18)	e. Unties shoes or hat, as an act of undressing				
	f. Unfastens clothing zipper that has a large pull tab				
(21)	g. Puts on hat				

Age (Months)		Curriculum Sequences	Date:	Date:	Date:	Date:
	h.	Puts on socks, loose shoes, and "stretch" pants				
(24)	i.	Removes simple clothing (e.g., open shirt or jacket, "stretch" pants)				
	18.	**Self-Help Skills: Grooming**				
(9)	a.	Enjoys playing in water (same as item 19f.)				
(15)	b.	Cooperates in hand-washing and drying				
(18)	c.	Allows his or her teeth to be brushed				
(21)	d.	Washes own hands				
(24)	e.	Wipes nose, if given a tissue				
	19.	**Fine Motor Skills: Tactile Integration**				
(3)	a.	Responds differently to warm/cold rough/smooth (same as item 5a.)				
	b.	Permits hands, feet, or body to be moved over soft, smooth-texture surfaces; or spontaneously moves them over such surfaces				
(6)	c.	Reacts to tactile stimulation with movement				
	d.	Permits hands, feet, or body to be moved over rough-textured surfaces; or spontaneously moves them over such surfaces				
	e.	Explores objects with fingers				
(9)	f.	Plays in water (same as item 18a.)				
	g.	Finds an object that is hidden in textured material				
(12)	h.	Plays with soft-textured materials				
(15)	i.	Spreads soft materials with fingers				
(18)	j.	Spreads firmer materials with hands				
(21)	k.	Pokes or plays with clay				
	20.	**Fine Motor Skills: Reaching, Grasping, and Releasing**				
(3)	a.	Actively moves arm when he or she sees or hears an object				
	b.	Bats at object at chest level				
	c.	Grasps object that is placed in his or her hand (i.e., not reflexive grasp)				
	d.	Reaches out and grasps objects near body				
	e.	Displays extended reach and grasp				

Age (Months)		Curriculum Sequences	Date: ___	Date: ___	Date: ___	Date: ___
(6)	f.	Rakes and scoops small objects (i.e., fingers against palm)				
	g.	Releases one object to take another				
	h.	Grasps an object, using thumb against index and middle fingers				
	i.	Uses inferior pincer grasp (i.e., thumb against side of index finger)				
	j.	Uses index finger to poke				
(9)	k.	Uses neat pincer grasp (i.e., thumb against tip of index finger)				
	l.	Releases four objects into a container				
(12)	m.	Imitates building a 2-block tower				
	n.	Imitates building 3–4-block tower				
	o.	Releases many objects into a container				
(15)	p.	Grasps two small objects with one hand				
(18)	q.	Imitates building 6–8-block tower				
(21)	r.	Puts a small object through a small hole in a container				
(24)	s.	Puts one pellet into a bottle				
	21.	**Fine Motor Skills: Manipulation**				
	a.	Looks to one side at a hand or a toy				
	b.	Looks at or manipulates a toy that is placed in the hands at midline				
	c.	Brings a toy and the hand into visual field and looks at them when the toy is placed in the hand (i.e., may move head or hand), or moves a toy to the mouth at midline (if the child has a visual impairment)				
(3)	d.	Watches hands at midline—actively moves and watches results				
	e.	Plays with own feet or toes				
(6)	f.	Glances from one toy to another when a toy is placed in each hand, or alternately plays with the toys				
	g.	Reaches out for toys and picks them up when toys and hand are in visual field (modify for a child with visual impairment)				

Age (Months)		Curriculum Sequences	Date:	Date:	Date:	Date:
	h.	Reaches out for toys and gets them when the toys (not the child's hands) are in the visual field (modify for a child with a visual impairment)				
	i.	Looks toward an object and visually directs the reach, or adjusts the reach to get a noisy object (if has no functional vision)				
(9)	j.	Manipulates objects with hands and fingers				
(12)	k.	Removes rings from a post				
	l.	Removes small round pegs from holes				
(15)	m.	Puts one large round peg in a hole				
	n.	Puts one small round peg in a hole				
	o.	Puts 5–6 small round pegs in holes (completes task)				
(18)	p.	Unwraps an edible item or other small object				
(21)	q.	Turns pages one at a time				
(24)	r.	Turns a doorknob with forearm rotation				
	22.	**Fine Motor Skills: Bilateral Skills**				
(3)	a.	Raises both hands when object is presented—hands partially open				
	b.	Brings hands together at midline				
	c.	Places both hands on a toy at midline				
(6)	d.	Transfers objects from hand to hand				
(9)	e.	Claps hands				
	f.	Uses both hands to perform the same action				
(12)	g.	Plays with toys at midline; one hand holds the toy and the other manipulates it				
	h.	Pulls apart pop beads				
(15)	i.	Holds a dowel in one hand and places a ring over it				
(18)	j.	Puts a pencil through a hole in a piece of cardboard				
	k.	Unscrews small lids				
(21)	l.	Puts loose pop beads together				
(24)	m.	Strings 3 large beads				

Age (Months)		Curriculum Sequences	Date: ___	Date: ___	Date: ___	Date: ___
	23.	**Visual-Motor Skills: Pencil Control and Copying**				
(15)	a.	Marks paper with writing implement				
(18)	b.	Scribbles spontaneously				
(21)	c.	Makes single vertical stroke, in imitation				
(24)	d.	Shifts from scribble to stroke and back, in imitation				
	24.	**Gross Motor Skills: Prone (On Stomach)**				
	a.	Lifts head, freeing nose; arms and legs flexed				
(3)	b.	Lifts head to 45° angle; arms and legs partially flexed				
	c.	Extends head, arms, trunk, and legs in prone position				
	d.	Bears weight on elbows in prone position				
	e.	Rolls from stomach to back				
	f.	Reaches while supported on one elbow				
	g.	Supports self on hands with arms extended and head at 90°				
(6)	h.	Pivots in prone position				
	i.	Pulls forward in prone position				
	j.	Pulls self to hands and knees				
	k.	Rocks forward and backward while on hands and knees				
(9)	l.	Plays with toys in an asymmetrical half-sitting position				
	m.	Moves forward (creeps) while on hands and knees				
(12)	n.	Raises one hand high while on hands and knees				
	o.	Creeps up stairs				
(15)	p.	Creeps down stairs, backward				
	25.	**Gross Motor Skills: Supine (On Back)**				
	a.	Turns head from side to side in response to auditory or visual stimulus				
	b.	Bends and straightens arms and legs				
	c.	Brings hands to mouth				
(3)	d.	Maintains head in midline position while supine				

Age (Months)		Curriculum Sequences	Date:	Date:	Date:	Date:
	e.	Reaches out with arm while in a supine position				
	f.	Holds feet in air for play				
(6)	g.	Rolls from stomach to back				
	26.	**Gross Motor Skills: Upright**				
(3)	a.	Holds head steady when held				
(6)	b.	Holds trunk steady when held at hips				
(9)	c.	Moves to a sitting position from stomach or all-fours position				
	d.	Sits alone				
	e.	Pulls self to standing position				
	f.	Steps sideways holding a support				
	g.	Stoops to pick up a toy while holding a support				
	h.	Removes hands from support and stands independently				
(12)	i.	Takes independent steps				
(15)	j.	Moves from hands and knees, to hands and feet, to standing				
	26–I.	**Gross Motor Skills: Upright — Posture and locomotion**				
	a.	Walks sideways				
(18)	b.	Walks backward				
	c.	Squats in play				
(21)	d.	Runs stiffly				
(24)	e.	Runs well				
	26–II.	**Gross Motor Skills: Upright — Stairs**				
	a.	Walks up stairs with railing, same-step foot placement				
(18)	b.	Walks down stairs with railing, same-step foot placement				
(21)	c.	Walks up stairs without railing, same-step foot placement				
(24)	d.	Walks down stairs without railing, same-step foot placement				
	26–III.	**Gross Motor Skills: Upright — Jumping**				
(21)	a.	Jumps off floor with both feet				

SAMPLE

Age (Months)		Curriculum Sequences	Date: ___	Date: ___	Date: ___	Date: ___
(24)	b.	Jumps off step with both feet				
26–IV.		**Gross Motor Skills: Upright Balance**				
(18)	a.	Stands on one foot while hands are held				
(21)	b.	Walks with one foot on the walking board and one foot on the floor				
	c.	Stands on one foot without help				
(24)	d.	Walks on line, following general direction				

CCITSN Developmental Progress Chart

Dates of Testing (Fill in circle with color used on the chart):

- ○ 1. _____
- ○ 2. _____
- ○ 3. _____
- ○ 4. _____

Child: _____

Interventionist: _____

(The hatch marks indicate that no normative data are available.)

[watermark: SAMPLE]

	CCITSN Curriculum Sequence	0–3 mo.	3–6 mo.	6–9 mo.	9–12 mo.	12–15 mo.	15–18 mo.	18–21 mo.	21–24 mo.
Cognition	1. Visual Pursuit and Object Permanence	a b c d e	f	g	h	▨	▨	▨	▨
	2. Object Permanence: Motor and Visual	a b c	d e	f g	h	▨	▨	▨	▨
	3. Auditory Localization and Object Permanence	a b	c d	e f g	h ■	i	j k	l m	n
	4. Attention and Memory	a	b	c	d	e	f g	h i j	k l m n
	5. Concept Development	a	b	c	d e	f	g	h i	j k l
	6. Understanding Space	a	b	c d	e	f	g	h i j	k
	7. Functional Use of Objects and Symbolic Play	a	b c d e	f g	h	i	j k	l m	n
	8. Problem Solving		a	b	c d	e	f g	h i	j k
	9. Visual Perception	a	b c	d e f	g	h	i	g h	i
Communication	10. Prevocabulary/Vocabulary	a	b	c d	e f	g h	i j	k l	m
	11. Imitation: Sound and Gestures	a	b c d e	f	g h	i j	k l m	n o	p q
	12. Responses to Communication from Others	a	b c d	e f	g h	i	j	k l	m
	13. Conversation Skills	a b	c d e f g h i j k	l	m n o	p q	r s t	u v	w x y z aa bb
Social Adaptation	14. Self-Direction	a b c	d e	f	g	h	i	f g	h i
	15. Social Skills	a b c	d e f	g h i j	k l	m n	o p	q r s	s t
	16. Self-Help Skills: Eating	a b	c d e f g	h i j k l	m	n	o p	q r s	t u
	17. Self-Help Skills: Dressing		c d e f g	h i j k l				f g	h i
	18. Self-Help Skills: Grooming			a	a	b	c	d	e
Fine Motor Skills	19. Fine Motor Skills: Tactile Integration	a	b c	d e f	g	h	j	k	
	20. Fine Motor Skills: Reaching, Grasping, and Releasing	a	b c d e f	g h i j	k	l	j	q	r s
	21. Fine Motor Skills: Manipulation	a b c d	e	f	g h i j k	l m n o	n o p	q	r
	22. Fine Motor Skills: Bilateral Skills	a b	c d	e f	g h	i j	k	l	m
	23. Visual-Motor Skills: Pencil Control and Copying				a	a	b	c	d
Gross Motor Skills	24. Gross Motor Skills: Prone (On Stomach)	a b	c d e f g	a					
	25. Gross Motor Skills: Supine (On Back)	a b c d	e f g						
	26. Gross Motor Skills: Upright	a	b	c	d e f g h i	j			
	26–I. Gross Motor Skills: Upright, Posture and locomotion						a b	c d	e
	26–II. Gross Motor Skills: Upright, Stairs						a b	c	d
	26–III. Gross Motor Skills: Upright, Jumping						a	a	b
	26–IV. Gross Motor Skills: Upright, Balance							b	c d

Developmental Progress Chart: CCITSN and CCPSN (12 mo.–3 yrs.)

Child: _____

Interventionist: _____

Dates of Testing (Fill in circle with color used on chart.):

- ○ 1. _____
- ○ 2. _____
- ○ 3. _____
- ○ 4. _____

(The hatch marks indicate that no normative data are available.)

Domain	CCITSN Curriculum Sequences	12–15 mo.	15–18 mo.	18–21 mo.	21–24 mo.	2–2.5 yrs.	2.5–3 yrs.	CCPSN Curriculum Sequences
Cognition	1. Visual Pursuit and Object Permanence	i j	k	(hatched)	(hatched)			
	2. Object Permanence: Motor and Visual			(hatched)	(hatched)			
	3. Auditory Localization and Object Permanence	h		(hatched)	(hatched)			
	4. Attention and Memory	e	f	g h	i j k l m n	a b c d	e f g h	1. Attention and Memory — e (I.)
	5. Concept Development	f	g	h	j k	a b	c d e	2. Concepts — c d e (I.) e (II.)
	6. Understanding Space	h i	j	l	m n	a b	c d e	
	7. Functional Use of Objects and Symbolic Play	i	j	k	l	a b	c d	3. Symbolic Play
	8. Problem Solving	h	i	j	k	a	b	4. Reasoning
	9. Visual Perception	a	b c d	e f g h	i	a b	c d	5. Visual Perception — (I.) b c (II.) d
Communication	10. Prevocabulary/Vocabulary	h	i	k l	m	a b c d e f	g h	6. Expressive Vocabulary
	11. Imitation: Sound and Gestures	m n	o	p	q	a	b c	7. Interest in Sounds and Language Functions
	12. Response to Communication from Others	i j	k l m	n o	p q r s	a b c d	e f g h	8. Receptive Skills
	13. Conversation Skills	p q	r s t	u v	w x y z aa bb	a b c d e	f g h	9. Conversation Skills
						a b c d e	f g h i j	10. Sentence Construction
Social Adaptation	14. Self-Direction	b c	d	e	f g h i	a b	b	11. Responsibility
	15. Social Skills	m n	o	p	q r s t	a b c d	c d e f	12. Self Concept
	16. Self-Help Skills: Eating	n o	p q	r s	t u	a b c d	e f g	13. Interpersonal Skills
	17. Self-Help Skills: Dressing	c d	e	f g	h i	a b c	d e	14. Self-Help Skills — (I.)
	18. Self-Help Skills: Grooming	b	c	d	e	a	b	(II.) (III.) (IV.)

66

Fine Motor Skills

No.	Category	Codes
19.	Fine Motor Skills: Tactile Integration	m · i · o · p · q · r · s
20.	Fine Motor Skills: Reaching, Grasping, and Releasing	l · m · n · o · p · q · r
21.	Fine Motor Skills: Manipulation	i · j · k · l · m
22.	Fine Motor Skills: Bilateral Skills	
23.	Visual-Motor Skills: Pencil Control and Copying	a · b · c · d

Gross Motor Skills

No.	Category	Codes
24.	Gross Motor Skills: Prone (On Stomach)	o · p — I. a b c d e
25.	Gross Motor Skills: Supine (On Back)	II. a b c d
26.	Gross Motor Skills: Upright	j — III. a b — IV. a b c d

(continued)

No.	Category	Levels / Codes
15.	Fine Motor Skills: Hand Use	a b c d
16.	Fine Motor Skills: Manipulation	a b c d
17.	Fine Motor Skills: Bilateral Skills	a b c d
18.	Fine Motor Skills: Tool Use	a b
19.	Visual-Motor Skills	I. a b c d · II. a b · III.
20.	Locomotion	I. a b c · II. a b · III. · IV. a b · V.
21.	Stairs	I. a b c d e · II. a b
22.	Jumping	I. a b · II. a b · III. a
23.	Balance	I. a b c · II. a b c d e f
24.	Balls	I. a b c · II. a
25.	Outdoor Equipment	a b c

Curriculum
Sequences

1.

Visual Pursuit
and Object Permanence

A CHILD'S ABILITY to visually explore his or her world is critical to the development of many concepts in the first 2 years of life. Early items in this sequence should be included in the intervention program of children who are functioning under the 2 month developmental level, even if they have been diagnosed as being blind, since such a diagnosis is frequently incorrect in children during this developmental period.

Object permanence is the recognition that an object continues to exist although it can no longer be seen, touched, or heard. Jean Piaget (1952) considered this concept to be critical to a child's development of language and abstract thought. Recent research suggests that children recognize the permanence of objects at much younger ages than they demonstrate through the usual Piagetian procedures (e.g., removing covers). Furthermore, this research casts doubt on the relationship between language acquisition and object permanence that is so measured. Nevertheless, this aspect of development remains important both because it relates to the child's emerging concept of objects and because searching for objects and remembering their location are indicators of memory and attention—important elements of cognition.

The first part of this sequence (items 1a.–1f.) focuses on developing visual tracking skills and instilling the understanding that objects continue to exist even if they disappear for a few seconds. The latter part of the sequence (items 1g.–1l.) is specifically designed for children whose handicaps prevent them from reaching, grasping, and removing covers from objects to indicate that they remember where objects are even when they are out of sight several minutes. Thus items 1g. through 1l. should be omitted for children who are able to do sequence 2., Object Permanence: Motor and Visual (pp. 83–91).

REFERENCE

Piaget, J. (1952). *The origins of intelligence in children.* New York: International Universities Press.

1. Visual Pursuit and Object Permanence

a. Visually fixates for at least 3 seconds
b. Visually tracks object from side to side
c. Visually tracks object from forehead to chest
d. Visually tracks object moving in a circle
e. Gaze lingers where object or person disappears
f. Continues to look at caregiver when caregiver's face is covered with a cloth

---

Omit the following for children physically able to do sequence 2.

---

g. Looks at cover under which object has disappeared after a momentary distraction

h. Looks to the correct place when object is hidden in 1 of 2 places
i. Looks to the correct place when object is hidden in 1 of 3 places
j. Looks at correct place for an object after seeing it covered in 3 places successively
k. Looks successively at 2 different covers until an object is found that was hidden from the child's view (i.e., invisible displacement)
l. Looks systematically at 3 different covers until an object is uncovered that was hidden from the child's view

AREA: **1. Visual Pursuit and Object Permanence**
BEHAVIOR: 1a. Visually fixates for at least 3 seconds

Materials: A variety of interesting objects (e.g., silver ball, red pom-pom, red flashlight, small checkerboard, bull's-eye drawn on a card)

Procedures:

Hold object 6–10 inches from the child's eyes, wiggling it gently to attract his or her attention. Repeat with a different object.

Note: Sometimes it is very difficult to get certain infants with handicaps to look at anything. Usually such infants respond best to something very bright and shiny like a large Christmas ball that reflects images. Some infants will only respond to a bright light in a darkened room. Experiment to find what objects and what degree of room light get the best responses.

Use in Daily Routines:

Keep the toys you plan to use near the changing table and work on this activity every time you change the child's diaper.

Adaptations:

Visually Impaired: Continue to work on this item even if a child has been described as "cortically blind" and is making no responses. In many cases the child's nervous system has not matured to the point that the child can attend to the sight. Given time and stimulation, that attention may develop. Consultants to this curriculum project state, "Do not assume that a child cannot see unless both eyes have been removed."

Also, be aware that some children with visual impairments will not fixate at the midline, but rather to one side or the other. Try various locations of the object as you work on this item.

Criterion: The child looks at an object for 3 seconds or longer, several times a day on several different days. It is all right to begin working on visual tracking (item 1b.) if the child will only respond to one object, but it is important to continue working on this item (1a.) until the child will look at several kinds of objects.

AREA: **1. Visual Pursuit and Object Permanence**
BEHAVIOR: 1b. Visually tracks object from side to side

Materials: A variety of toys for which the child has shown preference

---

Procedures:

Present an object at midline, about 12 inches from the child's face. When the child looks at it, move it slowly to one side, and then to the other side (e.g., 5–8 inches to either side).

Use additional objects in the same manner. Try to hold the child's attention on the object and track it from side to side for 2–3 minutes.

If the child does not track at all, try one of the following until he or she begins to do so:
Vary the distance of the objects from the child's eyes.

(continued)

Use noisy objects.
Vary the illumination of the room and the brightness of the object.

Use in Daily Routines:

Identifying one or more daily care activities (e.g., diaper changes, playtime before or after meals) that are appropriate for practicing visual tracking. Keep the materials near the place(s) where the event(s) occur, so that it will be easy to remember to practice the tracking each time the child is there.

Adaptations:

Visually Impaired: Experiment with materials and lighting with a child with a visual impairment to determine which items give the best responses.

Criterion: The child visually tracks at least 3 different objects from one side of his or her visual field to the other, crossing the midline smoothly several times on several different days.

AREA: **1. Visual Pursuit and Object Permanence**
BEHAVIOR: 1c. Visually tracks objects from forehead to chest

Materials: Bright, shiny objects, especially those for which the child has previously shown preference

---

Procedures:

Present a bright object directly in front of the child, about 18 inches from his or her eyes, or closer, if you know the child cannot see at that distance. When the child looks at the object, move it slowly to the level of the child's chest and then back to the height of his or her forehead.

Use a variety of objects, following this procedure for about 3–5 minutes.

If the child does not track the object with his or her eyes at all, try one of the following until the child begins to do so:

Vary the distance of the object from the child's eyes and the speed with which it is moved.
Wiggle the toy to try to get and maintain the child's visual attention to it.
Use noisy objects.
Vary the illumination of the room and the brightness of the object.

Use in Daily Routines:

Work this activity into one or more regularly occurring daily care events as described in items 1a. and 1b.

Adaptations:

Visually Impaired: See the Visually Impaired Adaptations section of item 1b.

Criterion: The child visually tracks at least 3 different objects at midline from chest level to forehead level and back again, several times on several different days.

AREA: 1. **Visual Pursuit and Object Permanence**
BEHAVIOR: 1d. Visually tracks object moving in a circle

Materials: A variety of bright, shiny objects for which the child has previously shown a preference

---

Procedures:

Present an object at midline and attract the child's attention to it. Move the object slowly to one side and then move it in a circle a little larger than the child's face.

Use a variety of objects, continuing for 3–5 trials with each of several different objects for 2–3 minutes.

If the child does not track the object for the full circle, do one or more of the following until the complete track is achieved:

Vary the distance of the object from the child's eyes and the speed with which it is moved (usually move it more slowly).

Wiggle the toy to try to get and maintain the child's visual attention to it.

Use a noisy toy, but make noise with it only at 3 or 4 points in the circle, making noise at the points where the child looks away.

Vary the illumination of the room and the brightness of the object.

Use in Daily Routines:

Work this activity into the child's daily routine, several times each day (as described in items 1a. and 1b.).

Adaptations:

Visually Impaired: See the Visually Impaired Adaptations section of item 1b.

Criterion: The child tracks at least 3 different objects through a full circle, several times a day, on several different days.

AREA: 1. **Visual Pursuit and Object Permanence**
BEHAVIOR: 1e. Gaze lingers where object or person disappears

Materials: A variety of bright, shiny objects for which the child has previously shown a preference

---

Procedures:

Present an object at midline and move it slowly to the left and then to the right.

Let the object drop from sight at the child's right. As it drops, talk about it (e.g., "Where's the ball? Where did it go?")

Wait 5 seconds and make the object reappear at the same place and comment on its reappearance (e.g., "Here it is!"). When the child looks at the object or at the place it disappeared, bring it closer for the child to inspect. Help the child touch the object, make a noise with it, or otherwise enjoy it.

Repeat the same procedure, but this time drop the toy on the child's opposite side. Vary the side where the object disappears randomly as you continue this activity.

Make this activity as much fun as possible. You may, on some trials, want to substitute yourself for the object, making this a kind of peek-a-boo game.

(continued)

Use in Daily Routines:

It is easy to do this activity at any time that you stop to attend to the child. Just do it once or twice and then go on to something else.

If other children are around, teach them to play this kind of peek-a-boo game with the child, sometimes using an object and sometimes using themselves.

Adaptations:

Visually Impaired: If the child with a visual impairment tracks an object (i.e., previous items in this sequence), but he or she does not show any tendency to wait for the object to reappear, try to reinforce looking by mkaing a noise with the object as you present it and again when it is out of view (but not as it moves across the line of vision). Once a response is established, try to phase out the auditory stimulus.

Motor Impaired: If you have difficulty getting the child with the motor impairment to respond to the object in this item, seek advice from a physician or occupational therapist. The child may not be properly positioned and thus unable to offer the optimal response.

Criterion: The child's gaze lingers for 3 or more seconds at the point at which the object or person disappeared from sight. This should occur several times a day on several different days.

AREA: **1.   Visual Pursuit and Object Permanence**
BEHAVIOR: 1f.   Continues to look at caregiver when caregiver's face
is covered with a cloth

Materials: Cloth or light scarf

Procedures:

Place a cloth over your head, saying, "Where's _____?" Wait a few seconds and remove the cloth quickly. Note whether or not the child is still looking at you. Always come out from under the cloth smiling, talking, or laughing to reinforce the child for looking.

If the child does not maintain his or her gaze toward you, do one of the following:

Continue talking to the child for the full time your face is covered to see if he or she maintains attention; gradually reduce the amount of talking you do until you are silent.
Cover your head for a shorter period of time (i.e., brief enough to maintain the child's gaze). Gradually increase the time your head is covered until the child will maintain his or her gaze at least 5 seconds.

Note: If it is difficult to tell whether the child is continuing to look at you, use a brightly colored semi-sheer scarf through which you can see reasonably well, but which makes it difficult for the child to see your face.

Or, use a paper with a small hole in the middle that will allow you to see through.

Or, have one person watch the child's responses while the other plays with the child. If other children are available, they might enjoy covering their faces while you observe the child's responses.

Use in Daily Routines:

Play this game with the child during routine care activities such as diaper changes or before or after meals.

(continued)

Adaptations:

Visually Impaired: Be sure to be close enough for the child with limited vision to see you. Also, choose materials that contrast significantly with your skin and hair to make it more likely that the child will know your face is covered. Talk to the child to maintain attention, if necessary, but gradually eliminate the talking while the face is covered.

Motor Impaired: See the Motor Impaired Adaptations section of item 1e.

Criterion: The child maintains his or her gaze toward the caregiver for several seconds when the caregiver's face is covered and is quiet. This should occur several times on several different days.

AREA: 1.   Visual Pursuit and Object Permanence

BEHAVIOR: 1g.   Looks at cover under which object has disappeared after a momentary distraction (for children whose motor impairments preclude reaching to remove covers)

Materials: A variety of toys that the child enjoys; a collection of different covers (e.g., handkerchief, cup, can, box, pan)

Procedures:

Place an object in front of the child. Name it and talk about it. Cover the object completely, then call the child's name or distract him or her so he or she will look away from the covered object momentarily. When the child returns his or her attention to you, ask, "Where is the _____?"

If the child looks back at the covered object, say, "That's right, it is under the _____." Lift the cover and show the child the object, talk about it some more, help the child play with it, and so forth. Repeat the procedure with the same toy, but with a different cover.

If the child does not look at the cover, say, "Let's find the _____. I'll bet it is here under this _____ (lift the cover). Here it is!" Then repeat the procedure without this prompt.

Use in Daily Routines:

Do this activity with the child several times a day as you get out (or change) toys for him or her. Almost all children love hiding games and do not tire of them as long as there are not too many repetitions at one time.

For some trials, you may want to cover something edible and allow the child to eat it after he or she looks at the cover. This would be a good activity at the end of a meal when you may be providing something sweet to eat.

Adaptations:

Visually Impaired: Depending on the severity of the child's visual impairment, it may be necessary to omit this item and rely on those in sequence 3 (Auditory Localization and Object Permanence) to teach object permanence.

Hearing Impaired: Use gestures as well as words to communicate "Where is it?" with a child with a hearing impairment.

Criterion: After having been distracted momentarily, the child looks back at a cover, under which an object has been hidden, or responds by looking at the cover when asked, "Where is the _____?" This should occur several times in 1 play session and on more than 1 day.

AREA: **1.   Visual Pursuit and Object Permanence**
BEHAVIOR: 1h.   Looks to the correct place when object is hidden in 1 of 2 places
(for children whose motor impairments preclude reaching to remove covers)

Materials: Several of the child's favorite toys; a variety of cloths, boxes, or other objects that can be
used to cover the toys

Procedures:

Placed 2 crumpled cloths or 2 containers in front of the child. Take a toy and place
it in the child's hands, rub it against the child, or otherwise help the child to focus attention on it.

Place the toy under one of the covers as you talk about what you are doing (be sure
the child is watching).

Call the child by name and try to get him or her to look at you; then say, "Where is
the _____?" If the child looks at the correct cover, take it off and give the toy to the child,
make the toy produce a noise, or do whatever is appropriate to the toy and pleasing to the
child.

Repeat several times, randomly changing the side under which the toy is hidden.
Do not just alternate sides.

If the child does not look at the correct cover, say, "Uh-oh, that's not where it is,"
and lift the other cover and show the child the toy. Lower the cover slowly and ask again
where it is.

Note: It is important to teach the child to look at you or at something else at the
midline momentarily before looking for the toy. Only in this way can you be sure the
child remembers where the toy is. Likewise, you will avoid giving extra cues about
where the toy is if you remember to return your hands to the midline after you have
placed the cover over the toy.

It is much harder for a child to learn to use eye gaze to indicate location than
it is for one to reach or point. It may take patience to teach the child to make a clear
response. Experiment with placement of the covers so that you feel sure which one
the child is looking at. Ask an occupational therapist for assistance if you have difficulty determining the best placement.

Use in Daily Routines:

Do this activity several times a day at times when you are getting toys out for the
child, preparing to play with the child, or beginning another activity.

Adaptations:

Visually Impaired: Use sequence 3 (Auditory Localization and Object Permanence) to
teach object permanence to a child with a motor handicap and a significant visual impairment.

Hearing Impaired: See Hearing Impaired Adaptations section in item 1g.

Criterion: The child looks to the correct cover when an object is hidden under 1 of 2 covers. The
child should be able to do this with few errors during several trials.

AREA: **1. Visual Pursuit and Object Permanence**
BEHAVIOR: 1i. Looks to the correct place when object is hidden in 1 of 3 places
(for children whose motor impairments preclude reaching to remove covers)

Materials: Several favorite toys; a variety of "covers"

___

Procedures:

Place 3 crumpled cloths or 3 inverted containers in front of the child. Introduce a
toy to the child, which you will later hide under one of the covers. Help the child play with
the toy briefly in order to help focus his or her attention on it.

Place the toy under one of the covers as you talk about hiding the toy (be sure the
child watches what you do).

Call the child by name to get him or her to look at you; then say, "Where is the
_____?" If the child looks at the correct cover, take it off and help the child play with it.

Repeat this activity several times, randomly changing where the toy is hidden.

If a child does not look at the correct cover, say, "Uh-oh, that's not where it is," lift
the correct cover, and say, "Here it is." Lower the cover slowly and ask where it is again.
Make sure the child is watching. Try this activity again in a new location.

Use in Daily Routines:

Integrate this activity into the daily care routine by hiding the child's dessert or
other favorite food at mealtime (but *not* at the beginning of the meal when the child is
especially hungry), by hiding a crib toy as you are putting the child to bed, or by hiding a
bath toy as you give the child a bath. Always make it fun!

Be sure to place the 3 covers far enough apart so that you can tell when the child is
looking at each one. This may involve placing the covers on a shelf or table near the child's
eye level so that you can easily see his or her eyes.

If it is too difficult to tell where the child is looking when the covers are in a row,
it may be necessary to construct an object board like that described in the appendix on
pages 367–368 to aid in this activity. You may also request help from an occupational
therapist or other professional who has had experience training children to use eye gaze to
augment nonvocal communication.

Adaptations:

See Adaptations sections of 1a.–1h.

___

Criterion: The child looks at the correct place to find a toy after it has been hidden in 1 of 3 places.
This should be done with few errors, on several trials.

___

AREA: **1. Visual Pursuit and Object Permanence**
BEHAVIOR: 1j. Looks at correct place for an object after seeing it covered in 3 places
successively (for children whose motor impairments preclude reaching to remove covers)

Materials: Several favorite toys; a variety of covers

___

Procedures:

Place 3 covers in front of the child in positions to allow good judgment of where he
or she is looking (see Procedures sections of items 1a.–1i.).

___

(continued)

Show the child the toy that you will use in this activity, then slowly place it under one cover. Take it out, let the child see it, and then place it under the next cover in sequence. Let the child see it again as you take it out and then put it under the last cover. Leave it there and show the child that your hand is empty.

Get the child to look at you and then ask where is the toy. If the child looks toward the correct cover, uncover the toy and help him or her play with it.

On the next trial, place the object under the covers in the opposite direction. On subsequent trials, have the final placement be in one of the 3 places randomly.

If the child does not look correctly, lift the cover where the child looked and say, "Oops, it's not there. Look again." Continue until the toy is found. Always act excited when the child finds the toy and let him or her play with it at the end of the trial.

Note: Sometimes it helps to exaggerate your actions as you hide and expose the toy under the covers by moving the toy close to the child before and after each action.

If necessary, use an object board to facilitate your discrimination of the child's direction of gaze (see the appendix on pp. 367–368).

Use in Daily Routines:

See the Use on Daily Routines section in item 1i. for appropriate example.

Adaptations:

See the Adaptation sections of items 1a.–1i.

Criterion: The child looks at the correct place to find a toy after it has been successively placed under 3 covers. This should be done with few errors on several trials a day throughout at least a week.

AREA: **1.   Visual Pursuit and Object Permanence**
BEHAVIOR: 1k.   Looks successively at 2 different covers until an object is found that was hidden from the child's view (i.e., invisible displacement) (for children whose motor impairments preclude reaching to remove covers)

Materials: Several favorite small toys; a variety of covers

Procedures:

Place 1 cover in front of the child. Show the child a toy small enough to be hidden in your hand. Close your hand around the toy. Put your hand under the cover and leave the toy. Bring out your hand, closed so that it still looks like the toy is in it. Then open your hand and say, "Uh-oh, it's gone! Where is the _____?" Uncover the toy and praise the child if he or she looked at the cover. If the child does not look at the cover, attract his or her attention to the cover, remove it, and talk about finding the toy.

As soon as the child is looking for the toy under 1 cover, introduce another cover, far enough apart to allow easy judgment of when the child moves gaze from one to the other. Put the toy in your hand. Place your hand under one of the covers momentarily, remove it (still closed) and put it under the second cover. Leave the toy under the second cover, remove your hand from under the cover, open it, and say, "It's gone. Where is the _____?"

Lift the cover the child looks at. If the cover is not the one with the item under it, say, "That isn't where it is. Where could it be?" Remove the correct cover when he or she looks at it (or after a few seconds if the child seems confused about where to look).

(continued)

Repeat the item, randomly varying the hiding place under the right and left covers *and* varying whether you leave the toy under the first cover your hand enters or under the second.

> *Note:* The child cannot know where you left the toy in this item since he or she did not see it between trials. The point of this item is that the child solves the problem of the search by systematically checking possibilities. In this case, there are only two alternatives. It does not matter which the child chooses first as long as he or she consistently chooses the second alternative when the first is incorrect.
>
> You may wish to vary this activity by putting the toy in a box and placing the box successively under each cover, emptying it under one of them. When doing this, it is important that the same amount of noise be made when dumping or not dumping the toy and that the child not see the toy from under the cover.

Use in Daily Routines:

See the Use in Daily Routines sections of items 1a.–1j.

Adaptations:

See the Adaptation sections of items 1a.–1j.

Criterion: The child looks at 2 covers in succession until a toy is found that was hidden from the child's view under one of them. This should occur on enough trials that the child must look at the second alternative several times.

AREA: **1.   Visual Pursuit and Object Permanence**

BEHAVIOR: 1l.   Looks systematically at 3 different covers until an object is uncovered that was hidden from the child's view (for children whose motor impairments preclude reaching to remove covers)

Materials: Several favorite small toys; a variety of covers

Procedures:

Place 3 covers in front of the child, in positions that will allow you to determine where he or she is looking.

Place a small toy in your hand or in a box. Show it to the child and then close your hand or turn the box so that the child cannot see the toy. Move it under one cover, out and under the next, then out and under the third, leaving the toy under one of the covers. Do not allow toy to be seen between covers.

Show the child your empty hand or the empty box at the end and say, "It's gone, where's the _____?"

Wherever the child looks, lift the cover. If it is not there, say, "Oops, not there. Now where should we look?" Continue until the toy is found, then let the child play with the toy.

Repeat this activity, leaving the toy in a different place (not always the last place you had your hand). Each time the toy is found, reward the child with the toy and a lot of excitement. Do not always work from right to left or left to right when hiding the toy. Vary the order of going under the covers as well, but always go under all three.

If the child stops looking after one incorrect response, encourage him or her by saying, "Look at this one. Let's try it." Wait for the child to look and then lift the cover.

(continued)

Note: Remember that the child cannot know where the toy is in this activity. What you are interested in teaching him or her is a systematic search strategy as well as the memory and perseverance to carry it through.

Use in Daily Routines:

See the Use in Daily Routines sections of items 1a.–1k.

Adaptations:

See the Adaptations sections of items 1a.–1k.

Criterion: The child uses a systematic search pattern in looking at the covers to find a toy that was hidden from his or her view. This should occur several times throughout the activity.

2.

Object Permanence: Motor and Visual

THIS SEQUENCE IS useful for teaching children to attend to and remember objects that are presented to them. It is intended for children who do not have serious visual impairments and who have the ability to use their hands and arms sufficiently well to reach, grasp, pull, and release. Prerequisites for the sequence include items 1a. through 1f. in sequence 1., Visual Pursuit and Object Permanence (pp. 73–77) and items 20a. through 20g. in sequence 20., Fine Motor Skills: Reaching, Grasping, and Releasing (pp. 287–291).

2. Object Permanence: Motor and Visual

a. Pulls cloth from face
b. Pulls cloth from caregiver's face
c. Uncovers partially hidden toy
d. Uncovers fully hidden toy
e. Finds toy hidden under a cover, when 2 covers are present
f. Finds toy when it is hidden under 1 of 2 covers, alternately
g. Removes cover when object is hidden under 1 of 3 covers

h. Finds toy hidden under 3 superimposed covers
i. Finds toy after seeing it covered in 3 places, successively (i.e., visible displacement)
j. Finds object after it is covered in 2 places, successively (i.e., invisible placement)
k. Finds object under 1 of 3 covers after a systematic search (i.e., invisible displacement)

AREA: 2.   Object Permanence: Motor and Visual
BEHAVIOR: 2a.   Pulls cloth from face

Materials: A soft cloth, diaper, towel, or scarf

Procedures:

When a child is looking at you, play a Peek-a-boo game by putting a cloth over his or her face (leave mouth uncovered). Say, "Where's _____ (baby's name)?" Pause to allow the child the opportunity to remove the cloth on his or her own. Continue the game through several trials, smiling as the child removes the cloth.

If the child does not pull the cloth off, remove it for him or her, saying, "There you are!" Try again.

Note: In this item, attend to the child's movements that suggest he or she is attempting to remove the cloth. Assist his or her movements by removing the cloth, then decrease your help as the child is able to do more for him- or herself.

Some children are afraid of having a cloth placed on their faces. You may have to gradually introduce the cloth by initially placing it on only part of the face or body, or by using a relatively sheer cloth that allows the child to still see his or her surroundings.

Use in Daily Routines:

Hiding games are usually one of a child's favorite activities. Build this game into many care activities throughout the day (e.g., diapering, putting the child to bed, getting child up in the morning or from a nap). Always express joy when you see the child's face again.

Adaptations:

Visually Impaired: Adjust your position or distance from the child with a visual impairment to accommodate his or her usable vision.

Hearing Impaired: Be sure to be very animated while playing with the child with a hearing impairment, letting your facial expressions aid in communication.

Motor Impaired: More help may be required for a child to remove the cloth if he or she has a motor impairment. Provide as much help as necessary. Also, experiment with different kinds of cloths and different placements on the child's face. Some cloths may be easier than others for the child to remove.

Criterion: The child completely removes a cloth placed over his or her face in a Peek-a-boo game. This should be consistently done several times on a number of different days.

AREA: 2.   Object Permanence: Motor and Visual
BEHAVIOR: 2b.   Pulls cloth from caregiver's face (item e in sequence 20 [Reaching, Grasping, and Releasing] is a prerequisite skill for the remainder of the items in this sequence)

Materials: A soft cloth, diaper, towel, or brightly colored scarf

---

Procedures:

Talk to and smile at the child. When you have his or her attention, place a cloth over your face, saying, "Where's _____ (e.g., Mother, other caregiver's name)?"

(continued)

Pause to allow the child to remove the cloth. Say, "Here I am!" Then repeat this activity.

If the child does not pull the cloth off, remove it yourself and smile at him or her as your face reappears. Then put it over your face again.

Note: Attend to movements that indicate the child's attempt to remove the cloth. Assist him or her with removing the cloth, then decrease your help as the child is able to do more for him- or herself.

If the child seems afraid when the caregiver covers her- or himself with the cloth, help the child adapt to the game by hiding behind sheer scarves or objects that can easily be pushed aside.

Use in Daily Routines:

Play this game frequently throughout the day. Some of the easiest times to initiate this activity are when changing diapers or when you are near the crib where cloths are handy.

Adaptations:

Visually Impaired: Experiment with the position and the kind of cover that you use with a child with a visual impairment to maximize his or her use of residual vision. Bright colored or high contrast cloths may be the most appropriate.

Hearing Impaired: Be sure to be especially animated with a child with a hearing impairment to facilitate communication.

Motor Impaired: Experiment with the position and the kind of cover that you use with a child with a motor impairment to determine what will be the easiest for him or her to remove.

Criterion: The child completely removes a cloth that is placed over an adult's face in a peek-a-boo game, several times a day on a number of days.

AREA: 2.   Object Permanence: Motor and Visual
BEHAVIOR: 2c.   Uncovers partially hidden toy

Materials: A variety of toys or objects, including ones for which the child has shown preference (e.g., car keys, small rubber doll, brightly colored beads, small car); various covers (e.g., cloths, cushions, scarfs, boxes)

Procedures:

Show an object to the child. As the child reaches for it, cover more than half of the object with a cover. If the child removes the cover, allow him or her to have the object.

If the child seems to show no interest in the object after it is partially covered, say, "Where's the _____? Oh, there it is!" as you cover and uncover it several times. Then partially cover it again and wait for a response.

If the child does not remove the cover, but tries to do so, assist him or her with the task, then gradually decrease your help as he or she is better able to do it him- or herself.

Note: Experiment with the kind of objects that you hide. A few children will only look for food or an object that makes noise.

(continued)

Use in Daily Routines:

Encourage searching for objects in play throughout the day. For example, as you put the child to bed, cover all but one leg of a favorite teddy bear, and say, "Now what did I do with Teddy? Where's your bear?"

Adaptations:

Visually Impaired: Be sure there is a large contrast in color and/or brightness in the cover and the object that is being hidden for a child with a visual impairment. It may be necessary to use larger objects than ones suitable for children with adequate vision. It may also be useful to hide toys that make noise when they are touched, so that the child will get more feedback as he or she handles the cover.

Hearing Impaired: Use gestures to help communicate the need to look for the object that is covered when working with a child with a hearing impairment. Also, be especially animated with the child to aid communication.

Motor Impaired: Experiment with different types of covers to find one that the child with a motor impairment can most readily remove.

Also, experiment with different positions for the child. For some children, this item can be more easily accomplished in a side-lying position. Contact your physical or occupational therapist for advice on positioning children with motor impairments.

Criterion: The child removes a cover and gets a toy, several times a day on a number of days.

AREA: 2.   Object Permanence: Motor and Visual
BEHAVIOR: 2d.   Uncovers fully hidden toy

Materials: A variety of toys or objects for which the child has shown preference; various covers.

Procedures:

Proceed as in item 2c., except completely cover the object.

Note: Sometimes a child will begin putting objects under covers and then finding them again. Participate in this play by talking about what he or she is doing, taking turns hiding the toy and so forth.

Sometimes children will learn to pull a cloth off of a toy in order to get praise from an adult, rather than to retrieve the object that has been hidden. Observe the child's behavior carefully and do not move on to the next item until it is clear he or she is remembering and searching for the object beneath the cover, rather than pulling the cloth for adult praise. Be sure to hide objects that are of high interest to the child. Remember to vary the objects that are hidden so that the game does not become boring.

Use in Daily Routines:

Hide objects for the child throughout the day—under boxes, inside a pot with a lid, behind the door, and so forth. Be sure that the child watches you hide the object and act surprised or happy when he or she recovers it.

Adaptations:

See the Adaptations section of item 2c.

Criterion: The child removes a cover from a fully hidden toy and plays with the toy several times.

AREA: **2.   Object Permanence: Motor and Visual**
BEHAVIOR: 2e.   Finds toy hidden under a cover, when 2 covers are present

Materials: A variety of toys; various covers

Procedures:

Hide a toy under 1 cover. When the child uncovers it, introduce a second cover a few inches away from the first. Take the toy and hide it under the second cover while the child watches.

If the child looks under the cover where he or she previously found the toy, say, "Oops, where is it?" Encourage the child to remove the other cloth. If he or she does not, do it for the child to show him or her where it is.

Repeat this procedure, varying the side to which the second cover is introduced.

Note: If using scarfs or clothes, be sure to bunch them up so that the shape of the toys is not visible.

Use in Daily Routines:

Try only a few trials of this activity throughout the day. Also talk to the child about findings things when you are looking for something (e.g., "Where did I put my book? Maybe it is under the paper—let's see.").

Adaptations:

See the Adaptations section of item 2c.

Criterion: On several different occasions, the child finds a toy that is hidden under a second cover on the first try.

AREA: **2.   Object Permanence: Motor and Visual**
BEHAVIOR: 2f.   Finds toy when it is hidden under 1 or 2 covers, alternately

Materials: A variety of interesting toys and covers

Procedures:

Place 2 covers in front of the child. Show the child a toy and then hide it under 1 of the covers. When the child uncovers it, act excited, ask for the toy and then hide it under the second cover, while the child watches.

If the child looks under the cover where he or she previously found the toy, say, "Oops, where is it?" Encourage the child to remove the other cloth. If he or she does not, do it for the child and "find" the toy.

Repeat the procedure, varying the side under which you hide the toy (i.e., do not simply alternate sides; randomly select the side under which the toy will be hidden).

Note: If using scarfs or cloths, be sure to bunch both of them up before hiding the toy so that the shape of the toy is not visible.

If the child has difficulty with the task it may help to use 2 very different covers (e.g., a box and a scarf). Once the child masters that task try more similar covers (e.g., 2 scarfs of different colors; 2 boxes of different shapes or colors) and then, finally, 2 nearly identical covers.

(continued)

Use in Daily Routines:

> Build this activity into playtime throughout the day. Most children love to find objects that are hidden from them.

Adaptations:

> See the Adaptations section of item 2c.

Criterion: The child consistently finds the toy under the correct cover (3 or 4 consecutive correct trials) on several days.

AREA: **2.   Object Permanence: Motor and Visual**
BEHAVIOR: 2g.   Removes cover when object is hidden under 1 of 3 covers

Materials: A variety of interesting toys and covers

Procedures:

> Place 3 covers in front of the child. Show the child a toy and hide it under 1 of the 3 covers. Allow the child to look for it.
>
> If the child looks in the wrong place, encourage him or her to continue looking.
>
> On subsequent trials randomly vary the placement of the toy.
>
> *Note:*   It is common for children to look in the same place that they found the toy on the previous trial. Give the child feedback (e.g., "I fooled you. It is not there this time. Look again.") Also, exaggerate your movements as you hide the toy to focus the child's attention on the new location.

Use in Daily Routines:

> Try to do a few trials of this activitiy several times a day rather than many trials in a row, once a day. This will help maintain the child's interest and enthusiasm. Work the trials into routine care events (e.g., diapering, feeding) as well as into planned play sessions.
>
> When you are looking for something (even if you know where it is), ask the child to help you look. This will reinforce remembering where objects were last seen.

Adaptations:

> See the Adaptations section of item 2c.

Criterion: Child consistently finds a toy under 1 of 3 covers on several different days. That is, the child rarely makes an error on 3 or more consecutive trials.

AREA: **2.   Object Permanence: Motor and Visual**
BEHAVIOR: 2h.   Finds toy hidden under 3 superimposed covers

Materials: A variety of interesting toys and covers

(continued)

Procedures:

Present a toy to the child. When he or she looks at it, place it on the table. Cover it with 3 covers, added one at a time. Allow the child to remove the covers until the object is found.

Try additional objects with the same procedure for several times.

If the child does not retrieve the toy, try one of the following:

Repeat the procedure slowly, explaining that you are hiding the toy and that he or she is to find it.

Demonstrate the removal of 1 cover at a time, saying, "Is it under here? No . . . Is it here?" and so forth.

Note: The object of this item is to assist the child to remember there the object was hidden and to foster the perseverance to continue to remove the 3 covers in sequence. It may be helpful to hold each cover lightly and unobtrusively to prevent the child from removing all 3 at once.

Use in Daily Routines:

Look for ways to practice this activity at various times throughout the day. Also, this activity could be used to find ways to call a child's attention to objects in the home or school that may require some effort to retrieve.

Adaptations:

See the Adaptations section of item 2c.

Criterion: On several occasions, the child removes 3 superimposed covers one at a time, to retrieve a toy.

AREA: **2. Object Permanence: Motor and Visual**
BEHAVIOR: 2i. Finds toy after seeing it covered in 3 places, successively
(i.e., visible displacement)

Materials: A variety of interesting toys and covers

Procedures:

Place 3 covers in front of the child. Introduce a favorite toy or object. Allow the child to watch as you put the object under the cover on the child's left.

Bring the toy out from under the cover, letting the child see it. Then put it under the middle cover and bringing it out so the child can again see it. Repeat the same process with the third cover, but this time leave it under the cover.

Allow the child to search for the toy.

If the child does not look for the toy, demonstrate looking under each cover, saying, "Where did the _____ go? Here it is!"

Vary the sequence of placing the toy under the covers. For example, on one trial, go from left to right; on another, go from right to left; and on another place the toy first under the right cover, then under the left, and then leave it under the center cover.

Note: Some children will find this task easier if the covers are very different from one another. For others it will make no difference. Experiment to find what works best. Remember to be sure that the toy being hidden is more interesting to the child than any of the covers.

(continued)

Use in Daily Routines:

>   Try this activity several times a day in different situations (e.g., at mealtime, when getting ready to go outside). Make it more interesting to the child by hiding something that is essential to his or her next activity. For example, you might hide the child's shoes when you are getting him or her dressed.

Adaptations:

>   See the Adaptations section of item 2c.

Criterion: On several different occasions, the child finds toy without error after seeing it covered in 3 places, successively.

AREA: **2.   Object Permanence: Motor and Visual**
BEHAVIOR: 2j.   Finds object after it is covered in 2 places, successively
                      (i.e., invisible displacement)

Materials: A variety of covers; various toys small enough to be hidden in your hand or a small box

---

Procedures:

>   Place 2 covers on the table. Show the child a small object. When he or she looks at it, close your hand around it. Without the object being visible, slide your hand under the first cover and then bring it out (do not leave the toy there, but do not let the child see it in your hand).

>   Be sure the child is looking at your closed hand, then put it under the second cover. Leave the toy there, then show the child your empty hand. Encourage the child to look for the toy, lifting one or both covers as necessary.

>   On the next trial leave the toy under the first cover, but pretend you have it in your hand as you put your hand under the second cover. Then show the child your empty hand and encourage him or her to look for the toy.

>   On subsequent trials, vary the side on which you leave the toy.

>   *Note:*   When the child does not see you hide the toy, there is no way of knowing where it is. The object of this item is not to guess right every time, but to recognize that if the toy is not under one of the covers it is under the other. Make the errors a part of the game by laughing and saying, "I fooled you that time."

>   A variation on this activity is to take a toy in your hand, put your hands behind you, and transfer the toy to the other hand. Bring out both hands, closed, and ask the child to pick which hand the toy is in. Vary the hand in which you leave the toy so the child will have to guess.

>   Let the child try to imitate this activity by hiding the toy from you. Make mistakes deliberately as you search, but always model a systematic search for the object (i.e., if it is not under one cover, look under the other). Talk about attempts as you proceed.

Use in Daily Routines:

>   Try this activity several times throughout the day, selecting objects to be hidden and appropriate covers for the place, time, and activity of the day (i.e., hide the child's mittens and use as covers the child's hat, coat, and pants).

(continued)

Adaptations:

> See the Adaptations section of item 2c.

Criterion: The child looks under a second cover to find a toy when he or she fails to find it under the first. This should be done consistently and without adult prompts or encouragement.

AREA: 2.   Object Permanence: Motor and Visual
BEHAVIOR: 2k.   Finds object under 1 of 3 covers after a systematic search (i.e., invisible displacement)

Materials: A variety of interesting small toys and covers

Procedures:

> Proceed as in item 4j., sequence 4. (Attention and Memory), but use 3 covers. Vary where you leave the toy (e.g., left, middle, right) and do not allow the child to see the toy in your hand between covers.
>
> If necessary, ask the child to look for the toy. If the child gives up after looking under 1 or 2 covers, encourage him or her to continue looking.
>
> *Note:*   The important element of this item is that the child engage in a systematic search. That is, the child should not look under the same cover twice in one trial. It does not matter in what sequence the child lifts the covers, but each should be lifted only once as he or she searches for the toy.
>
> Take turns with the child, letting him or her hide the toy from you. Model a systematic search saying something like, "It's not there, I just looked there. Maybe it is here."

Use in Daily Routines:

> See Use in Daily Routines sections of items 2a.–2j.

Adaptations:

> See the Adaptations section of item 2c.

Criterion: The child finds object after a systematic search of 3 covers (lifting each cover no more than one time), several times.

3.

Auditory Localization and Object Permanence

AUDITORY LOCALIZATION AND object permanence are key skills in the developmental process. To expedite the acquisition of these skills, this sequence offers items that will assist in developing a child's ability to identify the direction from which sounds come. To further assist in skill development, the localization skills learned in the first items are used in the subsequent items to demonstrate the concept of object permanence. Items 3h., 3i., and 3j. are specifically designed for children with visual impairments, who cannot proceed through sequence 2., Object Permanence: Motor and Visual (pp. 83–91); these items should be omitted for other children.

Children with visual impairments have been noted to be very slow to develop the concept of object permanence, perhaps because they are denied the common appearance-disappearance-reappearance experiences (e.g., Peek-a-boo games) of children who have intact vision and because they cannot demonstrate object permanence in the standard fashion (e.g., removing covers from items that have been hidden). Thus, the last 2 items (3i. and 3j.) of the sequence are designed both to teach object permanence and to provide a means of demonstrating acquisition of this concept.

3. Auditory Localization and Object Permanence

a. Quiets when noise is presented
b. Visually searches for sound
c. Turns head and searches for or reaches toward ear-level sound while lying down
d. Turns head or reaches toward source of ear-level sound while sitting
e. Turns head toward sound and looks or reaches directly at noisemaker when noise is presented at shoulder level
f. Looks directly at (or reaches for) noisemaker when sound is presented to the side and at waist level
g. Turns head and looks back and forth to 2 sounds (or reaches to either side as sounds are presented)
h. Reaches for an object after it no longer makes noise (for children with visual impairments)
i. Reaches for an object that no longer makes noise, at midline and both sides, above and below shoulder level (for children wtih visual impairments)
j. Reaches in the correct direction for an object that has made noise in several places (for children with visual impairments)

93

AREA: 3.   **Auditory Localization and Object Permanence**
BEHAVIOR: 3a.   Quiets when noise is presented

Materials: A variety of noisy, shiny noisemakers

Procedures:

Make sounds with a noisemaker for 3–5 seconds about 6 inches from the child's ear at ear level. Begin with toys that make relatively soft and pleasant sounds.

Observe the child for any indications of decreased activity in response to the sound presented.

Present the same noisemaker to the other ear and observe.

Change noisemakers and try again. If a child does not respond, gradually increase the loudness of the sounds that are presented.

When the child quiets, bring noisemaker in view (and/or touch it to the child). Make the noise again.

Note: This response cannot be "taught," although you can experiment with noises to see what is most effective in promoting a response from the child (e.g., take the child to a very quiet room and do not talk prior to presenting the noisemaker, vary the distance of the noisemaker from the ear, try noisemakers with very different pitches or different intensities).

Some children habituate (i.e., stop responding) to sounds rather quickly, so it is important to change noisemakers frequently and to try this item for only 5–6 trials at one time.

Use in Daily Routines:

This is an easy item to try throughout the day (e.g., as you change a child's diaper, when you simply pass by the child throughout the day.) Keep noisemakers at the changing table and/or in a box or bag near the child.

Adaptations:

Hearing Impaired: If a child does not respond to any or to only a few of the noisemakers, refer him or her to an audiologist to have a hearing check. Seek advice from the audiologist for the best noisemakers to use to optimize the chance for a response from the child.

Sometimes other developmental problems make a child appear to have a hearing impairment. As the child develops further, the responses to sounds will begin to appear more like those of children who can hear. Be sure to share this kind of information with the child's audiologist.

Criterion: The child regularly quiets when a sound is presented. That is, you should see this response almost every time you present a novel sound over a period of several days.

AREA: 3.   **Auditory Localization and Object Permanence**
BEHAVIOR: 3b.   Visually searches for sound

Materials: A variety of noisemakers with interesting appearance

---

(continued)

Procedures:

Make sounds with a noisemaker for 3–5 seconds about 6 inches from the child's ear at ear level. Begin with noisemakers that make relatively soft and pleasant sounds.

Observe the child's eyes. If he or she does not look back and forth for the noise, attract his or her attention to the object by bringing it to the midline, making the noise, and then move it back and forth again, in an attempt to obtain the child's attention. Then, remove the object, wait for a few seconds, and present it at the child's side again.

Present the same noisemaker to the other ear and proceed as above.

Change noisemakers and repeat the trial. If a child does not respond, gradually increase the loudness of the sounds that are presented. Keep a record of the kinds of sounds to which the child responds.

Wiggle the toy again to create a visual effect, as well as a sound, when the child does not search for it.

Note: For some children, it will be necessary to work on this skill in a quiet room with no distracting noises.

Use in Daily Routines:

Take the opportunity throughout the day to watch the child's responses to environmental sounds (e.g., the telephone, closing doors, toys being used by other children).

Adaptations:

Visually Impaired: Many children with visual impairments will respond with searching eye movements, even if they cannot see the object. Look for this response as an indication of attention, and reinforce the response by touching the child with the object on the hand or cheek of the same side where the sound was presented. If a child with a visual impairment does not visually search, look for other indications of attention (e.g., moving head from side to side, increased motor activity).

Hearing Impaired: Seek the advice of an audiologist as to the kinds of sounds that are most likely to be heard by a child with a hearing impairment. Be especially careful to work with the child in a quiet situation.

Criterion: The child visually searches for a variety of sounds. This should be observed throughout the course of daily activities, not just in training sessions.

AREA: 3. Auditory Localization and Object Permanence
BEHAVIOR: 3c. Turns head and searches for or reaches toward ear-level sound while lying down

Materials: A variety of noisemakers (e.g., those that have gotten the best response in previous items)

Procedures:

Make sounds with a noisemaker about 6 inches from the child's ear at ear level and observe his or her response.

Randomly test one ear, then the other, with the noisemaker, changing toys frequently and giving only 6–8 trials at a time.

(continued)

If the child does not turn his or her head to find the toy, gain the child's visual attention to the toy at his or her midline, then move the toy to one side slowly while making noise. Remove the toy, wait for a few seconds and again present it at the side. If this procedure does not work after 5 trials, present the sound at the side and gently turn the child's head in the direction of the sound. As the child's head is turned, make the sound again and move the object in such a way as to produce an interesting visual effect.

> *Note:* It may be unclear whether a child has visual impairment. Always work for the visual response first, even if the child has been described as "cortically blind." If you cannot get any indication of the child's looking at the noisemaker, use the adaptation for children with visual impairments.

Use in Daily Routines:

Look for opportunities throughout the day to try this item for a few minutes (e.g., when changing a diaper, when placing the child on the floor to play). Many exposures throughout the day will work better than concentrated training sessions. Also, watch for the response to occur naturally to environmental sounds.

Adaptations:

Visually Impaired: Touch the face of a child with a visual impairment with the toy as you make a noise with it. Move the toy and make the sound on one side, guiding the child's hand to the toy. Remember to keep making the noise until you get a response or until you have prompted the response.

Hearing Impaired: Seek advice from the audiologist as to the best kinds of sounds to use with a child with a hearing impairment. Try to stimulate the child in a quiet room.

Motor Impaired: Some children with neurological impairments have unusual movement patterns that make it difficult for them to reach for an object when they turn their heads toward it (see description of Persistent Asymmetric Tonic Neck Pattern, p. 19). Seek the advice of the physical or occupational therapist regarding this activity if the child has an unusual movement pattern.

Criterion: The child turns his or her head in the direction of a sound and visually searches or reaches, when lying down. This should be observed during several trials on different days or in the everyday care of the child.

AREA: 3. Auditory Localization and Object Permanence
BEHAVIOR: 3d. Turns head or reaches toward source of ear-level sound while sitting

Materials: A variety of noisemakers

Procedures:

Make sounds about 6 inches from the child's ear at ear level and observe his or her response.

Randomly test one ear, then the other, with the noisemaker, changing toys frequently and giving only 6–8 trials at a time.

If the child does not turn his or her head to find the toy, gain the child's visual attention to the toy at his or her midline, then move the toy to one side slowly while making noise. Remove the toy, wait for a few seconds, then present it again at the side. If this

(continued)

procedure does not work after 5 trials, present the sound at the side and gently turn the child's head in the direction of the sound. As the child's head is turned, make the sound again and move the object in such a way as to produce an interesting visual effect.

Use in Daily Routines:

Try this activity for a few minutes, several times a day, when the child has been seated for some other activity (e.g., just after a meal).

Adaptations:

Visually Impaired: With a child with a visual impairment, try to have the noisemaker at ear level, but also enough forward of the body to facilitate reaching. If the child does not turn toward the object, gently turn his or her head as described above, but also prompt reaching for the object while it is making a noise. Experiment to find the best position and objects for both sound and sight. Remember that reaching toward a sound is more difficult than reaching for something that can be seen. A child who is totally blind will be slow to develop this response.

Hearing Impaired: Experiment to find objects that the child with hearing impairments can hear and that are of particular interest to him or her visually.

Motor Impaired: Head turning and/or reaching may be disrupted by physical impairments. A child may perform best when positioned on his or her stomach over a bolster or placed in other adaptive equipment. Seek the advice of the physical or occupational therapist as to the best positions for the child to learn to localize sounds.

Criterion: The child turns his or head or reaches toward the source of a sound while sitting. This response should occur not only in several training sessions, but spontaneously throughout the course of daily events.

AREA: **3. Auditory Localization and Object Permanence**
BEHAVIOR: 3e. Turns head toward sound and looks or reaches directly at noisemaker when noise is presented at shoulder level

Materials: A variety of noisemakers

Procedures:

Follow the procedures outlined in item 1d.; however, present the noise at shoulder level instead of at the child's midline.

Use in Daily Routines:

See the Use in Daily Routines section of item 3d.

Adaptations:

See the Adaptations section of item 3d.

Criterion: The child turns his or her head toward the sound and fixes his or her eyes on the noisemaker (or reaches directly for the noisemaker) on most trials in several training sessions and/or this behavior is observed on several occasions throughout the course of daily activities.

AREA: **3.   Auditory Localization and Object Permanence**
BEHAVIOR: 3f.   Looks directly at (or reaches for) noisemaker when sound is presented to
the side and at waist level

Materials: A variety of noisemakers

Procedures:

Make sounds with a noisemaker on one side of the child, about 8 inches from his
or her body at waist level.

Repeat this procedure on the child's other side, then randomly present the sound on
each side on successive trials. Many children will turn their heads to the correct side but will
not look down to find the noisemaker. If this occurs, make the noise again while the head is
turned. If the child still does not look down, bring the toy up to eye level and make a noise
with it as you move it down to waist level, trying to get the child to visually track it. Then,
attract the child's attention to you back at midline and again make the noise at waist level.

Whenever the child does look at the toy, be sure to move it, give it to the child, or
otherwise let him or her know it was good that he or she found the noisemaker.

Use in Daily Routines:

Keep noisemakers available throughout the child's living area. Try this item each
time you prepare to give one of these toys to the child to play with or just happen to pass
the child and can make use of a toy near him or her.

Adaptations:

Visually Impaired: Use large, bright colored and/or shiny noisemakers to maximize the
chances of the child with visual impairment seeing them. Be sure to keep making the noise
as the child tries to reach for it. If the child reaches in the right direction, move the toy to
the child's body until it touches him or her at the level where it was presented. Place the
child's hands over it, encouraging him or her to feel it. Move the noisemaker back to the
position where you initially presented the sound and introduce the sound again. Guide the
child's hand to where the toy is and give it to the child. Remember that this response will
be slow to develop in children who cannot see the objects that are being presented, that
learning to localize sounds is particularly important for children with visual impairments,
and that localization is always easier to the side than at midline.

Hearing Impaired: Seek the advice of the audiologist or speech-language pathologist as
to the best noisemakers to use with a child with hearing impairments. Be sure that they are
both visually attractive and create sounds that the child is most likely to hear.

Motor Impaired: With a child with motor impairments, seek the advice of a physical or
occupational therapist regarding how to position the child to acquire the best responses.

Criterion: The child turns his or her head toward a sound and looks at (or reaches for) the noisemaker when sound is presented at waist level, in several trials on different days throughout training,
or is observed to make this response frequently in the normal course of daily activities.

AREA: **3.   Auditory Localization and Object Permanence**
BEHAVIOR: 3g.   Turns head and looks back and forth to 2 sounds (or reaches to either
side as sounds are presented)

Materials: A variety of noisemakers with interesting visual characteristics

---

Procedures:

Hold a different toy in each hand, approximately 10–11 inches from the child's midline, at ear level, but 6–8 inches in front of his or her face. Make a noise with one of the toys for 2–3 seconds. Pause for 1–2 seconds, then make a noise with the other toy. Repeat, making three presentations with each sound.

Repeat this same procedure with 2 different toys.

If the child does not look at the toy that is making the noise, move it to midline to get the child's visual attention, and then take it slowly back to the side. Then make noise with the second toy. Bring it to midline and back if necessary to get the child's attention. Wait and be quiet for 5 seconds or more, then do it again.

If the child looks back and forth at the two toys, place them in the child's hands and let him or her manipulate or touch them.

Use in Daily Routines:

Keep noisemakers at the diaper changing area and in other areas where you frequently interact with the child. Do the above procedure each time you change the child and, periodically, when you take time to just play with the child.

Adaptations:

Visually Impaired: Make a noise with a toy in easy reaching distance anywhere between the shoulder and hip level of the child with a visual impairment. Continue making the noise until the child finds it. When the child reaches and touches the toy, give it to him or her and allow time for the child to explore and play. Then present another toy on the other side. Alternate sides and positions of objects to promote good localization of the objects. Do not physically assist the child unless he or she loses interest or gets too frustrated to continue reaching.

Hearing Impaired: Experiment with various noise-making materials to find those that foster the best responses for the child with a hearing impairment.

Criterion: The child turns his or her head and looks back and forth to 2 sounds (or reaches correctly when toys are presented alternately to each side) on several trials on different days.

AREA: **3.   Auditory Localization and Object Permanence**
BEHAVIOR: 3h.   Reaches for an object after it no longer makes noise (for children with
visual impairments)

Materials: A variety of noisemakers with interesting visual characteristics

---

Procedures:

Make a noise briefly (to one side at waist level) and wait for the child to reach. If he or she does not reach, make the sound a little longer, then stop and wait. Continue increas-

(continued)

ing the duration of the sound until the child reaches, but always stop the sound before he or she actually touches the object. Make the sound again only if necessary to maintain the child's effort to find the object.

Make sure there are not too many competing sounds when you try this activity.

Use in Daily Routines:

Keep noisemakers in places where you are apt to interact with the child frequently (e.g., diapering area, eating area, play area). Try this activity before, after, or during these other activities.

Adaptations:

Hearing Impaired: If a child has both visual and hearing impairments, seek the advice of the audiologist or speech-language pathologist as to the best noisemakers to use.

Motor Impaired: If the child cannot reach, seek assistance from the physical or occupational therapist in identifying a response that indicates that the child knows the toys are there, even though it can no longer be heard.

Criterion: The child reaches for an object on either side after it no longer makes noise, several times on a number of different days.

AREA: 3.   Auditory Localization and Object Permanence
BEHAVIOR: 3i.   Reaches for an object that no longer makes noise, at midline and both sides, above and below shoulder level (for children with visual impairments)

Materials: A variety of bright, shiny noisemakers

Procedures:

Make a noise, briefly, with a toy and encourage the child to find it. If the child does not, make the sound a little longer, then stop and wait again. Increase the duration of the sound as necessary to promote reaching. Vary the position of the toy—from above shoulder level to hip level, from far left through midline to far right. Talk to the child as he or she searches, to give the child feedback as to how well he or she is doing. Make a slight noise with the noisemaker to aid in a continued search, if necessary. Always give the toy to the child to play with when he or she touches it or make a game of letting the child touch it, praising him or her and moving it to another location, whichever approach is best suited to the child.

Make this a game that is equivalent to hide-and-seek. Laugh with the child and talk about "tricking" him or her when mistakes are made.

Use in Daily Routines:

Plan to play this game many times throughout the day, as you change the child's diapers and engage in other care activities.

Adaptations:

Hearing Impaired: If a child has significant impairments of both vision and hearing, it will be very difficult for him or her to master this item. Seek assistance from the audiologist or speech-language pathologist for ideas about the best noisemakers.

(continued)

Motor Impaired: Seek help from the physical or occupational therapist to determine the best positions in which to place toys to allow the child with motor impairments to be successful in reaching.

Criterion: The child reaches for objects that are no longer making a noise above and below shoulder level, or to the right, left, and at midline. This response should be observed both in specific training sessions and in the normal routine of the day (e.g., when the child is sitting, he or she should be able to retrieve a dropped toy if it makes a noise as it lands).

AREA: **3.   Auditory Localization and Object Permanence**

BEHAVIOR: 3j.   Reaches in the correct direction for an object that has made noise in several places (for children with visual impairments)

Materials: A variety of bright, shiny noisemakers

Procedures:

Make a brief noise with a toy in one location (e.g., above the child's head); move the toy (e.g., to waist level) and make the noise again. Wait. Observe where the child reaches. If he or she reaches toward where the toy that first made noise, repeat the sound in the last location again and wait for the child to find the toy. Talk about what happened (e.g., "I fooled you; its over here. Can you find it?"). Gradually work up to moving the toy rapidly through four places, making the noise momentarily in each. Reward the child's attempts with praise and let him or her have the toy with which to play.

Watch for favorite toys to use for this game. Make the game fun!

Use in Daily Routines:

Keep toys appropriate for this activity in all areas where you frequently interact with the child. Do this activity prior to changing the child, after meals, before or during a free play time, and at other convenient times throughout the day.

Adaptations:

Hearing Impaired: See the Hearing Impaired Adaptations section of item 3i.

Motor Impaired: See the Motor Impaired Adaptations section of item 3i.

Criterion: The child reaches for a toy in the right direction when it has made noise in 3 or 4 places. This should be observed to occur most of the time, both in training sessions and in daily events (e.g., finding a toy that drops and rolls or bounces to a new location).

4.

Attention
and Memory

ATTENTION AND MEMORY are necessary components of most learning. The activities included in this sequence for facilitating the development of attention and memory are basically the same activities that are included in other sequences that facilitate language, teach cause and effect relationships, and provide an understanding of where objects are located in space. For example, you use games to teach the child turn-taking behaviors that are an important precursor of communication, but you also use these same games to help the child learn to recognize (i.e., remember) a sequence of activities. However, for the purpose of better understanding the child and the factors that facilitate or interfere with his or her learning, it is useful to assess and record progress in attention and memory separately from those skills developed when using the same activities in other sequences.

4. Attention and Memory

a. Shows anticipation of regularly occurring events in everyday care
b. Anticipates frequently occurring events in familiar "games" (e.g., nursery rhymes) after 2 or 3 trials
c. Anticipates frequently occurring events in familiar "games" on first trial
d. Remembers location of objects that are put down for a few minutes
e. Reacts to a change in a familiar game or routine
f. Recognizes familiar toys, people, and places
g. Imitates adult actions with novel objects several hours after observing actions

h. Retrieves own toys from usual locations
i. Imitates novel action involving a combination of objects several hours after observing the action
j. Recognizes own and others' clothing, toys, and personal belongings
k. Retrieves household objects from usual locations on request (i.e., signed, spoken)
l. Puts objects away in correct place
m. Says or acts out parts of rhymes or songs independently
n. Repeats a 2-word or 2-number sequence

AREA: **4. Attention and Memory**
BEHAVIOR: 4a.   Shows anticipation of regularly occurring events in everyday care

Materials: A normal home or group care environment

___

Procedures and Use in Daily Routines:

The most important way to "teach" this item is to provide a consistent environment for the child. It should be consistent in terms of the people providing most of the care and the settings in which the care is provided. Routines should be established in diapering, preparations for eating, bathing, bedtime, and so forth. After routines have been established, begin to watch for signs that the child is anticipating the next part of the routine. For example, when the child is hungry, does he or she stop crying when the sounds of food preparation are heard? Or, does he or she get excited when hearing the bath water being drawn?

Adaptations:

Visually Impaired: Be sure to develop routines that have strong auditory cues that are easy for the child with a visual impairment to discriminate.

Be sensitive to cues other than eye gaze and smiling that indicate that the child is anticipating events.

Hearing Impaired: Be sure to develop routines for a child with a hearing impairment that have strong visual cues.

___

Criterion: The child shows anticipation of 2 or more regularly occurring events in everyday care. These should be observed on several occasions and at least 2 different people should be able to agree that the child's behavior indicates anticipation.

AREA: **4: Attention and Memory**
BEHAVIOR: 4b.   Anticipates frequently occurring events in familiar "games" (e.g., nursery rhymes) after 2 or 3 trials
BEHAVIOR: 4c.   Anticipates frequently occurring events in familiar "games" on first trial

Materials: A normal home or group care environment

___

Procedures and Use in Daily Routines:

Play "games" with the child throughout daily care activities. For example, when bathing or dressing the child, play "This little piggy" with his or her toes, or play body part games, such as "Head knocker, eye blinker, nose blower, mouth eater, chin chucker, chin chucker, chin chucker chin" (touching each part and then tickling under the chin). When the child is accustomed to the game and enjoying it, wait a few seconds before a critical line and observe the child. Does he or she say "wee, wee" or touch a toe for the last little piggy or pull up the shoulders expecting the tickle when you get to "chin chucker"?

Note: Children generally enjoy games that include touching or tickling and it is easy to observe their anticipation as they prepare for the tickle or the touch to come. However, some do not enjoy either touch or tickle. Play other games that rely on interesting sounds for their effects.

Most book stores have a collection of books with rhyming games for children. Look up and try some new ones!

___

(continued)

Adaptations:

> *Visually Impaired:* Emphasize games involving touch and sound for a child with a visual impairment.
>
> *Hearing Impaired:* Emphasize games involving touch and sight for a child with a hearing impairment.

Criterion for item 4b.: The child shows anticipation of an event in 1 or more familiar "games" after it is played 2 or 3 times in sequence. This should be observed on a number of occasions over a period of several days.

Criterion for item 4c.: On several different days, the child shows anticipation of an event in 1 or more familiar "games," the first time it is played on a given day.

AREA: **4. Attention and Memory**

BEHAVIOR: 4d. Remembers location of objects that are put down for a few minutes

Materials: A normal home or group care environment

Procedures and Use in Daily Routines:

Observe the child periodically as he or she is examining or playing with toys or other objects. What happens when the child puts the object down, out of sight (drops it behind his or her back or puts it down and turns away from it)? If the child picks up the object again, does he or she seem to pick it up because it again came into view or does the child turn to the right location and pick up the toy as if expecting to find it there?

If the child is not ever observed to retrieve a toy that has been dropped and is out of sight, try to set up the situation artificially, using one of his or her favorite toys. As he or she drops it or puts it down, quickly distract the child so that he or she turns far enough away, rendering the toy to be out of sight. Wait for a few minutes to see if the child turns back to the toy. If he or she does not go back to toy, talk about it and, if necessary, show it to him or her and then put it back out of sight. Try this activity again with different toys.

Adaptations:

Visually Impaired: If a child has a significant visual impairment, it is difficult to learn locations of objects, especially if he or she moves during instruction. It is important to teach the child at an early age to search for objects by passing his or her hands over the floor, table, or other surface. The child with a visual impairment who searches with his or her hands in a location where the toy was last placed or dropped would pass this item.

Motor Impaired: A child with a severe motor impairment may not be able to demonstrate memory for location by picking up an object. With such children, it will be difficult to be sure of their knowledge of location until they are capable of understanding the question, "Where is the _____?" and can either point or use eye gaze to indicate location.

Criterion: On several occasions, the child demonstrates that he or she remembers the location of an object that was put down for a few minutes by deliberately retrieving the object or indicating where it is in response to a question.

AREA: **4.   Attention and Memory**
BEHAVIOR: 4e.   Reacts to a change in a familiar game or routine

Materials: A normal home or group care environment

Procedures and Use in Daily Routines:

Once a child is showing anticipation of events in "games" or the household routine, begin checking his or her understanding by deliberately doing something "wrong." For example, instead of giving the baby his or her bottle, begin to feed a doll or pretend to drink it yourself. Or, you might try to do "This little piggy" on the child's fingers instead of his or her toes. Observe the child's reactions. Laughter, a look of "puzzlement," trying to correct what you are doing, or fussing may be indicators of an understanding that you are making a mistake. Respond appropriately to what the child does. Laugh at yourself and say, "Oops, Mommy made a mistake. That's not the way we do it," and then do it right.

Adaptations:

No adaptations are necessary.

Criterion: The child reacts to a change in a familiar game or routine. This should be observed to occur in several different games or in the same one on a number of different days.

AREA: **4.   Attention and Memory**
BEHAVIOR: 4f.   Recognizes familiar toys, people, and places

Materials: A normal home or group care environment

Procedures and Use in Daily Routines:

The best way to help a child learn to recognize things that are familiar is to provide a consistent and predictable environment. For example, the child will learn more effectively if he or she has only a few toys present to play with at one time, if there are relatively few people providing his or her primary care, and so forth. Observe the child carefully in situations where something or someone new is introduced and in situations where there is a "reunion" with someone or something familiar. Watch for signs that the child recognizes people, toys, or places. Signs of recognition may include smiling, reaching for, going to a place in a room where a special toy has been kept for his or her visits, and so forth.

If the child is not showing signs of recognition of "the familiar," make an effort to increase his or her attention to people, places, and objects in the environment. Go with the child to explore, talk about what you see, hand items to the child, and help him or her look, feel, smell, listen to them. Put an item away that the child has played with every day. Bring it out again several days later but present it with one or two other objects or toys that have continued to be around. Observe the child's responses.

Adaptations:

Visually Impaired: For a child with visual impairments, be sure to include items in his or her environment that have distinctly different textures or shapes to aid in recognition.

Motor Impaired: The child with severe motor impairments may be limited in his or her ability to communicate recognition by movement toward the familiar. It may be necessary to rely primarily on indications of pleasure.

(continued)

Criterion: The child demonstrates recognition of familiar toys, people, and places. It is important that recognition be observed in several situations by more than one adult.

AREA: **4. Attention and Memory**
BEHAVIOR: 4g. Imitates adult actions with novel objects several hours
after observing actions

Materials: A few toys or objects that are unfamiliar to the child, are not similar to other toys that the child has manipulated, and have characteristics that could suggest a variety of actions (New toys are appropriate, but not necessary. Objects found around the house [e.g., spools of thread, packing materials, tools] are also effective.)

Procedures:

Show the child a new toy or object and demonstrate, 2 to 3 times, what can be done with it. Then put it away without letting the child try it. Demonstrate a different action on another object, something quite different than the first. Again, put the object away without letting the child try it. Repeat the procedure with a third object. One example of three different simple action-object combinations are: shaking a plastic egg that has something inside that makes noise, letting go of a string to allow a helium balloon to go to the ceiling, and pushing a button to make an electronic toy work.

After 2 or 3 hours (or even the next day) bring out the objects and give them to the child. Observe the child's actions with the toys. Does he or she try to do what you did with the objects? If not, let the child explore the toys in his or her own way, and then demonstrate your actions again, and see if the child will imitate having just seen the action. (If not, he or she may need more practice on immediate imitation before proceeding with this item).

Repeat this procedure with two or three other new objects.

Use in Daily Routines:

Pay attention to what the child does with various objects in the home or group care setting. Frequently, children watch an adult or another child do something and then come back later and do it themselves. This indicates that the child is remembering the action without having practiced it—the essence of this item.

Adaptations:

Visually Impaired: If the child has a sufficient visual impairment, it will be difficult to teach and assess memory in this way. The most likely opportunity for observing this kind of deferred imitation would be in a situation where a person makes a particular exclamation (or other noise, such as a clap) in response to a sound and the child is later heard to make the same exclamation (or noise) to the same sound.

Motor Impaired: If the child has a motor impairment, be sure to select actions that are within his or her motor capabilities. For some children with severe motor impairments, no imitation except vocalizations will be possible. For some, even imitation of vocalizations will be impossible, making this item inappropriate for those children.

Criterion: The child imitates adult actions with novel objects several hours after observing the activity. The child should imitate at least 2 of 3 actions that were demonstrated at one time.

AREA: **4. Attention and Memory**
BEHAVIOR: 4h.   Retrieves own toys from usual locations

Materials: A normal home or group care environment

Procedures and Use in Daily Routines:

Store the child's toys in consistent locations and have the child assist with "clean up." Observe the child to see if he or she deliberately goes to get a particular toy from its usual location. For example, the child might be playing with a train engine, then go back to his or her room to get a train car to go with the engine, or he or she might find a block, then go retrieve a box of blocks to use with it.

Ask a child to get a particular toy and bring it to you so that you can play with it together.

Adaptations:

Visually Impaired: It is especially important to keep the belongings of a child with visual impairments in consistent locations. It may help the child to locate objects and to remember where they are. It may also be helpful to create "cubbyholes" for storage that have different textured materials attached to the edges (e.g., squares of corduroy for blocks, circles of sandpaper for balls) so that the child has additional cues about the location of desired objects.

Motor Impaired: A child with significant motor impairments may not be able to retrieve objects. You may assess the child's memory for the objects' locations by deliberately putting objects in the "wrong" place and checking the child's reactions. Always accompany this action by correcting your error and talking about it to the child.

Criterion: The child retrieves his or her own toys from usual locations either on his or her own or in response to a request. This should be observed for 3 or more toys and care should be taken to determine that the child wanted a particular toy and knew where it was rather than just picking up whatever was handy.

AREA: **4. Attention and Memory**
BEHAVIOR: 4i.   Imitates novel action involving a combination of objects several hours
after observing the action

Materials: A collection of pairs of objects that are unfamiliar to the child and that can be combined to create interesting effects

---

Procedures:

Show the child a pair of objects and demonstrate, 2 to 3 times, how they can be combined to create a certain effect (e.g., hit an empty can with a large nail). Then put the objects away without letting the child try them. Demonstrate a different action with two other objects, ones that are quite different than the first. Repeat the procedure with a third pair of objects. Then, put all of the objects away.

After 2 or 3 hours (or even the next day), bring out the objects and give them all to the child. Observe the child's actions with the toys. Does he or she try to do what you did with them? If not, let the child explore in his or her own way, and then demonstrate your actions and see if the child will imitate you, having just seen the action.

Repeat this procedure with two or three other new pairs of objects.

(continued)

Use in Daily Routines:

Watch for naturally occurring examples of this kind of deferred imitation. For example, you may find the child has "gotten into" daddy's tool kit and is imitating actions with the tools that he or she has never had an opportunity to practice.

Adaptations:

Visually Impaired: For children with visual impairments that are too severe to see any of the adult's actions, this item is inappropriate. Continue to work on variations of item 4g. Also, work on teaching the child particular actions to go with particular songs, and observe if the child demonstrates memory for those actions when he or she hears the song.

Motor Impaired: For a child with motor impairments, select actions that are within his or her motor capabilities. If the child's impairments are severe, this item is inappropriate.

Criterion: The child imitates a novel action involving a combination of objects several hours after observing the action. This should be observed with at least 2 of 3 pairs of objects that are demonstrated at a given time.

AREA: 4. Attention and Memory
BEHAVIOR: 4j. Recognizes own and others' clothing, toys, and personal belongings

Materials: A normal home or group care environment

Procedures and Use in Daily Routines:

Throughout the day make a point of identifying the ownership of objects within the child's environment. It is important that the child learn that some objects belong to everyone in the family or group care setting, while others belong to specific people. When dressing the child, talk about his or her clothing. You can teach a child many other basic concepts in the context of talking about personal belongings. For example, "There're Daddy's shoes. Look how big they are. See you little shoe" or "Susie's coat is blue, LaChandra's is green, and you have a red coat."

Periodically check on the child's knowledge of ownership by asking questions or giving instructions (e.g., "Where is your coat?" "Bring me Daddy's hat." "Take this to Sarah's room."). Correct errors by gently suggesting that the child made a mistake (e.g., "Uh-oh, that's not your coat. That is Derrick's coat. Your coat is right there [pointing]. Please bring it to me.").

You can also check on the child's knowledge by "tricking" him or her (e.g., start to put his or her coat on yourself, start to put your shoes on him or her, mix up other articles that have clear ownership). Watch for the child's reactions. If the child does not laugh or do something to indicate that he or she knows this is "wrong," say, "Oops, what did I do? I started to put Johnny's coat on you. Let's give it to Johnny. Can you help me find your coat?" Make this a joking and fun exchange.

Adaptations:

Visually Impaired: If the child is blind, help him or her learn to associate the feel and sound of objects with the people who own them. At home, make a point of considering textures when buying toys and clothing, not only for the child with a visual impairment, but also for all members of the family, so that the child will have that cue to help him or her identify objects and their owners. Also, use the location of objects to help identify owner-

(continued)

ship. Help the child become aware of sounds that are associated with different people (e.g., footsteps, noises of particular objects).

In a group care setting, mark the children's "cubbyholes" with different textured fabrics. This will help a child who is visually impaired locate his or her own cubby by both feeling these fabrics and by its general location. This will help the child learn to locate the cubbys that belong to each of the other children. Encourage the other children to let the child with the visual impairment touch their clothing, toys, or other belongings as you talk about them.

Hearing Impaired: For a child with a hearing impairment, communicate ownership through both speech and gestures.

Motor Impaired: It may be necessary to check the understanding of ownership of a child with motor impairments by having him or her use eye gaze to indicate which of 2 items belongs to a particular person or by relying on the child's response to your giving the "wrong" item to someone.

Criterion: The child recognizes his or her own and others' clothing, toys, and personal belongings. That is, the child should be able to identify ownership of at least 8 different items, no more than half of which belong to him- or herself.

AREA: **4.   Attention and Memory**
BEHAVIOR: 4k.   Retrieves household objects from usual locations on request
(i.e., signed, spoken)

Materials: A normal home or group care environment

Procedures and Use in Daily Routines:

Throughout the day, involve the child in your activities. Especially encourage the child to "help" you with various tasks. Ask the child to go get items for you that are within his or her reach. If the child returns without the item you requested or acts confused, make the request again, specifying the exact location of the item. If the child is still unsuccessful, take him or her with you to find the item. Talk about where it is and then let the child carry it back to your task location. It is important to act pleased and to praise the child when he or she is able to respond to your requests. It is even more important that you not be critical or negative when the child is unsuccessful in locating the object you requested. By giving the child additional instructions or by going with him or her to find the object and then letting the child carry it to the task location, you will be ensuring that he or she will feel successful and willing to try another time.

Adaptations:

Visually Impaired: Be especially careful to keep household items in consistent places so that the child with a visual impairment will not have to search.

Hearing Impaired: See Hearing Impaired Adaptations in previous items.

Motor Impaired: You may need to decrease your requests for the child to retrieve objects, based on the extent of his or her motor impairment. This item is inappropriate for children with severe limitations of movement.

Criterion: The child retrieves household objects from usual locations on a daily basis when requested to do so (i.e., signed, spoken).

AREA: 4. Attention and Memory
BEHAVIOR: 41. Puts objects away in correct place

Materials: A normal home or group care environment

Procedures and Use in Daily Routines:

Involve the child in your activities throughout the day. Praise him or her for helping to pick up and put away toys and any other items that are not where they should be. When the child picks up an item for you, do not tell him or her where it belongs; instead, ask him or her to put it away (e.g., "Do you know where this goes? Would you put it away for me please?"). If the child indicates that he or she does not know where the item belongs, tell him or her the location.

If the child makes an error in putting something away, say, "Oops, that's not quite right. I think it goes here because. . . . Bring it here, please." Then, praise the child for getting it right. Always ensure success!

Adaptations:

Visually Impaired: The child with a visual impairment may need additional assistance in finding the right location for items. Provide containers of different sizes and shapes to be used for storing different objects. As described before, attach fabric scraps or other textured materials to the containers to provide additional cues to help the child identify the correct location for objects. For example, you might glue sandpaper to one end of a plastic tub that is used to store sandbox toys, or a piece of imitation fur to a basket that is used to store stuffed animals. Provide whatever help is necessary for the child to learn correct locations, but be sure to make requests similar to those you would make of a child without a visual impairment.

Hearing Impaired: See the Hearing Impaired Adaptations in previous items.

Motor Impaired: Adjust your requests for the child with motor impairments to "put away" objects to accommodate his or her impairments. This item is not appropriate for a child with severe motor impairments. Your best way to assess such a child's knowledge of locations is by asking questions like "Where do we keep the _____?" (using eye gaze for an answer, if necessary) or by putting things in the "wrong" place and observing the child's response.

Criterion: The child puts objects away in their correct place. Objects should include most of the child's belongings as well as 5 or 6 that do not belong to him or her. The child should put the objects away without the adult's assistance, but not necessarily without the adult's request.

AREA: 4. Attention and Memory
BEHAVIOR: 4m. Says or acts out parts of rhymes or songs independently

Materials: A normal home or group care environment

Procedures:

Frequently read rhymes or sing songs to the child. Try to include many that have actions to them (e.g., "The Itsy, Bitsy Spider," "The Wheels on the Bus," "Little Jack Horner"). After the child is imitating your actions well, begin to wait slightly before you

(continued)

do the actions to see if the child will do them without your model; or, after the child has learned to sing along with you, start a song and see if the child can sing part of it without you. Again, help as needed.

Use in Daily Routines:

Singing songs or saying rhymes is a good way to keep a child entertained when you are riding in the car, waiting in a doctor's office, or waiting for other events. A singing-songs period is also an important part of a group care schedule. The children learn from one another as well as the adult.

Adaptations:

Visually Impaired: If necessary, physically guide the hands of a child with a visual impairment through the movements for songs. Also, select songs that have a variety of different sounds rather than (or in addition to) relying on hand movements (e.g., "Old MacDonald Had a Farm," "The Wheels on the Bus").

Hearing Impaired: Even children with severe hearing impairments respond well to the rhythm of songs and rhymes. Be sure to emphasize the rhythm as you sing and make movements to the songs. Also, use signs along with the words to some songs and show pictures as you sing songs such as "Old MacDonald Had a Farm."

Motor Impaired: If possible, sing songs with movements that are within the child's motor capabilities. If the child has severe impairments that interfere both with speech and with hand movements, include him or her in singing activities, but do not use this item as part of his or her intervention plan.

Criterion: The child says or acts out parts of 2 or more rhymes or songs independently. The adult may start the song, but the child must say or sing one phrase without the adult singing or must do a good approximation of at least one of the movements associated with the song at the appropriate time without an adult concurrently modeling the movements.

AREA: **4. Attention and Memory**
BEHAVIOR: 4n.   Repeats a 2-word or 2-number sequence

Materials: A normal home or group care environment

Procedures:

Play games with the child that involve repeating. Most children at this age love words and will try to imitate almost anything. Always start easy, that is, with only 1 number or a short word. Then move on to a 2-word or 2-number sequence (e.g., "Say apple," "Say Daddy," "Now say apple, Daddy"). If the child gets a 2-word sequence correct after having repeated each word alone first, try a new 2-word sequence.

If several children are together, play a memory game where you say one word and point to a child who repeats it after you. Move on to 2-word or 2-number sequences. Young children may have trouble waiting their turns and several will call it out. Do not be critical of this in young children. Just say, "You remembered it, now let's see if Diedre can do the next one all by herself."

Use in Daily Routines:

This is another activity that can keep children occupied in situations where they are confined and waiting (e.g., riding in the car, sitting in a doctor's office).

(continued)

Adaptations:

> *Hearing Impaired:*   If necessary, substitute a 2-sign sequence for a child with a hearing impairment.

> *Motor Impaired:*   If a child's motor impairments prevent both speech and movement, this item is inappropriate.

Criterion: The child repeats 5 or more 2-word or 2-number sequences on several occasions.

5.

Concept Development

IN THE PERIOD between birth and 2 years, a child progresses from making simple discriminations to attaching labels to relatively abstract characteristics of objects (e.g., color, size, shape). This sequence represents an attempt to challenge the child to attach meaning to the discriminations that are made at early developmental levels. It also attempts to help caregivers understand the importance of being sure that a child is able to discriminate objects on the basis of important characteristics before trying to teach him or her labels for those characteristics. Thus, sorting and/or matching precede identifying by name.

5. Concept Development

a. Responds differently to warm/cold, rough/smooth (same as item 19a.)
b. Responds differently to family members and strangers (same as item 15h.)
c. Responds differently to adults and children (either familiar or unfamiliar)
d. Reacts to a "different" object in a group of similar objects
e. Laughs or smiles at adults who are engaging in "baby" or other unexpected behaviors
f. Is puzzled or surprised when objects "vanish" or cease to function in usual ways
g. Points to objects or pictures by simple category names (e.g., dog, cat, house)
h. Sorts objects into categories
i. Sorts by color
j. Sorts "big" and "little"
k. Points to or otherwise identifies "round" and "square"
l. Points to or otherwise identifies "big" and "little"

AREA: **5. Concept Development**
BEHAVIOR: 5a.   Responds differently to warm/cold, rough/smooth (same as item 19a.)

Materials: Objects with a wide variety of textures, some of which are metal and can be warmed or cooled rapidly (e.g., a piece of indoor-outdoor carpet, spoons, texture ball, stuffed animals, rubber "hedgehog" or "porcupine")

Procedures, Use in Daily Routines, and Adaptations:

See the Procedures, Use in Daily Routines, and Adaptations sections of item 17a., sequence 17., Fine Motor Skills: Tactile Integration.

Criterion: The child responds differently to the two stimuli that are presented.

AREA: **5. Concept Development**
BEHAVIOR: 5b.   Responds differently to family members and strangers (same as item 15h.)

Materials: A normal home or group care environment

Procedures, Use in Daily Routines, and Adaptations:

See the Procedures, Use in Daily Routines, and Adaptations sections of item 15h., sequence 15., Social Skills.

Criterion: The child regularly responds differently to family members and strangers (or to family members and day care providers). It should be possible for two adults to agree on the response differences observed.

AREA: **5. Concept Development**
BEHAVIOR: 5c.   Responds differently to adults and children (either familiar or unfamiliar)

Materials: A normal home or group care environment

Procedures and Use in Daily Routines:

Try to provide the child with many opportunities to be around children and adults. Observe the way the child responds to these people and try to determine if he or she is responding differently. Commonly, children prefer to be with children. They will stop fussing if placed on the edge of a group of playing children, will watch children quietly for much longer periods of time than if left with adults who are not directly interacting with them, will show more excitement (e.g., body movement, often vocalization) when a child approaches, and so forth.

Adaptations:

Visually Impaired: The child with a severe visual impairment may be quite late in developing this skill because the discrimination must be made on the basis of voice, smell, activity level, and other nonvisual characteristics. Be sure to give the child with a visual

(continued)

impairment opportunities to be with other children and adults and experience size and other differences by tactile exploration.

Criterion: The child responds differently to adults and children on several occasions. Two adults should agree on the response differences that were observed.

AREA: 5.   Concept Development
BEHAVIOR: 5d.   Reacts to a "different" object in a group of similar objects

Materials: Several "sets" of objects in which there are 7–10 similar or identical objects and one that is different in size, shape, function, or several notable characteristics (e.g., 8 blocks and a bell of similar size, 6–8 beads with large holes in them and 1 solid block of similar size, 6–8 small "wooden people" [e.g., those made by Fisher-Price] and one small car)

Procedures:

Give the child a container of one of the sets of objects or simply place the objects out on a surface in front of the child. Observe the child as he or she explores the objects. Pay close attention to the child's behavior when he or she picks up the "different" object. Watch for behavior that would indicate that the child recognizes it as different (e.g., looking at it longer, handling it longer, trying different activities with it, tossing it away).

Note: This activity can be continued with the child long after he or she has demonstrated that the difference in simple objects is recognized. Simply increase the complexity of the discrimination to be made. For example, give the child several dolls and one similarly sized animal, or 5 spoons and 1 fork. This is a good way to entertain the child and will give you an idea of the child's growing powers of discrimination and categorization.

Use in Daily Routines:

Keep a set of objects, as described earlier, in a container to give to the child when you are busy, but are in a position to observe what he or she does. It will keep you both entertained.

Adaptations:

Visually Impaired: Select objects that differ in terms of their shapes, textures, or sounds they produce for a child with a visual impairment. Begin with objects that are markedly different, as these discriminations may be more difficult for the child with a visual impairment.

Motor Impaired: If the child's motor impairment precludes picking up and handling the objects, try placing them one at a time in front of him or her, leaving each there until the child seems to be uninterested. Watch for facial expressions, signs of excitement, or longer interest to indicate a discrimination of the "different" object.

Criterion: The child reacts to a "different" object in a group of similar objects. This should occur with at least 2 sets of objects and the reaction should be clear enough that two adults can agree on the response differences observed.

AREA: 5. Concept Development

BEHAVIOR:　5e.　Laughs or smiles at adults who are engaging in "baby" or other unexpected behaviors

Materials:　A normal home or group care environment

Procedures and Use in Daily Routines:

As you go through your daily routines, occasionally "tease" the child by doing something you would not normally do. For example, prepare the baby's bottle, but pretend to drink it yourself; when the music comes on the radio, stop what you are doing and dance around vigorously; put your hat on upside down; or try to put a glove on your foot. Try not to laugh yourself until you see what the child is going to do. If he or she laughs, then you laugh too. If the child looks puzzled or troubled by what you have done, say something like "Silly me, look what I did," and laugh.

Sometime later, try a different "silly" behavior.

Note: It is important not to do these "silly" behaviors often or they will cease to be unexpected and, at this stage, you are really trying to determine if the child discriminates between usual and unusual behavior.

Adaptations:

Visually Impaired: Try to think of activities that you can do with a child with a visual impairment that do not depend on being seen to be recognized as unusual. For example, start to put the child's shoe on his or her hand.

Criterion:　The child laughs or smiles at adults who are engaging in "baby-like" or other unexpected behaviors on several occasions.

AREA: 5. Concept Development

BEHAVIOR:　5f.　Is puzzled or surprised when objects "vanish" or cease to function in usual ways

Materials:　A variety of toys, containers, miscellaneous objects found around the home

Procedures:

Play a simple guessing game with the child to challenge his or her understanding of what normally happens. For example, place a small toy in one hand and show it to the child. Place your hands behind you and move the object from the one hand to the other. Bring your hands out, still in fists, and let the child open each one to look for the toy. Do this several times, sometimes leaving the toy in the same hand shown to the child and at other times transferring it. Then, leave the toy behind you in your pocket, under a cushion, or someplace else out of sight. Observe what the child does when the toy is not in either hand.

Another game you could play would be to let the child drop 1 or 2 small toys into a container. Shake them up and let the child take them out. Do this a couple of times, then remove the toys from the container as you shake it (without letting the child see what you are doing). Give the child the empty container and observe what he or she does.

(continued)

Play with a wind-up toy that has an on/off switch, regularly presenting it to the child with the switch on after you have wound it. Then, wind it, and present it with the switch off.

Participate in the activities described, and look for signs of the child's surprise (e.g., laughter, a puzzled look on the face, looking in the place(s) where nothing was found another time, shaking the container, shaking the toy to make it work).

Use in Daily Routines:

In most households there are toys, appliances, or other objects that cease to work in the way they have always worked. Observe how the child responds when something does not "work." Act surprised yourself and say something like, "What's the matter? Uh-oh, it's broken."

After the child has had many opportunites to observe you pouring cereal into a bowl, tip an empty box over the bowl and shake it in the normal fashion. Or, when a small box is only about half full allow the child to try to pour cereal into his or her bowl. After several such experiences give the child an empty box. Observe to see if the child acts puzzled, shakes the box harder, and/or looks in the box to see what is "wrong."

Adaptations:

Visually Impaired: Rely on natural instances of toys, appliances, and other objects not working, especially those that make noise, or set up such a situation. It will be difficult for the child with a significant visual impairment to comprehend that items should not vanish until very complex search patterns have been developed.

Motor Impaired: If necessary, use eye gaze with a child with motor impairments as a signal for you to open a hand to expose a toy when you play the aforementioned guessing game.

Criterion: On several occasions, the child is puzzled or surprised when objects "vanish" or cease to function in their usual ways.

AREA: 5.   Concept Development
BEHAVIOR: 5g.   Points to objects or pictures by simple category names
(e.g., dog, cat, house)

Materials: A normal home or group care environment, including books, pictures, and/or magazines

---

Procedures:

Spend at least a few minutes every day "reading" to the child (i.e., sit down and look at a book, magazine, or pictures together). Point to objects, and name and describe them. Then begin to ask the child, "Where is the _____" or "Show me the _____."

Look for books or magazines that have pictures of several different kinds of dogs, cats, houses, and so forth. See if the child can point to the "dog," "cat," or "house" even though it is not the same dog, cat, or house that you have shown him or her in the past.

Note: At first, a child often develops overly inclusive categories. All animals may be identified as "dogs." Correct the child by saying something like, "No, that is a horse. The horse goes 'whinny, whinny' and the dog goes 'ruff, ruff.' Try to find some other examples of the two categories to reinforce a knowledge of the differences.

(continued)

Use in Daily Routines:

As you do daily household chores, make a conscious effort to expose the child to category names, beginning with simple ones like chair, table, rug, or brush. Then, keep the child occupied as you work by asking him or her to find several examples of the category you designate. For example, "Where's your chair? Where's another chair?" Or, you can give the child a dust cloth and say, "Please help me dust. Dust a chair. Now dust another chair." (The child is unlikely to dust acceptably, but will enjoy feeling like he or she is helping.)

You can also teach categories as you engage the child in "cleaning up" (e.g., "Lets pick up all of the trucks first. Now we'll get the blocks.").

As the child's knowledge increases, introduce more complex category names (e.g., furniture, dishes, animals).

Adaptations:

Visually Impaired: If the child has little or no useable vision, it may help to begin by teaching more inclusive categories that are related to how objects feel or sound. For example, the general term "Animal" may be easier to learn than a specific type of animal by feeling the fur of a stuffed animal. The child will not be able to point, but would be able to hand you objects such as "animals," "balls," or "trucks."

Hearing Impaired: Use signs as a supplement to words, if necessary, with a child with hearing impairments.

Motor Impaired: Rely on eye gaze as an indicator, if the the child with motor impairments is unable to point or to indicate yes or no, when asked, "Is this a _____ ?"

Criterion: The child points to objects or pictures by simple category names (or indicates knowledge of the names in some other fashion). The child should be able to demonstrate an understanding of at least 3 such category names.

AREA: **5.   Concept Development**
BEHAVIOR: 5h.   Sorts objects into categories

Materials: Several containers, a variety of toys and objects

Procedures:

Give the child 2 or 3 containers and a mixed group of toys or other objects. Select objects that could be easily sorted into the number of containers provided. For example, with 2 large and 1 small containers, you might give the child 5–6 small cars, 5–6 blocks, and 5–6 rubber bands. Suggest that the child put the objects into the containers. Observe whether the child makes an effort to sort the objects on the basis of some discernible categories, even though they may not be the ones you would choose.

If the child appears to randomly put the objects in the containers, show him or her how you would divide them, identifying each category by naming the items as you put them in the containers. Then give the child some objects representing other categories to put into the containers and observe his or her groupings.

(continued)

Use in Daily Routines:

Keep a collection of objects to sort near the telephone. When you are talking on the telephone or are busy in some other capacity, give the collection to the child to sort (changing it frequently so that the child will maintain interest).

Adaptations:

Visually Impaired: Select items to sort that can be identified by texture or sound with a child with a visual impairment.

Motor Impaired: Adjust the size of objects and container openings to accommodate the child's motor abilities. If the child cannot pick up and manipulate objects, put the objects and containers in front of him or her. Pick up an object and say, "Where should I put this one." Put it where the child indicates (i.e., through pointing, by eye gaze). Or, if the child can indicate yes/no, ask, "Should I put this one here?" It will help to have transparent containers so that the child can see the items already in the container as well as the one you plan to put in there.

Criterion: The child sorts objects into categories on several occasions. These need not be the categories that the adult had in mind, but it should be clear that the objects share common characteristics.

AREA: **5. Concept Development**
BEHAVIOR: 5i. Sorts by color

Materials: Objects and containers painted in primary colors

Procedures:

Present the child with a red container filled with red objects (e.g., blocks) and a blue container filled with blue objects. Dump them out and mix up the objects. Begin putting them back, one at a time, each time saying the color name and holding the object in front of the container to show how it matches. Then hand an object to the child and observe where he or she puts it.

Or, create piles of objects, each pile beginning with the object you place there. Then, identify each object by color, placing it in the appropriate pile.

If the child begins correctly placing the objects in the right pile, but then makes an error, say, "Oops, does that go there?" and help the child correct the error. However, if the child begins by randomly putting the objects in the container, let him or her finish. Dump them out and demonstrate again with several of the objects. If the child still does not match the objects by color, wait until another day and try two other primary colors or black and white.

When the child easily sorts two colors at a time, add a third, perhaps reducing the number of items of each color to avoid too much "clutter."

Note: A child who is "colorblind" may be able only to match black and white or a dark color and yellow. If you observe that the child is regularly successful with these combinations, but not with any of the others, continue to name colors but do not keep repeating this activity. Refer the child to an eye specialist.

Use in Daily Routines:

Have the child assist in sorting the socks when folding the laundry.

(continued)

Adaptations:

> *Visually Impaired:*   If the child has little or no useable vision, this item is inappropriate.

> *Motor Impaired:*   If the child with motor impairments is unable to sort or match the various colored objects for him- or herself, do the sorting with the child, indicating where each object is to go (i.e., through eye gaze, with a yes/no response, if necessary). See the appendix on pages 367–368 for a description of an object board that may be used for sorting activities.

Criterion: The child sorts by color on several occasions. These should include all primary colors. Also, the child should correct any errors, spontaneously, or when asked, "Does that one go there?"

AREA: 5.   Concept Development
BEHAVIOR: 5j.   Sorts "big" and "little"

Materials: Similar toys that are of distinctly different sizes (e.g., "matchbox" cars and cars 6–8 inches long; stuffed animals that are 3–4 inches long and 8–10 inches long)

Procedures:

> Use the terms "big" and "little" frequently as you talk about or show objects to the child. Occasionally collect some toys together and tell the child that you want him or her to place them in 2 piles, "all of the big ones here and all of the little ones here." Put an example of each item in the two locations. If there is a toy of intermediate size, talk about the fact that maybe it is a big object because it is much larger than the smallest one, but that it might also be a little object because it is littler than the biggest one. Let the child decide where it should go.

Use in Daily Routines:

> When cleaning up or sorting laundry, get the child to help by sorting clothing according to size (e.g., "Daddy's big socks go here and your little socks go here.).

Adaptations:

> *Visually Impaired:*   Help the child with a visual impairment to feel objects carefully in order to get a sense of size. Then, talk about size. Select items to sort that are even more different in size than those you would select for a child who sees well.

> *Motor Impaired:*   If necessary, do the sorting with the child with a motor impairment, indicating through pointing, eye gaze, or a yes/no response where the objects are to be placed. See the appendix on pages 367–368 for a description of an object board that may be used for sorting activities.

Criterion: The child sorts "big" and "little" objects, using 2 or more groups of objects.

AREA: 5.   Concept Development
BEHAVIOR: 5k.   Points to or otherwise identifies "round" and "square"

Materials: A variety of objects that are square and round (e.g., blocks, balls, cut-outs of construction paper)

(continued)

Procedures:

Be sure that the child can sort by shape. (See items 9d.–9f., sequence 9, Visual Perception). Check the skill by placing several square and round objects in front of the child and say, "Let's put all of the square ones here (as you place a square there for a model) and all of the round ones here (as you place a round one)."

If the child is able to sort accurately, mix the objects up and say, "Let's see if you can find something square. Now, let's see if you can find something round."

Use in Daily Routines:

Describe objects that you come across in your daily routines as square or round (e.g., point out signs when traveling or walking out doors, talk about the shapes of toys).

When looking at books, riding in the car, waiting in the grocery line, and so forth, play a game where you say, "I see something square (or round). Can you find something square (or round)?"

Adaptations:

Visually Impaired: Help the child with a visual impairment to feel round and square objects as you name them. Give the child plenty of practice sorting by square and round.

Hearing Impaired: Use signs to communicate with a child with hearing impairments, if necessary.

Motor Impaired: Use eye gaze or other indicators if the child's impairments prevent pointing and speech.

Criterion: The child points to or otherwise identifies "round" and "square" objects on several occasions.

AREA: **5. Concept Development**
BEHAVIOR: 51. Points to or otherwise identifies "big" and "little"

Materials: Toys and other objects that vary in size

Procedures:

Place two toys in front of the child and say, "Give me the big _____" or "Give me the little _____ ." If the child makes an error, ask, "Is that the big one? I think this one is the big one."

Repeat with other pairs of toys or objects. As the child becomes accurate with his or her labeling of "big" and "little," decrease the size difference between the 2 objects.

Use in Daily Routines:

As you give instructions to the child, include the terms big and little. Ask him or her to make size discriminations in bringing objects to you (e.g., "Please bring me the little cup.").

Adaptations:

Visually Impaired: It will be important to present objects of very different sizes and to decrease the difference more gradually with children with visual impairments, than for children with good vision.

(continued)

Motor Impaired: Use eye gaze or other indicators with children with motor impairments, if necessary.

Criterion: The child regularly points to or otherwise identifies "big" and "little" with a variety of objects, including pairs with relatively small differences in size.

6.

Understanding Space

Two IMPORTANT COGNITIVE tasks for infants to learn are: where they are in relation to the space around them, and where objects are in relation to one another in space. This sequence is the same as sequence 5., Spatial Concepts (pp. 99–109) in the first edition of this curriculum (Johnson-Martin, Jens, Attermeier, 1986) and is directed toward the development of those concepts. Most of the items have a fairly strong motor component. Research evidence suggests that spatial concepts are most readily developed by the experience of actively moving through space; neither passive movement through space nor simply observing movement of objects and people through space is as effective as active experience in promoting a good sense of distance, spatial orientation, and spatial relationships.

For children with severe motor impairments, the items in this sequence will become increasingly inappropriate after item 6f. Some modifications of items are suggested in the "Adaptations" sections of the items. However, these will certainly not apply to all children with limited motor capabilities. Curriculum users are encouraged to modify items to fit a child's motor capabilites as much as possible, but also to be creative in designing alternative items that actively engage the child in the exploration of space. Headsticks, scooter boards, and other devices that involve self-initiated and monitored movement may be particularly useful to incorporate into alternative items. As a last resort, passive observation accompanied by verbal descriptions may be used to teach spatial concepts. Under these circumstances, the child's understanding may be assessed by asking the child questions and using eye gaze or some other indicator response to specify a reply.

REFERENCE

Johnson-Martin, N., Jens, K.G., & Attermeier, S.M. (1986). *The Carolina curriculum for handicapped infants and infants at risk*. Baltimore: Paul H. Brookes Publishing Co.

6. Understanding Space

a. Shifts attention (i.e., visual fixation, body orientation) from one object to another

b. Looks for or reaches toward objects in sight that touch the body (omit for children with visual impairments)

c. Looks for or reaches toward objects out of sight that touch the body

d. Looks for or reaches toward objects that fall from view while making a noise

e. Looks for or reaches toward objects that fall quietly from view

f. Looks or moves in the right direction for objects that fall and roll or bounce to a new location

g. Searches for objects moved out of visual field or away from midline

h. Retrieves toys from a container when they have been dropped through a hole in the top

i. Pulls string to get object from behind a barrier

j. Reaches object from behind a barrier

k. Moves self around a barrier to get an object

l. Retrieves familiar objects from usual locations in another room, upon request

m. Puts objects away in correct places

n. Uses "tools" to deal with spatial problems (e.g., extends reach with a stick, extends height with a stool (same as item 8k.)

AREA: 6.   Understanding Space
BEHAVIOR: 6a.   Shifts attention (i.e., visual fixation, body orientation) from one object to another

Materials: A variety of brightly colored toys of different sizes, shapes, and textures, including some that make noise

---

Procedures:

Present a toy to the child, holding it about 10–14 inches from his or her face, at eye level, and 6–8 inches to the left or right of midline. When the child's attention is fixed on the object, present a second object at the same distance on the opposite side.

Alternately shake or wiggle the 2 objects for 20 seconds.

Observe whether the child shifts attention from one object to another (indicated by looking back and forth or moving head from side to side).

On every trial in which the child fails to shift attention between the 2 objects, do one or more of the following until the response is achieved:

Alternately move the items into the midline and closer to the child to attract his or her attention, and then move them back to their original position and try to alternately attract attention to them again.

Alternately present an item on either side, removing one as you present the other.

Note: Change the toys frequently in order to maintain the child's interest. Make notes regarding which toys the child seems to prefer. Use these preferences in selecting toys for future teaching sessions.

Use in Daily Routines:

Try this item during diaper changes or at other times when you usually play with the child. It sometimes helps to keep a couple of toys in your pockets so that you can present them to the child for a few minutes as you put him or her down for a nap or when you just pass by the child in the course of other activities.

Adaptations:

Visually Impaired: Select toys that make pleasant but different noises for a child with a visual impairment. Emphasize the sounds made by the toys and reinforce the child for orienting to them by touching the toy to the child's face or hand on the side where the toy was located. For the child with visual impairments item 3g. in sequence 3. Auditory Localization and Object Performance can be substituted for this item.

Criterion: The child shifts his or her attention (i.e., visual fixation, body orientation) from 1 object to another and back again as the objects are alternately jiggled or waved. Repeat the procedures several times with a variety of objects.

AREA: 6.   Understanding Space
BEHAVIOR: 6b.   Looks for or reaches toward objects in sight that touch the body (omit for children with visual impairments)

Materials: A variety of toys of different sizes, shapes, and textures, including some that make noise

---

(continued)

Procedures:

Observe where a child is looking, and touch his or her body with one of the objects that are well within his or her line of vision.

Note whether the child looks at the toy. Talk about the toy, wiggle it, and place it in the child's hand (or allow the child to take it if he or she reaches for it).

Touch the child's body with a different toy in another area outside of his or her direct line of vision, but where he or she could easily see (e.g., on the hand, on the leg). Observe to see if the child looks. Again, talk about the toy, wiggle it, or place it in the child's hands.

On every trial in which the child fails to look or reach for the object, do one or more of the following until the response is achieved:

Choose a different object and touch the child.

Gently rub the child's skin with the object or apply slightly more pressure as you touch him or her with the toy.

Attract the child's attention to the object at eye level. Then move it slowly to the place where it touched the child, trying to keep the child's gaze on the object. Touch him or her with toy again.

Physically guide the child's hand to the object.

Notes: Be sure that the child has tactile sensitivity in the areas that are being stimulated.

Avoid multiple trials of this item at one time. A child may habituate (i.e., cease to notice the stimulus) if he or she is touched in the same place several times in a row.

Also, avoid light touching or rubbing in areas where the child is known to be tactilely defensive (i.e., withdraws or cries when touched). For a child who is tactilely defensive, it helps if he or she sees the object as it touches him or her. In addition, firm pressure is less likely to provoke a negative reaction than is light pressure.

Use in Daily Routines:

Try this item once or twice, each time you change the child's diaper or have other opportunities to play with the child for a few minutes.

Adaptations:

Visually Impaired: Using a noisy toy may help the child with a visual impairment locate where the toy touched him or her. While one should attempt to get a child to look at the place he or she is being touched, that is not essential for learning to locate the source of the stimulation. For the child with a visual impairment, reaching toward the stimulation is a good substitute for looking toward it.

This item can be combined with the following item (6c.) for the child with a serious visual impairment.

Motor Impaired: Some children with significant motor impairments have reduced tactile sensitivity. It will be important to assess the child's sensitivity on different parts of his or her body in order to determine the best sites for the stimulation that is necessary for this item.

Severe motor impairments may interfere with a child's ability to turn his or her head to look directly at a stimulus, as well as limit his or her ability to reach toward the object. If a child seems to be aware of being touched (e.g., moves the area being touched),

(continued)

but does not look or reach, seek the help of the physical or occupational therapist. Careful positioning or other adaptations may improve the child's ability to respond.

Criterion: On several occasions, the child looks for or reaches toward objects that touch him or her within easy sight.

AREA: 6.   **Understanding Space**
BEHAVIOR: 6c.   Looks for or reaches toward objects out of sight that touch the body

Materials: A variety of interesting toys of different sizes, shapes, and textures, including some that make noise

Procedures:

Touch an object on the child's bare skin, outside his or her visual field (e.g., on the back of the child's leg or arm, on the side of his or her abdomen).

Observe whether the child looks for and/or reaches toward the object.

Vary the objects and the location at which the child is touched, again keeping the object from being seen by the child before it touches his or her body.

On trials in which the child fails to look at or reach for the object after being touched, bring the item into the child's view, get his or her attention with the object, and then touch the area again. Physically guide the child's hand to the toy, if necessary.

Notes: Be sure that the child has tactile sensitivity in the areas that are being stimulated.

Avoid multiple trials of this item at one time. A child may habituate (i.e., cease to notice the stimulus) if he or she is touched in the same place several times in a row.

Also, avoid light touching or rubbing in areas where the child is known to be tactilely defensive. For a child who is tactilely defensive, it helps to show him or her the object as it touches his or her body. In addition, firm pressure is less likely to provoke a negative reaction than light pressure.

Use in Daily Routines:

Carry toys in your pockets or keep them available in various parts of the house or room. Try this item when playing with or changing the baby and several times a day as you are handling him or her for other purposes (e.g., putting him or her down or getting up from naps, putting on floor or in playpen to play).

Adaptations:

Visually Impaired: Use noisy toys to assist in localization. There is no difference between items 6b. and 6c. for a child with a serious visual impairment. Credit both items if the child meets the criterion for 6c.

Motor Impaired: Some children with significant motor impairments have reduced tactile sensitivity. It will be important to assess the child's sensitivity on different parts of his or her body in order to determine the best sites for the stimulation that is necessary for this item.

Severe motor impairments may interfere with a child's ability to turn his or her head to look directly at or reach toward a stimulus. If a child seems to be aware of being touched (e.g., moves the area being touched), but does not look or reach, seek the help of

(continued)

the physical or occupational therapist. Careful positioning or other adaptations may improve the child's ability to respond.

Criterion: On several occasions, the child looks for or reaches toward an object that touches his or her body, out of sight.

AREA: **6.   Understanding Space**
BEHAVIOR: 6d.   Looks for or reaches toward objects that fall from view while making a noise

Materials: Spoon, bell, rattle, and other objects that would make a noise when striking the floor or other surface around the child

---

Procedures:

Hold an object at eye level, making sure that the child's attention is focused upon it.

Drop an item from view, making sure it makes a noise loud enough to be heard by the child when it hits the floor (or other surface) and that it does not touch the child as it falls.

Observe whether the child searches visually or reaches toward the object in the appropriate direction.

If the child does not look or reach, try one or both of the following:

Show the toy to the child again, bang it on the table (or other surface near him or her), then drop it. Then, bang it on the floor (or other lower surface), trying to attract the child's attention to it there. Return it to the table, and again, bang it, then drop it.

Hold the object at eye level, make a noise with it to attract the child's attention, move it slowly downward to the floor (or other surface below the child's waist level), and make the noise again. Physically assist the child in reaching for the object, if necessary, and allow him or her to play with it. After 2 or 3 trials, try dropping the object again. If necessary, again physically assist the child to reach toward the object, give it to him or her and allow some play time.

Use in Daily Routines:

This is a good activity to try when the child is seated for other activities (e.g., eating, playing). Most children enjoy looking for objects that drop and will eventually drop them to amuse themselves.

Note whether the child looks for or reaches toward an object after dropping it.

Adaptations:

Visually Impaired: This item will be more difficult for a child with a visual impairment than for the child with good vision, as it is easier to look in the direction an object has fallen than to reach for it. Use toys that are fairly large and as visually stimulating as possible. It may be necessary to physically guide the child's hand toward the toy for many trials. Teaching this item to a child with a visual impairment will be very similar to teaching him or her item 3h., in sequence 3., Auditory Localization and Object Permanence. (Reaches for an object after it no longer makes noise.)

Hearing Impaired: Toys should be selected that make particularly loud noises for a child with a hearing impairment. It may also be necessary to work with the child on a concrete,

(continued)

tile, or formica surface, where the noise of a falling object is exaggerated. For a child with a severe hearing loss, this item can be combined with item 6e.

Motor Impaired: Severe motor impairments may interfere with a child's ability to turn his or her head to look directly at and reach toward a stimulus. Seek the help of the physical or occupational therapist to determine whether careful positioning or other adaptations may improve the child's ability to respond.

Criterion: The child regularly looks for or reaches toward objects that fall from view while making a noise.

AREA: **6.   Understanding Space**
BEHAVIOR: 6e.   Looks for or reaches toward objects that fall quietly from view

Materials: Stuffed animals or other soft toys that will make minimal noise when dropped on the floor

---

Procedures:

Hold an object at eye level, making sure that the child's attention is fixed on the object, then drop it from his or her view.

Watch carefully to see if the child looks for or reaches toward the dropped object. Vary the objects used and the positions from which they are dropped (e.g., away from midline but easily within view of the child).

If the child does not look for or reach toward the fallen object, hold it at midline eye level, then, slowly move it vertically out of the child's sight. Move the object slowly enough to allow the child to visually track it.

Use in Daily Routines:

Do this activity whenever the child is seated in an appropriate location (e.g., before or after meals, sitting in an infant chair with toys on the tray). It could also be done as a way of entertaining the child while he or she is riding in a car seat in the back seat of a car.

Adaptations:

Visually Impaired: Give the child with a visual impairment a toy that does not make a noise when dropped. When the child drops it, say, "Uh-oh, you dropped it. Can you find it?" Physically guide the child to reach in the right direction and pat the surface to find the toy. Talk about what you are doing as you do it. Let the child play with the toy when his or her hand finds it.

Motor Impaired: Severe motor impairments may interfere with a child's ability to turn his or her head to look directly at or reach toward a stimulus. Seek the help of the physical or occupational therapist to determine whether careful positioning or other adaptations may improve the child's ability to respond.

Criterion: The child frequently looks for or reaches toward objects that have fallen quietly from view.

AREA: **6. Understanding Space**

BEHAVIOR: 6f. Looks or moves in the right direction for objects that fall and roll or
bounce to a new location

Materials: A variety of interesting toys that combine visual and auditory stimulation and that, when
dropped, will bounce and/or roll from the child (e.g., squeaky toys, balls with bells inside)

Procedures:

Hold the object at eye level, making sure that the child is attending to it. Drop the
object within the child's view and in an area that allows it to bounce and/or roll, while
remaining within the child's sight.

If the child does not look around to find the object, call his or her attention to where
it is and say something about its having rolled or bounced. Try again with a different
object, perhaps one that is larger and/or makes a noise as it rolls or bounces.

Note: As you do this item, think about the language you are using. Stress concepts such as "Uh-oh, *where* did it go?", "Is it *next to* the chair?", or "Maybe it went
under the chair."

Use in Daily Routines:

Note what the child does when objects are dropped accidentally throughout the
course of the day. If the child does not look around, use the situation for a brief training
session (i.e., show the child where the object went and then try dropping it again).

Adaptations:

Visually Impaired: For a child with a visual impairment, use large, brightly colored,
shiny toys that will make optimal use of the child's residual vision. Work on expanding the
surface that the child "pats" when searching for an object that he or she has dropped. Talk
about what is happening (e.g., "Look next to your leg.", "Try over by the table."). Begin
to use more advanced direction concepts such as "to the left," "in back of," and so forth.
The child with a visual impairment will be more dependent on such verbal descriptions
than the child who has adequate vision, and he or she should be exposed to these descriptions early and in as many situations as possible. The experience of finding the toys will
reinforce the meaning of the words.

Hearing Impaired: With a child with a hearing impairment, combine gestures and signs
with words as you encourage him or her to look for the object. Remember to talk about
where the object has gone.

Motor Impaired: Severe motor impairments may interfere with a child's ability to turn
his or her head to look directly at or reach and move toward a stimulus. Seek the help of the
physical or occupational therapist to determine whether careful positioning or other adaptations may improve the child's ability to respond.

Criterion: The child looks or moves in the right direction for an object that has fallen and rolls or
bounces. This should occur consistently if the child is attending to the object before it falls.

AREA: 6. Understanding Space

BEHAVIOR: 6g.   Searches for objects moved out of visual field or away from midline

Materials: A variety of interesting and noisy toys, as well as toys that do not make noise

---

Procedures:

Elicit the child's attention to a toy at midline and eye level. Move the toy slowly out of the child's visual field (e.g., behind the child, behind you, behind some other barrier).

Vary the toys that are used, as well as the speed and direction of movement of the toys as they are moved.

Watch for indications that the child knows where to look for the object (e.g., he or she tries to look or reach behind you, he or she moves in the right direction). Make finding the toy a game—talk about where the toy has gone.

If the child does not search in the right direction, make a noise with the object and bring it back into view. Then, move it away again. Change objects frequently to maintain his or her interest.

Use in Daily Routines:

Children love to play hiding games. Try playing these type games whenever you have a free moment with the child. Carry a special toy with you so that you can do the item quickly before, during, or after some other care activity (e.g., diapering, feeding, preparing for bedtime).

Adaptations:

Visually Impaired: If the child has a visual impairment, choose objects that make a constant noise as you move them from the midline. Begin by letting the child hold his or her hand over yours as you move the toy. Then move it without the child's hand on yours, and see if he or she can locate the toy by the sound.

Motor Impaired: A child with significant motor impairments may "search" for objects out of his or her visual field with eye movements. That is, the child may look at your arm and then at you to indicate that the toy is still in the hand behind you. You can encourage good use of eye movements by asking, "Where is it?" and then talking about where the child is looking (e.g., "You're looking at my arm. Do you think it is in that hand? Let's see.").

Criterion: On several occasions, the child searches for objects that are moved out of his or her visual field or away from the midline by reaching or moving toward it or by using eye gaze or some other indicator response to show that he or she knows the object's location. When using eye gaze, 2 or more adults should independently interpret the behavior.

AREA: 6. Understanding Space

BEHAVIOR: 6h.   Retrieves toys from a container when they have been dropped through
a hole in the top

Materials: A variety of small toys; containers with holes to drop objects through (e.g., Fisher-Price Mail Box, shape boxes, a round oatmeal box with one or more holes cut in the top) (The holes should be just large enough to accommodate the toys. It should be somewhat difficult to see the toys in the container after they have been dropped through the hole.)

(continued)

Procedures:

Drop 1 or more toys through the opening at the top of the container, saying, "Oops, where did it go?" Wait to see if the child lifts up the box, removes the lid, or does some other appropriate activity in an effort to retrieve the toy that indicates an understanding of where the toy is and how to get it back.

If the child does not attempt to retrieve the toy, demonstrate how it can be done. Physically assist the child, if necessary, as he or she tries to get the toy.

Note: While shape boxes are appropriate for teaching this activity, they may be frustrating to some children. If the child is having difficulty getting the toy into the container through the hole, change containers. It may be helpful to make your own containers from boxes and begin with only one hole so that the child is not having to master shape or size discrimination along with the goals of this item.

Use in Daily Routines:

Look around the environment that you and the child are in to identify containers in use that would demonstrate the principles being taught in this item (i.e., the object is present when it goes out of sight, it drops down when you let it go, and it can be retrieved). For example, if there is a trash can with a swinging lid, you can show the child that the trash goes into another container inside, which is then carried outside. Give the child the experience of putting the trash in the basket. Talk about what is happening—use the words, "down," "where," "out," "in," and so forth.

Adaptations:

Visually Impaired: For a child with a visual impairment, choose toys that are large, brightly colored, or shiny to maximize the use of residual vision. Use containers with only one hole or several similar holes, so that the child does not have to combine shape discrimination with learning that objects drop down through a hole and can be found again. Guide the child's hands so that he or she can feel the container and explore its characteristics as you talk about it. Talk the child through getting the object in the hole and finding it afterwards. Be sure to emphasize location words so that the child is mastering these concepts.

Motor Impaired: With a child with a motor impairment, select toys and containers that will maximize his or her chances for success in putting the toy through the hole. Holes may need to be larger for these children. If the child has severe motor impairments and cannot pick up or release objects, the cognitive component of this item will have to be learned by observing a careprovider and/or other children. For these children, it is particularly important to talk about what is happening and then to check the child's understanding by asking questions, by relying on his or her verbal replies, eye gaze, or other communicative acts for answers (e.g., you might use a relatively tall container so that eye gaze would be easier to judge, and ask the child, "Where did the toy go?" The child could be credited with a correct response if he or she looked at the bottom of the container).

Criterion: On several occasions, the child retrieves toys from a container after they have been dropped through a hole in the top (or, if the child is unable to retrieve the toys, he or she indicates their location). The child is credited for this item even if he or she does not retrieve the toys until an adult asks where they are (i.e., the child may have the spatial concept, but not the motivation to retrieve those particular toys until asked).

AREA: **6. Understanding Space**
BEHAVIOR: 6i. Pulls string to get object from behind a barrier

Materials: A variety of barriers common in the child's environment (e.g., partially opened door, upholstered armchair, cardboard box, box lid), various toys with strings attached (e.g., stuffed animal with a long tail, pull toys)

Procedures:

Show the child a toy, being sure that he or she is attending to and interested in it.

Place the toy slightly out of the child's reach and demonstrate pulling the string to get it. Place the toy out of reach again, with the string near the child's hand. Wait to see if the child pulls the string to get the toy. If he or she does not, physically prompt pulling the string. Let the child play with the toy.

While the child is watching, place a toy behind a barrier (e.g., behind the door or a piece of furniture, under or inside an open box) with the string near the child. See if he or she pulls the string to get the toy. If the child does not pull the string, pull it toward the child and let him or her play with the toy for a few minutes. During this process, talk to the child about what is happening (e.g., "Where did it go?", "Is it behind the door?", "Can you get it?").

Note: Item 8c., Pulls string to obtain an object or make an effect, sequence 8., Problem Solving, and this item can be worked on at the same time.

Use in Daily Routines:

When the child is playing with a pull toy or other toy that could readily be used for this item, stop to play with him or her for a few minutes and try this item using a magazine, box lid, or nearby piece of furniture for a barrier. Most children love hiding games and will respond well to this, even if it interrupts an ongoing activity for a few minutes.

Adaptations:

Visually Impaired: Help the child with a visual impairment feel the string and the toy. Help the child practice pulling the string to get the toy, talking about what he or she is doing throughout. When you place the toy behind the barrier, talk about it (e.g., "Where is the dog? Maybe it is behind this chair. Here's its string. What will happen if you pull it?"). Help the child find and pull the string to teach him or her that the toy can be pulled from behind the barrier (or, in some cases, over the top or under the bottom of the barrier).

Motor Impaired: Modify the materials you use to enable the child with motor impairments to use whatever abilities he or she has. It may help to put a loop in the end of the string or to attach a large bead at the end to make it easier to grasp and pull. Some children will be unable to reach, grasp, or pull. The only way they will learn the concepts involved in this item is for you to show him or her what happens and to talk about it as you demonstrate. Show the child what you mean by "top," "bottom," "behind," and "under," with gestures. Entertain the child with this hiding game and hope that he or she is learning from it even though there is no way to communicate the knowledge.

Criterion: The child retrieves an object from behind (inside or under) a barrier by pulling a string. This should occur with several different objects and several different barriers. The child should know what to do on the first trial when a new toy and barrier are introduced.

AREA: **6.   Understanding Space**
BEHAVIOR: 6j.   Reaches object from behind a barrier

Materials: A variety of barriers that are common in the child's environment (e.g., partially opened door, upholstered armchair, cardboard box, box lid), various toys, including some known to be the child's favorites

---

Procedures:

Show the child a preferred toy and make sure that he or she is paying attention to it.

While the child is watching, hide the toy behind a barrier, close enough to the child so that he or she can reach behind it. If the child does not reach behind (or move the barrier) to get the toy, demonstrate how to do so.

Make this a game. Laugh and talk as you play, making comments like: "Here's bunny."; "Oops, there goes bunny."; "Where's bunny?"; "I found bunny."; and "Can you find bunny?"

Use in Daily Routines:

Look for opportunities throughout the day to join the child's play and try this item with a toy that he or she has nearby. Use furniture, magazines, curtains, or anything else that is handy for a barrier. The greater the variety of materials, the better the child's understanding.

Adaptations:

Visually Impaired: Help the child with a visual impairment feel the barrier. Talk about it. Use more physical assistance when proceeding through this item.

Motor Impaired: Select toys and barriers for the child with a motor impairment to minimize the amount of movement that is necessary to master this task. If the child is severely motor impaired and is unable to reach or move independently, you will have to try to teach this and other spatial concepts through demonstration and verbal description of what is happening. It may be useful for the child to observe other children playing this game, as well as to have an adult demonstrate it to him or her.

Criterion: The child retrieves several different objects from behind a variety of different barriers. The child should know what to do on the first trial with a toy and a barrier that have not been used for training.

AREA: **6.   Understanding Space**
BEHAVIOR: 6k.   Moves self around a barrier to get an object

Materials: A variety of barriers common to the environment (e.g., furniture, doors, curtains, boxes), numerous interesting toys

---

Procedures:

While the child is watching, place a preferred toy behind a barrier that the child must go around in order to get to the toy (e.g., drop the toy behind a chair, toss a toy behind the door). If the child does not go around the barrier to get the toy, go around the barrier and call to him or her, talking about the toy that is there. If necessary, put the toy out in the child's view, shake it to attract attention, then put it back behind the barrier.

(continued)

Talk about how lonesome the toy is for the child, how you miss the toy and would like for the child to get it, and so forth.

Use in Daily Routines:

As with previous items, you should try this one several times a day, when the child is playing with toys near natural barriers. Try this hiding game only once or twice at a time, varying the materials and the barriers.

Adaptations:

Visually Impaired: A child with a visual impairment frequently encounters barriers as he or she moves around his or her environment. Help the child feel the barrier to determine its limits and to figure out how to get around it. If the child cannot see well enough to see you place an object behind a barrier, just place the object and tell the child that it is "behind the _____. See if you can find it." Provide as much physical assistance as necessary, and talk the child through the activity. It may help to use a music box or some other toy that will continue to make noise as the child tries to retrieve it.

Motor Impaired: If the child has a severe motor impairment, help him or her move around a barrier, talking about it as you carry him or her to find the toy. Try to assess the child's understanding through responses to questions or effective responses.

Criterion: The child moves him- or herself around 2 or more different barriers to retrieve a hidden toy. The child should be able to go around a different barrier than the one used in training on the first trial.

AREA: **6.   Understanding Space**

BEHAVIOR: 6l.   Retrieves familiar objects from usual locations in another room,
upon request

Materials: Toys and normal household or school objects that are placed on shelves or in other areas that are accessible to the child

---

Procedures:

Keep the child's toys and other items in specific locations in the home or classroom whenever they are not in use.

Have the child observe you putting preferred objects away and removing them so that he or she know their location. Also, involve the child in "picking up" and "putting away." Always identify what goes where.

Talk to the child frequently about the location of items (e.g., "The ball goes on the bottom shelf.").

While the toys or other familiar items are in the same room as the child, ask him or her to get a particular item. When the child is able to do this, begin asking him or her to bring toys or objects from another room. Do not tell the child where the object is if it is in its expected or usual location. The point of this item is that the child has learned and remembers the usual location of objects and can get them when requested to do so.

If the child is unable to get an item, go with him or her to get it. Point out and label its location. Arrange an opportunity to ask for that same object later in the day to reinforce the child's memory.

(continued)

Use in Daily Routines:

Asking a child to get something for you is a normal part of daily life. It is important only to note how well the child remembers usual locations of objects.

Adaptations:

Visually Impaired: If the child has a severe visual impairment, it is even more important to store objects in the same place. "Labels," made from different textured materials, may be used on shelves to assist the child in remembering which objects belong in which area or compartment.

Hearing Impaired: With a child with a hearing impairment, it may be necessary to make requests for objects with both signs and words. It may also be necessary to describe where objects are kept with signs and gestures.

Motor Impaired: A child with significant motor impairments may not be able to move well enough to retrieve toys from another location. In such a case, teach the child the correct location of objects by keeping him or her with you as you pick up the toy, talking about what you are doing on the way to get the toy, and assisting the child to "help" you as much as possible. (He or she may be able to drop a block in the block box if you place the block in his or her hands.) Assess such a child's understanding of object location by asking questions (if the child is able to communicate adequately) or by placing a toy or another object in a wrong location while the child is watching and observe his or her reaction. You may be able to say, "I've forgotten, where does _____ belong?" and the child may be able to "tell you" by pointing or eye gaze.

Criterion: The child retrieves several objects from usual locations in another room, upon request (or, if his or her motor impairment is too severe, he or she can indicate through pointing or eye gaze where objects belong).

AREA: **6.   Understanding Space**
BEHAVIOR: 6m.   Puts objects away in correct places

Materials: A normal home or group care environment

Procedures:

Keep the child's toys and other items in specific locations in the home or at the group care facility, whenever they are not in use.

Have the child observe you putting items away and removing them from their location when they are brought out to be played with or used. Frequently talk to the child about the location of items as you put them away (e.g., "The ball goes on the bottom shelf.").

Ask the child to help you "pick up" and "put away" items that were used. Observe where the child puts the items. If they are not placed in the correct locations, say something like, "Oops, I think you got the ball in with the blocks. Can you put it over there in that tub with the other balls?"

Note: It is rare to find a child that enjoys picking up. If many toys are in sight, the child may be disorganized by so many stimuli. It will help if you organize the task (e.g., "Let's see if we can pick up all the blocks first. I will help you. Let's see how many blocks we can find."). Praise the child for helping you and tell others about what a good helper he or she was.

(continued)

Use in Daily Routines:

Putting items away is something that occurs (or should occur) every day. There will be ample opportunity to work on this item. The real issue in this item is to be attentive to when the child has learned the appropriate location for most of the items in his or her home or group care environment.

Adaptations:

Visually Impaired: The child with a visual impairment should be required to help pick up just as other children. He or she may need some special help in learning to feel compartments or other spaces in order to recognize which is appropriate for particular objects. Try to make the compartments/spaces more identifiable by attaching textured materials (e.g., sandpaper on top of the block box, fabric on the side of the box for dress up clothes).

Motor Impaired Try to include the child with motor impairments in picking up and putting away activities when possible. If the child uses a wheel chair or stroller, place objects on the child's lap and push the chair to each object's correct location. Praise the child for helping. For the children with more severe motor impairments, it may be necessary to assess their understanding of where items belong by having them "tell you" by pointing or eye gaze.

Criterion: The child puts familiar objects away in their correct place. The child should be able to put all familiar toys in correct places when asked (or, if his or her motor impairment is too severe, he or she is able to indicate the object's correct location).

AREA: **6. Understanding Space**

BEHAVIOR: 6n. Uses "tools" to deal with spatial problems (e.g., reach with a stick, extends height with a stool (same as item 8k.)

Materials: Small dowels, a broom, strings with loops at the ends, stools, chairs, a variety of toys. (Everything necessary for this item should be available in a normal home or group care environment.)

Procedures:

With "tools" available, create spatial problems for the child. For example, engage the child in playing with a set of blocks that includes one or more dowels. Show the child how you can pull a toy toward you with the dowel. A few minutes later, "accidentally" push a block or other toy out of reach, under a chair or other piece of furniture, and say, "Oops, I can't reach the block. How can we get it?" And/or, after using a stool several times to get something out of reach, place something up out of the child's reach and ask, "How do you think you could get that?"

If the child becomes frustrated, make suggestions and provide physical assistance so that he or she can solve the problem. Make a point of not solving problems for the child, but, instead, encourage him or her to solve them independently or with only hints or suggestions from you. For example, if the child is trying to reach something that is too far away, put the broom or some other object next to the child and say, "Do you think it would help to use this?"

(continued)

Use in Daily Routines:

When spatial problems occur naturally throughout the course of the day, observe the child's responses. Give the child hints or make suggestions that might help him or her solve the spatial problem. Also, model a problem-solving approach to daily events. For example, when you are trying to carry too many items and keep dropping one, put some of the items in a grocery bag; or when you can't reach something on the top shelf, pull a chair over and climb up to get it. As you do these activities, discuss what you are doing with the child.

Adaptations:

Visually Impaired: It may be difficult for a child with a visual impairment to develop a good understanding of space and to perceive potential solutions to spatial problems. More physical assistance and verbal cues will be needed with these children.

Motor Impaired: Carefully select the kind of spatial problems you arrange for a child with a motor impairment in order to ensure some success. A child with a severe motor impairment is generally surrounded with "tools" that affect his or her functioning (e.g., a wheelchair, a prone stander). Talk to the child about how these tools can help him or her do activities. Assume a problem-solving attitude about helping the child to accomplish tasks—talk about the things you are trying and why. These activities may teach the child about space and problem-solving, but he or she may not be able to experience it more directly.

Criterion: The child uses a tool to solve one or more spatial problems spontaneously (i.e., without any physical or verbal prompts).

7.

Functional
Use of Objects
and Symbolic Play

LEARNING TO USE objects in an adaptive and socially appropriate way lays the foundation for some aspects of problem solving, role taking, and other forms of imaginative play. One of the earliest means a child has of defining or understanding objects and, therefore, of developing concepts about categories or classes of objects is through the functions that each object serves. Normally, children spend a great deal of time maniuplating objects in order to understand their properties and potential uses.

The items in this sequence are designed to help children with disabilities develop appropriate ways to interact with objects and to play constructively within the constraints imposed by their disabilities. Although suggestions are included for modifying the items to meet the needs of children with visual, hearing, or motor impairments, further modifications will undoubtedly be necessary for children with multiple and/or severe disabilities. For example, for some children with severe disabilities, the only available mode of teaching may be to simply demonstrate appropriate object usage repeatedly and then check for learning by abruptly shifting to inappropriate usage and watching for signs of amusement, surprise, or dismay. It is especially important to keep daily records of such efforts to teach and to assess the child's learning, because "reading" the signals of these children is difficult. Their ability to understand is often underestimated. Good records may be the best evidence available to document their capabilities.

7. Functional Use of Objects and Symbolic Play

a. Moves hand to mouth
b. Explores objects with mouth
c. Plays with (e.g., shakes, bangs) toys placed in hand
d. Commonly performs 4 or more activities with objects
e. Explores objects and responds to their differences
f. Demonstrates appropriate activities with toys that have obviously different properties

g. Combines 2 objects in a functional manner
h. Imitates activities related to the function of objects
i. Plays spontaneously with a variety of objects, demonstrating their functions
j. Imitates adult behavior with props
k. Spontaneously engages in adult activities with props
l. "Talks" to dolls or animals and/or makes them interact with one another

AREA: **7.   Functional Use of Objects and Symbolic Play**
BEHAVIOR: 7a.   Moves hand to mouth

Materials: Sticky substances (e.g., jelly, syrup) that the child enjoys tasting

---

Procedures:

Watch for hand to mouth movement. The movement may already be spontaneously occurring. If it does not occur or is infrequent (e.g., 3–4 times a day), put a small amount of something sweet or "good tasting" on the back of the child's hand (e.g., on the knuckle below the index finger, wherever it will be easiest for the child to suck it off).

Grasp the child's elbow gently and use it to move the child's hand to his or her mouth. Hold it there until the child has a chance to taste the substance on it. Talk to the child in a soothing tone.

Release the child's elbow, put more sweet substance on his or her hand, and observe.

If the child does not take his or her hand to the mouth, repeat the above procedure several times, giving as little assistance as necessary.

Notes: As soon as hand-to-mouth movement is established, toys should be introduced and other activities encouraged. Hand-to-mouth activity is an important part of body awareness and exploration, but can become a powerful self-stimulating behavior in children with disabilities if not modified with more advanced behaviors.

Some children develop a "bite reflex" and will clamp down on anything touching their teeth. Do not work on this item if the child demonstrates this behavior. Seek assistance on this item from a speech pathologist, physical therapist, or occupational therapist if this behavior is demonstrated.

Use in Daily Routines:

It may be helpful to work on this activity just before feedings or when the child gets fussy and you are holding him or her. Mouthing the hands is usually a source of comfort to a child.

Adaptations:

Motor Impaired: More physical assistance may be required for a child with a severe motor impairment. Relaxation exercises prior to working on hand-to-mouth movement may be helpful. Side-lying is often a good position to encourage hand-to-mouth behavior in the child with motor impairments. Consult a physical or occupational therapist for advice.

Criterion: The child frequently moves his or her hand to the mouth spontaneously.

AREA: **7.   Functional Use of Objects and Symbolic Play**
BEHAVIOR: 7b.   Explores objects with mouth

Materials: A variety of small objects that are appropriate for holding and mouthing (e.g., teething toys, rattles) (Texture, temperature, and taste of these objects may be varied to increase the probability of mouthing.)

(continued)

Procedures:

Place a toy in the child's hand and observe. If the child does not carry it to his or her mouth in a reasonable amount of time, gently grasp the child's elbow and guide the hand and object toward the mouth.

If the child withdraws from the toy, try a different one. Talk in a soothing voice to the child as you try to help him or her explore the object with the mouth.

If the child drops the toy and puts his or her hand in the mouth, try other toys to see if some are easier for the child to grasp than others. Or, physically assist by keeping your hand over the child's hand and helping guide the toy to his or her mouth.

Notes: Mouthing is usually the first way babies explore the properties of objects. It is also useful in helping the child develop oral-motor skills. However, a child with a disability may get "stuck" at this level of development. Be sure to move on to the next items in this sequence as soon as the child is able to easily mouth toys.

Observe the child carefully. Some behaviors suggest abnormal reactions that require the help of a specialist (e.g., occupational or physical therapist). Among these are: the child seems to get objects to the mouth but then draws back suddenly when they get near the face, usually dropping the object; the child drops the object and extends the arm away from the body as he or she turns the head to look at the object.

Use in Daily Routines:

Try this item whenever you are holding the child. Keep some appropriate toys available in an apron pocket or on the table where you are apt to sit with the child.

Adaptations:

Motor Impaired: Side-lying is often a good position to encourage hand-to-mouth behavior in the child with motor impairments. A child with motor impairments may require more physical assistance to get a toy to his or her mouth. In some cases, the child will not be able, even with assistance, to hold a toy and explore it with his or her mouth. In these situations, try holding the toy near the child's mouth and observe his or her efforts to explore it with the mouth. Count this item as passed if the child frequently mouths objects held for him or her.

Criterion: The child explores most objects with the mouth that are placed in his or her hands.

AREA: **7.   Functional Use of Objects and Symbolic Play**
BEHAVIOR: 7c.   Plays with (e.g., shakes, bangs) toys placed in hand

Materials: A variety of small toys that produce sounds or a visual spectacle when shaken or dropped

---

Procedures:

Hold a toy out to the child and shake it. If the child does not spontaneously take it, place it in his or her hands.

If the child does not attempt to shake the toy, place your hand over the child's hand and help shake the toy. Then release the child's hand. If he or she still does not attempt to shake the object, assist by jiggling the arm at the elbow. Repeat with other toys.

Also try banging an object on a table or other surface to make the noise. Physically assist the child to bang an object, if necessary.

(continued)

Use in Daily Routines:

Give the child a rattle or bell several times throughout the day (e.g, when the child is lying in a crib, when he or she is on the floor, when the child is seated in a swing or chair). Also, provide something to "bang" whenever the child is seated by a table or in an infant chair with a tray. A spoon is often a favorite noisemaking object.

Adaptations:

Visually Impaired: Be sure to include a variety of noisemaking toys for a child with visual impairments, since he or she may not have the added reinforcement of seeing the objects that are provided.

Hearing Impaired: Choose objects that make particularly loud sounds and/or sounds that are within the frequencies best heard by a child with a hearing impairment. Seek the advice of a speech pathologist or audiologist, if necessary.

Motor Impaired: More preparation (e.g., relaxation exercises) and/or physical assistance may be necessary for a child with motor impairments. It may help to tie a noisemaker onto the child's arm for short periods of time so that there is immediate feedback about what happens when the arm is moved. Even the child with the most severe motor impairments may enjoy and benefit from this activity, although the child's actual participation may be limited. Credit the child with significant motor impairments with a pass on this item if he or she begins to move the arm(s) more as soon as a noisemaking toy is tied on or if he or she is able to continue the movement once you have helped to start it. You should continue this activity after the child reaches this criterion, however, in the hope that he or she will become more able to initiate it.

Criterion: The child spontaneously shakes or bangs several different objects.

AREA: **7.   Functional Use of Objects and Symbolic Play**
BEHAVIOR: 7d.   Commonly performs 4 or more activities with objects

Materials: A variety of small toys that reinforce particular behaviors (e.g., squeaky toys that respond to patting; rattles that respond to shaking or waving; textured toys that invite rubbing; hard toys that make a noise when they are "banged," soft toys that make no noise when hit against a surface; balls or toys with wheels that roll when pushed)

Procedures:

Present toys, one at a time, to the child and observe what he or she does with each.

If a child has only 1 or 2 activities that he or she does with objects (e.g., only mouthing and shaking), demonstrate another activity and physically assist the child in doing it (e.g., waving, patting, banging, pushing).

Use in Daily Routines:

Prepare a box of toys with varied characteristics (e.g., noisemaking toys, textured toys) and give it to the child to explore as he or she waits for a meal, while you are talking on the telephone, and so forth. Observe what the child does with the toys.

(continued)

Adaptations:

> *Visually Impaired:*   Select the kinds of toys that will give the most feedback to a child with a visual impairment. It may help you to identify these toys if you shut your eyes and explore a variety of toys for yourself.
>
> *Hearing Impaired:*   Be sure that noisemaking toys make sounds sufficiently loud or at the right frequencies for a child with a hearing impairment to hear. Look for toys that make different visual spectacles (e.g., cradle gym, "busy box") when different activities are done with them.
>
> *Motor Impaired:*   Because of the limited response capabilities of a child with severe motor impairment, you can proceed to the next item, even though fewer than 4 activities are engaged in commonly. It is important to continue trying to find even slightly different activities that the child can do with toys in order to promote development of whatever motor skills he or she has and in order to prevent stereotypic behaviors from developing.

Criterion: The child spontaneously performs 4 different activities with toys, throughout the course of a day (e.g., mouthing, shaking, banging, patting, rubbing, deliberately pushing, throwing, dropping).

AREA: 7.   Functional Use of Objects and Symbolic Play
BEHAVIOR: 7e.   Explores objects and responds to their differences

Materials: Three to five "sets" of toys (each set should have 3 similar toys and 1 that is different [e.g., 3 squeaky toys and a rattle, 3 blocks and a ball, 3 stuffed animals and a bell])

Procedures:

> Present the child with 1 set of toys and observe his or her play for 2–3 minutes. Watch for changes in activity when the child handles the toy that is "different." For example, the child may always begin exploration by shaking the toy. When given the blocks and the ball the child may try to shake each object, but, when they make no noise, he or she may try other activities such as banging. When the ball does not make a noise when hit on the table, he or she may then try some other activity or simply spend more time examining or feeling this "odd" toy.
>
> If the child does not respond to the differences in the toys, demonstrate what you can do with the toys and talk about them.

Use in Daily Routines:

> Continue presenting the child with a small collection of toys with varying characteristics (as used in item 7d.) at various times throughout the day. Observe how the child responds to the differences of the toys.

Adaptations:

> *Visually Impaired:*   Select toys carefully for a child with a visual impairment, so that he or she will be able to identify differences in them.
>
> *Hearing Impaired:*   Select toys with strong visual effects for a child with a hearing impairment.
>
> *Motor Impaired:*   If the child's impairment is too severe to allow him or her to pick up toys and to do different activities with toys, try doing the actions for the child and observ-

---

(continued)

ing his or her reactions. For example, squeak the 3 squeaky toys and then try to squeak the rattle. Act surprised that it does not squeak and say," "What else could I do with it? I think I'll shake it." Talk about the characteristics of the toys as you play with them whether you think the child can understand or not. Look for indications of surprise or pleasure when you do the "wrong" activity with a toy—this will let you know that the child understands the appropriate activity.

Criteria: The child responds differently to the one different object in several sets of objects when an adult is trying to teach this skill *and* he or she readily changes from one activity to another based on the characteristics of the toy, when playing with a variety of toys.

AREA: 7.   Functional Use of Objects and Symbolic Play
BEHAVIOR: 7f.   Demonstrates appropriate activities with toys that have obviously different properties

Materials: A collection of toys that usually elicit different responses (e.g., squeaky toys to be patted or squeezed; balls to be rolled; various shapes and textures to be felt; rattles and bells to be shaken; cars to be pushed; mirror to be looked into)

Procedures:

Present the child with 1 toy at a time, allowing him or her to play with it as long as he or she is interested in it. Note the behavior that the child shows with each toy.

Try to present toys in a sequence to maximize differences (e.g., follow a squeaky toy with a mirror or a car).

If the child does not change activities as a result of changes in toys, demonstrate an appropriate use of each toy before handing it to the child. Physically assist the child in such appropriate use if he or she does not imitate the demonstration.

Use in Daily Routines:

Give the child a collection of toys with different characteristics to play with at various times throughout the day (as in the two previous items). It is important to limit the number of toys around the child at any one time (limit: perhaps 3–5), because too many toys are often distracting to a child, making it difficult to attend to any one for more than a few seconds.

Adaptations:

Visually Impaired: Select toys that have high contrast in color, brightness, and texture, as well as in usage for a child with a visual impairment. Also, include toys that make different noises when the child does the appropriate activity (e.g., a bell that rings when shaken, a car that clangs when pushed, a ball that chimes when rolled).

Motor Impaired: Select toys that are responsive to the motor actions that a child with motor impairments is able to perform. The child with severe motor impairments may never be able to demonstrate appropriate activities with toys. However, he or she can demonstrate an understanding of object function by laughing, frowning, or otherwise communicating recognition when an adult deliberately does the "wrong" action with a toy. Therefore, it is important to keep showing the child what objects do and exposing him or her to other children who are appropriately playing with toys. Periodically, check the child's

(continued)

understanding by going through a series of toys doing the appropriate activities with most, but inappropriate actions with a few. Carefully observe the child's reactions.

Criterion: The child engages in appropriate activities with most familiar toys (or, if his or her motor impairment is too severe, he or she can indicate an understanding of appropriate toy usage).

AREA: **7.   Functional Use of Objects and Symbolic Play**
BEHAVIOR: 7g.   Combines 2 objects in a functional manner

Materials: A collection of functionally related objects that are familiar to the child (e.g., spoon and bowl, fork and plate, blocks and a container to put them in, "pound-a-peg" and hammer, dowel and "donut block")

Procedures:

Present the child with 2 objects that have some functional relationship, and observe him or her. If the child does not spontaneously combine the objects appropriately, demonstrate how it is done. Physically prompt the response if necessary.

Use in Daily Routines:

Provide toys that relate to each other in a functional manner for the child throughout the day. Also, point out to the child how objects relate to each other in daily living activities—when you are cooking or cleaning, at mealtime, bath time, and so forth. Note if the child combines objects in a way that indicates some understanding of function.

Adaptations:

Visually Impaired: It will be necessary to help a child with a severe visual impairment "see," by feeling objects and experiencing their functions as you demonstrate. For example, help the child find his or her bowl on the table with one hand and a spoon with the other. Talk about what they are and that we need to put the spoon in the bowl in order to get the food out. Guide the child's hand with the spoon to the bowl and help him or her to eat. Later, give the child an empty bowl and a spoon. Guide a hand to one or the other and then observe to see if the child seeks the other object and tries to combine them. Do this kind of activity throughout daily care activities, letting the child experience the soap and the soap dish, the soap and the washcloth, and so forth.

Motor Impaired: Carefully observe the child's attempts to combine objects that indicate an understanding of the relationships between the objects, even if the child cannot fully master the activity, due to a motor impairment. Also, continue as in item 7g. to try to determine the child's understanding through his or her responses to your doing the "wrong" activity with the objects.

Criterion: The child spontaneously combines several sets of objects appropriately. The combinations should be in different classes of objects. For example, if the child puts many different kinds of objects into many different kinds of containers, this is still only one example of combining objects. The child would have to demonstrate 1 or 2 other kinds of combinations to pass this item.

AREA: **7. Functional Use of Objects and Symbolic Play**
BEHAVIOR: 7h. Imitates activities related to the function of objects

Materials: A collection of objects that demonstrate many different functions (e.g., whistle, drum and stick, pound-a-peg and hammer, xylophone that can be pulled as a pull toy or hit to make music, other pull toys, windmill that can be blown)

Procedures:

Show the child an object (or 2 objects that will be combined to demonstrate a function) and demonstrate its use. For example, you might present the hairbrush and then brush your hair, the child's hair, and the doll's hair, talking all the time about the brush and hair. Then give the child the brush and observe what he or she does.

Demonstrate again and physically prompt the activity if necessary.

Note: It is important to introduce new objects/toys to the child while progressing through the items in this sequence. The understanding of function should be becoming more complex. That is, the child should move from simple activities with objects that he or she sees every day in the environment to identifying probable function(s) of a new object or toy simply by looking at it. Choose materials accordingly.

Use in Daily Routines:

Talk to the child throughout the day about the function of various objects. Show him or her how to squeeze the bottle to get the detergent to come out, how you flip the switch to make the lights come on, how you remove the lid to get something inside, and so forth. Let the child try it after you show him or her.

Adaptations:

Visually Impaired: Help the child with a visual impairment experience what you are demonstrating and talking about by guiding his or her hands through the activity. Help the child explore objects carefully by guiding his or her hands over them and talking about their characteristics as you do so.

Motor Impaired: Give the child with motor impairments credit for attempts to imitate, even if they are not successful. Physically assist the child as much as necessary to give him or her some experience with the function of objects. Continue to demonstrate and talk about what is happening whether imitation is a possibility or not.

Criterion: The child spontaneously imitates activities that are related to the function of several different objects.

AREA: **7. Functional Use of Objects and Symbolic Play**
BEHAVIOR: 7i. Plays spontaneously with a variety of objects, demonstrating their functions

Materials: A collection of objects that demonstrate many functions (e.g., hairbrushes, washcloths, squeaky toys, cup, spoon, doll, whistle, drum and stick, pound-a-peg and hammer, xylophone that can be pulled as a pull toy or hit to make music, other pull toys)

(*continued*)

Procedures:

Present the child with 3 or 4 of the objects and observe what he or she does with each one. If the child does not use the object in its functionally correct manner, say, "What can we do with that? Show me." If the child does not spontaneously use the items in its functionally correct manner, go back to modeling an appropriate use of the objects and encouraging the child to imitate.

Repeat with additional objects.

Use in Daily Routines:

Continue stressing the functions of objects in the environment and including the child in as many of your household and care routines as possible.

Adaptations:

Visually Impaired: Help a child with a visual impairment to explore new objects with his or her hands and whatever residual vision is available. Talk about possible object functions based on the characteristics of each object. Provide as much physical assistance as necessary to help the child get started with a new object.

Motor Impaired: Select objects that will respond to the child's limited motor abilities. If the child's disability is too severe and he or she is unable to interact with the objects/toys, continue demonstrating function and talking about it. Also, continue to check the child's understanding by occasionally doing the "wrong" activity with an object or toy.

Criterion: The child spontaneously plays with a variety of objects, demonstrating their functions.

AREA: **7.   Functional Use of Objects and Symbolic Play**
BEHAVIOR: 7j.   Imitates adult behavior with props
BEHAVIOR: 7k.   Spontaneously engages in adult activities with props

Materials: Objects normally found in the home or in the "Pretend Play" center in a classroom (e.g., child-sized broom, mop, adult hat, mirror, dust cloth, playhouse, dolls, toy animals, play telephone, old purses and/or briefcases)

Procedures:

Include the child in your everyday activities. Make a point of talking about what you are doing and giving the child a chance to try. For example, if you are sweeping, talk about sweeping up the dirt, show the child the pile and how you clean it up. Give the child a small broom so that he or she can "work" alongside you. Or, if you're using a hammer to build something, give the child a small hammer or wooden mallet and a piece of wood so that he or she can pretend to hammer. Or, ask the child to help you clean up spills by handing him or her a cloth to use while you use another.

Observe the child's spontaneous play. Watch to see if the child treats dolls or animals as people (e.g., putting them to bed, dressing them, feeding them) or if the child imitates household chores (e.g., tries to wipe off the table if given a cloth, tries to sweep or hold dustpan, tries to hammer with a hammer). If such activities rarely or never occur, select an object and show the child what to do with it and provide physical assistance to get him or her started. Watch to see if that activity spontaneously occurs again later in the day or in the next few days. Repeat with other objects.

(continued)

Use in Daily Routines:

This skill is best taught by including the child in adult activities throughout the day, both by providing him or her with materials with which to "work" alongside you and by supplying the child with a collection of props (e.g., clothes, tools) to promote pretend play.

Adaptations:

Visually Impaired: Because imitating adult actions is so closely related to seeing those actions, it will take more effort to teach the child with a visual impairment to imitate. As you go about your daily activities, talk about what you are doing. Mention, particularly, the parts of the materials you are using (e.g., the handle and the brush sections of the broom) and help the child feel these parts. Physically guide the child in the use of the materials. Then give him or her an opportunity to try it independently. Ask the child to help you, although you know that the child cannot see sufficiently to be of any genuine help.

Motor Impaired: Discuss the activities you are doing with the child who has motor impairments. Involve the child to whatever extent is possible. If the child has severe motor impairments, make a point of carefully showing him or her the materials you are using, touching them to the child's hands if he or she cannot reach and feel them independently. Check the child's understanding of the use of these props by occasionally using one incorrectly (e.g., trying to hammer with a screwdriver) to see if the child responds in a way to indicate that he or she understands that you are "teasing" or "tricking" him or her.

Criterion for item 7j.:   The child imitates several adult activities with props. This should occur spontaneously throughout the course of daily activities, not just during a "training session."

Criterion for item 7k.:   The child spontaneously engages in several adult activities with props. That is, the child does the activities without having just seen the adult do the same activity.

AREA: **7.   Functional Use of Objects and Symbolic Play**
BEHAVIOR: 7l.   "Talks" to dolls or animals and/or makes them interact with one another

Materials: A variety of toys that stimulate imaginative play (e.g., dolls, doll bed, bottle, small dishes, cars, trucks, toy animals, puppets, doll clothing)

Procedures:

Frequently play "pretend" with the child. Hug and kiss a baby doll or toy animal, take one for a ride in a car or truck, talk for them, and so forth. Encourage the child to participate (e.g., "The poor bear is hungry. Can you feed him some supper?").

Watch for the child's spontaneous use of fantasy play in which he or she talks to animals or dolls or has the animals or dolls interact with one another.

Use in Daily Routines:

Pretend play is a good way to play with a child when you have time to devote yourself to the play, but it is also an excellent way to entertain a child when you are busy doing something else. You can talk to the child, encouraging him or her to take dolls or animals on trips, to go get the one that is lonely and needs some company, and so forth.

(continued)

Adaptations:

> *Hearing Impaired:*   If the child with a hearing impairment is learning to sign as well as speak, try to make the dolls, puppets, or animals make simple signs as you engage in pretend play with them. For example, when you say, "This bear is hungry," move the bear's paw to his mouth. Credit the child for this item if he or she appears to be trying to make the toys sign, if he or she makes signs for them, or if he or she signs to them.

> *Motor Impaired:*   For the child with severe motor impairments, it may be necessary for the adult to do most of the playing, talking to the child about what is happening and asking him or her questions (e.g., "Does the baby need a kiss?"). Look for pretend activities that are suitable to the child's motor and language capabilities.

Criterion: On several occasions, the child spontaneously engages in imaginative play during which he or she talks to toy animals or dolls or has them interact with one another.

8.

Problem Solving

MOST OF THE items in this sequence come from sequence 7., Control over Physical Environment (121–127) of the first edition of this curriculum (Johnson-Martin, Jens, & Attermeier, 1986). The name was changed to provide more continuity with *The Carolina Curriculum for Preschoolers with Special Needs* (Johnson-Martin, Attermeier, & Hacker, 1990) but the purpose of the items remains the same. Problem solving in infancy begins when the child learns that his or her behaviors are effective in changing the environment and that the environment changes in predictable ways. Successful problem-solving experiences are critical for developing a sense of competence, maintaining motivation for learning, and for instilling the concept of cause and effect.

Some children's disabilities may be too severe to accomplish many of the items in this sequence. For those children, it is critical to continue to search for any behaviors that are, or can be shaped to become, voluntary. These behaviors can then be used either to activate toys or other objects (e.g., with electronic switches, if necessary) or to signal an adult of a desired interaction. The pleasure usually demonstrated by the child the first time he or she recognizes that he or she is in control of what is happening justifies whatever effort has been necessary for the child to get to that point. Furthermore, the foundation has been laid for the child to operate a communication board or other device, should this become necessary.

REFERENCES

Johnson-Martin, N.M., Attermeier, S.M., & Hacker, B. (1990). *The Carolina curriculum for preschoolers with special needs.* Baltimore: Paul H. Brookes Publishing Co.
Johnson-Martin, N., Jens, K.G., & Attermeier, S.M. (1986). *The Carolina curriculum for handicapped infants and infants at risk.* Baltimore: Paul H. Brookes Publishing Co.

8. Problem Solving

a. Repeats activity that produces an interesting result

b. Persists in efforts to obtain an object or make an effect

c. Pulls string to obtain an object or make an effect

d. Repeats an activity that elicits an interesting reaction from others

e. Overcomes obstacles to get toys
f. Plays with a variety of toys to produce effects
g. Increases rate of usual activity with a toy when it stops working or tries another activity to make the toy work (work on items 8h. and 8i. simultaneously)
h. Uses adults to solve problems (work on items 8g. and 8i. simultaneously)

i. Imitates an adult action to solve a problem (work on items 8g., 8h., and 8i. simultaneously)
j. Solves simple problems without adult assistance
k. Uses "tools" to solve problems (same as item 6n.)

AREA: **8.   Problem Solving**
BEHAVIOR: 8a.   Repeats activity that produces an interesting result

Materials: A variety of "responsive" toys (e.g., chime bells, crib mobiles, bells, squeaky toys (made of very soft rubber)

Procedures:

Provide the child with a variety of toys that respond to very simple movements on the part of the child. Place them where there will be an optimal chance of the child's contacting them.

If the child does not seem to repeat activities that produce noises or sights, tie a bell to the child's wrist or ankle with brightly colored ribbon for 15 minute periods, 3 or more times a day. Observe the child carefully during this time. Record the number of times the child moves the wrist or ankle in the 3 minutes prior to attaching the bell. Compare that number with the number of times the child's limb is moved in the 3 minutes after the bell has been attached (allowing 3 minutes immediately after the bell is attached for the child to discover that movement produces sound).

If the child does not spontaneously move his or her "belled" limb in the first minute, physically assist movement several times. Observe again to see if the child spontaneously moves.

Another approach is to attach a string to the child's wrist or ankle and to a mobile or other easily seen toy in his or her crib, so that limb movement causes the other object to move. Leave it attached for no more than 10–15 minutes. Observe to see if there are differences in the amount of movement when the child is not attached to the toy and when he or she is attached. DO NOT LEAVE THE CHILD UNATTENDED IF YOU HAVE ATTACHED A LIMB TO A TOY WITH A STRING.

Use in Daily Routines:

As you go about your daily routines, be sure that there are responsive toys available to the child. The child is often kept satisfied for a longer period of time when he or she wakes up and finds toys to look at, hear, and feel in the crib. Responsive toys will usually interest the child the longest.

Adaptations:

Visually Impaired: Select toys that make noise and have interesting textures for a child with a visual impairment.

Hearing Impaired: Select toys that produce interesting visual effects and particularly loud noises for a child with a hearing impairment.

Motor Impaired: Select toys that require minimal motor responses for a child with a motor impairment. Attaching toys to the child may be one of the few means of helping him or her to interact with the toys. Look for a variety of different toys with different effects that can be attached.

If the child cannot move any limb well enough to cause effects, identify a behavior you can readily discriminate (e.g., sticking out the tongue, turning the head to one side), then you make something happen (e.g., ring a bell, wiggle a stuffed animal) each time the child does the behavior. Observe and record the results carefully to determine if the behavior increases in the presence of the rewarding toy.

(continued)

Criterion: The child repeats an activity several times when it produces an interesting result or increases a behavior (e.g., moving the arm) when that behavior results in a particular effect (e.g., making an attached bell jingle). This change in behavior in response to its effects should be observed several times a day over a period of several days.

AREA: **8.   Problem Solving**
BEHAVIOR: 8b.   Persists in efforts to obtain an object or make an effect

Materials: A variety of interesting toys or household objects

---

Procedures:

Place a toy just beyond the reach of the child and observe his or her reactions. If the child cries or immediately loses interest, bounce the toy or do something else to make it attractive and place it a little closer. Make it possible for the child to get the toy, but with some persistence. Gradually increase the amount of effort necessary or the length of time the effort must take.

Sometimes dangling a toy from a string, so that it moves when the child tries to get it, will help promote persistence. Be sure to arrange the situation so that persistence pays off.

Use in Daily Routines:

Observe what the child does in situations where he or she wants an object that is out of immediate reach. Such events occur frequently in the course of any child's day. Do not immediately give the objects to the child if it looks like he or she is trying to get it independently. To avoid frustration, you may want to push the object slightly closer or help in some other minimal way that will let the child get the desired object without your actually giving it to him or her.

Adaptations:

Visually Impaired: Hold a favorite noisemaking toy slightly out of reach and encourage the child with a visual impairement to find it. Physically prompt reaching out further, leaning to the side, or whatever behavior would lead to obtaining the toy. It is important to have the toy continuously making noise, so that the child will know that it is still there.

Motor Impaired: Carefully assess the motor capabilities of the child with motor impairment and arrange situations that present a challenge and, therefore, require persistence; but, be sure that success is possible.

Criterion: The child consistently persists in an effort to obtain a desired object. This should occur in several different situations.

AREA: **8.   Problem Solving**
BEHAVIOR: 8c.   Pulls string to obtain an object or make an effect

Materials: String, interesting toys, crib gym, pull toys

(*continued*)

Procedures:

Dangle a toy by a string in front of the child and then place it out of reach, but with the string toward the child and within easy grasp. If the child does not pull the string and get the toy, demonstrate how to do it.

Or, place a toy on top of a cloth (e.g., diaper, small blanket) and show how you can get the toy by pulling the cloth toward you.

Repeat either activity and observe to see if the child pulls the string (or cloth) without further demonstration. If not, place the string in his or her hand. Wait. If there is no effort to pull the string (or cloth), physically prompt the child, providing only as much help as necessary and letting the child play with the toy when he or she gets it.

Use in Daily Routines:

Have one or two pull toys available in the areas where the child is throughout the day. Periodically place one toy near the child with the string toward him or her. Observe to see if the child pulls the string to bring the toy closer.

Have a crib gym in the child's crib (or attached to a frame that fits over an infant seat) that has rings or other "handles" to pull and create effects. Observe the child now and then to see if he or she is learning how to pull the string, ring, or other device to create an effect. Such a toy may keep the child entertained while you are doing other activities, but will become boring to the child if he or she is left alone with it too much of the time.

Adaptations:

Visually Impaired: Use toys that make noise with a child who has a visual impairment. Help the child feel the toy and the string as you talk about them. Place the toy slightly out of reach and put the string in the child's hand. Talk about getting the toy. If the child does not pull the string, put your hand over the child's hand and show him or her how to do it. Begin with a short string to assure success and work up to a longer one. As the child becomes more able to get the toy with the string, place the string on the table or floor where the child is and let him or her find it by patting the surface.

Motor Impaired: Adapt the materials for the child with motor impairments to his or her capabilities. It may be easier for the child to pick up the string if it is attached to ring, a spool, or some other object that the child can grasp. It may also be necessary to use a short string (the length determined by the child's ability to move his or her hand and arm).

If a child has severe motor impairments, this item may be impossible, even with adaptations. It is important to evaluate this kind of child to determine if there is any kind of electrical switch that he or she could operate. Such a switch can be connected to battery operated toys and give the child success in creating an effect with very limited movements.

Criterion: Child spontaneously (i.e., without an immediately preceding demonstration) pulls a string or a cloth to get a toy, or pulls or pushes some device to get an effect. Except in the child with severe motor impairments, this behavior should be seen in several different situations (in free play, in training sessions, using different toys).

AREA: **8. Problem Solving**
BEHAVIOR: 8d.   Repeats an activity that elicits an interesting reaction from others

Materials: None

(continued)

Procedures:

When the child is making a face, clapping hands, or making any desired response, immediately answer him or her by laughing, cheering, or imitating the child's response.

If the child does not repeat his or her own action, say something like, "That's wonderful! Let's do it again." If the action lends itself to physical prompts, assist the child in doing it again.

Note: Some children are initially startled by adults' responses and become quite subdued and even resistant to repeating the activity. If this occurs, make responses to the child's behaviors more muted, but make it clear you enjoyed what he or she did.

Use in Daily Routines:

This kind of situation will occur naturally throughout the day. It is not an activity that you can "set up."

Adaptations:

Visually Impaired: It will be important to give the child with a visual impairment tactile as well as auditory feedback about the activities that you enjoy. Touch and hug the child as well as laugh or praise when he or she does that special something for you.

Motor Impaired: Motor impairments will reduce the number of activities that a child can do. Be sure to look carefully for behaviors that you can respond to with real pleasure (e.g., looking at you when you talk, trying to adjust posture as you pick the child up).

Criterion: On several occasions, the child repeats activities that elicit interesting reactions from other people.

AREA: 8. Problem Solving
BEHAVIOR: 8e. Overcomes obstacles to get toys

Materials: Any favorite toys, various containers

Procedures:

Arrange a situation in which the child can see or hear an interesting toy, but must overcome some simple obstacle to get it. For example, place the toy in a transparent plastic container or behind a sheet of Plexiglas so that the child must dump the container, remove a loose-fitting lid, push a barrier aside, or do some other activity to get the toy.

If the child does not spontaneously overcome the obstacle, demonstrate how it can be done and/or physically guide the child through the process. Reduce the help given as rapidly as possible.

Once a child masters one kind of obstacle, try others. Make it a game!

Use in Daily Routines:

Having obstacles between us and what we want is a normal part of everyday life. Observe how the child copes with such situations. If the child does not try to overcome obstacles and either cries for help or just gives up, provide him or her with help in the form of encouragement, demonstration, and/or making the task a little easier. Do not solve the problem for the child, but help him or her to solve it with your guidance.

(continued)

Adaptations:

Visually Impaired: Limited vision is itself a major kind of obstacle! It will be necessary to teach the child with a visual impairment to explore objects with his or her hands as well as whatever residual vision is available to determine its properties so that problems can be solved. Place a toy in a container, shake it so that it can be heard. Talk about its being inside the container. Give the container to the child and help him or her feel the sides, the bottom, and the top. Help the child reach inside and get the toy. Once the child is competent with retrieving objects from various open containers, begin trying containers with loose-fitting lids.

The child with a visual impairment will have to learn to use verbal concepts to solve simple problems. When working on overcoming obstacles, teach the child such concepts as "on the other side of" by demonstrating (e.g., "Now the toy is here next to you. Feel it. Now I put it on the other side of the pillow. Can you get it?"). Guide the child through the actions.

Motor Impaired: Be creative when devising tasks for a child with a motor impairment, so that it will challenge, not overwhelm the child's motor capabilities. Children with very limited motor skills may do something as simple as touch your hand (perhaps moving their hands no more than one-half inch) to cause you to give a toy to him or her. Communication of this sort may be the only way the child can solve problems that are beyond his or her motor capabilities. Remember that it is important to demonstrate solving problems and to discuss solving problems for these children, so that they can learn by observation if not by doing.

Criterion: The child overcomes several different kinds of obstacles to get toys or other desired objects.

AREA: **8.   Problem Solving**
BEHAVIOR: 8f.   Plays with a variety of toys to produce effects

Materials: "Busy Box," other responsive toys (i.e., toys that have an effect when pushed, pulled, poked, squeezed, or rocked)

Procedures:

Observe the child's play with a variety of responsive toys. Does the child manipulate them in such a way as to produce sight or sound effects? Does the child experiment with novel toys or objects to determine what they can do? When the child tries these different activities with the toys, show interest and excitement about his or her accomplishments. Imitate what the child did with the toy or object.

If the child does not try different activities with toys to get varying effects, demonstrate and, if necessary, physically guide the child through manipulating the toys to produce the effects. Work toward as much variety of movement and activity as the child's limitations and temperament will allow.

Use in Daily Routines:

Be sure that responsive toys or objects are available throughout the living area where the child spends his or her time. Observe how the child interacts with these toys.

(continued)

Bath time is often a good time to observe the child's understanding of how water affects objects. For example, provide toys that sink as well as toys that float, show the child that sponges can be squeezed, offer him or her bottles that can be filled and squirted, and find other unique objects to share with the child.

Adaptations:

Visually Impaired: For the child with a visual impairment, look for toys that create tactile as well as auditory effects (e.g., a toy that emits a puff of air when squeezed). The bath activities noted above are also good for providing a variety of experiences with different kinds of materials for a child with a visual impairment.

Motor Impaired: For a child with motor impairments, look for toys and other materials that respond with minimal movement on the part of the child or that respond to the particular kind of movement that the child can make. Colored cellophane that "crinkles" when grabbed or shaken may be one of the few things that will produce a good effect for some children with motor impairments. For a child with a more severe motor impairment, it may be necessary to rely more on electronic or battery-operated toys that require only minimal response. If the child can only engage reliably in one motor behavior (e.g., pushing), try to maintain variety by attaching a push switch to different toys at different times. Avoid creating boredom by leaving the child with one toy for long periods of time or with a switch for long periods, even if the toys are changed frequently.

If other children are around the child with the motor impairments, make sure that he or she has the opportunity to observe what they are able to do with toys. Encourage the other children to show the child with motor impairments what they can do with different materials. Talk to the child about what he or she is seeing.

Criterion: The child plays with several different toys (or different parts of a "busy box") to produce interesting effects. A child with severe motor impairments may pass the item by reliably operating a switch to create effects in 2 or more toys.

AREA: 8.   Problem Solving

BEHAVIOR: 8g.   Increases rate of usual activity with a toy when it stops working or tries another activity to make the toy work (work on items 8h. and 8i. simultaneously)

Materials: Toys with moving parts, toys that "go" when something is pushed or pulled, other interesting toys

---

Procedures:

Observe what happens when a child is playing with a toy that breaks or stops working in the expected way. He or she may try doing the usual activity with the toy more frequently or with more force, or may examine the toy, shake it, try another activity with the toy, and so forth. If the child does none of these actions, but either cries or puts the toy aside, talk about what has happened and try several actions to make the toy work or to fix it. Try to explain to the child that if something doesn't work, you can try to do other things with it.

If no opportunities arise naturally to observe the child dealing with something that does not respond as expected, set up a situation to teach this kind of problem solving. For example, place a long gift wrap tube on a brick to form a small ramp so that the child can put cars in at the top and watch them come out the other end. After the child is accustomed to this "game," set the tube flat on the floor or on a very low support, so that the cars will not roll or will roll slowly. Observe what the child does. If the child does not try to figure out the problem on his or her own, demonstrate how to make the support higher so that the cars will come out the other end again.

Use in Daily Routines:

This kind of problem solving is best encouraged in natural events that occur throughout the day. Encourage and praise persistence in the child when he or she attempts to make something work.

Adaptations:

Visually Impaired: Physically guide a child with a visual impairment through problem solutions as you talk about them.

Criterion: The child increases his or her rate of a usual activity with a toy when the toy stops working, or he or she tries another activity to make a toy work. This should be observed on a number of occasions with different toys or objects.

AREA: **8. Problem Solving**
BEHAVIOR: 8h. Uses adults to solve problems
BEHAVIOR: 8i. Imitates an adult action to solve a problem (work on items 8g., 8h. and 8i. simultaneously)

Materials: Toys that create an interesting sight and/or sound for a period of time and then stop (e.g., windup toys, shape boxes, toy cash register, jack-in-the-box)

Procedures:

Select a toy that requires a new and/or moderately difficult motor response for the child. Show the child how to get the desired effect from the toy. For example, wind up a toy car and let it run down. Observe the child's reaction when the effect stops. If he or she loses interest, try a new toy or try the first one again, acting more excited about what happens.

If the child picks up the toy and tries, but cannot work it, or if he or she cries, hold out your hand and say, "Do you want some help?" Be sure that the child watches how you make the toy work. Observe his or her reaction when the effect stops again.

If the child makes no attempt to imitate what you did to make the toy work, place your hands over his or her hands and demonstrate what to do. When the effect stops, encourage the child to try it on his or her own. If the child is unsuccessful, offer your help again and assist him or her to do it. Try to reduce the amount of help you provide.

Use in Daily Routines:

Children frequently ask for help with some problem throughout the day. Do not simply do a task for the child. Demonstrate how it can be done and encourage the child to try. If he or she is unsuccessful, physically assist, but no more than necessary. Help the child feel that he or she has accomplished the task and that he or she should be proud of that fact.

Adaptations:

Visually Impaired: Choose toys carefully for a child with a visual impairment, looking for ones that make a good noise and for which the necessary action to make them "work"

(continued)

can be easily felt by the child. Physically guide the child through the actions as you talk about it.

Motor Impaired: To the extent possible, choose toys that the child has the motor capabilities to work. For children with more severe motor impairments, you may work on this item by introducing a new switch that requires a slightly different movement than the one the child is currently using with success.

Criterion for item 8h.: On several occasions, the child requests help from an adult to make a toy work (e.g., the request can be in the form of handing the toy to the adult or looking back and forth between the adult and the toy to communicate that the adult should do something).

Criterion for item 8i.: The child imitates adult actions to make several different toys work regardless of whether or not the imitation is successful.

AREA: 8. Problem Solving
BEHAVIOR: 8j.   Solves simple problems without adult assistance

Materials: A variety of toys, various containers, a normal home or group care environment

---

Procedures:

Collect a box of toys or materials that are new to the child and that will create some problems for him or her. Select materials carefully to fit a child's sensory and motor capabilities. Play with the child awhile, showing him or her how some of the items work, but without focusing too much attention on your actions. Then let the child play on his or her own as you observe, responding naturally to his or her attempts to involve you in play. Encourage the child to figure his or her problems out on his or her own, but give as much help as necessary to avoid undue frustration. Watch for the child's efforts to solve simple problems on his or her own (e.g., opening drawers to remove objects, removing various kinds of lids to get objects out of containers, finding an opening on a simple puzzle box).

Use in Daily Routines:

Observe the child's reactions to normal problems in the environment. At this developmental level, getting into drawers, closets, tool chests, and so forth is enjoyable for the child. While making the environment safe, allow the child to do some of this exploration. It will allow you to observe his or her problem-solving skills.

Adaptations:

Visually Impaired: Choose materials for the child with a visual impairment that will challenge his or her tactile and motor capacities but that will also provide enough sound or other effects to maintain his or her interest. Helping the child learn to solve the problems of mobility within the home or group care environment should be a part of this item.

Motor Impaired: Select materials for the child with motor impairments that fit his or her motor capabilities. For the child with a severe motor impairment, one way to assess and teach problem solving skills would be to present a new switch to the child, hooked up to a familiar and favorite toy. Observe the child's spontaneous efforts to try to make the switch work. Demonstrate how the switch can be turned on and off if necessary and then, again, observe.

Expose the child with motor impairments to other children who are solving problems. Talk about what they are doing. Have the children demonstrate for the child.

(continued)

Criterion: The child independently solves several simple problems.

AREA: **8. Problem Solving**

BEHAVIOR: 8k. Uses "tools" to solve problems (same as item 6n.)

Materials: A normal home or group care environment

Procedures and Use in Daily Routines:

In everyday interactions with the child, demonstrate how to solve problems with "tools." For example, if a ball rolls under the bed, use a broom to get it out; when an item is too high to reach, push a chair near the item and climb up to reach it. Always talk to the child about what you are doing, and make sure he or she attends to you.

When the child encounters similar situations, do not immediately solve the problem for the child. Ask what the child thinks he or she could do, call attention to a tool, or otherwise make a suggestion without actually directing the child to do a particular activity. If the suggestion is not effective, demonstrate what could be done so that the child can imitate your solution to the problem. If he or she fails to imitate your solution, physically guide him or her through the activity. Recreate the problem (e.g., put the ball back under the chair) and see if the child can now solve the problem without further assistance.

Adaptations:

Visually Impaired: With a child with a visual impairment, rely more on physical guidance for the demonstration of problem solving. Always talk about what you and the child are doing.

Motor Impaired: When a problem naturally occurs for a child with motor impairments, try to think of a way that he or she might possibly be able to solve the problem, rather than solving it in the typical manner. Demonstrate that solution.

For a child with a more severe motor impairment, problem solution will depend on calling on others to help solve the problem. Encourage the child to communicate and seek help if needed.

Criterion: The child spontaneously uses tools to solve several different problems.

9.

Visual Perception

THE ITEMS INCLUDED in this sequence were placed under sequence 20–I., Object Manipulation: Form manipulation (pp. 245–250), in the first edition of this curriculum (Johnson-Martin, Jens, & Attermeier, 1986). The intent of these items, however, is not the development of fine motor skill, but rather the understanding of form and space. Therefore, a new, separate sequence has been developed for these items, which also correlates with sequence 5–II., Visual Perception: Puzzles and matching (pp. 137–143), in *The Carolina Curriculum for Preschoolers with Special Needs* (Johnson-Martin, Attermeier, & Hacker, 1990).

Due to the heavy emphasis on visual information in this sequence, these activities are less appropriate for the young child with a severe visual impairment. While activities can be modified with tactile cues provided, it is likely that the child with a visual impairment would achieve these at an older age.

Both children with significant motor and visual impairments may have greater difficulty understanding spatial concepts due to their limited opportunities for experiencing space (e.g., climbing under, over, and around objects). Be sure to include ways to help these children physically experience space in order to lay the foundation for developing better spatial perception.

REFERENCES

Johnson-Martin, N.M., Attermeier, S.M., & Hacker, B. (1990). *The Carolina curriculum for preschoolers with special needs*. Baltimore: Paul H. Brookes Publishing Co.

Johnson-Martin, N., Jens, K.G., & Attermeier, S.M. (1986). *The Carolina curriculum for handicapped infants and infants at risk*. Baltimore: Paul H. Brookes Publishing Co.

9. Visual Perception

a. Places large round form in a form board
b. Places square form in a form board
c. Imitates building a "chair" with blocks
d. Places round and square forms in a form board when they are simultaneously presented
e. Places triangular form in a form with a triangular hole
f. Places round, square, and triangular forms in a form board when they are simultaneously presented
g. Completes simple puzzles
h. Places correct forms in a form ball
i. Imitates a block train

AREA: **9.   Visual Perception**
BEHAVIOR: 9a.   Places large round form in a form board

Materials: A round form, a form board with one round cutout

Procedures:

Present the form board and the round form to the child. Ask the child to put the shape in the hole. If the child does it correctly, praise him or her. If the child has difficulty, demonstrate placing the form and then ask him or her to try it. If necessary, physically help the child put the form in the hole. Encourage the child to use his or her fingers to feel the round shape of the objects and the cutout in the form board. Gradually fade your assistance.

Note: If available form boards have several shapes in them, leave the other shapes in while working with the round one. The other shapes may even be initially taped in place.

Use in Daily Routines:

Make a simple shape "box" by cutting a round hole in the plastic lid of a container. Have the child drop round beads through the hole.

Adaptations:

Visually Impaired: Help the child with a visual impairment to feel the form and the form board. Covering the bottom of the hole with a textured material may be helpful.

Motor Impaired: Forms with a large knob handle may be easier for the child to place. Some children with severe motor impairments will not be able to place forms in boards. Teach form discrimination through sorting and matching tasks. For example, have the child push all the circles into one pile and the squares into another. Or, have the child indicate through eyegaze where a form should be placed. See the appendix on pages 367–368 for a description of an object board that can be used for sorting tasks.

Criterion: The child puts a round form in a form board on several different occasions.

AREA: **9.   Visual Perception**
BEHAVIOR: 9b.   Places square form in a form board

Materials: A square form, a form board with a square hole

Procedures:

Present the form board and the square form to the child. Ask him or her to put the shape in the hole. If the child does it correctly, praise him or her. If he or she has difficulty with the task, demonstrate how to do it by placing the form in the board and then ask the child to try it. If necessary, physically help the child put the form in the hole. Encourage the child to use his or her fingers to feel the round shape of the objects and the cutout in the form board. Gradually fade your assistance.

Use in Daily Routines:

Make a simple shape "box" by cutting a square hole in the plastic lid of a container. Have the child drop square blocks through the hole.

(continued)

Adaptations:

> See the Adaptations section of item 9a.

Criterion: The child puts a square form in a form board on several different occasions.

AREA: 9. Visual Perception
BEHAVIOR: 9c.   Imitates building a "chair" with blocks

Materials: Six blocks of identical size (e.g., approximately 1"), a doll

---

Procedures:

> Place the blocks in front of the child. Tell the child you are going to make a chair with the blocks. Take 2 blocks and stack them and place the third block in front of the stack. Show the child how to sit a small doll on the chair. Ask the child to build a chair. Demonstrate the process several times and physically assist the child, if necessary.

Use in Daily Routines:

> Have blocks readily available to the child. Vary building a 'chair' with other simple block patterns (e.g., towers, rows of blocks) to keep the child's interest in playing with the blocks. The function of this item is to promote motor skill, imitation, and visual/motor coordination.

Adaptations:

> *Visually Impaired:*   Help the child with a visual impairment to feel the block "chair." A model that has been glued together may be helpful. Use of blocks with Velcro attached may facilitate learning to build a pattern without the added frustration of blocks falling over when there is poor aim.
>
> *Motor Impaired:*   Blocks with Velcro may be helpful for the child with poorly controlled hand and/or arm movements. Also, try various sizes and weights of blocks to see what works best for the child.

Criterion: The child builds a "chair" with three blocks on several different occasions.

AREA: 9. Visual Perception
BEHAVIOR: 9d.   Places round and square forms in a form board when they are simultaneously presented

Materials: Round and square forms, a form board with both round and square holes

---

Procedures:

> Present a form board to the child with both the round and the square forms in place. Remove the shapes (or ask child to). Encourage the child to feel the shapes of the forms and holes. Ask the child to put the forms in the holes.
>
> If the child has difficulty with the task, demonstrate how to do it and then place the blocks near the correct holes and ask the child to try the task again. If necessary, physically guide the child's hand in placing the objects in the correct holes.

(continued)

Use in Daily Routines:

Keep a simple shape box available on a low shelf so that the child can play with it frequently.

Adaptations:

Visually Impaired: See Visually Impaired Adaptation section of item 9a.

Motor Impaired: Provide physical assistance as needed. If the child with motor impairments is unable to place the forms in the board, encourage him or her to indicate, by pointing or looking, where each shape should go. Also, encourage sorting shapes into separate piles.

Criterion: The child places both a round and a square form in form board on several different occasions.

AREA: **9.   Visual Perception**
BEHAVIOR: 9e.   Places triangular form in a board with a triangular hole

Materials: A triangular form, a form board with a triangular hole

---

Procedures:

Present a form board with the triangular form in place to the child. Remove the shapes (or ask the child to do so). Encourage the child to feel the shape of the form and the hole. Ask the child to put the form in the hole.

If the child has difficulty with the task, demonstrate how to do it and then place the blocks near the correct holes and ask the child to try the task again. If necessary, physically guide the child's hand in placing the objects in the correct holes.

Use in Daily Routines:

Keep a simple shape box in a place readily available to the child.

Adaptations:

See Adaptations section of item 9a.

Criterion: The child places a triangular form in a form board on several different occasions.

AREA: **9.   Visual Perception**
BEHAVIOR: 9f.   Places round, square, and triangular forms in a form board when they are simultaneously presented

Materials: A form board that has round, square, and triangular cutouts, along with shapes that fit into these spaces

---

Procedures:

Present a form board to the child with round, square, and triangular forms in place. Remove the shapes one at a time and place them on a table directly below the matching opening in the form board. Ask the child to put the shapes back into the form board.

(continued)

If the child has difficulty with the task, demonstrate how to do it and then place the blocks near the correct holes and ask the child to try the task again. If necessary, physically guide the child's hand in placing the objects in the correct holes. Gradually reduce your help, praising the child's effort in placing the forms without help.

After the child has been successful with placing the forms, mix the arrangement of the forms in front of the child and ask him or her to put them in again.

Use in Daily Routines:

Provide a simple shape "box" with which the child may play.

Adaptations:

See Adaptations section of item 9d.

Criterion: The child places round, square, and triangular forms correctly in a form board on several different occasions.

AREA: **9. Visual Perception**
BEHAVIOR: 9g. Completes simple puzzles

Materials: Large, simple puzzles with 4–5 independent pieces

Procedures:

Place a completed puzzle in front of the child. Draw his or her attention to the pictures in the puzzle. While the child watches, disassemble the puzzle and separate the pieces. Ask the child to put the puzzle back together.

If the child has difficulty with the task, place all the pieces in except 1. Help the child put the last piece in. When the child is able to place the 1 piece correctly, leave 2 pieces out, and so on. Provide physical prompting as needed. Remind the child to turn or rotate puzzle pieces, if needed, in order to make them fit.

When the child learns to complete that puzzle, change to another puzzle. When the child has had success with a number of puzzles with 4–5 pieces, gradually increase the complexity of puzzles that are offered.

Note: Puzzles come in a large variety of sizes, ranging from simple to difficult. Start with recognizable picture puzzles of familiar objects and with pieces that are easy to manipulate.

Use in Daily Routines:

Keep puzzles available to the child throughout the day.

Adaptations:

Visually Impaired: Use textured materials of familiar shapes for a child with a visual impairment. Also, look for puzzles that have plastic pieces with distinguishing physical characteristics.

Motor Impaired: See Motor Impaired Adaptation section of item 9d.

Criterion: The child completes two different simple puzzles.

AREA: **9. Visual Perception**
BEHAVIOR: 9h.   Places correct forms in a form ball

Materials: Form ball with at least six different shapes

Procedures:

Present the child with a form ball and matching shapes. Ask the child to put the objects in the correct holes. If the child has difficulty with the task, demonstrate how to place the shapes in and then ask the child to try the task again.

Physically assist the child, if necessary, at first, by holding the form ball so that most holes are covered by your hands, leaving only 1 or 2 holes open for the child to attempt to place a form through. Gradually allow the child to have more forms and choices (e.g., holes) available to place a form through.

Note: It is important for the child to correct his or her own errors when possible. At this stage, many children do the task by trial and error rather than by good form discrimination. Give assistance primarily when the child is frustrated.

Use in Daily Routines:

Store form ball where child can get it to play on his or her own.

Adaptations:

See Adaptations section of item 9d.

Criterion: The child places 5–6 different forms in a form ball on several different occasions.

AREA: **9. Visual Perception**
BEHAVIOR: 9i.   Imitates a block train

Materials: Ten 1-inch blocks

Procedures:

Place 10 blocks on the table in front of the child. Tell the child that you are going to make a train with the blocks. Align 4 of the blocks in a straight line. Place a fifth block on top of the first block. Push your "train" along the table while making a train sound. Then ask the child to use the rest of the blocks to make a train like yours. Leave your train in sight, but out of reach. Demonstrate this activity several times and give the child physical assistance, if necessary.

Use in Daily Routines:

At playtime, help the child use large wooden or cardboard blocks to make trains, as well as other vehicles. Reinforce language and spatial concepts by making and talking about trains of different sizes and lengths.

Adaptations:

See Adaptations section of item 9c.

Criterion: The child imitates a block train on several different occasions.

10.

Prevocabulary/ Vocabulary

THE COMMUNICATION SKILLS of a very young child are difficult to neatly divide into categories more commonly used for older children. Yet, it is important to identify the skills that serve as foundations for later communication skills. In the first edition of this curriculum (Johnson-Martin, Jens, & Attermeier, 1986), the skills that the authors believed to be the building blocks of later vocabulary and expressive language were included in one sequence 13., Vocal Communication (pp. 175–188). In this edition, the communication domain has been expanded and changed conceptually. Items from the Vocal Communication sequence are now included in two sequences, this sequence, and sequence 13., Conversation Skills (pp. 207–225), thereby separating expressive vocabulary from the more pragmatic aspects of communication.

The "expressive vocabulary" of the child who is functioning under a 9 month development level is primarily made up of vocalizations and gestures that express feelings or needs. Some of these items are placed in this sequence, as "prevocabulary," and others can be found in sequence 13., Conversation Skills (pp. 207–225). The division is, perhaps, arbitrary, but was useful in limiting the number of items in sequence 13., which is already the longest. Above the 9-month developmental level, the items in this sequence are more clearly expressive vocabulary, both in the form of words and manual signs.

REFERENCE

Johnson-Martin, N., Jens, K.G., & Attermeier, S.M. (1986). *The Carolina curriculum for handicapped infants and infants at risk*. Baltimore: Paul H. Brookes Publishing Co.

10.   Prevocabulary/Vocabulary

a. Provides constant signals for states of hunger, distress, and pleasure

b. Vocalizes 5 or more consonant and vowel sounds

c. Laughs

d. Vocalizes 3 or more feelings

e. Vocalizes repetitive consonant-vowel combinations

f. Uses 2 or more gestures associated with verbal concepts (e.g., "all gone," "so big," "more," "bye-bye")

g. Uses 2 or more words or signs to label objects or to name people

h. Uses 3 or more words or signs to label objects or to name people

i. Uses one or more exclamations or signs that stand for an exclamation

j. Uses 7 or more words or signs

k. Meaningfully says or signs "no"

l. Appropriately uses 15 words or signs

m. Names or makes appropriate signs for 3 or more pictures of familiar objects

AREA: **10.   Prevocabulary/Vocabulary**
BEHAVIOR: 10a.   Provides consistent signals for states of hunger, distress, and pleasure

Materials: A normal home or group care environment

Procedures and Use in Daily Routines:

Pay close attention to the way in which the child indicates his or her internal states. Initially, note the primary discrimination that can be made is between the child's indication of pleasure/satisfaction and hunger/distress. When the child cries to indicate distress, some cries are more intense than others, usually communicating the intensity of the child's needs. Gradually, it should be possible to determine if the child's cry communicates hunger (or other discomfort), anger, or boredom. Likewise, the early quiet and peaceful state that occurs after feedings or other comforting events will differentiate into a variety of indicators of pleasure (e.g., cooing sounds, smiles). The child's ability to produce consistent signals for different states depends, in large part, on caregivers' attending to different behaviors, guessing from context what they mean, and responding on the basis of that guess. If the child's behavior suggests the guess was "wrong," the caregiver tries something else. In this process, the child learns what signals the adult reads and the adult learns to read signals more accurately. For example, if a child is "just fussing a little," the caregiver may try moving him or her to a new area of the room, talking to him or her, or otherwise trying to provide a change in stimulation. If the fussiness increases in intensity, the caregiver may intervene more (e.g., change a diaper, pick up and rock the child, offer milk). In this exchange, the child learns the kind of cry that produces particular results and the adult learns to discriminate various cries from one another.

Note: It is very important to respond to a child's cries rather than ignoring them, out of concern about "spoiling" the child. Cries are especially important sources of communication when other forms of communication have not developed. Responding to cries teaches the child that he or she has some control over the environment and that communication is important. The child will substitute other forms of communication for crying as they develop. It is more likely that a child will become a chronic crier if caregivers respond inconsistently to crying than if they respond consistently. However, a child may also become a chronic crier if caregivers respond to crying, but are not sensitive to other communicative cues or signals from the child (e.g., changes in activity level, different vocalizations).

Adaptations:

None are necessary.

Criterion: Child provides consistent signals for states of hunger, distress, and pleasure that can be discriminated by the primary caregiver(s). That is, the caregiver should be able to label the state and appropriately respond. This should occur daily, although there may be periods in which a child will again become "difficult to read," usually during periods of illness or when new behaviors are emerging.

AREA: **10.   Prevocabulary/Vocabulary**
BEHAVIOR: 10b.   Vocalizes 5 or more consonant and vowel sounds

Materials: A normal home or group care environment

(*continued*)

Procedures and Use in Daily Routines:

>   Throughout the day, take time to look directly at the child, try to establish mutual gaze, and then talk to the child. This should occur as part of all routine care activities.

>   Listen to the child. As he or she begins to vocalize, imitate those vocalizations or talk back as if having a conversation.

>   Attach a nonbreakable mirror on the child's crib or on the wall by the crib or mat where the child spends time, so that the child can see his or her face as different sounds are made.

>   Make sure that the child knows you think vocal sound production is fun!

Adaptations:

>   *Visually Impaired:* For a child with a visual impairment, place his or her hand on your mouth as you make different sounds, so that the child can "feel" these sounds as well as hear them. Occasionally, help the child touch his or her own mouth when he or she is making different sounds.

>   *Hearing Impaired:* Help the child with a hearing impairment to "feel" sounds by letting him or her touch your mouth or larynx; also by having the child touch his or her own mouth or larynx. It may also help to amplify the child's vocalizations with a microphone and speakers, so that he or she can hear the sounds. Seek the advice of a speech pathologist or other specialist in language training for a child with a hearing impairment.

Criterion: The child vocalizes 5 or more consonants and vowel sounds.

AREA: 10. Prevocabulary/Vocabulary
BEHAVIOR: 10c. Laughs

Materials: A normal home or group care environment

Procedures and Use in Daily Routines:

>   Situations during which the child experiences touching or noises are generally most effective in eliciting laughter at early ages (e.g., tickling the child's face or stomach; making popping sounds).

>   Take time during daily care activities and at times set aside for playing to interact with the child making various noises, tickling him or her gently, and/or saying nursery rhymes or songs that include tactile stimulation (e.g., Pat-a-cake, "This little piggy . . . "). Always laugh, repeat the activity, or otherwise respond with enthusiasm when the child smiles or laughs.

Adaptations:

>   *Motor Impaired:* Some motor impairments, particularly tight or loose muscle tone, interfere with a child's ability to smile and laugh. It frequently takes longer for the child to "build up to" or "organize" a smile or laugh. If you are getting few of these responses, try waiting for a longer time between episodes of play. For example, after wiggling the little toe and saying, "And this little piggy cried, 'wee,' 'wee,' 'wee,' all the way home," wait (10–20 seconds) before going on to repeat the rhyme or to do some other activity. If you get a delayed smile or laugh, try to regularly build extra time into "games" to allow these smiles and laughs to occur.

Criterion: The child frequently laughs.

AREA: **10.   Prevocabulary/Vocabulary**
BEHAVIOR: 10d.   Vocalizes 3 or more feelings

Materials: A normal home or group care environment

___

Procedures and Use in Daily Routines:

Listen carefully to the child's vocalizations. Try to determine if they are different when he or she is showing enjoyment, interest, boredom, protest, and so forth.

Provide feedback for such vocalization. If the child's vocalization sounds like a protest, say, "Oh, you don't like this; well, let's change it"; if the vocalization sounds like pleasure, say, "That's fun. Let's do it again!"

It is important that the child learn, through your actions, that his or her vocalizations are being discriminated and are, therefore, affecting his or her environment.

Adaptations:

Hearing Impaired: For a child with a hearing impairment, use signs/gestures as well as words to communicate your interpretation of his or her sounds.

___

Criterion: The caregiver can discriminate 3 or more feelings from the child's vocalizations. At this stage, the feelings and the signals should be more complex than those for item 10a. That is, it should be possible to identify 2 or more kinds of pleasure and/or to distinguish discomfort from anger.

AREA: **10.   Prevocabulary/Vocabulary**
BEHAVIOR: 10e.   Vocalizes repetitive consonant-vowel combinations

Materials: A normal home or group care environment

___

Procedures and Use in Daily Routines:

Carefully listen to the child's vocalizations. Note any consonant-vowel combinations that he or she makes (e.g., "ba," "da," "ma," "pa"). Talk back to the child by stringing together repetitions of one of the child's frequent sounds (e.g., "ba, ba, ba, ba," using an interesting inflection pattern). Listen to see if the child repeats a syllable, either the one you modeled or another one.

Mealtime is an especially good time to stimulate sound production. As you feed the child, make sounds (e.g., "Mmmmm, Mmmmm, good"). If the child does not vocalize, you may occasionally apply gently rhythmic pressure at the child's lips with the spoon or your finger as you say, "ma, ma, ma," making it more likely that a sound will be made as pressure is released.

Always try to make vocalizing fun for the child. Make it into a turn-taking game and be excited when the child takes his or her turn!

Adaptations:

Hearing Impaired: Work in front of a mirror so that the child with a hearing impairment can see both you and him- or herself as you vocalize. Place the child's hand alternately on your throat and on his or her own throat as sounds are made.

___

Criterion: The child frequently vocalizes at least 2 repetitive consonant-vowel combinations.

AREA: 10. Prevocabulary/Vocabulary

BEHAVIOR: 10f. Uses 2 or more gestures associated with verbal concepts (e.g., "all gone," "so big," "more," "bye-bye")

Materials: A normal home or group care environment

Procedures and Use in Daily Routines:

Use gestures when you talk to the child. For example, when you get to the end of the applesauce at mealtime, show the child the empty container and say, "All gone," as you also gesture "all gone." Similarly, gesture "more," as you ask the child, "Do you want more?"

Wave as you say, "Bye-bye," when it is time to go somewhere or when someone is leaving. Physically prompt the child to wave if he or she does not imitate. Then, begin saying "Bye-bye" slightly before you wave to see if the child will wave on the verbal cue alone.

Play games that have gestures that are associated with word concepts, such as, "How big is Johnny? So big!" (as you raise the hands up as high as you can reach). See if the baby will imitate and, later, if he or she will answer the question, "How big is Johnny?" by holding up his or her hands.

Adaptations:

Visually Impaired: The child with significant visual impairments will probably learn words before gestures. This item is inappropriate.

Hearing Impaired: Be sure to learn and use standard signs with the child with a hearing impairment if the speech pathologist feels it is appropriate.

Motor Impaired: For a child with motor impairments, use gestures that are within his or her motor capabilities. The child should get credit on this item for gestures that are less precise than those required of the child without motor impairment. The issue is that the motor movement that the child makes is consistently used in association with the words or as a means of communicating. For children with severe motor impairments, this item may be inappropriate.

Criterion: The child uses several gestures/signs associated with verbal concepts. Each should be used either spontaneously by the child in an appropriate situation or during a child's "turn" in a turn-taking game (i.e., it may be difficult to judge what is spontaneous and what is imitation).

AREA: 10. Prevocabulary/Vocabulary

BEHAVIOR: 10g. Uses 2 or more words or signs to label objects or to name people
BEHAVIOR: 10h. Uses 3 or more words or signs to label objects or to name people

Materials: A normal home or group care environment

Procedures and Use in Daily Routines:

Listen to see if the child makes any attempt to approximate words (e.g., "Daddy," "bottle," "doggie," "Mama"). When the child reaches to indicate that he or she wants something, name it and wait momentarily to see if the child will make some effort to imitate the word.

(continued)

If the child is very slow to attempt to say words, try holding the desired object out of reach until some vocalization is heard; gradually require a closer approximation to the name before giving the object to the child. *Do not* unduly frustrate the child, however. It is more important the he or she learn that communication of any form (e.g., pointing) is valuable, than that the child produce a particular word. If you have been making little progress with speech production, you may want to try a total communication approach (e.g., signs/gestures + speech), so that the child may learn signs to use until speech becomes easier for him or her.

Always show your pleasure when the child says a new word!

Adaptations:

Visually Impaired: Children with visual impairments often imitate speech well, but have difficulty establishing the meaning of words. Make a special effort to help the child explore objects by feeling and handling them and to experience people by touching their hair and faces as well as by hearing their voices to help them establish and understand the object or person.

Hearing Impaired: Use both signs and speech when talking to a child with a hearing impairment. Accept approximate signs as you would accept approximations of sounds, but model the correct sign and sometimes physically assist the child to form it if he or she is making little progress through imitation.

Motor Impaired: A child's motor impairments may interfere with his or her articulation. Listen carefully and accept poorer approximations than you might for other children. Consult a speech pathologist for help in developing an augmentative communication system if the child's word production is lagging far behind his or her understanding of language.

Criterion for item 10g.:   The child spontaneously (not in imitation) says or signs 2 words to label objects or to name people.

Criterion for item 10h.:   The child spontaneously says or signs 3 or more words to label objects or to name people (or, consistently makes choices between objects that stand for other objects or events; or makes choices between pictures that stand for objects or events).

AREA: **10.   Prevocabulary/Vocabulary**

BEHAVIOR: 10i.   Uses one or more exclamations or signs that stand for an exclamation

Materials: A normal home or group care environment

Procedures and Use in Daily Routines:

Use exclamations in a natural way throughout the day. Frequently, the exclamation that a child learns first is "Uh-oh," which is said whenever something is dropped or spilled. Try to be consistent in the expressions you use for particular events and listen for the child's attempts to imitate and appropriately use them.

Occasionally play with the child using puppets, dolls, or stuffed animals. Say "Ouch" when you make the puppet fall down, and "uh-oh" or other exclamations when appropriate to the events you create. After you have done this several times, pause to see if the child will insert the exclamation.

(continued)

Adaptations:

> *Visually Impaired:*   It may be harder for a child with a visual impairment to associate the exclamation with the event that prompted it. Be sure to help the child make these associations by showing him or her what has happened. For example, when a cup is tipped over and spills say, "Uh-oh," and guide the child's hand to feel both the cup and the milk.

> *Hearing Impaired:*   Use both a sign and words for a child with a hearing impairment in situations that normally call for an exclamation.

Criterion: The child uses at least 1 appropriate exclamation on several different occasions.

AREA: **10.   Prevocabulary/Vocabulary**
BEHAVIOR: 10j.   Uses 7 or more words or signs

Materials: A normal home or group care environment

Procedures and Use in Daily Routines:

> Talk to the child throughout the day naming objects, describing what you are doing, and so forth. Be particularly attentive to objects at which the child is looking or with which he or she is playing. Their labels will be easier to learn since they already have the child's interest and attention.

> *Note:*   Do not be concerned about articulation when the child is trying to learn many new words. A vocalization can be counted as a word for the child if it is used consistently for the same object or event, even if it is quite different from the standard form of the word. Continue modeling the correct pronunciation, but do not require the child to repeat the word. Respond to the communication, not to the pronunciation!

Adaptations:

> *Visually Impaired:*   Help a child with a visual impairment experience the objects and events in his or her environment through handling the items and by hearing the activities. By assisting the child in this manner, he or she will be better able to develop a meaningful vocabulary and understand what others are trying to communicate.

> *Hearing Impaired:*   Use signs as well as words with a child with a hearing impairment.

> *Motor Impaired:*   If a child's motor impairment interferes with his or her speech development, work toward establishing and implementing an augmentative communication system. A speech pathologist can help you design object or picture boards that will allow the child to communicate without speaking intelligibly.

Criterion: The child uses 7 or more words or signs (or, can choose 7 objects, events, or people using a communication board).

AREA: **10.   Prevocabulary/Vocabulary**
BEHAVIOR: 10k.   Meaningfully says or signs "no"

Materials: A normal home or group care environment

(continued)

Procedures and Use in Daily Routines:

Consistently say "no" when the child engages in inappropriate activities. Use a logical restraining action, if necessary (e.g., remove the child from the area).

Be sure that the child also hears "no" in other contexts (e.g., to indicate refusal or denial). For example, the child may be giving you some of his or her crackers. After a few, say, "No more, I'm too full"; or, if the child indicates that he or she wants something that cannot be provided, say, "No, you can't have that."

When the child begins to say "no," it is important to communicate respect for his or her feelings. If it is reasonable, stop doing whatever prompted the "no," allow the child to refuse a particular food, and so forth. In situations where it is not reasonable to let the child have his or her own way, say something to indicate that you understand the child's wishes, but have to make a different decision (e.g., "I know you don't want to take a bath, but look at all that dirt. We have to get you clean."). Offer some incentive to the child for complying with your wishes (e.g., "Would you like to take this cup and bowl to play with in the water?").

Notes: Many children will say "no" or "no-no" when they are about to do something they know is forbidden. This is an appropriate use of the word. Reinforce it by saying, "You're right, that is a no-no. Let's do this" (providing an alternative activity).

When children first learn to say "no," they frequently say it to any question, regardless of what they really mean. Respond to such "no's" as if they were intended. That is, if the child says "no" to an offer of juice, start to put the juice away. If the child protests, say, "You said no, you must mean yes. Say, 'yes'?" Whether or not the child says "yes," give him or her the juice. Gradually, the child will learn not to say "no" automatically to questions.

Adaptations:

Hearing Impaired: Sign "no" each time you say it when conversing with a child with a hearing impairment.

Motor Impaired: If children have significant motor impairments, they are often slow to learn the meaning of "no," because they are rarely told "no" to stop an ongoing activity. Try to help the child understand and use "no" by emphasizing the word in other situations (e.g., if the child turns away from his or her carrots, say, "Don't you want your carrots? *No* carrots?" [and take them away]). Shake your head as you emphasize the word "no." The child may learn to shake his or her head to indicate "no" before being able to say the word.

Criterion: The child meaningfully says or signs (or shakes head) "no" on several occasions.

AREA: **10. Prevocabulary/Vocabulary**
BEHAVIOR: 101. Appropriately uses 15 words or signs

Materials: A normal home or group care environment

Procedures and Use in Daily Routines:

See the Procedures and Use in Daily Routines sections in item 10j.

Adaptations:

See the Adaptations section in item 10j.

(continued)

Criterion: The child appropriately uses 15 words or signs (or makes 15 different choices using an augmentative communication system).

AREA: **10.   Prevocabulary/Vocabulary**

BEHAVIOR: 10m.   Names or makes appropriate signs for 3 or more pictures of familiar objects

Materials: A normal home or group care environment

Procedures:

>At least once each day, spend time "reading" to the child. Find books or magazines with large, colorful picture. As you go through the books or magazines, point to pictures and name what you see. Encourage the child to point, by asking, "Where is the _____?". If the child points, name whatever he or she points at. Then begin to ask the child, "What's that?" as you point to a picture. Try to be sure that you are asking the child to name a picture of something that is familiar to the child and can be found in the daily environment.

Use in Daily Routines:

>Keep sturdy books around for the child to play with when you are not directly involved with him or her. If the child brings it to you to show you a picture, name it or ask him or her what it is. Let the child know that books and pictures are important.

Adaptations:

>*Visually Impaired:*   Create a book for a child with a visual impairment that is full of textured surfaces with which the child is familiar. For example, put in a piece of bark from a tree, some pine needles, a piece of terry cloth, a piece of rug. Go through the book with the child and name these items (e.g., "tree," "pine needles," "towel," "rug"). Let the child feel them. Open a page where two or three items are present and ask the child to find one of them. Work up to asking the child to name items as he or she touches them.

>*Hearing Impaired:*   Sign, as well as say, the names for objects in books for a child with a hearing impairment.

>*Motor Impaired:*   Read to the child with motor impairments. If he or she cannot name or point to pictures, use eye gaze as an indicator response so that the child can show you pictures as you name them. Continue to work on receptive vocabulary if the child is unable to talk or sign.

Criterion: On several occasions, the child names or makes appropriate signs for 3 or more pictures of familiar objects.

11.

Imitation: Sound and Gestures

T HE FIRST EDITION of this curriculum (Johnson-Martin, Jens, & Attermeier, 1986) included two sequences that were related to imitation: sequence 10., Gestural Imitation (pp. 151–156), and sequence 12., Vocal Imitation (pp. 167–173). In this edition, the authors combined the two sequences to make this sequence. This seemed appropriate because adults converse with young children using both gestures and speech, thereby modeling both behaviors at the same time and children vary as to whether they first imitate sounds or gestures. Both should be appreciated by caregivers. Perhaps the most important factor for later communication is that imitation develops and becomes more precise.

REFERENCE

Johnson-Martin, N., Jens, K.G., & Attermeier, S.M. (1986). *The Carolina curriculum for handicapped infants and infants at risk*. Baltimore: Paul H. Brookes Publishing Co.

11.   Imitation: Sounds and Gestures

a.   Quiets to voice

b.   Looks at person who is talking and gesturing

c.   Repeats sounds just made when imitated by a caregiver

d.   Continues a movement if it is imitated by a caregiver

e.   Shifts sounds—imitates sounds in repertoire when made by a caregiver

f.   Imitates an activity in repertoire after observing the caregiver doing that activity

g.   Imitates inflection (i.e., pitch)

h.   Attempts to match new sounds

i.   Imitates familiar movements

j.   Imitates familiar 2-syllable words (e.g., baba, dada, mama)

k.   Experiments with making own mouth move like that of the adult

l.   Imitates familiar 2-syllable words with syllable changes (e.g., baby, uh-oh, all gone) *or* Imitates 2 signs that stand for words (e.g., Daddy, all gone, more, eat, drink)

m.   Imitates most new one-syllable words *or* Imitates most simple signs that stand for words

n. Imitates familiar words overheard in conversation *or* Imitates signs observed in others' conversation

o. Imitates environmental sounds during play

p. Imitates 2-word sentences *or* Imitates sequence of 2 signs

q. Imitates 3-syllable words

AREA: **11.   Imitation: Sound and Gestures**
BEHAVIOR: 11a.   Quiets to voice

Materials: A normal home or group care environment

Procedures and Use in Daily Routines:

When the child is lying down, but alert, or when the child is just beginning to fuss, move over to him or her and talk in an animated, but comforting, fashion. Observe to see if the child's motor activity quiets, if he or she stops fussing, or if there is some other behavioral change to suggest that the child is listening and interested.

Begin to talk to the child before you are in view of him or her. Observe to see if the behavior changes to just the voice or to both the sight and sound of the caregiver.

Note: Be sure to give the child time to respond. Some children seem to either process information very slowly or to have difficulty organizing a response to incoming information.

Adaptations:

Visually Impaired: Touch the child with a visual impairment as you talk to him or her to provide more associations to the voice.

Hearing Impaired: Depending on the extent of the child's hearing problem, this item may be inappropriate. If so, move on to the next item.

Criterion: The child quiets to a voice on several different occasions. That is, the child's motor activity decreases or fussing diminishes upon hearing a voice. This should occur prior to seeing the person who is talking.

AREA: **11.   Imitation: Sound and Gestures**
BEHAVIOR: 11b.   Looks at person who is talking and gesturing

Materials: A normal home or group care environment

Procedures and Use in Daily Routines:

Talk to the child in an animated fashion, using hand gestures that are appropriate to what you are saying. If the child looks at you, continue to speak and touch him or her, smile, and/or pick him or her up. Try to maintain eye contact for as long as you can.

Adaptations:

Visually Impaired: If the child with the visual impairment appears to be unable to see you, physically guide his or her face to a position directly opposite you. Work on sequence 3., Auditory Localization and Object Permanence, using your voice as the stimulus some of the time. Guide the child's hand to your face as you speak to one side or the other. Also, physically guide his or her head in that direction. This gives the child the experience of orienting to the direction of the speaker.

Hearing Impaired: Keep gestures simple and visible to the child with a hearing impairment.

Criterion: On several different occasions, the child looks at the person who is talking and gesturing. The child should orient to the person as he or she begins to talk and continue looking at the talker for at least 1 minute, although there may be momentary looking away and then back again.

AREA: **11.   Imitation: Sound and Gestures**
BEHAVIOR: 11c.   Repeats sounds just made when imitated by a caregiver

Materials: A normal home or group care environment

Procedures and Use in Daily Routines:

Attend to sounds that the child spontaneously makes. Imitate the sound a child makes and pause to see if he or she makes the sound again. If the child makes another sound, imitate that one, then, again, wait.

Note: There is a period in the development of many children when they will become very quiet if a person talks when they are talking. If the child does stop vocalizing when you attempt to start this turn-taking game, just wait until the next vocalization and try again. Eventually, the child will learn the turn-taking pattern.

Adaptations:

Hearing Impaired: Be sure that the child with a hearing impairment is looking at you and exaggerate your mouth movements as you imitate the sound that he or she is making. The child may be cued to continue vocalizing by seeing you as well as by whatever he or she is able to hear. If the child seems unaware of your vocalizing, go on to item 11d., which lays the foundation for imitation of gestures, rather than sounds.

Criterion: The child frequently repeats sounds just made when imitated by the caregiver.

AREA: **11.   Imitation: Sound and Gestures**
BEHAVIOR: 11d.   Continues a movement if it is imitated by a caregiver

Materials: A normal home or group care environment

Procedures and Use in Daily Routines:

When you are sitting with the child (e.g., mealtimes), observe his or her actions. Identify a motor behavior the child does fairly frequently (e.g., slapping the table). Imitate that behavior just after the child does it and then wait to see if he or she will do it again. If the child does something else, imitate that behavior. When the child does repeat a behavior after you have imitated it, you should imitate it again. Try to make it into a turn-taking game.

Adaptations:

Visually Impaired: Select behaviors that produce noise for the child with a visual impairment, so that he or she will know you are imitating.

Motor Impaired: Observe the child with motor impairments carefully and consult with the physical or occupational therapist to determine which movements are under the child's volitional control. Imitate as above. Be sure to allow a little extra time for the child to imitate, as motor impairments often slow down response times.

Criterion: On several occasions, the child continues a movement if it is imitated by a caregiver. Unless the child has a severe motor impairment, at least 2 different behaviors should be continued for several "turns."

AREA: 11. Imitation: Sound and Gestures
BEHAVIOR: 11e. Shifts sounds—imitates sounds in repertoire when made by a caregiver

Materials: A normal home or group care environment

Procedures and Use in Daily Routines:

When you are engaged in a turn-taking game with the child in which you are imitating his or her sounds and the child is making those sounds again, change the rules of the game. Instead of imitating the child, answer the child's vocalization with a different sound, one that you have heard the child make on other occasions. Wait to see what the child does. If he or she repeats the original sound, say a different sound again. Watch for the child to make an effort to change his or her sounds to match yours.

Adaptations:

Hearing Impaired: If the child has a severe hearing impairment and is unable to hear, thus, imitate you, do a similar activity with gestures. That is, imitate what the child does for several turns and then change your action. For example, after several turns in which each of you bangs the table once, bang it twice on your turn; or, after several turns of banging the table, clap your hands on your turn.

Criterion: On several different occasions, the child shifts sounds when the caregiver responds to the child's vocalization with another sound from the child's repertoire. If a child has a severe hearing impairment, a shift from one motor action to another, in imitation, may be credited for this item.

AREA: 11. Imitation: Sound and Gestures
BEHAVIOR: 11f. Imitates an activity in repertoire after observing the caregiver doing that activity

Materials: A normal home or group care environment

Procedures and Use in Daily Routines:

As you talk or play with the child, model some simple motor activity that you have seen the child engage in at other times. For example, you might clap your hands or stick out your tongue. Watch to see if the child will imitate you.

If the child does not imitate, repeat the action. If feasible, physically prompt the child to do the action and then, repeat it again.

Adaptations:

Visually Impaired: Remember to use actions that the child with a visual impairment has previously done and that he or she can identify by the sounds it created (e.g., clapping hands, banging the table, patting the hand on the mouth while making a noise).

Motor Impaired: Carefully select actions for the child with motor impairments, so that they are easy for him or her to perform. Give sufficient time for the child to organize a response.

Criterion: On several occasions, the child imitates an activity that is already in his or her repertoire after observing a caregiver do the activity. Unless a child has a very limited repertoire of movements, at least 2 different activities should be imitated.

AREA: **11. Imitation: Sound and Gestures**
BEHAVIOR: 11g. Imitates inflection (i.e., pitch)

Materials: A normal home or group care environment

Procedures and Use in Daily Routines:

When engaging in vocal turn-taking with the child, introduce some exaggerated inflection pattern(s). For example, if you are saying, "ba ba ba ba ba" in a normal tone of voice, begin to say it with a high-pitched, squeaky voice. Watch the child's reactions and wait to see if he or she attempts to imitate. If the child does not attempt to imitate, go back to the normal voice for a few turns and then, again try the squeaky voice or, perhaps, a big, deep voice.

Note: Some children will find exaggerated shifts in pitch amusing and will smile or laugh instead of trying to imitate. Laugh along with them, but try again.

Adaptations:

Hearing Impaired: Try to identify the pitches to which the child with a hearing impairment responds best. Use those for this item. If you get no responses, the item may be inappropriate.

Criterion: On several occasions, the child changes his or her pitch in an attempt to imitate a caregiver's pitch changes.

AREA: **11. Imitation: Sound and Gestures**
BEHAVIOR: 11h. Attempts to match new sounds

Materials: A normal home or group care environment

Procedures and Use in Daily Routines:

When playing a vocal turn-taking game with the child, introduce a sound you have heard the child make. After he or she imitates it, introduce another sound, one you have not yet heard the child make. For example, the child may be saying, "dadada, bababa, gagaga" and other sounds incorporating a consonant and an "ah" sound and may readily change from one to the other in imitation of you. If so, you might introduce one of the same consonants with an "oo" sound (e.g., "doo, doo, doo," "boo boo boo," "goo goo goo"). Pause a while to allow the child time to imitate the sound.

Always play these vocal games with a lot of smiling, laughter, and enthusiasm, as though having an interesting conversation.

Adaptations:

Visually Impaired: Occasionally place the hand of a child with a visual impairment near or on your mouth as you make sounds so that he or she can feel the shape of your mouth and the force of the air expelled as well as hear the sound.

Hearing Impaired: Be sure the child with a hearing impairment is looking at you. Exaggerate your mouth movements as you make a new sound.

Criterion: The child frequently attempts to match new sounds. The imitation does not have to be exact, but it should be evident that the child is trying to change the way he or she shapes the mouth, moves the lips or tongue, and so forth.

AREA: 11.   Imitation: Sound and Gestures
BEHAVIOR: 11i.   Imitates unfamiliar movements

Materials: A normal home or group care environment

Procedures:

When you are engaging in a turn-taking game with the child in which you alternately make the same or similar motor actions (e.g., clapping, banging), introduce a new action (e.g., putting the hands over the eyes, raising the hands high above the head).

If the child does not change his or her behavior in an attempt to imitate the new action, again model the behavior and physically assist the child to do it. If the child does imitate you, respond by laughing, praising, or whatever is pleasing to the child.

It is often helpful (and fun!) to do this activity in front of a mirror.

Use in Daily Routines:

Use turn-taking games to occupy the child in situations that are likely to produce boredom and fussiness (e.g., waiting in grocery lines, waiting for lunch to cook).

Adaptations:

Visually Impaired: If the child's visual impairment is so severe the he or she cannot see the caregiver's actions, this item is inappropriate.

Hearing Impaired: Introduce the child with a hearing impairment to some easy standard signs during these turn-taking games.

Motor Impaired: Be creative in identifying actions that the child with motor impairments can use in turn-taking games. In children with very severe impairments, this item may be inappropriate.

Criterion: The child imitates several unfamiliar actions on several different occasions.

AREA: 11.   Imitation: Sound and Gestures
BEHAVIOR: 11j.   Imitates familiar 2-syllable words (e.g., baba, dada, mama)

Materials: A normal home or group care environment

Procedures and Use in Daily Routines:

During play or caregiving activities, initiate a vocal imitation game. After several turns, begin to say a simple and familiar word like "Dada" or "Mama." Pause and wait to see if the child will imitate.

You may be most successful if you introduce a word when the child is making sounds similar to that word. For example, children frequently babble "Dadadada" long before they actually say, "Dada" (stopping after two syllables). When the child babbles "Dadadada," you say "Dada" with uneven emphasis on the two syllables, making it sound more like a single word than part of a stream of babble. Again wait for the child to imitate. If he or she continues to babble, continue to take your turn with similar sounds, but in word form.

(continued)

Adaptations:

> *Hearing Impaired:* Be sure that the child with a hearing impairment is looking at you as you try to play vocal turn-taking games. Speak clearly and with exaggerated mouth movements as you form different sounds.

Criterion: The child imitates at least 2 familiar 2-syllable words on several occasions.

AREA: 11. Imitation: Sound and Gestures
BEHAVIOR: 11k: Experiments with making own mouth move like that of the adult

Materials: A normal home or group care environment

Procedures and Use in Daily Routines:

> Spend time holding the child on your lap or in another position that allows him or her to see and reach for your face as you talk. Allow the child to touch your face and mouth.
>
> Watch the child's mouth as you talk. Notice whether the child moves his or her mouth as you talk, as if trying to do what you are doing. Exaggerate your mouth movements (e.g., make a big "O," whistle, tighten your lips for an "Mm-mm-mm-mm").
>
> *Note:* This item is different from earlier efforts in which the child attempts to move his or her mouth when seeing the adult talking, in that now the child is both more deliberate and more precise in his or her imitations and is actively interested in the mouth of the speaker and the sounds it produces.

Adaptations:

> *Visually Impaired:* It is especially important to encourage the child with a visual impairment to touch your mouth as you talk and to make vocal noises. Occasionally, take the child's hand from your mouth to his or her mouth and then back to yours. Try this when you blow, do a "Bronx cheer," or other action in which the lips are active.
>
> *Hearing Impaired:* Encourage the child with a hearing impairment not only to touch your mouth, but to hold his or her hand on your throat to feel the vibrations of your speech. Take the child's hands to his or her own throat to help compare the way it feels.
>
> *Motor Impaired:* Sometimes a child with motor impairments will not be able to reach for your mouth. However, the child may watch you intently as you talk. Observe the child as you do exaggerated mouth movements to see if he or she attempts to imitate.

Criterion: On several occasions, the child experiments with making his or her own mouth move in a manner similar to that of the adult.

AREA: 11. Imitation: Sound and Gestures
BEHAVIOR: 11l.   Imitates familiar 2-syllable words with syllable changes
(e.g., baby, uh-oh, all gone) *or* Imitates 2 signs that stand for words
(e.g., Daddy, all gone, more, eat, drink)

Materials: A normal home or group care environment

(continued)

Procedures and Use in Daily Routines:

Talk to the child throughout the day. Name people and objects. As you do so, wait and see if the child tries to imitate these names and labels. When the child produces a "baby version" of the word (e.g., "baba" for bottle), let the child know that you understand what he or she is trying to say by saying, "Baba. Yes, that's right. It is a bottle."

When playing vocal games, introduce 2-syllable words/expressions with syllable changes (e.g., baby, uh-oh, all gone).

Adaptations:

Visually Impaired: A child with a severe visual impairment will often be a proficient imitator, but have difficulty associating words with objects and events. Even when working on imitation, find ways to highlight the meaning of the words you are introducing.

Hearing Impaired: If the child with a hearing impairment is unable to imitate you vocally or is learning this imitation very slowly, stress imitating standard signs. Always talk to the child using signs, and watch for the child's attempts to imitate the signs. Show your pleasure and try to reinforce meaning when the child imitates even if the imitation is quite inaccurate (e.g., if the child imitates the sign for cookie, say "Yes, cookie," making the sign again as you speak and then give him or her the cookie).

Motor Impaired: If the child with motor impairments is unable to imitate either vocally or motorically, delete this item and all items that follow in this sequence from the child's educational program.

Criterion: On several occasions, the child imitates familiar 2-syllable words with syllable changes, *or,* if the child has a hearing impairment, he or she imitates 2 signs that stand for words.

AREA: **11. Imitation: Sound and Gestures**
BEHAVIOR: 11m. Imitates most new one-syllable words *or* Imitates most simple signs that stand for words

Materials: A normal home or group care environment

Procedures and Use in Daily Routines:

Talk to the child throughout the day. Notice what (or who) the child seems interested in and name those objects and people; describe events. Whenever you label something or someone, pause to see if the child will try to imitate that sound. If the child tries to imitate, repeat the label and let him or her approach, touch, have, or otherwise experience the object or person associated with the label. That is, teach meaning along with imitation.

Adaptations:

Hearing Impaired: Talk to the child with a hearing impairment as much as you would to any other child. Use signs along with your speech, emphasizing the signs (i.e., making the signs slowly and precisely) when you are naming objects or people. Watch for the child's attempts to imitate the signs, and respond enthusiastically to them.

If a child is very slow to learn to imitate, model a sign and then physically guide the child's hands to make that sign; model the sign again and wait to see if the child will imitate.

Criterion: The child imitates most new one-syllable words, *or,* if the child has a hearing impairment, he or she imitates most simple signs that stand for words.

AREA: **11.   Imitation: Sound and Gestures**
BEHAVIOR: 11n.   Imitates familiar words overheard in conversation *or* Imitates signs
observed in others' conversation

Materials: A normal home or group care environment

Procedures and Use in Daily Routines:

Periodically observe the child when you are talking to another adult or to another child to see if he or she is listening and repeating one or more of the words that are heard. Also, pay attention to the sounds that the child makes after the conversation is over. He or she may practice some of the words heard.

Adaptations:

Hearing Impaired: Use signs as you talk to people in the child's presence, even if those people are unfamiliar with signing. Observe the child to determine if he or she tries to imitate 1 or more of the signs observed in a conversation.

Criterion: On several occasions, the child imitates familiar words, *or,* if the child has a hearing impairment, he or she signs from others' conversations.

AREA: **11.   Imitation: Sound and Gestures**
BEHAVIOR: 11o.   Imitates environmental sounds during play

Materials: A normal home or group care environment

Procedures and Use in Daily Routines:

When you play with the child or read to him or her, make appropriate nonspeech noises that are associated with different animals or objects. For example, "moo" at the picture of a cow as well as say "cow," "bark" for the dog, "meow" for the cat, and make "rhmm, rhmm, rhmm," noises for a car. Children usually love these noises. After you have made each sound, listen to see if the child imitates the sound then, or, perhaps, minutes later, as the play continues.

Adaptations:

Visually Impaired: Help the child with a visual impairment associate the sounds with the objects/animals by encouraging tactile exploration of them. For example, the child may learn to make a motor noise when touching a car and discovering its wheels.

Hearing Impaired: Depending on the severity of the child's hearing impairment, this item may be inappropriate. However, it is worthwhile to explore the child's responses to environmental sounds as described above. The child may be able to hear some of these sounds and enjoy imitating them.

Criterion: The child imitates several different environmental sounds during play.

AREA: **11. Imitation: Sound and Gestures**
BEHAVIOR: 11p. Imitates 2-word sentences *or* Imitates sequences of 2 signs

Materials: A normal home or group care environment

Procedures and Use in Daily Routines:

As the child begins to use more single words to communicate, begin stressing 2- and 3-word sentences as you talk. For example, if the child says, "Ball," you say, "Big ball," and pause, giving the child an opportunity to try to say "Big ball." Always let the child know you like it when he or she imitates. Also, continue to provide experiences that reinforce the meaning of the words that you introduce.

Adaptations:

Hearing Impaired: As the child with a hearing impairment begins to use single signs to communicate, begin to stress 2-sign sequences to communicate with him or her. Watch for the child's attempts to imitate these sequences. If the child has difficulty imitating, physically guide him or her through the sequence, then repeat it yourself and wait for the child to try again.

Criterion: The child imitates several 2-word sentences, *or,* if the child has a hearing impairment, he or she imitates several sequences of 2 signs.

AREA: **11. Imitation: Sound and Gestures**
BEHAVIOR: 11q. Imitates 3-syllable words

Materials: A normal home or group care environment

Procedures and Use in Daily Routines:

Throughout the course of normal, day-to-day interactions, the child will hear many 3-syllable words. Pay attention to his or her efforts to begin to imitate more complex sound sequences: 3-syllable words (e.g., Grandaddy) or 2-word sentences containing 3 syllables (e.g., "Doggie gone"). Speak some of these words or phrases more slowly and distinctly to facilitate imitation. Show your pleasure at the child's attempts to imitate.

Adaptations:

Hearing Impaired: Depending on the extent of the child's hearing impairment, this item may be inappropriate and should be deleted from the educational program.

Criterion: The child imitates several 3-syllable words on different occasions.

12.

Responses to Communication from Others

THIS SEQUENCE IS concerned with how well a child understands the communicative efforts of others—a communicative act that is clearly not just receptive. Such communicative efforts are a part of ongoing interactions between the child and caregiver. The sensitivity of the caregiver in "reading" the child's responses is important both in the interpretation of how much the child understands and in the child's progress toward understanding. In order to learn the meaning of adult messages, the child must have feedback about his or her responses to those messages.

This sequence attempts to make the caregiver more aware of the child's responses and, thus, better capable of appropriately stimulating him or her. However, it is important to recognize that it may be very difficult to learn to "read" the signals of some children with significant disabilities. Unfortunately, in many cases a seemingly unresponsive child "teaches" caregivers to stop talking. To see this, one need only compare the verbal output of a caregiver to a normal 2-year-old with that to a child of the same age or older who has severe cerebral palsy and is nonverbal, even when cognitive functioning is normal. It is important that adults continue to talk and gesture to a child even when responses from the child are absent or hard to understand.

It is also vital to recognize that many children with disabilities will rely on some alternate form of communication at various times throughout their development. In this sequence, it is suggested that gestures and manual signing accompany speech for many children. Be sure to consult with your communication disorders specialist for advice on the extent to which manual signing is appropriate for any given child.

12. Responses to Communication from Others

a. Appropriately reacts to tone of voice and/or some facial expressions
b. Turns to the direction from which name is being called
c. Stops activity when name is called
d. Does previously learned task on verbal or gestural cue

e. Responds with correct gesture to "up" and "bye-bye"

f. Responds to "no" (i.e., briefly stops activity)

g. Identifies 3 objects or people that are spoken or signed

h. Responds to "give me" (spoken and/or signed) (same as 15l.)

i. Follows simple commands (spoken and/or signed)

j. Identifies most common objects when they are named and/or signed

k. Appropriately indicates "yes" or "no" in response to questions

l. Identifies 2 body parts when they are named or signed

m. Retrieves objects from the same room on verbal or signed request

n. Identifies at least 4 animals in pictures when they are named or signed

o. Identifies 15 or more pictures of common objects when they are named or signed

p. Understands 2 or more category words (e.g., animals)

q. Identifies 5 body parts

r. Correctly follows 3 different 2-part commands involving one object

s. Follows 3 different 3-part commands

AREA: **12.   Responses to Communication from Others**
BEHAVIOR: 12a.   Appropriately reacts to tone of voice and/or some facial expressions

Materials: A normal home or group care environment

Procedures and Use in Daily Routines:

Talk to the child often. Naturally express your feelings and try to reflect back to the child what you believe he or she is feeling. For example, if the child bites you (just as he or she chews on everything else in the environment) frown and say firmly, "No, that hurts me!"; or, if the child vigorously rejects some item of food, say, "Ooh, was that yucky?" exaggerating both the inflection pattern that indicates disgust and the facial expression associated with it.

Note: Without being aware of it, many adults exaggerate their facial expressions when talking to a baby or a young child. This probably helps the child associate facial expressions with other events in the environment and is, no doubt, useful. Listen to yourself and watch yourself in the mirror. If you are not doing this exaggeration, make a conscious effort to do so.

Adaptations:

Visually Impaired: Tone of voice will be especially important for a child with a visual impairment. Be particularly aware of communicating feelings through tone of voice when working with this child.

Hearing Impaired: Facial expressions will be particularly important for a child with a hearing impairment. Be especially aware of your facial expressions as you communicate with this child.

Criterion: The child appropriately reacts to tone of voice and/or facial expressions that are communicating at least 2 different emotional states. For example, the child might look solemn if the caregiver sounds angry or hurt; fearful, if the caregiver is afraid; excited, when the caregiver is excited; or smile, when the caregiver is happy or laughing. At least one other person besides the primary caregiver should be able to confirm that the child is responding differently to the different vocal and facial expressions.

AREA: **12.   Responses to Communication from Others**
BEHAVIOR: 12b.   Turns to direction from which name is being called
BEHAVIOR: 12c.   Stops activity when name is called

Materials: A normal home or group care environment

Procedures and Use in Daily Routines:

Regardless of how young a child is, call him or her by name as you talk.

Call the child's name in order to get his or her attention. Initially, the child will primarily attend because the voice alerts him or her. Soon, however, the name will be associated with the call to attention.

Note: Many families have 2 or more "pet" names for a child in addition to the given name. Children often enjoy these pet names. There is nothing wrong with using them, but it is important to use the given name more frequently than the pet names until the child learns to recognize it as his or her own name.

(continued)

Adaptations:

Visually Impaired: A child with a visual impairment will be slower to turn to a caregiver's call because the turning is not reinforced by seeing the person who spoke. Work on having the child turn his or her head or body to your voice, along with the auditory localization skills found in sequence 3, Auditory Localization and Object Permanence (pp. 93–101).

Provide tactile feedback on your location when you call the child. That is, stand nearby, call the child, then reach out and touch him or her, guiding his or her hand toward your face. Remember, it is much easier to localize sounds at the sides than at the midline, either in front or in back.

Hearing Impaired: Depending on the severity of the child's hearing impairment, it may not be possible for him or her to respond to his or her name being called. Always use the child's "name sign" as you say his or her name and find another way to elicit attention, if necessary. For example, sometimes a clap can be heard when a voice cannot. The clap can be used to attract attention and then the name sign can be given. Be sure to use a consistent signal so that the child will learn it means, "Look at me, I have something to tell you."

Motor Impaired: The child with motor impairments may be unable to turn his or her head easily. You may find that the response from this child is very delayed. Be sure to give him or her time to respond to a call before you repeat it.

Criterion 12b.: The child frequently turns toward a beckoning voice when his or her name is called (or, if the child has a hearing impairment, he or she turns to some other signal and looks at the adult to see his or her name sign).

Criterion 12c.: The child frequently stops his or her activity when his or her name is called (or, if the child has a hearing impairment, he or she stops his or her activity to the same signal that is used in 12b).

AREA: **12. Responses to Communication From Others**
BEHAVIOR: 12d. Does previously learned task on verbal or gestural cue

Materials: A normal home or group care environment

Procedures:

Select any behavior that a child has learned to do when playing with you (e.g., kissing, hugging, clapping, playing "pat-a-cake"). Try to initiate that activity with just a verbal cue. For example, say, "Pat-a-cake, Pat-a-cake" without doing any actions yourself. Wait momentarily to see if the child claps. If he or she does, go on and play the game. If the child does not clap, again say, "Pat-a-cake" and you start clapping or physically guide him or her to start clapping. Then play the game. The next time start again with just the verbal cue.

If the child is not yet participating in any activities that lend themselves to being initiated by a verbal cue, begin creating games that can be used in this way. For example, kiss the baby and then say, "Give me a kiss" or "Give me some sugar," placing your face close to the child; or lean toward the child so that his or her mouth touches your face and then hug him or her.

Other activities to try are: "How big is Johnny? So big" (raising the child's hands above his or her head); "Let's blow bubbles" (then do a Bronx cheer and wait for the child to imitate); or "Knock, knock" (as you rap on the table and then wait for the child to imitate).

(continued)

Use in Daily Routines:

Use games to fill in the moments throughout the day that the child needs attention. Teaching the child to play games on verbal cues will allow you to keep him or her entertained for short periods, while you are doing other activities.

Adaptations:

Hearing Impaired: Sign and gesture, as well as talk, when you play games with a child with a hearing impairment.

Motor Impaired: Try to create games that are suitable to the child's motor limitations. If the child cannot voluntarily move his or her arms or legs, you can create a "game" that requires only eye movements. For example, as you hold your hand in different positions, say "Look up, look down, look left, look right, look all around!" and then circle your finger toward the child's tummy and tickle him or her. This kind of a game will not only be fun for the child, but will develop good "visual pointing," which can be used in communication exchanges as the child develops further.

Criterion: On several occasions, the child does a previously learned task on spoken or signed cue.

AREA: **12.   Responses to Communication from Others**
BEHAVIOR: 12e.   Responds with correct gesture to "up" and "bye-bye"

Materials: A normal home or group care environment

Procedures and Use in Daily Routines:

Consistently match your verbalization of "up" and "bye-bye" with the appropriate gestures (i.e., reaching for the child, waving).

When it is time to get the child out of bed or you are getting ready to pick the child up, say, "Do you want to get up?" Hold your hands out but do not touch the child. Wait to see if he or she will reach for your hands. If not, reach down and take the child's hands and hold them a second or so before you pick him or her up. Gradually reduce the help you are providing. Instead of reaching down and taking the child's hands, just touch him or her gently on one arm and take your hands back, beckoning the child to reach.

Use a similar procedure to teach "bye-bye." When someone is leaving, say "Bye-bye," wave yourself, and then physically prompt the child to wave. Gradually reduce the amount of help you give the child, until he or she is waving in response to the situation and the verbal cue.

Adaptations:

Visually Impaired: It may be difficult for a child with a visual impairment to understand partings, in terms of other people leaving. The child may first learn "bye-bye" in response to going somewhere him- or herself.

Hearing Impaired: Sign, as well as talk, when teaching a child with a hearing impairment as in the above Procedures section.

Motor Impaired: If the child's motor impairments prevent his or her making even modified gestures to "up" and "bye-bye," delete this item from the intervention plan, but continue modeling the behaviors. These natural gestures help the child understand the meaning of these words.

Criterion: The child regularly responds with correct gestures to "up" and "bye-bye."

AREA: **12.   Responses to Communication from Others**
BEHAVIOR: 12f.   Responds to "no" (i.e., briefly stops activity)

Materials: A normal home or group care environment

Procedures and Use in Daily Routines:

When the child engages in inappropriate activity that should be stopped, say, "No," firmly, and distract the child with a new activity, move him or her to a different location, or do something else that stops the activity and communicates, "Do this, instead of that."

After you have said, "No," always respond to even momentary cessation of activity with praise and give the child special attention as he or she begins to do the substitute activity. It is important that the child learn "what to do" and well as "what not to do."

Adaptations:

Hearing Impaired: With a child with a hearing impairment, accompany "no" with a gesture that means "no" or "stop." Be sure that the child can see you.

Motor Impaired: If the child's motor impairment is too severe, there may be few opportunities to say "no" to him or her, and this item may be inappropriate. However, be sure that you teach the child the meaning of "no" in other contexts. That is, when it is appropriate, say "no" to mean, "I don't like it," "I don't want any," "Don't do that" (see sequence 10., Prevocabulary/Vocabulary, item 10k. (p. 178).

Criterion: The child usually briefly stops activity when told "no."

AREA: **12.   Responses to Communication from Others**
BEHAVIOR: 12g.   Identifies 3 objects or people that are named or signed

Materials: A normal home or group care environment

Procedures and Use in Daily Routines:

Throughout the day, notice what or who is capturing the child's attention. Talk about whatever the child seems to be interested in. Name the toys, animals, or people as you talk (e.g., "Here comes Daddy," "Nice doggie. Pat the nice doggie," "Ball. Roll the ball").

Call the child's attention to items that interest you by handing them to the child or by pointing to them as you call them by name. If you are carrying the child, let him or her touch the object and then back up a little so his or her arm is still extended toward the object, but not touching it as you talk about it and point with your free hand. If the child does not begin to imitate your pointing, hold up his or her arm in the direction that you pointed, as you say, "See the _____."

Begin to ask the child, "Where's _____?" or "Where is the _____?", beginning with things you have named several times for him or her. If the child does not point or otherwise indicate the object, you point and say, "There it is; right there. See the _____." Physically prompt the child to point if that is reasonable in the situation.

Adaptations:

Visually Impaired: If the child has little useable vision, he or she will not be able to point to objects. Instead, teach the child to identify objects by touch, smell, and sound. Name the items or people that the child is touching or otherwise attending to. Also teach the child to "scan" the environment by moving his or her hands around on surfaces to find out what is where. To check the child's understanding of names, place 2 or 3 objects within easy reach, and say, "Find the _____"; or, after a familiar person has entered the room, sat down, and talked, say, "Where's _____" to see if the child can go to that person. Correct errors by helping the child further explore the object you asked for and the one he or she identified, so that the differences will be more apparent.

Hearing Impaired: Sign, as well as talk, as you teach the child with a hearing impairment names of objects and people.

Motor Impaired: If the child with motor impairments is unable to point, use eye gaze as an indicator of understanding.

Criterion: The child identifies 3 objects or people that are named or signed, each on several occasions. Most children will point with the whole hand or a finger. It is also acceptable for the child to touch or pick up the objects that were named. Eye gaze may be used instead of pointing, if appropriate to the child's handicap.

AREA: **12. Responses to Communication from Others**
BEHAVIOR: 12h. Responds to "give me" (spoken and/or signed) (same as 15l.)

Materials: A normal home or group care environment

Procedures:

When the child is involved in playing with a small toy, say or sign, "Give me the _____," holding out your hand. If the child does not give you the toy, gently take it from him or her, say (or sign), "Thank you," and immediately give the toy back to the child. Make a game of taking and returning a variety of toys. Avoid asking for favorite toys until the child clearly understands that you will give them back. Do not take a toy if the child vigorously protests.

Use in Daily Routines:

Model "giving" throughout the day. That is, when the child reaches for something, say, "You want me to give you the _____? Here it is." Hand items to the child and others in the environment, saying, "Let me give you some _____," and so forth.

Adaptations:

Visually Impaired: If the child has a severe visual impairment and is unable to see a hand that is extended toward him or her, touch the child's hand as you say, "Give me the _____."

Hearing Impaired: Sign, as well as talk, for a child with a hearing impairment.

Motor Impaired: Omit this item from the intervention plan of a child with motor impairments, if he or she cannot release an object or push it toward you. Continue to talk about giving, however, as you offer items to the child or to others in the environment. Also, talk about giving kisses, hugs, or other forms of affection and try to create a way for the child to give in this form.

(continued)

Criterion: The child regularly responds to "give me" (spoken or signed) by giving whatever is requested.

AREA: **12.   Responses to Communication from Others**
BEHAVIOR: 12i.   Follows simple commands (spoken and/or signed)

Materials: A normal home or group care environment

Procedures and Use in Daily Routines:

Throughout the day, there will be opportunities and reasons for making requests of the child. Be sure to keep the requests simple (e.g., "Put the _____ down," "Bring the _____ to me," "Take this to Mary"). Always say "Thank you" or otherwise indicate your appreciation when the child complies. If the child does not do as requested, try to help him or her by demonstrating what you expected or physically guiding the child through the actions that are involved. If you guide the child through the actions, conclude with a "thank you," a hug, or some other indication of approval.

Adaptations:

Hearing Impaired: Sign, as well as talk, to a child with a hearing impairment.

Motor Impaired: If a child has a significant motor impairment, it is easy to forget to make requests of them. It is important to think carefully about what the child is capable of doing and how those behaviors can be used to teach an understanding of the language concepts that are involved in simple commands (e.g., in, up, here, there). If the child is not capable of any movement except eye gaze, begin with that form of requesting. Teach "Look at me," "Look at _____ ," "Look up," "Look down," and so forth. Also, be sure that the child is in situations where he or she has many opportunities to observe other children who are following instructions.

Criterion: The child follows at least 3 different simple commands, signed and/or spoken.

AREA: **12.   Responses to Communication from Others**
BEHAVIOR: 12j.   Identifies most common objects when they are named and/or signed

Materials: A normal home or group care environment

Procedures and Use in Daily Routines:

See Procedures and Use in Daily Routines sections in item 12g., Identifies 3 objects or people that are named or signed (p. 198).

Adaptations:

See Adaptations section of item 12g., Identifies 3 objects or people that are named or signed (p. 198).

Criterion: The child identifies most common objects (at least 10) when they are named and/or signed. Identification may be by any clear response, including touching, pointing, giving, and eye gaze.

AREA: **12. Responses to Communication from Others**
BEHAVIOR: 12k. Appropriately indicates "yes" or "no" in response to questions

Materials: A normal home or group care environment

Procedures and Use in Daily Routines:

Throughout the day, ask the child simple questions that require a yes/no answer (e.g., "Do you want some ice cream?" "Is this my shoe [as you hold the child's shoe up to your foot]?"). Begin with questions to which you are quite sure the child knows the answers.

Wait for a few seconds after the question to show the child that you are waiting for him or her to respond. If the child does not respond, demonstrate the expected response (e.g., nod your head and say, "Yes, you want some ice cream," shake your head and say, "No, that's not my shoe—it's your shoe!"). If the child does not yet make distinguishably different sounds for "Yes" and "No," physically assist him or her to appropriately nod or shake his or her head.

Correct the child if your question is one about an obvious fact (e.g., "Is this my shoe?"). However, if the child gives an unexpected response to a "do you want" question, do not "correct" him or her. Act on the basis of what the child says. For example, if the child shakes his or her head "no" when you offer ice cream, say, "No? I'll put it away then," or, "Well, I want some. I'll get some for me." If the child then acts upset, as if he or she really does want the ice cream, say, "You said "no" (shaking your head). Did you really mean "yes" (nodding your head)? Do you want some ice cream?)" If necessary, assist the child to nod his or her head. It is important for the child to learn that what he or she says (or gestures) is going to be believed and acted upon.

Note: Children frequently learn to indicate "no" before they indicate "yes," and may respond to every question with "no." Be sure to be consistent in acting on what a child says, rather than on what you think he or she means. This is the best way to help the child learn to communicate effectively.

Adaptations:

Hearing Impaired: Sign, as well as speak, the questions that you ask a child with a hearing impairment.

Motor Impaired: If the child with motor impairments can neither speak nor move his or her head well enough for you to distinguish between a "yes" and a "no" response, try to identify any two behaviors you can distinguish and can teach the child to use for "yes" and "no." For example, a simple vowel sound vocalization might be used for "yes" and a head turn for "no." When talking to the child and teaching him or her, use these behaviors along with your speech to model them for the child.

Criterion: The child regularly and appropriately indicates "yes" or "no" in response to questions. The appropriateness of the response is determined by the way in which the child behaves when the caregiver acts on what the child says.

AREA: **12. Responses to Communication from Others**
BEHAVIOR: 12l. Identifies 2 body parts when they are named or signed

Materials: A normal home or group care environment

(continued)

Procedures and Use in Daily Routines:

When you are dressing or bathing the child, talk about his or her hair, hands, feet, tummy, nose, eyes, ears, and other body parts as you touch them. Also, give instructions that aid in dressing and use the body part names (e.g., "Lift up your hands," "Let me wipe your nose").

When you are holding the child on your lap and he or she touches your mouth or nose, name these body parts and then touch the same parts on the child.

After doing the above activities on several different occasions, ask the child, "Nose? Where's your nose?" Or, if you're facing the child, ask, "Where's my nose?" If the child does not point to the correct body part or points incorrectly, show the child the body part yourself and then physically assist him or her to point correctly, naming the body part one or more times, again, as you do so.

When the child is playing with a stuffed animal or doll, ask the child to find the eyes, ears, feet, and so forth. Talk about the differences between the animals (e.g., the dog's big floppy ears and the mouse's little ears) or between a doll and an animal.

If in a group situation, sing songs that include pointing to (or otherwise indicating a knowledge of) body parts (e.g., "When you're happy and you know it, clap your hands [stomp your feet, shake your head, touch your nose, and so forth]").

Adaptations:

Visually Impaired: Take time to allow the child with a visual impairment to touch and feel your face, hands, feet, and so forth, as you are teaching him or her about his or her own body parts. For example, you might hold the child's hand, and say, "This is your hand. Here is my hand. See, my hand is bigger (while helping the child feel your hand with his or her free hand)." After the child has learned to identify his or her own body parts, begin asking the child to find your body parts.

Hearing Impaired: The signs for many body parts are simply pointing to the part. For this item, teach the child with a hearing impairment to point to his or her eye when you give his or her name sign, while you point to your eye; point to his or her foot when you give the name sign, while you point to your foot; and so forth. Then move on to dolls or stuffed animals, signing, "Show me doll's eye," "Show me dog's eye," and so forth.

Motor Impaired: If the child with motor impairments cannot point, use eye gaze or some other indicator response. You may also use a yes/no response (e.g., "Is this your nose?").

Criterion: The child points to or otherwise indicates 2 body parts when they are named. The child should be able to spontaneously do this (i.e., not only just after a period of trying to teach him or her) and to do it when asked by at least 2 different people.

AREA: 12. Responses to Communication from Others
BEHAVIOR: 12m. Retrieves objects from the same room on verbal or signed request

Materials: A normal home or group care environment

Procedures and Use in Daily Routines:

During the course of the day, include the child in your activities by asking him or her to hand items to you, get something for you that is across the room, and so forth. If the

---

(continued)

child looks puzzled when you ask for something, turn toward it and point to it. If the child picks up the wrong item, say, "No, I need the _____ ." If necessary, go over to the object and say, "This is the _____ . Please take it over there." Give as much help as necessary to assure that the child is successful. Always thank the child, give him or her a hug, call him or her a "good helper," and so forth.

Adaptations:

Visually Impaired: For a child with a visual impairment, keep objects in consistent places in his or her environment. Give the child the freedom to explore the environment. Label the objects that he or she touches and help him or her learn to distinguish between the objects on the basis of both feel and location. This will make it possible for the child to retrieve those objects for you.

Hearing Impaired: Sign, as well as speak, your requests to a child with a hearing impairment.

Motor Impaired: If the child with motor impairments is not mobile, this item is inappropriate. Continue to work on identifying objects. Also, try to give the child the experience of carrying something to another person by taking the child to get an object, helping him or her hold it, and deliver it to someone else.

Criterion: The child retrieves at least 3 different objects from the same room on verbal or signed request (without a caregiver pointing to the correct location).

AREA: 12. Responses to Communication from Others
BEHAVIOR: 12n. Identifies at least 4 animals in pictures when they are named or signed
BEHAVIOR: 12o. Identifies 15 or more pictures of common objects when they are named or signed

Materials: Books, magazines, picture cards

Procedures:

Spend at least 5–10 minutes each day "reading" to the child. Look at books together in which there are colorful pictures of animals and common objects. Point to these animals and objects and label them for the child. Ask the child to find them as you label them. If necessary, help the child point to or touch the pictures as you label them. Show enthusiasm for the pictures (i.e., in addition to naming them, talk about their color, size, activities, and so forth).

Use in Daily Routines:

When you are riding with the child in a car, at the grocery story, or in other situations where pictures are around on signs, food cartons, and so forth, point to and label what you see. Ask the child to find the items that you name.

Adaptations:

Visually Impaired: Experiment with different kinds of pictures (e.g., large, colorful pictures, ones with lots of contrast) to make use of the child's vision. If a child with a visual impairment cannot see well enough to identify any pictures, teach him or her to make an appropriate animal noise to the animal that you name (for item 12n.), create texture books as described in item 10m., and teach the child to identify objects in the book by feel (for item 12o.).

(continued)

Hearing Impaired: Sign, as well as speak, as you teach names of animals and objects for the child with a hearing impairment.

Motor Impaired: If the child with motor impairments cannot point, use eye gaze or some other reliable indicator response.

Criterion for 12n.: On several occasions, the child points to or otherwise indicates knowledge of at least 4 animals in pictures when they are named or signed (or, if the child has a visual impairment, he or she makes the correct animal sounds when the animal is named).

Criterion for 12o.: On several occasions, the child points to or otherwise indicates knowledge of at least 15 pictures of common objects.

AREA: **12. Responses to Communication from Others**
BEHAVIOR: 12p.   Understands 2 or more category words (e.g., animals)

Materials: A normal home or group care environment

Procedures and Use in Daily Routines:

As you talk to the child, you will probably introduce category words without being aware of it. One of the first category words that a child learns is "toys," because caregivers ask them to "Pick up the toys" or "Bring me the toys." When looking at a picture book of animals, it is natural to say, "Look at all these animals! Here's a pig, and here's a cow."

Pay attention to the words that you are using with the child. If you have not introduced category words or have introduced only a few, make a conscious effort to interject more new words. Some good ones to begin with are toys, clothes, dishes, animals, vegetables, fruits, and desserts. Help the child to understand what belongs in a particular category by sorting. For example, when picking up the toys you may find a sock or some other "nontoy" on the floor with the toys. Ask the child, "Is this a toy?" If the child says "yes," say "No, it is not a toy. It's a sock and should go in the basket with the dirty clothes." Or, when you are unloading the groceries, have the child help you sort the fruit and vegetables into separate piles.

> *Note:* There will always be some confusion about categories because an object may belong to one or another depending on usage or other characteristics. For example, doll clothes may be put in the pile with the toys, rather than in the hamper with the clothes of family members. When a child sorts in a way you would not sort, try to figure out his or her reasoning. Talk about it with the child.

Adaptations:

Visually Impaired: The child with a visual impairment may use different characteristics to determine what belongs in a category than does the child with good vision. Be aware of characteristics of objects that are salient to the child with a visual impairment (e.g., sounds, texture, usage) as you help him or her try to sort items into categories.

Hearing Impaired: Use signs, as well as talk, with the child with a hearing impairment.

Motor Impaired: If the child with motor impairments is unable to sort by moving objects into separate areas or piles, help the child understand categories by watching you sort and by having you ask yes/no questions (e.g., "Look at this puppet. Does it go here with the clothes or does it go here with the toys?").

Criterion: The child understands 2 or more category words. This may be demonstrated by sorting, by correctly indicating how someone else should sort, or by any other means, as long as it is clear that the child understands the categories.

AREA: 12. Responses to Communication from Others
BEHAVIOR: 12q. Identifies 5 body parts

Materials: A normal home or group care environment

Procedures and Use in Daily Routines:

See Procedures and Use in Daily Routines sections of item 12l., Identifies 2 body parts when they are named or signed (p. 202).

Adaptations:

See Adaptations section of item 12l., Identifies 2 body parts when they are named or signed (p. 202).

Criterion: On several occasions, the child points to or otherwise identifies at least 5 body parts.

AREA: 12. Responses to Communication from Others
BEHAVIOR: 12r. Correctly follows 3 different 2-part commands involving one object
BEHAVIOR: 12s. Follows 3 different 3-part commands

Materials: A normal home or group care environment

Procedures and Use in Daily Routines:

Throughout the day, include the child in your activities by asking him or her to do tasks with you and for you. Pay attention to the complexity of the instructions that you give the child. If the child is bringing or giving items to you at your request, he or she is following one-part commands with one object. Begin to make more complex requests that involve doing 2 tasks with one object (e.g., "Pick up the doll and put it on the chair," "Find your socks and bring them to me").

As the child begins to be successful with 2-part commands, introduce 3-part commands, as follows:

1 action and 3 objects (e.g., "Bring me the doll, the brush, and the comb.")

3 actions and one object (e.g., "Take this spoon, go in the dining room, and put it on the table.")

3 objects that are related by an activity (e.g., "Put your baby in the bed, and give her a bottle.")

Always give the child enough help to be successful, and demonstrate your pleasure and appreciation of his or her success. Help may consist of pointing and other gestures, physically assisting the child, and so forth.

Adaptations:

Visually Impaired: Carefully think about the instructions that you give to a child with a visual impairment, so that you are not making requests that are too difficult, given the child's visual capabilities.

Hearing Impaired: Sign, as well as speak, instructions to a child with a hearing impairment.

Motor Impaired: If a child has severe motor impairments, it may challenge your creativity to find activities that you can ask the child to do. Go as far as you can and make sure

(continued)

that the child also has many opportunities to observe other children following instructions. Make this observation more meaningful by talking to the child about what the other children are doing.

Criterion for 12r.:   The child correctly follows 3 different 2-part commands involving one object. This should be done without additional prompts from the caregiver (i.e., with pointing, repeating, or physically assisting).

Criterion for 12s.:   The child correctly follows 3 different 3-part commands. This should be done without additional prompts from the caregiver.

13.

Conversation Skills

THIS SEQUENCE IS the heart of all of the communication sequences. The child's ability to communicate is highly dependent upon interaction with an adult who is sensitive to his or her needs and behaviors. Early conversations are not made up of words but of reciprocal interactions. These interactions are the foundation for developing a desire to communicate, generating the meaning of communicative acts, and establishing the "rules" of communication exchanges.

At the same time, these interactions are the basis for the child's social and emotional development. The link between social/emotional development and interaction/communication development is especially strong in infancy and early childhood. The child who can maintain interactive play, make requests, and demonstrate basic expectations regarding the behavior of others has the building blocks for healthy social/emotional development as well as the basis for good communication skills. However, the development of these capabilities is highly dependent upon the sensitivity and responsivity of the adults who care for the child.

Early in a child's life, adults probably attribute more intentional communication to the child than is actually there. This attribution is important, however, because the adult acts on the child's "message" and the child begins to learn which of his or her behaviors influence the behaviors of others. This is the beginning of communication. For example, when a child first begins to say, "Da da," he or she is simply experimenting with sounds. When a parent repeatedly calls the child's attention to his or her father when the child says "Da da," the stage is set for the child to use the sound intentionally to identify the father. The same is true of nonverbal communications. A child learns to hold his or her hands up to mean "I want to be picked up," only after many experiences of raising the arms in anticipation of being picked up and having a parent interpret arms up as a wish to be picked up.

Handicapping conditions interfere with the vocal and motor behaviors that normally form the basis for early communicative acts. Because these conditions limit the child's repertoire of behaviors, adults may cease to attribute intentional communication and may interact with the child less frequently, slowing the development of the child's intentional communication. Therefore, it is especially important that caregivers for young children with disabilities remain alert to behaviors that can be interpreted and used in communication exchanges.

13. Conversation Skills

a. Smiles to person who is talking and/or gesturing

b. Protests by vocalizing disapproval of actions and/or events

c. Repeats vocalizations and/or gestures that elicit reactions

d. Indicates interest in a toy or object through eye gaze, reaching, or vocalization

e. "Requests" continued action of familiar toy, song, or activity by starting body movements, eye contact, and/or vocalization

f. Waits for adult to take his or her "turn"

g. Begins to listen—coordinates looking with listening

h. Makes requests by directing caregiver's attention

i. Indicates "no more" and "I don't like this" by turning or pushing away

j. Notices and vocalizes when primary caregiver prepares to leave

k. Uses eye gaze to select other person as partner in communication exchange

l. Changes pitch/volume to signify intensity of desires

m. Raises arms to be picked up

n. Indicates desire to "get down" or "get out" in some consistent fashion other than fussing or crying

o. Plays reciprocal games (e.g., taking turns making sounds, playing the Peek-a-boo game, clapping your hands)

p. Uses words or signs to express wants

q. Seeks adult's assistance in exploring the environment through vocalizations, pointing, or other communicative signals

r. Uses inflection pattern(s) when vocalizing (or uses gestures as if signing)

s. Greets familiar people with an appropriate vocalization or sign

t. Directs caregiver to provide information through questioning look, vocal inflection, and/or words

u. Uses inflection patterns in a sentence with 1 or 2 understandable words (or mixes recognizable signs in with other gestures)

v. Experiments with 2-word utterances (or 2-sign gestures) to achieve specific goals (e.g., "Me go," "Doggie up," "Daddy sit")

w. Spontaneously says (or signs) familiar greetings and farewells at appropriate times

x. Says (or signs) "no" to protest when something is taken away

y. Spontaneously uses words (or signs) in pretend play

z. Uses word (or sign) combinations to describe remote event

aa. Uses word(s) (or sign[s]) to request action

bb. Answers simple questions with a verbal response, gesture, or sign

AREA: **13.   Conversation Skills**
BEHAVIOR: 13a.   Smiles to person who is talking or gesturing

Materials: A normal home or group care environment

Procedures and Use in Daily Routines:

Talk to the child frequently throughout the day (e.g., when you are providing care such as feeding, diapering, bathing; when you walk by as the child is lying awake; when you can just take a few minutes to sit and hold the child for a "conversation"). At first, the child may just watch you. Try to elicit a smile by being especially animated as you talk and by touching or patting the child. Soon, just talking will be enough to elicit the smile.

Note: Most of a child's earliest smiles (1–2 months in youngsters without handicaps) are in response to inner states such as feeling full or comfortable. Thereafter, the child begins to smile at certain tactile stimuli (e.g., being kissed, patted, tickled, rubbed) and at sounds. It is important to respond to all of these early smiles by talking, gesturing, and otherwise interacting with the child. In this way the smiles become truly interpersonal and a part of the child's communication system.

Adaptations:

Visually Impaired: A child with little useable vision may seem inattentive when you talk to him or her because eye contact is not established. Smiling may also be delayed. Look for other signs of attention to the "conversation." Frequently it will be seen in changes in movement, particularly in the hands.

Hearing Impaired: Be sure to gesture and/or sign when you talk to the child with a hearing impairment.

Criterion: The child frequently smiles to the person who is talking and/or gesturing to him or her.

AREA: **13.   Conversation Skills**
BEHAVIOR: 13b.   Protests by vocalizing disapproval of actions and/or events

Materials: A normal home or group care environment

Procedures and Use in Daily Routines:

No effort needs to be made to teach the child to protest by vocalizing disapproval, but it is important to respond appropriately to it when it occurs.

When, in the natural course of events, you give the child something he or she does not like (e.g., a new food), there is a loud noise or other startling event, or the child is hurt, respond appropriately to the crying or other protest. Take the rejected food away to, perhaps, try again another time; pick the child up to comfort him or her; and so forth. Cries and other vocalizations of protest may begin as simple reactions to the situation but rapidly become an intentional communication if adults respond to them as communication.

Adaptations:

None are necessary.

Criterion: The child regularly protests by vocalizing disapproval of actions and/or events.

AREA: 13. Conversation Skills
BEHAVIOR: 13c.   Repeats vocalizations and/or gestures that elicit reactions

Materials: A normal home or group care environment

Procedures and Use in Daily Routines:

> Attend to the child's vocalizations. Imitate the sounds that he or she makes, or smile and say something to the child as if he or she had just made a statement to you. At times you will spontaneously laugh because the child will make a funny sound. Watch to see if the child vocalizes again. If so, respond again. These exchanges are the basis for later conversations.

Adaptations:

> *Hearing Impaired:*   Always respond to the vocalizations made by a child with a hearing impairment, whether or not you believe the child can hear you. Speak slowly and clearly but with animation to make the most of the child's residual hearing. Always combine gestures/signs with your speech.

Criterion: The child frequently repeats vocalizations and/or gestures that elicit reactions. The child may repeat the same sound or experiment with a new one, as long as the vocalization and/or gesture appears to be in response to the reaction of the adult.

AREA: 13. Conversation Skills
BEHAVIOR: 13d.   Indicates interest in a toy or object through eye gaze,
reaching, or vocalization

Materials: A normal home or group care environment

Procedures and Use in Daily Routines:

> Observe what the child attends to throughout the day. When he or she is looking at a particular object, reaching toward an object, or vocalizing as the object appears, talk about it, take the child to it to look at it more closely, point to it, or pick it up and give it to the child. Such actions let the child know that you are interested in the object in which he or she is interested. The more you respond to the child's interests in this way, the more he or she will try to communicate with you.
>
> *Note:*   At this stage, the child is probably not intentionally trying to get you to attend to an object. However, as the child discovers that you attend to what he or she is attending to, he or she will learn to use eye gaze, reaching, and vocalizing to communicate in a more intentional manner.

Adaptations:

> *Visually Impaired:*   Provide the child with a visual impairment with several toys at a time so that he or she can explore them. Talk about the toy that the child explores. Watch the child's activities closely throughout the day and comment on what he or she appears to be attending to. The child's interest may be expressed by tactile exploration, by cocking the head or otherwise listening carefully, and so forth.

Criterion: The child's interest in objects is usually apparent through behaviors such as eye gaze, reaching, or vocalization.

AREA: 13.   Conversation Skills

BEHAVIOR: 13e.   "Requests" continued action of familiar toy, song, or activity by starting body movements, eye contact, and/or vocalization

Materials: Normal home or group care setting

Procedures and Use in Daily Routines:

Play games with the child such as "Ride a horsey" (bouncing the child on your knee) or "Pat-a-cake" (clapping hands). Stop while the game is still pleasing to the child and wait to see if he or she will signal you to continue. Signaling may be in the form of beginning to bounce in the "Ride a horsey" game, taking your hands and trying to make them clap in the "Pat-a-cake" game, and so forth. As soon as you believe the child is signaling you to continue, begin the game again. If the child makes no such signal, try to prompt one. For example, you may jiggle the child a bit rather than bouncing him or her and this may help the child to start moving. When he or she moves, begin the "Ride a horsey" bouncing game again.

Make a toy "go" by winding it up, rocking it, pushing it, and so forth. While the child is enjoying this activity, make the toy "stop" and wait to see what the child does. The child may signal you to continue the activity by looking back and forth between you and the toy, by looking at the toy and vocalizing, by pushing the toy toward you, or by some other behavior appropriate to the situation. As soon as you believe the child is signaling you to continue, immediately make the toy "go" again.

Note: A child's signals to continue may be somewhat unclear at first. It is better to assume you are getting a signal from the child when you are not than to fail to respond to an intended signal. Your responses to the child's signals will make it more likely that he or she will try to signal again the next time the game stops. After awhile you may want to delay your continuation of the activity to see if the child will give a more vigorous or clear signal. In this way you can "shape up" clear communicative signals.

Adaptations:

Hearing Impaired: Choose activities and toys that depend on movement and visual spectacles.

Visually Impaired: Choose activities and toys that depend on movement and sound.

Motor Impaired: It may be more difficult for the child with a motor impairment to "request" by moving as most children without impairments do. You will need to be especially sensitive to directed eye gaze as a communicative signal.

Criterion: Child frequently requests continued action of familiar toys, songs, or activities by starting body movements, directed eye gaze, vocalization, or other consistent communicative signals.

AREA: 13.   Conversation Skills

BEHAVIOR: 13f.   Waits for adult to take his or her "turn"

Materials: A normal home or group care environment

(continued)

Procedures and Use in Daily Routines:

Throughout the day as you interact with the child, make up "games" to play. These can be as simple as imitating something that the child does (e.g., making a particular sound, banging on the table) and waiting for the child to do it again; or as complex as Peek-a-boo or other games with words. The point is to set up a turn-taking routine. Observe to see if the child waits after his or her action so that you can take your turn.

The best way to "teach" a child to wait for you to take a turn is for you to frequently "model" this behavior. That is, you imitate the child and wait for him or her to act again; or, you put a paper between you and the child and play Peek-a-boo several times and then wait for the child to peer around and look for you. In this way, you are showing the child how to take turns and how much fun it is!

> *Note:* This activity should continue long after the child has met the criterion for passing this item, because it promotes a good social interaction and lays the foundation for the child to develop increasingly complex imitation skills. Once a turn-taking routine is established, challenge the child's imitative skills. For example, begin a game by imitating the child. Once you have each had two or three turns, do a new behavior and see if the child will imitate the new action.

Adaptations:

Visually Impaired: Vocal turn-taking is one of the easier turn-taking games to play with a child with a visual impairment. It is also possible to set up other games that involve sounds by imitating an action that the child does that makes noise.

Motor Impaired: Be creative in developing games for a child with a motor impairment. Any voluntary act (e.g., movement, vocalization, eye gaze) can constitute the child's turn. Your role is to make whatever you do on your turn interesting enough for the child to want to imitate you.

Criterion: The child waits for an adult to take his or her "turn" in an exchange. The child should pick up on the turn-taking routine and wait for the adult after only a few turns in any newly initiated game.

AREA: **13. Conversation Skills**
BEHAVIOR: 13g. Begins to listen—coordinates looking with listening

Materials: A normal home or group care environment

Procedures and Use in Daily Routines:

As you care for and interact with the child during the day, pay attention to that in which the child appears to be interested. Talk about that object or person, take the child to it, bring it to the child. Observe to see if the child maintains interest as you talk, occasionally looking back and forth between you and the object.

Begin to try to expand the child's interests. Point at or take the child up to something in which you are interested and talk about it. Watch for the child to begin listening and focusing his or her attention on that object about which you are talking.

Adaptations:

Visually Impaired: Generally, the interest of a child with a visual impairment will be directed by what is heard and touched. Hand objects to the child and talk about them as he

(continued)

or she explores them. Use the coordination of listening with exploration or other indications of attention as alternate criteria for passing this item.

Hearing Impaired: A child with residual hearing is apt to coordinate looking with listening much like a child without hearing impairments. If total communication is being used, the child will often indicate attention and "listening" by glancing back and forth between the speaker (or signer) and the object that is being discussed.

Criterion: The child occasionally coordinates looking with listening as an adult calls attention to and talks about an object, person, or event of interest.

AREA: **13.   Conversation Skills**
BEHAVIOR: 13h.   Makes requests by directing caregiver's attention

Materials: A normal home or group care environment

Procedures and Use in Daily Routines:

This is an extension of item 13d. After routines of joint attention have been established, the child will begin to deliberately direct the adult's attention by reaching out toward objects to indicate a desire for them; by looking at the adult and crying to indicate a need for comfort; by looking back and forth between the object and the adult to indicate a desire for the adult to do something with the object; and so forth. It is critical for the adult to be sensitive to these early communicative signals: giving or showing the child those items that he or she appears to be desiring, comforting when the child seems to need comfort, and so forth.

Note: If the child wants something that he or she cannot have or touch, do not ignore the communicative signal. Talk about the object to communicate your desire to share his or her interests and then distract the child with some other interesting object or interaction.

Adaptations:

Visually Impaired: The child with a visual impairment may be slow to make requests for objects because he or she may not be aware of their presence. Whenever possible, present the child with two objects so that he or she can practice making choices. For example, if the child seems bored, get two toys and place one in each hand or place both on the floor in front of the child and guide his or her hand to one and then the other. Ask, "Which one do you want?" and then talk about the one that the child chooses.

Motor Impaired: Depending on the severity of the motor impairment, the child's primary means of making requests may be limited to using eye gaze. If the child appears to be using eye gaze to direct the adult to get objects, begin training the child to use eye gaze to make choices. That is, hold up two objects (e.g., juice and cereal, a music box and a soft toy animal) and say, "What do you want?" Give the child whatever he or she looks at. Do this as much as possible throughout the day.

Criterion: The child frequently makes requests by directing the caregiver's attention through reaching, vocalizing, alternating gaze between the adult and object, and so forth.

AREA: **13. Conversation Skills**
BEHAVIOR: 13i.   Indicates "no more" and "I don't like this" by turning or pushing away

Materials: A normal home or group care environment

Procedures and Use in Daily Routines:

Usually, the indicating of preference by turning or pushing away first occurs during feedings. It is important to respond to the child's turning away as a valid communication attempt. Put words to the child's behavior (e.g., "Oh, you don't want any spinach," "No more?"). It is all right to offer the child the same item again (e.g., "Please try some spinach"), but if the child continues to indicate rejection, do not insist. It is important that the child learns that you understand and respect his or her communication.

Adaptations:

Visually Impaired: The child with a visual impairment may have to rely on smell or texture to identify foods (or other stimuli) that he or she knows are unacceptable. Give the child a chance to smell food before you put it in his or her mouth.

Motor Impaired: Some children have such severe impairments that they cannot turn away. If this is the case, be sensitive to other cues that indicate that the child is full or wishes to reject whatever you are presenting. Give words to those cues and treat them as genuine communications.

Criterion: On several occasions, the child indicates "no more" and "I don't like this" by turning his or her head or body away or by pushing what is not wanted.

AREA: **13. Conversation Skills**
BEHAVIOR: 13j.   Notices and vocalizes when primary caregiver prepares to leave

Materials: A normal home or group care environment

Procedures and Use in Daily Routines:

To facilitate the emergence of the skill of noticing and vocalizing when the primary caregiver prepares to leave, make sure the child has an opportunity to observe the routines that lead up to the person's departure. It is important for the caregiver to announce his or her intent to leave (e.g., by saying "bye, bye"; by waving) and, if the child appears distressed, to respond to the child with words and gestures of reassurance.

Note: Sometimes parents will try to "sneak" away to avoid the child's protest about their leaving. This is apt to make the child more insecure because he or she can't predict whether a parent will be there or not. It is much better to say goodbye with reassurances as necessary (keeping this to a very brief exchange) and then make a point of seeking out the child and demonstrating affection upon return.

Adaptations:

Visually Impaired: It will be harder for the child with a visual impairment to identify the parents' "going out" route. The parents should talk to the child, describing what they are doing and where they are going. A point should be made of announcing both departure and return.

(continued)

Hearing Impaired: Be sure that the child with a hearing impairment has the opportunity to see his or her primary caregiver's preparations for leaving.

Motor Impaired: When a child with a motor impairment is not mobile, he or she misses much of what goes on in a home unless the caregiver makes a point of wheeling or carrying him or her to the room where the action is taking place.

Criterion: The child usually notices and vocalizes when the primary caregiver is preparing to leave. The child's responses should occur during preparations for leaving, not just when the caregiver opens the door and steps out. Vocalization may be in the form of crying or other protest.

AREA: **13.   Conversation Skills**
BEHAVIOR: 13k.   Uses eye gaze to select other person as partner in communication exchange

Materials: A normal home or group care environment

Procedures and Use in Daily Routines:

Make a point of saying something to the child each time he or she establishes eye contact with you. If this is occurring infrequently, make a point of leaning over the child and waiting until he or she looks at you. Then begin talking. It is not necessary to talk for more than a few seconds, but try to engage the child. Do this frequently throughout the day.

Observe the child when several other people are nearby. Does he or she use eye gaze to try to engage you or one of the other people?

Adaptations:

Visually Impaired: If the child's visual impairment is significant, this item is inappropriate. Watch for other cues that the child is trying to engage someone in a communication exchange (e.g., reaching out toward a person who is talking).

Hearing Impaired: Combine gestures with speech in communication exchanges with a child with hearing impairments.

Criterion: Frequently and in a variety of settings, the child uses eye gaze to select another person as a partner in a communication exchange.

AREA: **13.   Conversation Skills**
BEHAVIOR: 13l.   Changes pitch/volume to signify intensity of desires

Materials: A normal home or group care environment

Procedures and Use in Daily Routines:

Attend to the sounds that the child makes. Early in life, a baby tends to fuss and then work into a louder, more intense cry if attention does not come. Gradually, the child learns that more intense vocalizations get quicker results and he or she begins to use the more intense vocalizations (e.g., crying, yelling) to signal an intense need or desire. In order to facilitate the child's intentional use of pitch and/or volume to indicate intensity of

(*continued*)

desire, respond differently to different kinds of vocalizations; respond especially quickly to more intense (e.g., louder, higher pitched) vocalizations.

Adaptations:

Hearing Impaired: Children with hearing impairments often change pitch and volume to indicate preference in much the same way as children without handicaps. It is also important, however, to be sensitive to communicative cues other than changes in voice (e.g., activity level, hand movements).

Criterion: The child frequently changes pitch and/or volume to signify his or her intensity of desires.

AREA: **13. Conversation Skills**
BEHAVIOR: 13m.   Raises arms to be picked up

Materials: A normal home or group care environment

Procedures and Use in Daily Routines:

When you begin to pick up the child, put your arms out and say something like, "Do you want to get up?" or "Up we go." Wait for a few seconds to see if the child will raise his or her arms toward you. If the child does not raise his or her arms, touch your hands to the child's hands and again wait a few seconds.

Observe to see if the child raises his or her arms when you come near or when you ask, "Do you want to get up?" but before you put out your arms.

Always respond to the child's outstretched arms. If you cannot pick him or her up at that moment, say something to indicate that you understand that he or she wants to be picked up, but will have to wait.

Adaptations:

Visually Impaired: Always touch your hands to the hands of a child with a visual impairment as you approach to pick him or her up. Then, lift the child's hands up toward you, let go and pick the child up. This will begin to occur naturally as the child reaches to hold on to you as you lift him or her up. Then, begin to wait to see if child will initiate holding his or her hands out to be picked up when you approach.

Motor Impaired: The child with motor impairments may not be able to raise his or her arms. Try to shape some response that is possible for the child. Ask the physical or occupational therapist for suggestions.

Criterion: The child frequently raises his or her arms to be picked up. This must occur before the adult has put out his or her arms, but may be in response to a question such as, "Do you want up?"

AREA: **13. Conversation Skills**
BEHAVIOR: 13n.   Indicates desire to "get down" or "get out" in some consistent fashion
other than fussing or crying

Materials: A normal home or group care environment

(continued)

Procedures and Use in Daily Routines:

When you are holding the child or he or she is sitting in a high chair, watch for signals that the child wants to get down or get out of whatever is confining him or her (e.g., increased restlessness, reaching for the floor, fussiness): Ask something like, "Do you want to get down?" or "Want out?" and remove the child to some other situation. Check out your interpretation of the child's behavior by his or her response to being moved (e.g., does the child seem happy or does the behavior that prompted you to move the child persist?). If getting down or getting out doesn't seem to satisfy the child, try again to determine what he or she really wants!

Note: When young children are bored or uncomfortable, they usually work through a series of behaviors that culminate in fussing or crying when the other behaviors do not "work." Try to notice cues that indicate that the child may want to get down or get out before the fussing and crying begin so that you can teach the child that behaviors other than crying are an effective means of communication.

Adaptations:

Motor Impaired: It may be particularly hard for the child with severe motor impairments to give cues, other than crying, for wanting a change. Be especially attentive to try to identify the relatively subtle cues that may be unique to each child.

Criterion: The child regularly indicates desire to "get down" or "get out" in some consistent fashion other than fussing or crying.

AREA: 13. Conversation Skills
BEHAVIOR: 13o. Plays reciprocal games (e.g., taking turns making sounds, playing the Peek-a-boo game, clapping your hands)

Materials: A normal home or group care environment

Procedures:

One of the best ways to start "games" with a young child is to pay attention to what he or she is doing, identify some simple behavior, imitate that behavior, and wait for the child to do the behavior again (see item 13f.). For example, you may imitate hitting a hand on the table for a particular sound. As the child's skills develop, make these games more complex by expanding on something that the child does rather than imitating it exactly (e.g., after several turns of each of you hitting the table once, hit it twice on your turn; after several turns of saying "baba," change to "dada").

Also, introduce turn-taking games that are not just simple imitation such as the Peek-a-boo game (e.g., your turn is saying, "Where's _____? and the child's turn is peeking around the corner of a barrier) or the Pat-a-cake game (e.g., you say all the words, but stop the hand movements at particular intervals and wait for the child to do them).

Note: Children vary as to how long it takes them to organize themselves to "take a turn." This is especially true of many youngsters with Down syndrome. The adult must learn to wait (e.g., count to 10 or 15) after doing his or her turn to allow the child time to prepare to take a turn. Timing is critical for helping a child learn to play reciprocal games.

(continued)

Use in Daily Routines:

The aforementioned games are excellent ways to entertain a child in situations where you are waiting (e.g., in the grocery store line, in a doctor's office, riding in a car).

Adaptations:

Visually Impaired: Choose games that depend on sound for their effects when playing with a child with a visual impairment.

Hearing Impaired: Choose games that depend on sight and movement for effects when playing with a child with a hearing impairment.

Motor Impaired: The more severe the motor impairment, the more difficult it will be to identify behaviors in the child's repertoire that can be incorporated into games. Create games that accommodate the child's motor capabilities. Also, be sensitive to timing. Some children with motor impairments are slow to respond. Learn to wait longer for them to take their turns.

Criterion: The child plays several reciprocal games. That is, the child will take his or her turn as soon as the adult starts the familiar game.

AREA: **13.   Conversation Skills**
BEHAVIOR: 13p.   Uses words or signs to express wants

Materials: A normal home or group care environment

Procedures and Use in Daily Routines:

Attend to the child's attempts to communicate both vocally and through gestures or signs. Try to guess from context cues what the child wants if the vocalizations are unintelligible or the gestures or signs are unclear. Check your guesses with the child (e.g., "Do you want some juice?", "Juice?") and continue guessing until you get it right. Let the child know that you respect and will respond to his or her requests. Repeating what you think the child is saying will help the child refine his or her gestures or articulation of the word.

Adaptations:

Visually Impaired: Because the child with a visual impairment cannot look at what he or she wants, it may be more difficult to guess what he or she is trying to say. Try to be particularly sensitive to other kinds of cues, such as time of day, items that are frequently associated with an ongoing activity, and so forth.

Hearing Impaired: Use signs as well as speech when communicating with the child with a hearing impairment. Your producing the correct sign for the object or event that the child wants will help the child refine his or her own signs.

Motor Impaired: If the child's motor impairments interfere with speech, work toward an alternative system of communication to supplement vocal communication. Try to determine a good indicator response (e.g., pointing, eye gaze) and encourage the child to use that response to make choices. For example, hold a glass of orange juice in one hand and a glass of milk in the other, and say, "Here's some orange juice and here's some milk. Which one do you want?" Give the child whichever he or she looks at or points toward. For further information about working toward an augmentative communication system see

(continued)

Volume 7, Number 2, of *Physical and Occupational Therapy in Pediatrics* (Summer, 1987) devoted to augmentative communication.

Criterion: The child frequently uses words or signs to express wants (or, if the child has a severe motor impairment, is able to make choices through eye gaze or other indicator response).

AREA: **13.   Conversation Skills**
BEHAVIOR: 13q.   Seeks adult's assistance in exploring the environment through vocalizations, pointing, or other communicative signals

Materials: A normal home or group care environment

Procedures and Use in Daily Routines:

Respond to the child's efforts to engage you in helping him or her explore the environment. For example, when the child points at objects, name them, give them to him or her (if appropriate), lift the child so that he or she can see them more clearly, and so forth. This can occur throughout the day as you go about your other daily activities. The child's interest and exploration will often be guided by the activities in which you are engaged.

Note: This item is one example of the child's learning to coordinate attention to objects and people. Look for other indications of this as well (e.g., the child's bringing objects to the adult, the child's sharing his or her food with the adult).

Adaptations:

Visually Impaired: Vocalization will probably be the primary way in which the child with a visual impairment tries to engage a caregiver. It is especially important to respond and to take the time necessary to help the child explore constructively. For example, if the child touches an object in an unfamiliar environment, name the object for the child and, if necessary, direct his or her attention to those features that can distinguish it for the child (e.g., "That's a stool. Can you find it's legs? Feel how wide it is. Sometimes people rest their feet on it. Let me show you.").

Hearing Impaired: Be especially attentive to the gestures of a child with hearing impairments.

Motor Impaired: If a child has severe motor impairments, he or she may be limited to a few sounds and have no pointing responses. Be especially attentive to where the child looks as an indication of his or her interests (as in item 13k.). Try to expand the child's ability to signal that he or she wants to communicate with you. This may be done by selectively responding to different vocalizations so that one is shaped up to mean, "Hey you, pay attention to where I am looking and help me learn more about it"; or, perhaps, by developing a switch that the child can operate that rings a bell or turns on a light to attract the adult's attention.

Criterion: The child regularly engages the caregiver's assistance in exploring the environment through vocalizations, pointing, or other clear communicative signals.

AREA: **13.   Conversation Skills**
BEHAVIOR: 13r.   Uses inflection pattern(s) when vocalizing (or uses
gestures as if signing)

Materials: A normal home or group care environment

___

Procedures and Use in Daily Routines:

> Frequently talk to the child and pay attention to his or her vocalizations. Listen for the beginnings of vocalizations that sound like sentences even though no individual words can be understood. Respond to these vocalizations as if they were sentences. You can do this by repeating back to the child what you heard, by saying in clearly articulated words what you thought the child might be saying under these circumstances, by answering as if the child said a particular comment, and so forth. Often the child is not particularly interested in the content of what you say, but is very interested in the fact that you respond as if having a conversation. Your talking to the child gives more examples of the inflection patterns he or she is learning.

Adaptations:

> *Hearing Impaired:*   Seek the advice of the speech therapist as to the optimal loudness and pitch for speaking to the child with a hearing impairment and provide models of inflection patterns. Also, sign as you speak if this has been recommended by the therapist. For some children with hearing impairments, normal inflection patterns will not develop or will develop very slowly. Children who have been exposed to signing may begin to "babble" with signs (i.e., gesturing as if signing, although no standard signs are discernible). This behavior can receive credit for this item.

> *Motor Impaired:*   Some children with severe motor impairments will not be able to vocalize well enough to develop inflection patterns. If this is true, move on to other items in the sequence.

___

Criterion: The child routinely uses inflection pattern(s) when vocalizing.

AREA: **13.   Conversation Skills**
BEHAVIOR: 13s.   Greets familiar people with an appropriate vocalization or sign

Materials: A normal home or group care environment

___

Procedures and Use in Daily Routines:

> Always greet the child and others in an appropriate fashion (e.g., "Good morning, Bobby," "Hi, Bobby"). Encourage the child to greet others as well (e.g., "Say hi to Mary"), but do not repeat instructions to greet others several times. The child will learn best by having those whom he or she greets respond appropriately (e.g., greet the child, give him or her a hug).

Adaptations:

> *Visually Impaired:*   If the child with a visual impairment does not see sufficiently well to identify a person or to know a new person is entering the room, it is important to let him or her know who is approaching as well as to greet that person. This will help the child understand the function of a greeting.

___

(continued)

Hearing Impaired: Always use signs along with words with a child with a hearing impairment, so that he or she can learn the appropriate greeting signs. Teach the other adults and children in this child's environment to sign as well as to say their greetings.

Motor Impaired: If the child's motor impairment limits his or her speech, try to identify a vocalization, a gesture, or some other behavior that can be shaped to be a greeting. Let others in the environment know that this is the child's greeting, so that they can respond appropriately to it.

Criterion: The child frequently greets familiar people with an appropriate vocalizations or sign. This should be observed with several individuals in addition to the immediate family.

AREA: **13.   Conversation Skills**
BEHAVIOR: 13t.   Directs caregiver to provide information through questioning look, vocal inflection, and/or words

Materials: A normal home or group care environment

Procedures and Use in Daily Routines:

Respond to the child's attempts to communicate. Try to determine what he or she is trying to tell you both through the vocalizations and gestures as well as through being aware of objects and events in the environment. Particularly be sensitive to the child's attempts to elicit more information. Listen for the inflection pattern of a question and/or a word (e.g., "That?" + a pointing finger = "What's that?"); also look for a puzzled look on the child's face as he or she looks to you. Answer the question you think the child is asking, or, repeat the question that you think the child is asking and then answer it. Let the child know that you are interested in his or her questions!

Adaptations:

Hearing Impaired: Use gestures/signs as you talk to the child with a hearing impairment. Model asking questions. Look for gestures/signs that suggest questions.

Motor Impaired: When a child has severe limitations of pointing and speech, it may be necessary to be particularly attentive to quizzical looks.

Criterion: The child directs caregiver to provide information through questioning look, vocal inflection, or words on a daily basis.

AREA: **13.   Conversation Skills**
BEHAVIOR: 13u.   Uses inflection patterns in a sentence with 1 or 2 understandable words (or mixes recognizable signs in with other gestures)

Materials: A normal home or group care environment

Procedures and Use in Daily Routines:

After a child has begun to vocalize inflection patterns (something that sounds like a sentence), it will usually not be long until you are able to distinguish one or more words

---

(continued)

in such a vocalization. Listen carefully, try to extract the child's meaning and respond appropriately.

Adaptations:

Hearing Impaired: With a child with a hearing impairment, pay particular attention to his or her words in isolation as well as to the child's attempts to communicate through gestures and signs. Respond appropriately. Credit signs mixed in with other gestures if the child is being exposed to signs.

Motor Impaired: If the child with motor impairments is unable to use inflection patterns, he or she may still use isolated words. Try to ascertain the child's meaning and respond appropriately. Continue to work toward augmentative communication, if appropriate, and skip this item.

Criterion: The child often uses inflection patterns in a sentence with 1 or 2 understandable words.

AREA: **13.   Conversation Skills**
BEHAVIOR: 13v.   Experiments with 2-word utterances (2-sign gestures) to achieve specific goals (e.g., "Me go," "Doggie up," "Daddy sit")

Materials: A normal home or group care environment

Procedures and Use in Daily Routines:

When the child is making one-word utterances to communicate, "expand" the child's statement with a 2- or 3-word sentence. For example, if the child looks at you and says, "Sit," sit down, and as you do so say, "Daddy sit down." As the child begins to put 2 words together, expand with 3- and 4-word sentences. (You will probably do this automatically if you are spending much time alone with the child. It becomes particularly important to think about it, however, if you are caring for the child in a group care environment where it is easy to talk "over" the children to other adults.)

Adaptations:

Hearing Impaired: Communicate with the child with a hearing impairment using both speech and signs. The child is likely to combine 2 signs before combining 2 words. Combined signs meets the criterion for this item.

Motor Impaired: If the child with motor impairments is not able to talk, but is using an augmentative communication device, any procedure that results in achieving specific goals beyond the simple request for an object meets the criterion for this item. That is, pointing to a picture of a glass to get a drink *would not* meet this criterion, but pointing to 2 pictures (e.g., mama + glass, me + glass) *would* meet this criterion. Also, this criterion would be met by selecting 1 picture that communicates 2 ideas (e.g., the board includes pictures of glasses with different colored liquids and the child chooses the one that is orange to communicate that he or she wants orange juice).

Criterion: The child frequently experiments with 2-word utterances (signed or spoken) to achieve specific goals (or communicates 2 ideas through an augmentative communication device).

AREA: 13.   Conversation Skills

BEHAVIOR: 13w.   Spontaneously says (or signs) familiar greetings and farewells at appropriate times

Materials: A normal home or group care environment

Procedures and Use in Daily Routines:

Model appropriate greetings and farewells whenever another person comes into the room, when meeting someone outside the home, when someone leaves, and so forth. Encourage the child to imitate, but do not pressure him or her to do so. The best encouragement will be the response of others when the child does say (or sign or gesture) "Hi," "Bye-bye," and so forth.

Note: In group care environments, it is appropriate to occasionally encourage the group to imitate the caregiver in greetings and farewells when a visitor comes to visit (e.g., "Let's say it all together, 'Good morning, Mr. Edwards.' "). There are also songs that children can sing that include such greetings (e.g., "Where is thumbkin . . . Here I am . . . How are you today, sir? Very well, thank you, ...").

Adaptations:

Visually Impaired: Continue to let the child with a visual impairment know when someone is approaching that should be greeted.

Hearing Impaired: Encourage the child with hearing impairments to sign greetings and farewells, as well as speaking them. Teach friends and family to also sign greetings and farewells to the child as well as to talk to him or her.

Motor Impaired: Be sure to continue making appropriate greetings and farewells to the child with motor impairments whether he or she can speak or not. Try to identify some behaviors that the child can use for greetings and farewells if neither speech nor common gestures are possible.

Criterion: The child spontaneously says (or signs) familiar greetings and farewells at appropriate times.

AREA: 13.   Conversation Skills

BEHAVIOR: 13x.   Says (or signs) "no" to protest when something is taken away

Materials: A normal home or group care environment

Procedures and Use in Daily Routines:

Do not set up an artificial situation to teach or assess this skill. Simply observe what the child does in situations where something must be taken from him or her or where other children are present and the normal competition for toys is taking place. Let the child know that you have heard and are sympathetic to his or her protest (e.g., "Mary, give the ball back to Greg. He was playing with it."), although in some cases the child must still be parted from the object in question (e.g., "I know you want the ball, but we must put it away now and have dinner").

(continued)

Adaptations:

Hearing Impaired: Sign and say "no" in appropriate situations, so that the child with a hearing impairment has the experience of both symbols. Respect the child's signing "no" as much as his or her speech and be sure that others in the environment recognize the sign as well.

Motor Impaired: If the child's motor impairment interferes with his or her speech, find an alternative behavior that can be used to indicate "no" or "I don't like that." Help the child learn to use this behavior appropriately.

Criterion: The child frequently says or signs "no" to protest when something is taken away.

AREA: **13. Conversation Skills**
BEHAVIOR: 13y. Spontaneously uses words (or signs) in pretend play

Materials: A normal home or group care environment

Procedures:

Frequently engage in pretend play with the child. For example, talk for dolls, stuffed animals, or puppets; have them engage in activities that are familiar to the child (e.g., eating, going to bed, taking a bath); have them ask the child questions or otherwise involve the child in the play; have pretend tea parties where you and the child share "cookies and juice" from empty containers; build houses and roads with blocks and talk about them; take animals or other toys for rides in trucks or cars and talk about where they are going, whom they will visit, what they will do, and so forth.

Use in Daily Routines:

Pretend play is an effective way to entertain a child while waiting, riding in a car, or while doing routine activities around the house. It is an excellent way for the child to hear new words and to think about their meanings.

Adaptations:

Visually Impaired: Much of pretend play is built upon observations of the behavior of others; "pretending" is based on acting as if something is present when you cannot see it or acting as if one object is really something else. Visual images are important in such play. The child with severe visual impairments may be slow to develop complex pretend play. Talking and sound become even more critical elements. Reading stories to the child and then recreating the characters from the stories is a good way to stimulate pretend play. For example, after reading a story about a big bad wolf, you might play a game in which you say, "I'm the big bad wolf and I'm going to catch you. You'd better get away" or "Are you the big bad wolf? I had better run away."

Hearing Impaired: Use both signs and speech in pretend play with a child with a hearing impairment.

Motor Impaired: Motor impairments may limit both the child's ability to speak and the extent to which he or she can be motorically involved with pretend play. Involve the child as much as possible.

Criterion: The child spontaneously uses words (or signs) in pretend play. These should not just be immediate imitation of what a partner has said, but an integral part of the child's play.

AREA: **13. Conversation Skills**

BEHAVIOR: 13z.   Uses word (or sign) combinations to describe remote event

BEHAVIOR: 13aa.   Uses word(s) (or sign[s]) to request action

BEHAVIOR: 13bb.   Answers simple questions with a verbal response, gesture, or sign

Materials: A normal home or group care environment

Procedures and Use in Daily Routines:

Frequently engage in conversations with the child. Talk about what the child is doing or what he or she did earlier in the day. Listen carefully to what the child tries to say. Repeat back what you think you understand to check it out with the child. Ask the child questions about what he or she wants, what he or she is doing, and so forth. Listen for the different kinds of communications listed above:

z.   Does the child combine 2 or more words or signs to describe something that happened in another room or earlier in the day?

aa.   Does the child request that you do something with words or signs (e.g., "Give ball," "Come," "Push swing")?

bb.   Does the child answer simple questions with 1 or 2 words or gestures (e.g., "Where's Mommy?", "What is that?")?

Adaptations:

Hearing Impaired: Sign and/or gesture as well as speak to the child with hearing impairments. Respond to the child's communications in whatever form.

Motor Impaired: Help facilitate augmentative communication with the child with motor impairments if necessary.

Criterion for item 13z.:   The child occasionally uses word or sign combinations to describe remote events.

Criterion for item 13aa.:   The child uses words or signs to request at least 3 different actions.

Criterion for item 13bb.:   The child regularly answers simple questions with a verbal response or gesture.

14.

Self-Direction

BETWEEN 12 AND 24 months of age, it becomes increasingly important for children to be allowed to initiate and direct their own activities. This aspect of development is often overlooked in curricula and too much emphasis is frequently put on adult-directed learning. In fact, self-initiated activity is sometimes regarded with negativism and is considered to be a nuisance in intervention programs, rather than as a necessary component of active learning.

The primary prerequisite for beginning items in this sequence is some ability to communicate on the part of the child. This can be a very simple form of communication, such as making noises, pointing, moving toward an activity or item, or merely using eye gaze to indicate a preference or choice.

Several items in this sequence require motor responses that are necessary for active exploration and self-initiated movement away from the caregiver. If children with motor impairments are unable to make these responses, the focus will have to be on helping them comfortably separate from their primary caregiver and making choices between adult-determined activities. For example, a child may be shown two pictures, one of an indoor play area and the other of a swing, and asked if he or she wants to play inside or go outside and swing (i.e., pointing to the appropriate picture as the question is asked). Thus, the child is choosing his or her next activity by pointing to or looking at one of the pictures.

Although not stressed in the items themselves, it should be recognized that learning to deal with rules is a part of self-direction. While encouraging independence, curiosity, and exploration, the caregiver should also provide firm boundaries with clear consequences for transgressing them. Children with disabilities frequently suffer from overindulgence and/or overprotection. Both of these tendencies should be avoided.

14. Self-Direction

a. Moves away from the primary caregiver who is in same room

b. Moves partially out of the primary caregiver's sight for short periods of play

c. Makes choices (e.g., has preferred toys, foods, clothes. storybooks)

d. Gets toys with which to play from a box or shelf of toys

e. Plays alone with toys for 15 minutes
f. Approaches peer or adult to initiate play
g. Explores

h. Resists attempts from others to assist with feeding
i. "Asks" for snacks or drinks

AREA: **14.   Self-Direction**

BEHAVIOR: 14a.   Moves away from the primary caregiver who is in same room

Materials: A variety of toys or objects with which the child likes to play

Procedures:

Set up the room so that there are interesting and enticing activities or toys in various parts of the room that are away from where the primary caregiver and child are located.

Engage the primary caregiver in conversation, while basically leaving the child alone close to the interesting and enticing new toys or activities.

Watch the child. If he or she does not move to engage in play activities, have another adult or child begin to interact with the objects and/or encourage the child to join in the fun.

Use in Daily Routines:

Parents will appreciate suggestions that facilitate this move toward independence at home. They can make toys available in a corner of a room where they are working or relaxing and encourage play there. Teachers can do the same in a classroom setting.

Adaptations:

Visually Impaired: Try to attract the child with a visual impairment away from his or her primary caregiver by activating a noisy toy in another part of the room, at first just a few feet away from the caregiver and then, later, further away. Ask the caregiver to talk to the child as he or she plays, to assure him or her of the caregiver's continued presence.

Motor Impaired: Be sure to adapt ways in which a child with motor impairments can effectively move (or indicate to a caregiver that he or she wants to move) to interesting activities.

Criterion: The child moves away from the primary caregiver to play when attractive toys are available in another location.

AREA: **14.   Self-Direction**

BEHAVIOR: 14b.   Moves partially out of the primary caregiver's sight for
short periods of play

Materials: A variety of toys or objects with which the child likes to play

Procedures:

Set up an area nearby, but away from the immediate presence of the primary caregiver (e.g., just inside the doorway to another room, in an alcove, on the other side of a room divider), that contains something of interest to the child.

Engage the primary caregiver in conversation, while basically leaving the child alone. Do keep an eye on him or her, however.

If the child does not move to engage in the activity that was set up away from the caregiver, point out the items that are available to play with or have another adult or child act upon object(s) in the nearby area and entice the child to join in the fun.

(continued)

Use in Daily Routines:

Children will be torn between wanting to be close to the caregiver and wanting to play with his or her favorite toys or objects that are now in different locations. Be sure to encourage the child to move toward the new play areas and to reinforce "nice playing" when it occurs alone for a few minutes at a time.

Adaptations:

Visually Impaired: It will be necessary for an adult to activate noisy toys with which the child with the visual impairment can play that are located some distance away from the primary caregiver. By activating the toys, the child will become aware of the new, interesting and enticing toys. Have the caregiver continue to talk to the child while moving away to encourage the child and help him or her to understand what he or she is doing.

Motor Impaired: Be sure to make adaptations for the child with motor impairments, so that he or she can effectively move or indicate a desire to be moved to various activities.

Criterion: The child moves partially out of the primary caregiver's sight for short periods of play.

AREA: 14. Self-Direction
BEHAVIOR: 14c. Makes choices (e.g., has preferred toys, foods, clothes, storybooks)

Materials: Two or more of preferred objects to be presented to the child (e.g., toys, shirts when dressing, books when reading)

Procedures:

Provide the child with many opportunities to make choices. Rather than just giving the child a toy, put 2 toys (or 2 choices of food at a meal; 2 shirts when dressing) in front of him or her and ask which one he or she wants. Encourage the child to respond in any way he or she can (e.g., visually, verbally, physically).

When the child indicates a choice, be sure to let him or her have it, and verbalize the choice that was made (e.g., "Oh, you want the _____"). It is possible to insist on a choice by simply waiting until the child looks at or reaches for one of the items, then giving that one.

To be sure the child is actually choosing, however, select items for which the child has always shown strong and opposite reactions (e.g., banana pudding and spinach, a favorite toy and an uninteresting toy), and after a series of such choices (e.g., 8–10), jokingly offer the item not chosen.

Use in Daily Routines:

Encourage choice-making in dressing, eating, and play activities every day. Offering choices teaches the child that he or she can have some control over his or her significant events. Sometimes children will have to be encouraged to point out which food they "want first," so they don't inadvertently learn that they only have to eat items of which they are especially fond.

Adaptations:

Visually Impaired: The child with a visual impairment should be encouraged to taste foods, feel clothing (e.g., texture, long vs. short sleeves/legs), and touch toys to assist him or her in choosing items that he or she prefers.

(continued)

Motor Impaired: For the child with severe motor impairments and limitations, this item provides a good opportunity to teach and reinforce choice-making through the use of eye gaze.

Criteria: The child shows preferences and is allowed to make choices every day, *and* either laughs or protests when a nonchosen item is given to him or her.

AREA: **14.   Self-Direction**
BEHAVIOR: 14d.   Gets toys with which to play from a box or shelf of toys

Materials: A variety of toys that are regularly kept in a toy box or on a special shelf that the child can reach

---

Procedures:

Make the child aware that toys are always available in a given place (e.g., the toy box, a shelf). When he or she is unoccupied or begins to cling, guide him or her to where the toys are kept. Encourage the child to make a choice from among the toys, then move away when he or she selects one.

If the child continues to seek interaction, encourage another choice of toys, asking, "Are you finished with the _____?", "Now what would you like, the _____?" As soon as the child begins to play alone, be sure to offer verbal praise and reassurance that you are nearby.

Use in Daily Routines:

This item is most readily done as part of normal daily activities. It can be encouraged at home or in any caregiving environment. It requires only that toys be picked up and kept in given places and that children be observed to note when they are unoccupied.

Adaptations:

Visually Impaired: The child with a visual impairment will need to be guided to these areas initially and taught to feel physical attributes that signify being in the right place (e.g., a row of thumb tacks embedded in the edge of the shelf; a special edge or handle on the box).

Motor Impaired: For the child with motor impairments, it is especially important to make toys accessible or to provide physical assistance, so that the child has regular opportunities to get objects and to make choices.

Criterion: The child gets toys by him- or herself with which he or she can play, from a box or shelf where they are regularly kept.

AREA: **14.   Self-Direction**
BEHAVIOR: 14e.   Plays alone with toys for 15 minutes

Materials: A variety of toys or objects that will be selected by the child for play

---

Procedures and Use in Daily Routines:

Set up an area with a few toys or objects that are interesting to the child. Be sure that he or she is comfortable (e.g., in a good position if a physical disability is present).

(continued)

Give the child opportunities to play with these toys alone in this selected place, where he or she can be checked every few minutes. Start the child playing and then withdraw to the next room or become involved in another activity in the same room (e.g., reading, writing notes).

Be sure to "look in" and offer verbal reinforcement for "good playing" every few minutes. Be careful to reinforce his or her playing only when it is actually occurring, so that the child does not merely sit idle. If he or she is found to be idle or stressed, help him or her to redirect to another activity or temporarily move the child back into your proximity.

Notes: If self-stimulatory behaviors are observed during free play, search for more responsive and interesting toys and, if necessary, increase adult interaction. The adult should give attention after a short period of non–self-stimulatory behavior, rather than at the point that the self-stimulating behaviors occur.

Adaptations:

None are necessary.

Criterion: The child plays alone for 15 or more minutes, several times a week.

AREA: **14.   Self-Direction**
BEHAVIOR: 14f.   Approaches peer or adult to initiate play

Materials: None required

Procedures:

Watch for the child to seek interactions that will result in play (e.g., bringing toys to share, taking your hand to lead you to a play activity). These are early attempts to determine what and with whom he or she wants to play. Reinforce this activity by asking, "Do you want to _____?" or "Shall we play with the _____?", then allow the child to direct the sharing/playing roles of the two of you for a few minutes.

Use in Daily Routines:

Initiating play is a normal daily activity for children who are more than 18 months old. Allow them to lead in the selection of play activities. Reinforce them for staying occupied with given activities after they have chosen them. This will help them to increase their ability to stay with given tasks.

Adaptations:

Visually Impaired: When a child has a visual impairment, it is particularly important to reinforce his or her attempts to direct the course of interactive activities. Be sure to say, for example, "I'm really glad you want to play with me," when approached by the child.

Criterion: The child approaches a peer or an adult to initiate play at least once a day.

AREA: **14.   Self-Direction**
BEHAVIOR: 14g.   Explores

Materials: A variety of natural environments

(continued)

Procedures:

After child-proofing the house, encourage the child to explore by placing his or her favorite toys in unfamiliar places or by putting particularly interesting new toys or materials in corners, under tables, in accessible drawers, or in other places that the child usually does not go. At first, show the child the object and where you are placing it; later, simply place it so that it is partially visible and will invite exploration.

Take the child with you when you shop, visit friends, or go into a new room or area. If the child can move about, encourage him or her to investigate the new environment (see Note). If necessary, help the child explore a new environment; however, fade your presence as soon as possible.

Note: Be sure to be alert to potential hazards before allowing the child the freedom to explore.

Use in Daily Routines:

Exploring can be encouraged anywhere, but be very alert to potential sources of danger. Children can be allowed to explore, with guidance, in public buildings, shopping malls, parks, and many other places other than the home.

Adaptations:

Visually Impaired: For a child with a serious visual impairment or blindness, more adult involvement will be necessary to encourage movement away from the familiar. Begin with exploring contents of boxes that are clearly distinguishable by shape and texture, then go to a part of the room away from the child. Make noise with a toy and call to the child. When he or she comes, help him or her feel and manipulate the toy and the environment while you talk about it (e.g., "This is the corner, feel how the walls come together. Now, can you find the chair? Reach behind you."). Try to watch the child as he or she begins to explore, so that you can talk about what he or she is experiencing. Help him or her understand this new experience.

Motor Impaired: If the child with motor impairments cannot move independently, place him or her in an area near something of interest, and frequently check back with him or her. If the child can use his or her hands, present a variety of containers, some familiar and some unfamiliar, with different toys in them. Credit the child for choosing a new container and exploring the contents.

Criterion: The child explores his or her environment, both at home and away from home.

AREA: **14.   Self-Direction**
BEHAVIOR: 14h.   Resists attempts from others to assist with feeding

Materials: Normal mealtime foods or mid-day snacks

Procedures:

There is a fine line between the point in time when a child really needs assistance with feeding and when it saves the caregiver time and minimizes mess to continue providing this help. At some time it is appropriate for the child to resist being helped—even if he or she is somewhat slow and messy. Reinforce these attempts to do activities independently. Make sure that foods can be easily picked up and utensils (e.g., spoon, fork) are appropriate for the child's physical capabilities.

(continued)

It is also normal for the child to tire of his or her attempts to feed him- or herself and to suddenly want help. This is an important activity in the early transition from dependence to independence.

Use in Daily Routines:

Resisting assistance in feeding is a natural part of a child's development when he or she is seeking to become independent. Be tolerant and remember that it represents a step toward independent feeding.

Adaptations:

Visually Impaired: Special spoons and dishes with sides against which children can scoop their food are helpful for children with visual impairments. These utensils can be particularly helpful to children with visual impairment when they are learning to feed themselves.

Motor Impaired: If a child has a physical impairment that affects both his or her hands and arms, a physical or occupational therapist will be helpful in properly adapting eating utensils.

Criterion: The child resists attempts from others to feed him or her, so that self-feeding can be attempted.

AREA: **14. Self-Direction**
BEHAVIOR: 14i. "Asks" for snacks or drinks

Materials: Foods and drinks normally provided as snacks

Procedures:

Put snacks (e.g., fruit, cereal) out of the child's reach, but where they can easily be seen by the child. You may want to do this only once or twice between regular mealtimes. Do not offer the snacks to the child, but rather, wait for him or her to clearly indicate that a snack and/or a drink is wanted.

Be sure to respond to appropriate verbal or gestural communication from the child, but do not respond to whining, tugging at your clothes, or other inappropriate behaviors that a child might use when trying to get a snack.

Use in Daily Routines:

Requesting is a normal daily routine. Whether you are working with one child or several, wait for one to "ask" for a snack or if it's "snack time." Point out to others that "_____ asked for a snack," and ask, "Does anyone else want one?" This will help children to learn to ask for items that they want.

Adaptations:

Hearing Impaired: A child with a hearing impairment or language delay should be encouraged to use gestures and to give a "sign" when he or she wants a snack.

Motor Impaired: Special attention will have to be paid to a child with motor impairments or severe language delays. His or her attempt to be self-directive in asking for a snack or a drink will frequently be more subtle than attempts made by other children. It is important to regularly respond to these requests.

Criterion: The child asks for snacks or drinks once a day.

15.

Social Skills

L EARNING TO ENGAGE in reciprocal social interactions is a critical aspect of devel-opment. Parents and caregivers are eager to see young children comforted by and responsive to their interactions. Thus, it is distressing when children with disabilities are delayed in their ability to reinforce the interactions of caregivers and peers through smiling, laughing, game playing, and the like. Lack of development of social skills often makes it difficult for a caregiver to maintain the personal motivation to work with a child in other developmental areas.

In developing an intervention plan, the interaction between the caregiver and the child should be a primary focus. In the birth to 12-month period, one must be particularly aware of the need to "orchestrate" interactions so that appropriate turn-taking occurs. For example, many children with disabilities take considerably longer than usual to respond to social overtures on the part of caregivers. It is important to be patient and to look for smiles, waves, or other appropriate responses to stimulation that may be offered even after lengthy delays, which are generally not expected of children without disabilities.

The interventionist may need to help family members and caregivers modify their rate or intensity of responding to young children with disabilities. With some children who have severe motor impairments, it may even be necessary to help the caregiver identify facial expressions that are the functional equivalent of smiles or indications of responsiveness, even though they may not look like the smiles or re-sponses of other children.

During the 12- to 24-month developmental period, emphasis should shift to helping children initiate social interactions and respond to social overtures of peers and a broader range of adults.

15.   Social Skills

a.   Stops crying when sees (or touches) bottle or breast

b.   Can be comforted by talking to, hold-ing, or rocking

c.   Smiles to auditory and tactile stimula-tion

d.   Smiles reciprocally

e.   Smiles at familiar person

f.   Smiles at mirror image (omit for children with significant visual impairments)

g.   Tries to attract attention by making sounds, smiling, eye contact, or body language

h. Responds differently to family members and strangers (same as item 5b.)

i. Participates in simple games

j. Repeats activity that elicits laughter from observer(s)

k. Initiates game-playing

l. "Gives" items to others upon request (same as item 12h.)

m. Spontaneously shares with adults

n. Shows affection (e.g., hugs, kisses)

o. Tries to please others

p. Plays alongside other children—some exchange of toys

q. Provides "help" in simple household tasks—imitates adults

r. "Performs" for others

s. Tries to comfort others in distress

t. Spontaneously shares with peers

AREA: **15. Social Skills**
BEHAVIOR: 15a. Stops crying when sees (or touches) bottle or breast

Materials: Baby's bottle or mother's breast (feeding time)

Procedures:

Mother or caregiver should give the child ample time to see the bottle or breast before feeding begins.

Observe to see if the child quiets when he or she sees that he or she is about to be fed. Try to get the child's attention by briefly holding the bottle in his or her line of sight before presenting it.

Notes: The criterion on this item is not a prerequisite for proceeding through the remainder of the sequence. This item is primarily important because it helps the child establish connections between his or her communicating a need (i.e., through crying), a person responding to that need, and the child's changing his or her communication (i.e., through ceasing to cry).

Use in Daily Routines:

Opportunities to work on this behavior will occur naturally when the young child is hungry. Use these times to communicate with the child that feeding is about to begin.

Adaptations:

Visually Impaired: For the child with a visual impairment, talk about the bottle or breast and touch it to the child's hand prior to putting it in his or her mouth.

Criterion: The child stops crying upon seeing or touching the bottle or breast.

AREA: **15. Social Skills**
BEHAVIOR: 15b. Can be comforted by talking to, holding, or rocking

Materials: None required, but a small blanket may be helpful

Procedures:

When a child shows distress and crying, try to comfort him or her by, first, talking softly to the child without touching him or her or picking him or her up.

If the child does not quiet in response to talking, touch him or her gently while continuing to speak softly.

If the child is still showing distress, pick him or her up and hold him or her gently, but restraining the child from a great deal of body movement—especially by holding the child's arm folded across his or her body. Some children respond well to being swaddled in a small blanket.

If the child is still not comforted, rock him or her while holding him or her swaddled in the blanket.

Notes: Be sure to try comforting the child by going through the aforementioned steps in the order in which they are presented in this item. Offer minimal assistance to the child in the first steps and allow him or her to assist in comforting him- or herself.

(continued)

Use in Daily Routines:

It is important to comfort a child fairly quickly when distress is noted. It is important for the child to learn that help will come soon. However, it is also important to be responsive to behaviors other than crying or the child may learn that the only way to get attention is through crying.

Adaptations:

None are necessary.

Criterion: Children are very different in the way in which they show distress and respond to comforting. There is no criterion to be met before other items can be worked on, but try to quiet the child with as little intrusion on your part as possible. Do respond to the child's distress without too much delay though!

AREA: **15.   Social Skills**
BEHAVIOR: 15c.   Smiles to auditory and tactile stimulation

Materials: None required

Procedures and Use in Daily Routines:

Play with the child, making funny noises with your mouth, tickling him or her, blowing on his or her tummy, and so on. Do this as part of your normal caregiving routine as well as during special "play times" during the day.

When the child begins to smile, be sure to let him or her know you like the smile by changing your voice, facial expression, or other stimulation.

Note: Work on items 15c. and 15d. simultaneously.

Adaptations:

None are necessary.

Criterion: This activity can go on through early childhood. Look for smiling and laughter that appears to be contingent upon the stimulation. It should occur quite regularly.

AREA: **15.   Social Skills**
BEHAVIOR: 15d.   Smiles reciprocally

Materials: None required

Procedures and Use in Daily Routines:

The first smiles of a child appear to be responses to internal events, such as "feelings of satisfaction," and so forth, rather than responses to social events. It is your smiling at the child and your response to the child when he or she smiles that creates social interactions.

In all caregiving activities, it is very important to talk to the child and to smile often. Try to maintain eye contact with the child (even if he or she is diagnosed as "cor-

---

(*continued*)

tically blind," since sometimes that diagnosis is faulty) and provide physical contact (e.g., holding, stroking).

When smiles begin to occur, take note of what you were doing that seemed to promote smiling and respond with enthusiasm to the smile! Make it clear to the child by the change in your tone of voice, a hug, a bounce, and so on, that you like his or her smiling.

Watch briefly for the child to smile when he or she sees or hears you or any other person, before offering any tactile stimulation or picking him or her up.

Note: Work on items 15c. and 15d. simultaneously.

Adaptations:

Visually Impaired: A child with a visual impairment will learn to respond with a smile in response to hearing a familiar person's voice. Be sure to frequently talk to the child.

Criterion: Smiling in response to another person's smile is almost always an adaptive behavior. Look for smiling in response to your interaction with the child on a daily basis.

AREA: **15. Social Skills**
BEHAVIOR: 15e. Smiles at familiar person

Materials: None required

Procedures:

This is a difficult item to teach, but it is an important marker of developmental progress. A good way to promote its development is to ensure that the child has a small number of primary caregivers who regularly interact with him or her and who consistently reinforce social responses.

It is also important that the child has normal contact with a variety of strangers (e.g., in the grocery store, at church) whenever feasible.

The essence of this item is that the child smiles in recognition of a familiar person and does not smile to a stranger. Or the child smiles in a clearly different fashion to strangers versus familiar people (e.g., the child may smile equally often to both, but the smile in response to the stranger is preceded by a long pause in which the child seems to "study" the person, whereas the smile to the familiar person is more spontaneous). Use naturally occurring situations (e.g., return of parent after babysitting) to score.

Use in Daily Routines:

Parents and caregivers should be quite vocal and show happiness when seeing the child after a period of separation. Play the "Hi. How are you?" game for a few minutes after naps and periods of separation (e.g., when picking the child up from nursery or preschool).

Adaptations:

Visually Impaired: For a child with a visual impairment, it is important that the primary caregiver provide a great deal of tactile stimulation (e.g., stroking, cuddling) as well as talking in order to increase the number of associations that the child has with that person.

Criterion: The child shows a different smiling response to a familiar person than he or she does to an unfamiliar person.

AREA: **15. Social Skills**

BEHAVIOR: 15f.   Smiles at mirror image (omit for children with significant
visual impairments)

Materials: Mirror (8″ × 10″ or larger)

Procedures:

Place a mirror in front of the child in a position that allows the child to see him- or herself, but not you. Observe the child's reactions.

If the child does not smile upon seeing him- or herself in the mirror, do something with the child in front of the mirror that usually elicits smiles (e.g., tickle, play the peek-a-boo game, look over top of the mirror, let the child see your smiling face in the mirror). Observe the child's response to seeing him- or herself smile. Take the mirror away for a few seconds and then repeat the activity. Make a game of this activity with the child.

Note: Omit this item for children with significant visual impairments.

Use in Daily Routines:

This activity can be played in front of any mirror in the home. Pick the child up and move him or her away from and in front of the mirror, saying, "Who's that?" or "There's _____!"

Adaptations:

None are necessary for children with motor or hearing impairments.

Criterion: The child smiles when his or her image becomes visible in the mirror.

AREA: **15. Social Skills**

BEHAVIOR: 15g.   Tries to attract attention by making sounds, smiling, eye contact,
or body language

Materials: None required

Procedures:

The behavior of trying to attract attention is most easily observed in natural settings, particularly in situations where adults are interacting with one another and a child might feel that he or she is being ignored. The child may look to adults as they speak, wave his or her hands, or vocalize. When one of the adults looks at the child, the child is likely to smile.

When this occurs, reinforce the child by smiling back and attending to him or her for a few minutes, especially if the child has a physical disability and cannot get attention in more active ways.

After the child is smiling regularly in response to the smiles of his or her primary caregivers, deliberately approach the child with a neutral face and without talking or establishing eye contact, but wait for the child to smile before interacting with him or her. After he or she does smile or attempt to attract your attention, smile in return and react naturally (e.g., "Well, hi! How are you?").

(continued)

Use in Daily Routines:

> Observe the child when he or she is on the periphery of social interactions in the home, or elsewhere. Children frequently seek recognition and opportunities to be recognized or to interact with conversing adults.

Adaptations:

> *Visually Impaired:*   Always respond to smiles with some kind of physical contact and talking with a child with a visual impairment. Say, for example, "That is a beautiful smile," as you hug him or her. Also watch for other "body language" that may indicate a desire to be picked up or attended to. Pay particular attention to hand movements, and respond in a consistent way.

> *Motor Impaired:*   Note the aforementioned suggestion under Procedures for use with children with motor impairments.

Criterion: The child tries to get the attention of others by repeating sounds, smiles, eye gaze, or motions.

AREA: **15.   Social Skills**
BEHAVIOR: 15h.   Responds differently to family members and strangers
(same as item 5b.)

Materials: A normal home or group care environment

Procedures and Use in Daily Routines:

> At home, have the child present for family activities. Everyone in the family should spend time in face-to-face contact with the child, holding, touching and or talking to him or her. Watch the child for signs of recognition of family members (usually smiles). Then, pay careful attention to what the child does when an unfamiliar person visits the home or when the child is approached by an unfamiliar person away from home. Indications of knowing the difference between family members and strangers may be in facial expression (e.g., smiling at family and "studying" strangers), in activity level (e.g., excitement or quieting), or in other behaviors. Each child tends to have his or her own unique ways of responding.

>> *Note:*   If the child is in a group care environment, it is important that it provides a consistent setting where a limited number of people provide primary care. The child may learn to respond differently to strangers who visit the child care setting, but it is more likely that he or she will simply begin responding differently to the group care provider and the family member who picks up (or drops off) him or her.

Adaptations:

> *Visually Impaired:*   It will be especially important for family members and other caregivers to talk to the child with a visual impairment while holding him or her. The child may use touch, smell, and sound to identify people.

> It may be more difficult to identify the responses of a child with a visual impairment that indicate recognition. Such a child may be less likely to smile and establish eye contact. Pay special attention to hand and other body movements that may communicate the child's feelings.

(continued)

Criterion: The child regularly responds differently to family members and strangers (or to family members and day care providers). It should be possible for two adults to agree on the response differences that were observed.

AREA: **15.   Social Skills**

BEHAVIOR: 15i.   Participates in simple games

Materials: Those appropriate for the game to be played

Procedures:

During daily activities, play 1 or 2 games. Examples of games to begin with include: Peek-a-boo, "Here comes a little bug" (i.e., "walk" your fingers up the child's arm to child's tummy and then tickle him or her), and "This little piggy went to market" (i.e., touching the toes). As you begin playing a game, try to get the child to smile or laugh.

Once the child smiles during games, try to get him or her to become more actively involved. When you play the peek-a-boo game, wait a few seconds to see if the child will try to pull off the cover or if he or she looks to one side to anticipate your reappearance.

Stop other games part way through to see if the child will try to get you to continue them to completion.

Use in Daily Routines:

This activity is most easily done during normal interactions with the child throughout the day (e.g., when changing clothes, when getting up from a nap). Do it frequently!

Adaptations:

Visually Impaired: Choose games that emphasize auditory, tactile, and kinesthetic stimulation of the child.

Hearing Impaired: Choose games that emphasize visual, tactile, and kinesthetic stimulation of the child.

Criterion: The child laughs during social interactions and tries to "participate" in the game.

AREA: **15.   Social Skills**

BEHAVIOR: 15j.   Repeats activity that elicits laughter from observer(s)

Materials: A variety of small toys with which the child likes to play

Procedures:

This item should be worked on during daily routines, rather than at a specific time that has been set aside.

Whenever the child does something amusing, laugh at him or her and watch to see if he or she repeats the activity. If the child does not spontaneously repeat an activity when you laugh at him or her, try to get the child to do it again by imitating what he or she just did or by physically assisting him or her to repeat it. If necessary, combine your laughter with clapping or some other gesture to indicate pleasure with what the child has done.

(continued)

Use in Daily Routines:

Opportunities to laugh at a child's antics are presented throughout the day. Watch for them in play (especially imitation) situations, when dressing or undressing, or when playing simple games.

Adaptations:

Hearing Impaired: If you are working with a child with a hearing impairment, it is important to touch him or her or otherwise get his or her attention and then to clap along with laughing at his or her activity.

Motor Impaired: If the child with motor impairments has very limited movement and motor control, you will need to be sensitive to subtle movements.

Criterion: The child regularly repeats activities that elicit laughter from observer(s). Observe this activity over the period of a week or two to determine whether it has actually developed.

AREA: 15. Social Skills
BEHAVIOR: 15k. Initiates game-playing

Materials: None required

Procedures:

Watch for the child's efforts to start games that you have previously played with him or her (e.g., Peek-a-boo, "Ride-a-cock-horse," "This little piggy went to market . . ." or new activities (i.e., the child may hand you toys, showing that he or she wants you to play with him or her).

You can increase the likelihood of the child's initiating social play by responding quickly and regularly to any of his or her efforts to draw you into play. Stopping to play for even 30 seconds will make him or her more likely to initiate game-playing in the future.

Use in Daily Routines:

The child is likely to initiate game-playing throughout the day, especially when he or she would like attention. When getting dressed or undressed, the child may present his or her feet (e.g., hoping to play "This little piggy . . .") or try to get on your foot when you are sitting cross-legged (e.g., for a ride). You can play in this manner even while carrying on a conversation with another adult!

Adaptations:

None are necessary.

Criterion: The child seeks social play several times a day.

AREA: 15. Social Skills
BEHAVIOR: 15l. "Gives" items to others upon request (same as item 12h.)

Materials: Any toys and objects that are available in the child's natural environment

(continued)

Procedures:

When feeding or playing with the child, make a point of giving him or her objects while saying, for example, "Mommy gives it to (child's name)." Then ask the child for the object, holding out your hand. If he or she does not respond, try different objects or demonstrate with another child or adult.

Notes: Vary the words used (e.g., "give," "may I have") to increase generalization. Do not force the giving; prompt by gesturing with the outreached hand. The issue here is not the communication of meaning, but the pleasure of sharing.

Use in Daily Routines:

"Requesting" is especially easy to work on while dressing (e.g., "give me the shoe, sock"—which you previously put in the child's hand) or during meals. You can also do it with blocks, pop-beads, and other small toys while playing.

Adaptations:

Visually Impaired: Touch the hand of the child with a visual impairment lightly while asking for objects. Physically prompt if that seems necessary.

Hearing Impaired: Combine words with appropriate signs or gestures to convey the message "give (it) (to) me" for a child with a hearing impairment.

Motor Impaired: Use objects the child with motor impairments is able to grasp and release easily. With a child with severe motor impairments, watch for "interest" or attempts to "give" objects to an interested party.

Criterion: The child "gives" items at least 3 or 4 times when asked to do so.

AREA: **15. Social Skills**
BEHAVIOR: 15m. Spontaneously shares with adults

Materials: None required

Procedures:

Young children frequently like to play a sharing game while eating or doing other activities with caregivers.

Offer the child a bit of cracker and then ask, "Do you want to give me a bite?" as you hand the child the cracker and lean toward him or her. Do similar actions when playing with blocks (e.g., "Do you want to give me one?" after you have given several to the child).

Wait long enough so that the child has a chance to offer items to you without being asked for them, but do ask and extend your hand for items if they are not offered. Be sure to say "thank you" each time the child gives you an item. Also, offer items to him or her in return.

Use in Daily Routines:

The sharing that is required in this item is very similar to that found in item 15l., however, here, you are trying to get the child to offer you items that are not requested. You will have to be especially alert to offers from a child that may be easy to overlook or ignore. Take the time to accept items that are offered by the child and don't forget to model

(continued)

this behavior by asking, "Do you want some _____?", while holding it out to the child fairly often.

Adaptations:

Hearing Impaired: Include signs and gestures in interactions with the child with a hearing impairment.

Motor Impaired: The child with severe motor impairments may not be able to give anything to another person. Continue to model sharing by giving the child parts of your food. Also, ask the child, "May I have some of your _____?" and look for a smile, a nod, or other indications that the child is communicating "yes." Take some for yourself and say, "Thank you."

Criterion: The child spontaneously shares, without prompting, especially when a sharing game has been initiated.

AREA: **15. Social Skills**

BEHAVIOR: 15n. Shows affection (e.g., hugs, kisses)

Materials: None required

Procedures:

Freely show affection to the child. Pat him or her gently, hug and kiss on occasion, and tell the child that you really like him or her!

After a kiss, put your cheek close to the child's mouth and ask for a kiss; if necessary, press your cheek against his or her lips and then act pleased and kiss the child again. Likewise, place the child's arms around your neck and ask for a hug. Help the child hug you, if necessary. Respond to the child with another hug and/or a kiss.

Notes: There are family and personal differences regarding the type and amount of affection that is demonstrated. These should be respected when implementing this item. The issue is to help the child learn to give and receive affection. Note other specific signs of affection that are offered by the child.

Use in Daily Routines:

There is no one right time for an activity like this. Do it whenever it feels appropriate (e.g., after a nap or bath, when playing, when picking the child up from "school" or sitter, just because he or she has "been good" for a period of time). Do it frequently!

Adaptations:

None are necessary.

Criterion: The child shows affection via hugs and kisses, or another reliable behavior, to familiar adults and peers.

AREA: **15. Social Skills**

BEHAVIOR: 15o. Tries to please others

Materials: None required

(continued)

Procedures:

The behavior of trying to please others is a natural result from items 15l., 15m., and 15n. Watch the child for the following (or similar) behaviors:

The child does an activity that has gotten a positive response earlier in the day or on previous days.
The child looks to parents or others for approval after doing a task.
The child hugs, kisses, pats, without the benefit of modeling or prompting.

Always naturally and positively respond to these overtures by the child.

Use in Daily Routines:

This behavior can be facilitated by making opportunities to share or to show affection readily available. Be alert for opportunities to let the child "help" and for demonstrations of affection. When the child "shares" or "helps," be sure to respond positively and with enthusiasm.

Adaptations:

None are necessary.

Criterion: The child tries to please others by doing actions that he or she has done in the past; then looks for approval. This behavior should be indefinitely nurtured.

AREA: **15. Social Skills**
BEHAVIOR: 15p. Plays alongside other children—some exchange of toys

Materials: Any toys that are attractive to the child

Procedures and Use in Daily Routines:

Give the child as many opportunities to be around other children as possible. Watch for:

New and different behaviors (e.g., longer or shorter attention span, more looking around) in the presence of other children, as opposed to when playing alone
Positive responses to being with other children
Play that is nondisruptive in the presence of other children (except for occasional, but not deliberately hostile, "toy snatching")
Play alongside other children that lasts for 10–15 minutes

Be sure to reinforce any of these activities, telling the child that he or she is playing nicely near others.

Play alongside other children is a very natural activity to set up at home or in another caregiving environment. Children can be positioned near each other, each with their own sets of toys. If both have some blocks, kitchen utensils, cars, books, and so on, that are different from those of the other person, exchange of items will be more likely. Don't forget to reinforce sharing!

Notes: Deliberately disruptive behavior should be dealt with by momentarily removing the child from the situation, reintroducing him or her, and then observing him or her carefully to see if the disrupting continues. If it does, you need to determine its function. Is it a reaction to another child? If so, try to assess the appropriateness of the behavior of both children relative to the situation. Is it general discomfort in any group setting? If so, try to introduce the child to a setting with just

(continued)

one other child. Is it primarily a bid for adult attention? If so, it may be helpful for the adult to try to engage that child and another in a joint activity. If nondisruptive behavior cannot be sustained without constant adult attention, it may be necessary to seek the help of a psychologist in setting up a behavior management program.

Adaptations:

Motor Impaired: If the child with motor impairments cannot sit independently, adaptive seating for the floor may be needed. Consult an occupational or physical therapist.

If the child with motor impairments cannot actively exchange toys, intervene occasionally to ask another child to trade toys with him or her.

Criterion: The child plays alongside other children for periods of at least 10 minutes, with occasional sharing of toys.

AREA: **15. Social Skills**
BEHAVIOR: 15q. Provides "help" in simple household tasks—imitates adults

Materials: None required

Procedures and Use in Daily Routines:

When doing routine jobs in the house or yard, try to think of ways in which the child can provide "help," for example:

When cleaning up after meals, let the child try to wipe off his or her own tray or the table.
Let the child have a few dishes in a pan to wash.
Let the child drop his or her dirty clothes in the hamper.
Let the child have a cloth with which to dust.

Adaptations:

Visually Impaired: Provide physical guidance to the child with a visual impairment, taking him or her through simple tasks one step at a time. Be sure to verbally describe all that you are doing.

Motor Impaired: Look for tasks for the child with motor impairments that are within his or her motor capabilities. If the child has a severe impairment, have him or her "help" by indicating choices.

Criterion: The child goes through the motion of "helping" with several different household tasks on various occasions.

AREA: **15. Social Skills**
BEHAVIOR: 15r. "Performs" for others

Materials: None required

Procedures and Use in Daily Routines:

Young children like to please adults and to "show off" for them. They will do this spontaneously, as well as upon request at times. They like, and should be encouraged, to:

(continued)

sing songs, "say" short nursery rhymes, do tricks, and generally show that they are developing skills and competencies of which they are proud. When children "perform," be sure to show excitement and to praise and applaud their efforts!

Parents like their children to "perform." This is exemplified with comments from parents, such as "Do you want to sing _____ for Grandma?", "Show _____ how you can _____.", and "Let's do our _____ trick for Daddy." These are all ways of helping children to develop this behavior.

Adaptations:

Children with visual, motor, or hearing impairments will need much encouragement and, perhaps, some assistance to "show off." Pay attention to their special needs.

Criterion: The child has been observed "performing" for others on several separate occasions.

AREA: **15.   Social Skills**
BEHAVIOR: 15s.   Tries to comfort others in distress

Materials: None required

Procedures and Use in Daily Routines:

Model "comforting" people in natural ways when they show distress (e.g., kissing hurt places; patting or hugging a crying person). Request this kind of attention from the child (e.g., ask child to "kiss it better" when you hurt your finger). Suggest that the child comfort a hurt doll or stuffed animal.

Children can also comfort each other when they bump themselves, fall down, and the like during the day. Reinforce them for doing this. Show that you appreciate the fact that they are showing concern for others.

Adaptations:

Motor Impaired: The child with severe physical impairments can comfort others and should be encouraged to do so. Watch for any attempt to comfort another person, whether spontaneously, in imitation, on request, or in compliance with a prompt.

Criterion: The child tries to comfort others in distress on several separate occasions.

AREA: **15.   Social Skills**
BEHAVIOR: 15t.   Spontaneously shares with peers

Materials: Any toys or objects with which the child enjoys playing (e.g., a telephone, dishes, tools, objects that are better used with 2 people)

Procedures and Use in Daily Routines:

Spontaneously sharing with peers is a natural activity whenever two children are playing together. Pretend kitchens and "meal preparation" items, block building, car and truck games, dolls and dresses, and playing in sand or water are all activities that facilitate sharing.

(continued)

When playing with dishes, pretend foods, clothes, and so forth, the child may take an item to another child and give it to or set it near the child—whether it is actually accepted or not. Reinforce the child for doing this (e.g., "Good sharing!", "Is [child's name] having lunch with you?", "Are you letting [child's name] help you with the dishes?").

Children frequently use a great deal of verbal jargon while doing this kind of sharing—especially as they give objects and, later, retrieve them. Thus, this offers a chance to work on early communication skills. Sharing can be facilitated by suggesting that "_____ might like to play" or by guiding a child to share items and then commenting that others like such sharing.

Don't forget to reinforce sharing when it is observed.

Adaptations:

Motor Impaired: The child with severe motor impairments may not be able to indicate a desire to share. Encourage the child to share by asking questions such as, "Would you like to share some of your juice with Mary?" Praise any indication of a positive response to such questions, divide the materials between the two children, and encourage the second child to thank the child who shared.

Criterion: The child gives objects to peers while playing, without being prompted to do so.

16.

Self-Help Skills: Eating

IT IS IMPORTANT to encourage young children with disabilities, at an early age, to be as independent as possible in self-care activities. This sequence of items is directed toward the establishment of appropriate feeding patterns and, later, the development of independent eating. When working with children who have physical disabilities, it will frequently be important to seek consultation and assistance from a person who is knowledgeable about oral-motor problems (e.g., a communication disorders specialist, a physical therapist, or an occupational therapist) who can assist in establishing the best possible program for developing feeding/eating skills during the child's first year.

When working on the development of self-feeding skills, it may be necessary to both devise and use adaptive equipment that facilitates self-feeding. An occupational therapist should be able to offer suggestions on how to adapt eating utensils for each child. Regardless of the nature or the sophistication of the adaptive equipment, beginning feeders will usually be very messy. It is important that the interventionist help caregivers to understand that some mess is to be expected and must be tolerated in order for children to learn self-feeding.

16. Self-Help Skills: Eating

a. Smoothly sucks from nipple
b. Infrequently "roots" toward food or objects
c. Infrequently bites down on spoon
d. Infrequently gags—only when appropriate
e. Munches food—chewing up and down
f. Uses purposeful tongue movements
g. Pulls food off spoon with lips
h. Holds own bottle (omit for breast-fed infants)

i. Assists in drinking from cup that is held by an adult
j. Eats junior or mashed table food without gagging
k. Cleans lower lip with teeth
l. Chews with a rotary/side-to-side action
m. Feeds self with fingers
n. Holds and drinks from cup
o. Brings spoon to mouth and eats food off of it
p. Scoops food from dish with spoon

q. Chews well

r. No longer uses bottle or breast

s. Feeds self without spilling—almost no help

t. Feeds self a meal with spoon and cup as main utensils

u. Distinguishes between edible and non-edible substances

AREA: **16. Self-Help Skills: Eating**
BEHAVIOR: 16a. Smoothly sucks from nipple

Materials: Baby's bottle or mother's breast at feeding time

Procedures:

Get the child's attention by making sure that he or she sees the breast or bottle before feeding begins. Help him or her adjust to a comfortable position and angle for sucking. Closely observe, especially while very young, to make sure the child obtains good grasp of the nipple.

Note: No child should be given a bottle while lying on his or her back, particularly if mobility is limited. Not only is choking more likely, but if the child's oral-motor function is abnormal, liquid may flow into the ear canals, causing infection. A child should be able to smoothly suck and swallow a few days after birth.

Because sucking problems are often early signs of neurological problems, they are frequently a sign that professional assistance is needed. Arrange for a physical therapist, occupational therapist, or pediatrician to see the child if a feeding problem exists.

Use in Daily Routines:

Sucking is a natural activity that is part of each day's feeding routine. Make the feeding routine a relaxing time for both caregiver and baby.

Adaptations:

None are necessary.

Criterion: The child is able to take liquids from a bottle or the breast without choking, withdrawing, or becoming tense.

AREA: **16. Self-Help Skills: Eating**
BEHAVIOR: 16b. Infrequently "roots" toward food or objects

Materials: None required

Procedures:

Touch the child lightly on the cheek and see if he or she turns his or her head as if to find and suck on your finger. This movement is called the "rooting reflex." It is present at birth, and should begin to disappear by 3–4 months. It appears to be inhibited by hand-to-mouth activity, so, if the child is bringing his or her hands to the mouth, no further intervention should be necessary.

If the child is not bringing his or her hands to the mouth, and if he or she has an active rooting reflex, hand-to-mouth activity should be promoted. Experiment with putting the child in several positions to see which increases the probability of hand-to-mouth activity (often side-lying is best). Then you may physically guide the child's hand to his or her mouth and prompt mouthing by placing a good-tasting substance on his or her hand.

You may also touch around the child's mouth with your fingers, using first a firm and then a light touch. Do this several times a day. The rooting reflex will always be more

(continued)

easily elicited when the child is hungry than when he or she is sleepy or upset. Testing should be done with the infant alert and midway between feedings.

>   *Note:* Some children cannot tolerate being touched around the mouth without arching their backs or becoming irritable. If this is the case, you should seek the advice of a physical, occupational, or speech therapist.

Use in Daily Routines:

>   While playing with the child, help him or her to bring his or her hands to the mouth. Put a drop of jam, or another sweet substance, on the back of his or her hand near the thumb. When the child tastes this, he or she may try to bring his or her hand to the mouth more readily.

Adaptations:

>   None are necessary.

Criterion: The child does not automatically turn his or her head in response to his or her cheek being touched.

AREA: **16.   Self-Help Skills: Eating**
BEHAVIOR: 16c.   Infrequently bites down on spoon

Materials: Baby food, small spoon

Procedures:

>   Place a small amount of baby food on a spoon and put it on the child's tongue, touching the bottom gums. Wait to see if the child's jaws close tightly. This is called a "bite reflex."

>   A normal baby will be able to immediately open his or her mouth. Inability to do so is a likely sign of neurological problems and indicates the need for treatment by a therapist.

>   The bite reflex normally fades as the child begins to eat solid foods. Some techniques to use if the bite reflex is too strong are:

Rub the gums with your finger prior to feeding
Use a smaller spoon
Use baby foods that encourage munching and chewing

>   *Note:*   If a child has a strong bite reflex, never place your fingers into his or her mouth! If a child is biting down hard on something and cannot release it, wait a few seconds for the child to relax and release his or her bite. If the child does not release his or her bite, press your fingers on the muscles at the back of the jaw or hold the child's nose (the physiological need for air will cause the child's mouth to open). Do not pull the spoon from the child's mouth. This increases the bite reflex and could damage his or her mouth.

Use in Daily Routines:

>   A strong bite reflex is something to naturally watch for at feeding times. You can also rub the child's gums with your finger while holding him or her, allowing the child to take small amounts of desired foods (e.g., jam, applesauce) from your fingertip while you do this.

(continued)

Adaptations:

> *Motor Impaired:*   If the child with motor impairments persists in biting on a spoon during feeding, use a small coated spoon or one made of sturdy plastic.

Criterion: The child does not bite down on a spoon or tightly hold it in his or her mouth.

AREA: **16.   Self-Help Skills: Eating**
BEHAVIOR: 16d.   Infrequently gags—only when appropriate

Materials: Baby foods

Procedures:

> Gradually introduce different tastes and textures of pureed or strained foods. If gagging occurs, dilute the foods a little, choosing only those foods that are the smoothest. When the child tolerates those foods, gradually work up to more textured foods.
>
> Adding small amounts of baby cereal to strained foods will increase their texture and stimulate tolerance for textured foods.
>
> One technique that may reduce gagging is "tongue walking" (i.e., pressing firmly on the tongue with the tip of a small spoon, working from the front to the middle of the tongue).
>
> Be sure to hold the child as upright as possible and to provide good head support while feeding. Never feed a child in a lying position.
>
> *Note:*   If a child frequently gags beyond 6 months of age or if he or she never gags on food in the back of the mouth before 6 months of age, consult a therapist.

Use in Daily Routines:

> Eating should be a pleasant routine. Have several foods available and change between less and more textured ones while feeding.

Adaptations:

> None are necessary.

Criterion: The child eats strained foods, including cereal, without gagging.

AREA: **16.   Self-Help Skills: Eating**
BEHAVIOR: 16e.   Munches food—chewing up and down

Materials: Strained baby foods, infant cereals

Procedures:

> Place food in the child's mouth and observe his or her reaction. If the child pushes it out with his or her tongue, try placing the next spoonful in the side of his or her mouth. Pushing food out of the mouth with the tongue may be reflexive at first and is not necessarily a rejection of the food that is being offered.
>
> Watch for the child to start moving his or her jaws up and down while using the tongue to mash food against the roof of his or her mouth.

(continued)

Note: If a child persists in pushing food out of his or her mouth beyond 6 months of age, or has not developed a munching pattern, consult a therapist.

Use in Daily Routines:

The child's chewing patterns can be observed during normal feeding times. Allow plenty of time so that the child doesn't feel hurried while eating.

Adaptations:

Motor Impaired: Make sure the child is positioned comfortably in sitting with head flexed slightly forward. Try presenting food to either side of mouth between gums.

Criterion: The child chews with an up and down motion with food in his or her mouth.

AREA: 16.   Self-Help Skills: Eating
BEHAVIOR: 16f.   Uses purposeful tongue movements

Materials: Regular meals; sticky foods, such as oatmeal

Procedures:

Observe the child eating. Notice if the child moves his or her tongue to touch the food at the sides and the top of his or her mouth or if he or she pulls the tongue back while either eating or babbling. If you are not readily seeing tongue movement, try placing small amounts of sticky foods, such as oatmeal or jam, on the roof of the child's mouth, near the front, and between the cheek and gums. Observe the child's use of his or her tongue to retrieve these foods. If you note that the child is having difficulty with this activity, work on it for only a few minutes at each feeding, placing preferred foods at the front of the mouth so as to require tongue action for retrieval.

Note: Peanut butter is frequently used to promote tongue mobility, but must be used very cautiously. Since it does not readily dissolve, there is some danger of aspiration.

Use in Daily Routines:

While feeding, occasionally put a small amount of food on the child's upper or lower lip, so he or she will have to lick it clean. When he or she does, act excited. Imitate the child, or let him or her see him- or herself in a mirror.

Adaptations:

None are necessary.

Criterion: The child moves his or her tongue both to the side and to the top of his or her mouth.

AREA: 16.   Self-Help Skills: Eating
BEHAVIOR: 16g.   Pulls food off spoon with lips

Materials: Usually eaten foods

(continued)

Procedures:

Place a spoonful of food in the child's mouth, touching the lower lip only. Do not scrape the food off against the upper lip. Watch for the child to move his or her upper lip toward the spoon to clean it off—move the spoon up a little, if necessary, to help the child get the food.

If there are no lip movements, try alternately touching the top and bottom lips with the spoon, waiting for lip closure. Use this method with the child's favorite sticky foods (e.g., fruit, pudding). If that proves unsuccessful, try touching just above the child's lip with your finger and thus, putting light pressure on the spoon with his or her upper lip.

> *Note:* If a strong bite reflex is present, it may be triggered by the spoon touching the teeth. If this is a problem, use a very small spoon and avoid the teeth, pressing the spoon firmly on the front of the tongue. Pay special attention to keeping the child as relaxed as possible.

Use in Daily Routines:

Everyday feeding provides opportunities for this spoon feeding activity. It also encourages the child to be active in the feeding process. Let the child take the food from the spoon, rather than giving it to him or her.

Adaptations:

> *Motor Impaired:* Be sure that the child with motor impairments is well positioned in a fairly upright position with his or her head slightly flexed. Present the spoon at midline, putting slight pressure on the child's tongue and wait for him or her to pull the food off.

Criterion: The child uses his or her lips to clean food off of a spoon.

AREA: **16. Self-Help Skills: Eating**
BEHAVIOR: 16h. Holds own bottle (omit for breast-fed infants)

Materials: Plastic baby bottles (a small "preemie" bottle or one made to fit a baby's hands, if the child can't handle a regular bottle).

Procedures:

Present the child with a bottle by placing the nipple in his or her mouth while you continue to hold it. Once the child is comfortably sucking on the bottle, gently place his or her hands on the bottle. Over time, the child will take a firmer grip on the bottle.

Hold the bottle a few inches from the child's mouth and wait to see if he or she will reach out for it. As these reaching skills improve, gradually release your hold on the bottle. Occasionally check to see that the child hasn't dropped the bottle.

> *Note:* Do not put a child in bed with his or her bottle. Let the child drink first and then go to bed. Bottle drinking in bed is associated with both an increase in middle ear infection and tooth decay.

Use in Daily Routines:

You and the child will both enjoy his or her first steps toward independent feeding. Be sure to regularly check to see if the child needs help retrieving a bottle that was dropped, with positioning, or with grasping.

(continued)

Adaptations:

> *Motor Impaired:* A child with motor impairments frequently shows difficulties with reaching and grasping. Make sure he or she is as relaxed as possible during feeding (see "Handling" subsection in Chapter 3, p. 23). You may have more success feeding a child with disabilities by positioning him or her on a pillow in your lap, directly facing you.

Criterion: The child holds his or her bottle alone while drinking.

AREA: 16. Self-Help Skills: Eating
BEHAVIOR: 16i. Assists in drinking from cup that is held by an adult

Materials: Preferred liquids (avoid sugared beverages); several kinds of cups and small juice glasses; plastic cup with a weighted bottom; plastic cup with one side cut out so the top does not hit the child's nose

Procedures:

> Start with a small amount of liquid in a cup. Bring the cup to the child's mouth and tip it slightly, waiting for the child to actively cooperate by closing his or her lips around the cup. Hold the cup about an inch away from the child's mouth and wait for him or her to lean toward the cup.

> It is frequently helpful to start teaching cup drinking by using thicker liquids (e.g., milk, a light mixture of milk and cereal), which are easier for the child to handle.

> *Note:* Closed cups with spouts are not very helpful in teaching the head and lip control that is needed for drinking from a cup. Choose a cup without a spout or minimally use one with a spout.

Use in Daily Routines:

> Watch for the child to open his or her mouth as a cup approaches it. Talk about the procedure, saying, for example, "Want a drink?" or "Here's your drink," as cues to the child to get ready to drink.

Adaptations:

> *Motor Impaired:* Make sure the child with motor impairments is well positioned with his or her head slightly flexed. Use a small plastic cup with one side cut out. If the child has significant difficulty consult an occupational or physical therapist.

Criterion: The child leans toward a cup and drinks without excessive spilling or choking.

AREA: 16. Self-Help Skills: Eating
BEHAVIOR: 16j. Eats junior or mashed table food without gagging

Materials: Both smooth and textured foods (e.g., infant and junior baby foods, graham crackers, special infant crackers)

Procedures:

> Upon reaching 6–7 months of age, a child should be able to tolerate textures in foods without gagging. Such food may be encouraged in children who are that age and

(continued)

older, who refuse textured foods or who gag on them, by very gradually increasing texture (e.g., adding a little baby cereal or wheat germ to strained foods and allowing adjustment to that before moving on to junior foods).

Sometimes an overactive gag reflex can be modified by placing the spoon of food on the front of the tongue, lifting spoon slightly and placing it a little further back on the tongue, and so on, to the point the child starts to gag, and then returning it to the front to introduce food. This might be done 2 or 3 times during each feeding.

Note: If the gag reflex remains strong enough so that a child cannot tolerate junior foods after 9 months of age, seek professional help.

Use in Daily Routines:

Change foods that you feed the child daily. Just like adults, children appreciate changes in their meals and different tastes. Try to offer foods of at least 2, or even 3, different consistencies at any given meal.

Adaptations:

Motor Impaired: A child with motor and oral-motor disabilities needs to be in a relaxed state and proper sitting position to reduce the abnormal postures and reflexes that inhibit eating and promote gagging and teeth clenching. If the child is underweight, use mashed table foods, which have more calories, as well as being less expensive than commercially prepared baby foods. Try placing the food on either side of the child's mouth to encourage munching and to decrease gagging.

Criterion: The child eats junior or mashed foods at every meal without gagging.

AREA: **16. Self-Help Skills: Eating**
BEHAVIOR: 16k. Cleans lower lip with teeth

Materials: Usual, semi-solid foods (e.g., baby foods; mashed, well cooked regular foods)

Procedures:

Look for "lip cleaning" to spontaneously occur as the child is eating and when food sticks to his or her lower lip. Do not routinely wipe the child's mouth off after every bite. If the child is not starting to use his or her teeth to clean food off the lower lip, place favored sticky foods on the lip so that the child will have to retrieve them in order to get the taste. It may help to gently touch the lower lip with the spoon.

Note: If the child has an oral-motor problem that makes cleaning the lower lip very difficult, don't work on it too persistently. Try it just once or twice, so that eating remains an enjoyable activity.

Use in Daily Routines:

Opportunities for the child to clean food from his or her lip can easily be created at mealtime. If they don't occur naturally, leave small bits of food on his or her lower lip as you withdraw the spoon from the child's mouth.

Adaptations:

None are necessary.

Criterion: The child spontaneously and routinely cleans his or her lower lip during meals.

AREA: **16.   Self-Help Skills: Eating**
BEHAVIOR: 16l.   Chews with a rotary/side-to-side action

Materials: A variety of textured foods (e.g., junior baby foods, mashed table foods, baby sausages and meats, rice, mashed spaghetti)

Procedures and Use in Daily Routines:

Observe the child's response to textured foods and watch for adult-like chewing movements (e.g., rotary, side-to-side movements of the jaw). Frequently, just the stimulation of textured foods in the mouth is enough to trigger those movements, and no further intervention is needed. However, if the movements are not occurring, try placing some of the child's favorite foods on one side of his or her mouth, between the cheek and teeth.

Adaptations:

Motor Impaired: Alternately present food to both sides of the mouth of a child with motor impairments. Provide slight pressure to lower gums and/or teeth, if needed. If the child does not respond, try applying light pressure to his or her jaw with your hand to physically prompt chewing. Consult a therapist if difficulty persists.

Criterion: The child spontaneously and consistently shows rotary jaw movements when chewing textured foods.

AREA: **16.   Self-Help Skills: Eating**
BEHAVIOR: 16m.   Feeds self with fingers

Materials: A variety of foods such as oatmeal, pudding, cereal bits, bread sticks or crackers

Procedures:

Introduce the idea of self-feeding by placing sticky foods, such as oatmeal or corn syrup, on the child's fingers so that he or she can lick them off.

Provide a bowl of pudding so that the child can place a hand in it and lick off the food. Progress to foods that are easy to grasp and which do not require finger release to place in the mouth (e.g., bread stick, cracker). When the child is proficient with these foods, gradually move to smaller items (e.g., cereal bits) that require hand opening to place in mouth. As in all feeding items, new skills should be presented gradually.

Use in Daily Routines:

Finger feeding can be quite messy at first. Prepare for the mess by putting a large bib or clothes that can be soiled on the child. Model finger feeding by putting your finger in the food (e.g., pudding) and then eating the food from your finger.

Adaptations:

Visually Impaired: Encourage the child with a visual impairment to feel foods, and physically prompt the bringing of food to the mouth. A child with a visual impairment may profit from an extended period of finger feeding before use of a spoon is introduced.

Motor Impaired: If the child with motor impairments has difficulty finger feeding, try alternating his or her position (e.g., change to sidelying, elevate his or her chair tray so that his or her hands are naturally closer to the mouth).

Criterion: The child picks up and eats small bits of food without help.

AREA: **16.   Self-Help Skills: Eating**
BEHAVIOR: 16n.   Holds and drinks from cup

Materials: Plastic, easily held cup

Procedures and Use in Daily Routines:

Fill the child's cup approximately one-third full with liquid and give it to the child when he or she is thirsty. If the child cannot hold a cup and bring it to his or her mouth to drink, help him or her by placing both hands on the cup and bringing it to his or her mouth to drink. Gradually reduce your assistance.

Give the child plenty of opportunities to drink from a cup during feeding, while pretend playing, and when he or she wants a drink during the day.

Note: Many different types of cups are available on the market. Experiment to see which type of cup the child handles most easily (e.g., a cup with 1 or 2 handles, big or small handles, cups with cutouts for drinking).

Adaptations:

Visually Impaired: Permit (and even encourage) the child with a visual impairment to place his or her finger into the cup to feel the liquid before drinking.

Motor Impaired: A child with motor impairments may never be able to hold a cup independently. He or she should be taught to drink through a straw, if possible.

Criterion: The child drinks from a cup without help.

AREA: **16.   Self-Help Skills: Eating**
BEHAVIOR: 16o.   Brings spoon to mouth and eats food off of it

Materials: Spoon, dish, a variety of foods that can be easily scooped

---

Procedures and Use in Daily Routines:

Place a bowl with food in it in front of the child. Fill the spoon and help the child grasp it. Tell the child "Eat your food." If the child is unable to successfully bring the spoon to his or her mouth try gently elevating his or her elbow with your hand. If more assistance is needed, put your arm under the child's arm and place your hand gently on top of his or her wrist while standing or sitting behind the child. In this manner, you can assist the child with added support and wrist guidance.

At first, help the child to get food into his or her mouth. Then, assist only to the point that the spoon is several inches from the child's mouth, letting him or her complete the task on his or her own. Gradually reduce all help until the child can do this skill on his or her own.

Note: Many children try to reach for a spoon as they are being fed. This should be encouraged, regardless of how messy it is at first. Do not tire a child by insisting that he or she feed him- or herself all of every meal at first. Have the child do the work when eating most preferred foods and those that best stick to the spoon.

Adaptations:

Visually Impaired: Allow the child with a visual impairment to feel food with one hand while holding a spoon in the other. A dish with sides that permits easy scooping will also be helpful.

(continued)

Motor Impaired: Use Dycem (or a thin piece of rubber) under the dish of a child with motor impairments to prevent it from moving. A scoop dish may also be helpful. The child's spoon may have to be adapted to facilitate his or her grasp. Consult an occupational therapist if problems persist.

Criterion: The child brings his or her spoon to the mouth and puts food in without help. Help getting food onto the spoon may be provided.

AREA: 16. Self-Help Skills: Eating
BEHAVIOR: 16p. Scoops food from dish with spoon

Materials: Spoon, dish, a variety of foods that are easy to scoop

Procedures and Use in Daily Routines:

Place a bowl of food in front of the child. Have the child grasp a spoon, and encourage him or her to eat. If the child brings the spoon to his or her mouth but does not successfully scoop food onto the spoon, show the child how to scoop food. If necessary, physically assist the child to scoop food, but decrease your assistance as quickly as possible.

Be sure to give the child plenty of time and opportunity to practice. Start with foods that adhere well to the spoon (e.g., pudding, mashed potatoes, mashed bananas).

Adaptations:

Visually Impaired: Allow the child with a visual impairment to feel his or her food with one hand while holding a spoon in the other. A dish with sides that permit easy scooping will also be helpful.

Motor Impaired: Use Dycem (or a thin piece of rubber) under the dish of a child with motor impairments to prevent it from moving. A scoop dish may also be helpful. The child's spoon may have to be adapted to facilitate his or her grasp as well. Consult an occupational therapist if problems persist.

Criterion: The child scoops food from a dish with a spoon without assistance.

AREA: 16. Self-Help Skills: Eating
BEHAVIOR: 16q. Chews well

Materials: A variety of foods

Procedures and Use in Daily Routines:

Give the child the opportunity to eat a variety of foods that have small lumps, different or unusual textures, and various consistencies.

Once the child begins to chew, try to encourage more mature chewing by giving the child different solids between his or her back teeth. Try foods like long strips of hard cheese, semi-cooked carrots, and so forth. If necessary, hold one end, while letting the child chew the other end. Move food to different places in the child's mouth to stimulate a combination of vertical, horizontal, and rotary jaw movements. Repeat this activity at each meal if the child does not protest.

(continued)

Adaptations:

> *Motor Impaired:*   Alternately present food to both sides of the mouth of a child with motor impairments. Provide slight pressure to the child's lower gums and/or teeth, if needed. If the child does not respond, try applying light pressure to his or her jaw with your hand to physically prompt chewing. Consult a therapist if difficulty persists.

Criterion: The child chews a normal variety of foods.

AREA: **16.   Self-Help Skills: Eating**
BEHAVIOR: 16r.   No longer uses bottle or breast

Materials: Bottle or cup

Procedures and Use in Daily Routines:

> As the child learns to drink from a cup (item 16n.), gradually reduce the quantity of liquid given in a bottle or the time spent nursing. Substitute other cuddling behaviors for the time that was normally spent holding the child for bottle or breast feeding.

> *Note:*   The child's giving up of the bottle is achieved over a wide range of ages. Many physicians and dentists recommend weaning from the bottle at or shortly after 12 months of age.

Adaptations:

> *Motor Impaired:*   If the child with motor impairments is having oral-motor difficulties, there may be reason to prolong bottle or breast feeding. Consult a therapist.

Criterion: The child does not drink from a bottle or the breast.

AREA: **16.   Self-Help Skills: Eating**
BEHAVIOR: 16s.   Feeds self without spilling—almost no help

Materials: Spoon, dish, a variety of foods that are easy to scoop

Procedures and Use in Daily Routines:

> Place food in a bowl or saucer with a high edge (e.g., one that a spoon can work against easily). Encourage the child to self-feed. Offer him or her the spoon and demonstrate the process, tasting the food in his or her dish.

Adaptations:

> *Visually Impaired:*   Always begin a meal by "showing" a child with a visual impairment where the plate and spoon are located. It is also helpful to guide the child's hand to the foods on his or her plate so that he or she knows everything's location.

> *Motor Impaired:*   Be sure that the dish of a child with motor impairments is one that does not easily slide and that his or her spoon is appropriate (i.e., modified, if necessary). Consult an occupational therapist if needed. A child with severe impairments may never independently feed him- or herself.

Criterion: The child feeds him- or herself with a spoon without much spilling.

AREA: **16.   Self-Help Skills: Eating**
BEHAVIOR: 16t.   Feeds self a meal with spoon and cup as main utensils

Materials: Spoon, dish, cup appropriate for children

Procedures and Use in Daily Routines:

Place food on a child's dish and serve it to the child, putting a spoon next to the plate and a cup of milk, water, or juice near it also. Encourage the child to eat his or her meal while you do the same. If the child loses interest or begins to play, prompt appropriate eating behavior, but resist feeding the child. Let him or her independently eat.

Adaptations:

Visually Impaired: Always begin a meal by "showng" a child with a visual impairment where the plate and spoon are located. It is also helpful to guide the child's hands to the foods on his or her plate so that he or she knows everything's location.

Motor Impaired: Be sure that the dish of the child with motor impairments is one that does not easily slide and that his or her spoon is appropriate (i.e., modified, if necessary). Consult an occupational therapist if needed. A child with severe motor impairments may never independently feed him- or herself.

Criterion: The child feeds him- or herself a complete meal.

AREA: **16.   Self-Help Skills: Eating**
BEHAVIOR: 16u.   Distinguishes between edible and nonedible substances

Materials: Edibles (i.e., foods), nonedibles (i.e., nonfood objects)

Procedures and Use in Daily Routines:

Observe whether or not the child mouths nonedibles in his or her play. If he or she does, remove them and provide him or her something else with which to play.

Offer the child 2 similar items (i.e., one edible and one nonedible). Praise the child when he or she eats the edible item and plays with the nonedible one. However, if the child still insists on putting nonedible item in his or her mouth, make a face and verbally ask him or her to take it out. Get the child to imitate you. If necessary, remove the nonedible item.

Observe the child's behavior when he or she plays alone. Ask the child to remove nonedible items from his or her mouth as necessary.

Adaptations:

None are necessary.

Criterion: The child distinguishes between familiar edible and nonedible substances *and* does not attempt to eat nonedible items.

17.

Self-Help Skills: Dressing

T HE INTENT of dressing and undressing activities presented in this sequence is simply to promote as much independence as possible on the part of a young child. Dressing and undressing skills will always require some degree of motor facility, especially as represented by items within sequence 20., Fine Motor Skills: Reaching, Grasping, and Releasing (pp. 285–297).

Caregivers are encouraged to be creative in selecting types of clothing. Adaptive clothing fasteners can be used to encourage a child to use what motor abilities he or she may have in the dressing process. Velcro can take the place of buttons, zippers, and even shoe strings. Loose fitting shirts will be pulled over a child's head much more easily than tight fitting ones.

A child with severe motor impairments may always be extremely limited, perhaps to the point of only being able to cooperate in the dressing process. When assisting a child in the dressing process, it is very important to talk to him or her about what is happening. Make comments about the clothing's color, how nice a given article of clothing may look on the child, and so forth, in order to engage the child cognitively in the dressing task, even if he or she cannot actively participate.

17. Self-Help Skills: Dressing

a. Cooperates in dressing and undressing (e.g., holds arm out for sleeve, foot out for shoe)

b. Removes socks and partially pulls shirt over head

c. Indicates need for change of soiled diaper or pants

d. Removes loose clothing (e.g., socks, mittens, hat, untied shoes)

e. Unties shoes or hat, as an act of undressing

f. Unfastens clothing zipper that has a large pull tab

g. Puts on hat

h. Puts on socks, loose shoes, and "stretch" pants

i. Removes simple clothing (e.g., open shirt or jacket, "stretch" pants)

AREA: **17.   Self-Help Skills: Dressing**
BEHAVIOR: 17a.   Cooperates in dressing and undressing (e.g., holds arm out for sleeve, foot out for shoe)

Materials: The child's clothing that is loose and easy to put on or pull off

---

Procedures:

While dressing the child, name his or her body parts as you touch them. Encourage the child to move the named body part (e.g., arm, leg).

Place the child's arm or leg partially in or out of a garment and encourage him or her to assist you during dressing or undressing (e.g., "Push your leg through here!", "Pull your arm out!"). Play the Peek-a-boo game with the child to encourage his or her "help," while putting the garment on or taking it off over his or her head.

Use in Daily Routines:

Dressing can be aversive to a child if shirts are pulled roughly over his or her head or if it is hurried. Talk to the child about what is being done. Allow plenty of time and try to get the child involved in helping you. Make it fun!

Adaptations:

Visually Impaired: When dressing a child with a visual impairment, be sure to talk about everything that is being done and to be gentle in your approach with the clothes. It is frightening to have something pulled over your head or to have your arm pulled when you don't expect it.

Motor Impaired: If a child with motor impairments tends to be stiff while dressing, you may need to engage in activities that are relaxing before this can be accomplished.

Criterion: The child cooperates in both dressing and undressing.

AREA: **17.   Self-Help Skills: Dressing**
BEHAVIOR: 17b.   Removes socks and partially pulls shirt over head

Materials: Shirts, undershirts, sweaters, socks

Procedures:

The first step in learning to remove clothing is to learn to pull things off that are already partially removed (e.g., a shirt pulled to the top of the head, socks that are partially removed). Make a game of this activity. Play Peek-a-boo when pulling a shirt over the child's head. Encourage and help him or her to finish pulling the shirt off. Do the same with a hat, pulling it over the child's eyes and prompting him or her to remove it. Help the child to grasp partially removed socks and to finish pulling them off.

Use in Daily Routines:

Whenever dressing or undressing the child, give him or her the opportunity to help (e.g., with jackets, caps, pajamas).

(continued)

Adaptations:

Visually Impaired: Be sure to talk about the process of dressing and undressing with a child with a visual impairment. Tell him or her what is going to happen and what is being put on or taken off. Discuss the differences in the way different clothes feel.

Motor Impaired: A child with motor impairments is likely to need prompting and physical assistance. Provide it as needed, but keep the goal of independent functioning well in mind. Try alternative positions such as supported sitting or lying down.

Criterion: The child pulls off his or her socks and shirt that have been partially removed by an adult.

AREA: **17. Self-Help Skills: Dressing**
BEHAVIOR: 17c.   Indicates need for change of soiled diaper or pants

Materials: Cloth or disposable diapers, pants

Procedures and Use in Daily Routines:

Sometime after the child is a year old, he or she will begin to give clear signals when his or her diaper is messy. Watch for these signs (e.g., vocalizations, pointing, walking with a wide gait) and ask, "Do you have dirty pants?", "Do you want me to change your diaper?"

Check to see if the diaper or pants are soiled. If they are, talk to the child about changing it as you go through the process. Talk about taking the dirty diaper/clothes off and putting a clean one on.

Note: If you are consistently checking and finding that a child's pants are not wet or messy, look carefully at the cues, either verbal or behavioral, to which you are responding. You may need to work to help the child give clearer signals or to be more discrete in picking up cues that the child is offering.

Adaptations:

None are necessary.

Criterion: The child clearly indicates a need to have a soiled diaper or pants changed. This can be done either verbally or nonverbally.

AREA: **17. Self-Help Skills: Dressing**
BEHAVIOR: 17d.   Removes loose clothing (e.g., socks, mittens, hats, untied shoes)

Materials: Socks, mittens, hats, shoes

Procedures and Use in Daily Routines:

Draw the child's attention to what you are doing when you undress him or her by both talking about the process and showing or helping him or her to feel it. Encourage the child to participate and help in the process.

(continued)

"Start" the process of removing clothing and have the child finish it (e.g., pull a sock just past the child's heel or pull a shirt partially over his or her head and then have the child remove the article of clothing the rest of the way). Assist the child through the process, and then gradually fade your assistance. Use different articles of clothing.

Adaptations:

Visually Impaired: Be sure to use clear verbal cues along with physical prompts with a child with visual impairments (e.g., say, "Take off your sock," while touching or giving a slight tug on sock).

Motor Impaired: It may be necessary to continue providing assistance to a child with motor impairments, even when it is very clear that he or she is trying to remove the clothing. Remember, independence is important. Help as little as necessary and work on eliminating your assistance altogether.

Criterion: The child removes loose clothing without assistance.

AREA: 17.   Self-Help Skills: Dressing
BEHAVIOR: 17e.   Unties shoes or hat, as an act of undressing

Materials: Shoes with laces, hat with tie, mirror

Procedures and Use in Daily Routines:

When you undress the child, describe what you are doing. As you untie the child's shoes, say, for example, "Now, let's untie your shoes and take them off." Have the child watch as you untie his or her shoes. Untying a hat in front of a mirror will make the process visible to the child.

Put your hands over the child's hands lightly and guide her or him through the process of pulling the ends of the shoestrings to untie them.

Adaptations:

Motor Impaired: For a child with motor impairments who is unable to grasp, small strings, plastic rings, bells, and so on may be attached to the ends of his or her laces. Shoes with Velcro fasteners may be easier for some children.

Criterion: The child unties his or her shoes or hat, as an act of undressing.

AREA: 17.   Self-Help Skills: Dressing
BEHAVIOR: 17f.   Unfastens clothing zipper that has a large pull tab

Materials: If the child's clothing has small zipper tabs, put small chains, string loops, or key tags on them to make them easier to grasp.

Procedures and Use in Daily Routines:

Show the child how to unfasten his or her coat or pants. Zip up the zipper and then ask the child to unzip it. If the child cannot, or does not grasp the pull tab on the zipper, assist him or her by placing the metal tab in his or her hand. If the child cannot maintain his

(continued)

or her grasp, then an adaptation to the pull tab may be necessary (e.g., larger plastic piece attached to it). If grasp is maintained, but the child does not unzip, then assist him or her by helping to "start" the motion. Physically assist only as much as necessary, fading support as quickly as possible.

Adaptations:

Motor Impaired: Velcro fasteners may be good substitutes for zippers for a child with motor impairments. They are frequently easier for a child to manipulate.

Criterion: The child unzips own clothing (or unfastens Velcro fasteners).

AREA: 17. Self-Help Skills: Dressing
BEHAVIOR: 17g. Puts on hat

Materials: Hats that are easy to put on and take off

Procedures:

Give the child a hat. While saying "Put the hat on your head," make the movement of placing a hat on your head with your hand. Put a hat on the child's head, remove it, and say, "You put it on."

Use a box of hats from which the child can choose; provide a mirror so that he or she can see what he or she has put on.

Use in Daily Routines:

Playing "dress-up" is a fun activity for young children to play. Encourage the child to put on hats as part of play activities. Provide different kinds and shapes of hats.

Adaptations:

Visually Impaired: Place a hat in the hands of a child with a visual impairment and ask him or her to put it on. If the child cannot, or does not, put the hat on his or her head, use gentle physical guidance to help him or her do so. Point out differences in hats via their feeling (e.g., soft hats, floppy hats, furry hats).

Motor Impaired: If the child with motor impairments cannot move his or her arms well enough to put on a hat, encourage the child to help as much as possible as you put it on him or her (e.g., "Lift your chin a little.", "Turn your head over here."). Praise efforts to help.

Criterion: The child puts a hat on without assistance.

AREA: 17. Self-Help Skills: Dressing
BEHAVIOR: 17h. Puts on socks, loose shoes, and "stretch" pants

Materials: Loose fitting shoes, socks, and pants with an elastic waistband

---

Procedures:

Show the child how to put on socks, shoes, or pants. Begin by putting them partially on and letting the child finish (e.g., pull up socks or pants). Then hand the child

---

(continued)

socks, one at a time, or pants and encourage him or her to try it alone. Provide physical assistance as needed, but be sure to do so only when it is really necessary. Gradually reduce the amount of assistance you give.

> *Note:*   Children do not differentiate right from left at this age. Some guidance with shoes and the front/back of pants may be necessary.

Use in Daily Routines:

Children like to play with adult clothes. Provide old shoes, shirts, and hats for the child, with which to play "dress-up." Encourage the child to try on clothes and/or to change sets of clothes while he or she plays.

Adaptations:

Visually Impaired: Hand a child with a visual impairment shoes, one at a time. If the shoes are put on the wrong feet, help the child remove them and tell him or her which foot each shoe goes on. Talk about how it "feels better" on the proper foot.

Motor Impaired: Select clothing that is especially easy to put on. If the child has a severe motor impairment, encourage him or her to help as much as possible.

Criterion: The child puts on loose fitting shoes, socks, and pants with an elastic waistband. Record the items that the child puts on.

AREA: 17.   Self-Help Skills: Dressing
BEHAVIOR: 17i.   Removes simple clothing (e.g., open shirt or jacket, "stretch" pants

Materials: Loose fitting shirts, jackets, and pants with an elastic waistband

---

Procedures:

This item is an extension of item 17d., Removes loose clothing. When a shirt has been opened in front, let the child take it off. Show him or her how to use one hand to pull the shirt from the other arm. Cue this behavior by saying, "Take your _____ off," and touching the proper place to begin.

If the child has difficulty, offer verbal encouragement and provide physical assistance to get the process started. Help only as much as is necessary.

Use in Daily Routines:

Dressing and undressing will occur at several natural times throughout the day. Encourage the child to do as much as possible alone. Praise him or her for independence in this activity.

Adaptations:

Motor Impaired: Select clothing that is especially easy to remove. If the child has a severe motor impairment, encourage him or her to help as you remove the clothing.

Criterion: The child removes simple articles of clothing (e.g., shirt, jacket, "stretch" pants) without assistance.

18.

Self-Help Skills: Grooming

NEEDLESS TO SAY, children under the age of 2 do not play an extremely active role in keeping themselves clean and properly groomed. The activities included in this sequence are preparatory to actual "self-care" activities. In general, the activities seek to develop cooperation with the caregiver, on the part of the child, in grooming activities. It is important for children to learn that being clean and properly groomed feels good.

If a child has physical disabilities that require him or her to be dependent upon others for grooming and personal hygiene, it is critical to talk to him or her about the grooming activities as they take place. Always talk to a child while helping him or her with these activities. Talk about what is being done and the importance of these activities for health and appearance. Upon completing an activity, be sure to praise the child for his or her cleanliness or improved appearance. The young child with a disability should not feel that someone is doing something to him or her, but that someone is engaging in important activities with him or her for very specific benefits.

18. Self-Help Skills: Grooming

a. Enjoys playing in water (same as item 19f.)

b. Cooperates in hand-washing and drying

c. Allows his or her teeth to be brushed

d. Washes own hands

e. Wipes nose, if given a tissue

AREA: **18.   Self-Help Skills: Grooming**
BEHAVIOR: 18a.   Enjoys playing in water (same as item 19f.)

Materials: A plastic dish pan or any similar container that will hold 2″ to 3″ of water

Procedures and Use in Daily Routines:

Put water in a pan and then give the child two or three objects with which to play in the water (e.g, a small cup, a figure shaped sponge, toys that float). Encourage the child to play and to get his or her hands into the water. After a few minutes of play, or if you see interest waning, ask if the child wants to dry his or her hands and offer assistance with a towel.

Incorporate playing in water in appropriate tasks and situations throughout a typical day.

Adaptations:

Visually Impaired: Talk to the child with a visual impairment about the pan of water and help him or her to feel it and splash in it. Demonstrate smooth, non-splashing water play, as well as splashy fun (e.g., help the child to hit the water to make a big splash). The child will learn how to play in the water by the feel and the consequence (e.g., does he or she just get his or her hands wet or does he or she also wet his or her face or clothes?).

Criterion: The child plays in a pan of water when the opportunity is presented.

AREA: **18.   Self-Help Skills: Grooming**
BEHAVIOR: 18b.   Cooperates in hand-washing and drying

Materials: Soap and water; something to stand on so that the child can comfortably get his or her hands into a sink

Procedures and Use in Daily Routines:

Provide opportunities for the child to wash his or her hands before meals and snacks, when coming in from outdoor play, and at other times throughout the day. Put water in a sink or basin and demonstrate by washing your hands next to the child. At the same time, encourage the child to put his or her hands in the water to also wash. Share a small bar of soap.

If the child is reluctant to wash his or her hands, try having him or her finger paint first, then talk of the need to get the paint off the hands and point out how the color comes off in the water.

Let the child help open the drain to let the water out and to get a towel to dry his or her hands.

Adaptations:

Visually Impaired: Guide the child with a visual impairment to the water. To help the child to feel the need to wash his or her hands, let the child play with something sticky (e.g., finger paints, pudding).

Motor Impaired: Take the water to the child with motor impairments that prevent him or her from standing at the sink or using a basin. Use a shallow pan with a small amount of

(continued)

water or simply a wet wash cloth. Ask the physical or occupational therapist about the best positioning of the child for this activity.

Criterion: The child does not resist involvement in washing and drying hands.

AREA: **18.   Self-Help Skills: Grooming**
BEHAVIOR: 18c.   Allows his or her teeth to be brushed

Materials: Toothbrush; a comfortable place to stand in front of a sink and mirror

Procedures and Use in Daily Routines:

Place the child in front of a mirror and tell him or her it is time to brush his or her teeth. Show the child the toothbrush and how you put toothpaste on it. Ask the child to open his or her mouth, and then proceed to brush his or her teeth (if the child does not open his or her mouth, gently open his or her lips manually and brush).

Try to make the experience pleasant. If the child does not attempt to hold the toothbrush, physically assist by placing it in the child's hand and physically guiding it to his or her mouth. If the child cannot use his or her hands and arms well enough to assist in that fashion, teach the child to turn his or her head, to open his or her mouth, and to spit out the toothpaste (i.e., anything within the child's capabilities that increases independence and participation in the process).

Note: Be sure to use a soft, child's toothbrush when beginning. You may even have to put a little toothpaste on your finger and "brush" with it before using an actual brush. Also, use a pleasant-tasting toothpaste, one children will like.

Adaptations:

None are necessary.

Criterion: The child allows his or her teeth to be brushed at least once a day.

AREA: **18.   Self-Help Skills: Grooming**
BEHAVIOR: 18d.   Washes own hands

Materials: Soap and water

Procedures:

After playing with substances or objects that get hands dirty (e.g., finger paints) or before meals or snacks, tell the child that it is time to wash his or her hands. Make sure that the child can reach the water in a sink or that someone is there to turn the water on and off for the child.

Hand the child soap and offer verbal encouragement. Provide physical assistance only if the child is resistant or is having difficulty. Decrease the amount of assistance you give gradually, but regularly.

Use in Daily Routines:

It is easy to arrange opportunities for handwashing by first providing opportunities for the child to get his or her hands dirty. Playing with finger paints, in sand, and many

(*continued*)

other substances will get hands dirty enough for you to suggest that they need to be washed.

Adaptations:

Motor Impaired: Promote as much independence as possible in handwashing. If the child with motor impairments cannot wash his or her hands at a sink, he or she may be able to soak his or her hands in a shallow pan of water, move his or her hands back and forth on a wet wash cloth, or just move one hand forward so that the adult can wash it more readily. Give credit to the child with severe impairments who is as independent as permitted by the motor limitations.

Criterion: The child independently washes his or her hands each time he or she is asked to do so.

AREA: **18.   Self-Help Skills: Grooming**
BEHAVIOR: 18e.   Wipes nose, if given a tissue

Materials: Soft tissues

Procedures and Use in Daily Routines:

When the child has a runny nose or sneezes, tell the child to wipe his or her nose and hand him or her a tissue. If the child makes no attempt to wipe his or her nose, physically assist him or her to do so. Gradually withdraw assistance on further trials. You may also demonstrate how to gently blow the nose. Encourage the child to imitate.

If the child cannot get his or her hands to the nose, work on getting the child to cooperate with you when you wipe his or her nose.

Sometimes a child can learn this response better if he or she is also given opportunities to "play" at wiping a doll's nose, your nose, and so forth.

Adaptations:

Visually Impaired: Guide the child's hand to his or her nose with a tissue. Talk about wiping the nose and making it clean.

Motor Impaired: If a child's motor impairment precludes independent nose wiping, encourage him or her to cooperate when you wipe his or her nose. Also, always precede your wiping with a question such as, "Do we need to wipe your nose?" Give credit on this item to a child with severe motor impairments if he or she responds affirmatively to the question *and* cooperates with the process.

Criterion: The child wipes his or her own nose when given a tissue and asked to do so.

19.

Fine Motor Skills: Tactile Integration

THE DEVELOPMENT OF fine motor skills has been divided into four areas, each representing a different aspect of development. This division is somewhat artificial and there is clearly overlap between the areas. The division allows the curriculum user to gain a better understanding of a child's strengths and weaknesses in order to provide more effective intervention. It is also important to remember that the items included in this sequence provide an important sensory foundation for the development of more sophisticated fine motor skills.

Although it has long been recognized that tactile stimulation is important to infant development, items that are related to tactile exploration and stimulation are rarely included in infant curricula. The reason for this could be because most curricula have been based on the developmental milestones that are included in standardized tests and the fact that those milestones that are pertinent to the acceptance of tactile stimulation have been hard to identify. The items included in the first part of this sequence primarily come from The Callier-Azusa Scale (Stillman, 1977), which was developed for children with both hearing and visual impairments. Experience suggests that these items are the least ordinal of any in the curriculum. Therefore, it is important to check all children with the 0- to 12-month items to determine appropriate intervention.

It is crucial to remember that many children with disabilities, as well as some children without apparent special needs, demonstrate very atypical responses to tactile stimulation. Some of these responses are "defensive," causing the child to withdraw from or to show distress at light or unexpected touch. These are often fussy infants, who may be bothered by certain clothing, bedding, or foods. They may withdraw from being held or cuddled. Other infants are underresponsive, apparently unaware of any stimulus until it reaches a painful level. Furthermore, many infants may also become fascinated, in a stereotypic way, with particular stimuli. Any one of the aforementioned problems should be called to the attention of an occupational therapist.

REFERENCES

Stillman, R. (Ed.). (1977). *The Callier-Azusa Scale*. Dallas: Callier Center for Communication Disorders, University of Texas.

19. Fine Motor Skills: Tactile Integration

a. Responds differently to warm/cold, rough/smooth (same as item 5a.)
b. Permits hands, feet, or body to be moved over soft, smooth-textured surfaces; or spontaneously moves them over such surfaces
c. Reacts to tactile stimulation with movement
d. Permits hands, feet, or body to be moved over rough-textured surfaces; or spontaneously moves them over such surfaces
e. Explores objects with fingers
f. Plays in water (same as item 18a.)
g. Finds an object that is hidden in textured material
h. Plays with soft-textured materials
i. Spreads soft materials with fingers
j. Spreads firmer materials with hands
k. Pokes or plays with clay

AREA: **19. Fine Motor Skills: Tactile Integration**
BEHAVIOR: 19a.   Responds differently to warm/cold, rough/smooth (same as item 5a.)

Materials: Objects with a wide variety of textures (e.g., metal object that can be warmed and cooled rapidly, a piece of indoor-outdoor carpet, spoon, fabric such as velvet)

Procedures:

Gently rub different objects over the child's skin for brief periods of time. Try stimulating the child's palms of hands, face, soles of feet, arms, and/or legs, waiting for a few seconds after each stimulation to observe his or her response. Vary the stimuli with each new trial.

If the child makes any response that indicates that he or she has felt the stimulus item, continue touching or rubbing with it until he or she stops responding. Then try a high-contrast stimulus to the same area (e.g., after using a rough piece of carpet or washcloth, try a piece of velvet or a metal spoon).

If the child does not respond, try varying the stimulus that is used. After three or four trials, stop offering that stimulus for the time being and introduce it again at a later point.

Note: If the child is underresponsive (i.e., does not react) or overresponsive (i.e., pulls away, becomes irritable), consult with an occupational therapist regarding appropriate activities and approaches.

Use in Daily Routines:

Incorporate this stimulus activity into play, dressing, and bathing with the child.

Adaptations:

Motor Impaired: Be sure to include stimulation to the palms of the hands of a child with motor impairments (relaxation may be necessary to get the hand open for stimulation).

Criterion: The child responds differently to the two stimuli presented.

AREA: **19. Fine Motor Skills: Tactile Integration**
BEHAVIOR: 19b.   Permits hands, feet, or body to be moved over soft, smooth-textured surfaces; or spontaneously moves them over such surfaces

Materials: A variety of soft, smooth toys and objects (e.g., stuffed animals, powder puffs)

Procedures:

Stimulate the child as in item 17a., but focus on stimuli that are soft and smooth. Rub these objects back and forth over the child's body for about 15–20 seconds. If the child withdraws from light touch or gentle rubbing with these objects, try stimulating him or her with a firmer touch. If the child tolerates the firmer touch, stimulate in that manner several times a day for at least 1 week. Then, conduct trial stimulations with a slightly lighter touch. Continue decreasing the pressure of the stimulation until the child can tolerate and/or enjoy gentle rubbing on his or her hands, arms, legs, and face.

Note: The items in this sequence are presented roughly in the order of their emergence in normal children. The order may vary considerably with children with

(continued)

disabilities. Several of the items may be worked on at the same time. Integrate them into daily care routines for the child.

Use in Daily Routines:

Incorporate this stimulating activity with soft, smooth-textured surfaces into daily care routines such as bathing, diapering, and dressing.

Adaptations:

None are necessary.

Criterion: The child permits soft, smooth-textured surfaces to be moved over his or her hands, feet, or body or spontaneously moves his or her body parts over such surfaces.

AREA: **19.   Fine Motor Skills: Tactile Integration**
BEHAVIOR: 19c.   Reacts to tactile stimulation with movement

Materials: A variety of toys made from different-textured materials (e.g., furry, coarse, smooth)

Procedures:

Rub a textured object lightly over the child's face, hands, arms, or legs, in a place where clear responses have been elicited in the past. Observe the child for any movement.

Stimulate the child again, moving the stimulus items away from and back toward the child, talking about what you are doing (e.g., "What was that? Let's see if we can find it.").

Use in Daily Routines:

Incorporate this activity into play, bathing, and dressing with the child.

Adaptations:

Motor Impaired: Tactile stimulation with a child with motor impairments may need to be preceded with a period of preparation:

For a child with stiff muscles, do relaxation activities first.

For a child with weak floppy muscles or very slow responses, try some "rough play," such as bouncing, prior to tactile input. Once the child is moving on his or her own, pause and resume the item.

Criterion: The child moves part of his or her body within 5 seconds following the initiation of tactile stimulation.

AREA: **19.   Fine Motor Skills: Tactile Integration**
BEHAVIOR: 19d.   Permits hands, feet, or body to be moved over rough-textured surfaces; or spontaneously moves them over such surfaces

Materials: Various rough-textured toys or materials (preferably objects that have not been used on previous items)

(continued)

Procedures and Use in Daily Routines:

Present an object to the child, rubbing your hands over it and talking about it. Use words to describe the object like "scratchy," "bumpy," and so forth, as appropriate. Place the object in front of the child within easy reach, and observe him or her.

If the child does not spontaneously explore the object by feeling it in some way, gently approach him or her with the object and rub it over a part of his or her body.

Make a game of it (e.g., "Here is the bumpy one," "Here comes the scratchy one").

Note: If the child cannot or does not spontaneously feel rough-textured objects, but does permit stimulation with them, it is particularly important to continue to provide stimulation every day. Emphasize the stimulation of the fingers and palms of the hands.

Adaptations:

Motor Impaired: See the Motor Impaired Adaptations section of item 19c.

Criterion: The child permits rough-textured surfaces to be moved over parts of his or her body, or he or she spontaneously moves over such surfaces.

AREA: 19. Fine Motor Skills: Tactile Integration
BEHAVIOR: 19e. Explores objects with fingers

Materials: Objects with holes or indentations in them and that have different textures

---

Procedures and Use in Daily Routines:

Show the child an object with holes or indentations in it while feeling and poking your fingers into the holes. Give the object to the child (e.g., put it in the child's lap, place it in the child's hands, put it wherever it will be easiest for the child to explore). Observe the child's actions.

If the child does not explore the object with his or her fingers, help the child rub his or her fingers over it. If the child's hands are tightly closed, tap on his or her wrist or elbow to loosen his or her fingers. Then, help the child poke his or her fingers into the object's holes. Talk about your actions as you are doing them.

Try to stimulate the child with different objects to see if any spontaneous exploration occurs. Make this a fun activity for the child.

Adaptations:

None are necessary.

Criterion: The child spontaneously explores a variety of different objects with his or her fingers.

AREA: 19. Fine Motor Skills: Tactile Integration
BEHAVIOR: 19f. Plays in water (same as item 18a.)

Materials: Water in a large basin

(continued)

Procedures:

Place the child's hands or body in water. Help him or her to splash, to push back and forth, and play in the water. Observe the child's behavior as he or she plays in the water.

Play games with the child, allowing him or her to splash you. Do not frighten the child by splashing his or her face. Try placing a few floating toys in the water for the child to reach for and to make move by hitting or splashing the water.

Use in Daily Routines:

This item is readily incorporated into bathtime. Have fun with it!

Adaptations:

Motor Impaired: Use water at a neutral temperature with a child with motor impairments, particularly if he or she has stiff muscles. If the water is too cold for this child, he or she may have more difficulty moving. Provide any support that may be needed for secure sitting, so that the child's hands may be free to play.

Criterion: The child plays or splashes in water.

AREA: **19. Fine Motor Skills: Tactile Integration**
BEHAVIOR: 19g. Finds an object that is hidden in textured material

Materials: A tub full of lentils, beans, rice, or sand; a favorite toy

---

Procedures:

Place the child's hands in the tub that is full of lentils, beans, rice, or sand and help him or her feel the materials. Place a smooth toy in the tub and push it into the lentils or other materials, until it is practically covered. Then pull the toy out (or let child pull it out). Next, push the toy back into the material and completely cover it, and then say, "Where did the _____ go? Can you get it?"

If the child makes no attempt to uncover the toy, take the child's hands and push the material aside until the toy is uncovered. Then pull the toy out and let the child play with it. Talk about where the toy was and what you are doing, as you hide it again.

If there are still no searching behaviors, repeat the game, just covering toy partially; or play the game of covering the child's own hand(s) with the material, so that the child must pull his or her hand(s) out to uncover them.

Note: Reasonable care should be taken to prevent the child from putting materials from the tub into his or her mouth. They could cause choking. If the child frequently mouths objects, this activity can be done with a tub of dry cereal.

Use in Daily Routines:

Play the game of hiding a favorite toy or the child's hand(s) while playing in a sandbox.

Adaptations:

Motor Impaired: A child with motor impairments may enjoy this activity but may be unable to move enough to ever uncover objects. Help him or her to continue playing in

---

(continued)

the material, changing the contents of the tub fairly often to alternate the stimulation that it offers.

Criterion: The child finds an object hidden in a tub of textured material on several different occasions.

AREA: **19. Fine Motor Skills: Tactile Integration**
BEHAVIOR: 19h.   Plays with soft-textured materials

Materials: Finger paint, cooked cornstarch mixture (i.e., to the consistency of pudding), Jell-O, pudding

Procedures:

Many children demonstrate enjoyment of soft-textured materials by feeling their food, squishing soap through their hands, and so on. If this is spontaneously observed, the item does not need to be worked on.

If it is not demonstrated, put a glob of the material in front of the child and help him or her run his or her fingers through it and explore it. If the child withdraws or cries, do not force him or her to keep his or her hands in contact with the material, but show the child what you can do with the substance. Then, leave the child for a few minutes and let him or her independently explore and play. Take the material away if the child continues to object to it, and try this activity again a few days later.

Add a few drops of food coloring to light colored materials to demonstrate color mixing.

Note: This item should be continued periodically throughout the first 3 years of life or longer, since it helps a child manipulate with his or her fingers. This also provides the child with tactile input. At times, you may wish to increase the tactile input by changing the material to sand, oatmeal, or some other "gritty" substance.

Use in Daily Routines:

Tactile stimulation with soft-textured materials will often occur during mealtime. This is considered to be a normal part of exploration, and assists the child as he or she learns to feed him- or herself.

Adaptations:

Motor Impaired: Be sure to create frequent opportunities for the child with motor impairments to play with and explore all types of tactile materials, since his or her ability to spontaneously seek out these experiences is often limited.

Criterion: The child plays with soft-textured materials for 3–5 minutes.

AREA: **19. Fine Motor Skills: Tactile Integration**
BEHAVIOR: 19i.   Spreads soft materials with fingers

Materials: Paper (e.g., a variety of shapes, colors, and textures), finger paints, paper towels, water for cleanup, paint shirts or smocks

(continued)

Procedures:

Place a piece of paper with paint on it in front of the child. Allow the child to touch and smear the paint, getting some on his or her fingers and hands as well as all over the piece of paper. If the child shows no interest in touching the paint, gently prompt him or her to do so, by taking the child's hand in yours and guiding it to the paint.

Demonstrate how to spread the paint on the paper. If the child does not respond to your modeling, again prompt the activity by taking his or her hand and manually moving it around the paper.

If the child is very resistant, try putting a small amount of paint in a plastic bag that can be sealed. The child can then "paint" by pushing/drawing on the outside of the bag.

Vary the texture of paints with flour, water, sand, and so on. Try painting with pudding instead of finger paints. Paint with foam made by mixing dishwashing detergent with water and paint and then whipping the mixture with an egg beater.

Use in Daily Routines:

Finger painting can be done in the tub prior to bathtime, making cleanup easy. Finger painting also makes a nice small group activity and can be used to facilitate sharing and communication.

Adaptations:

Visually Impaired: When presenting paints and other soft materials to a child with a visual impairment, describe them and how they feel (e.g., slippery, wet, cool, different colored).

Motor Impaired: Be sure that the child with motor impairments is well-positioned so that his or her hands are free for play. For some children, a prone stander works well. Give physical assistance as needed for the child to participate in this activity. Help the child open his or her hands and place them flat on paper and paint. Help the child use his or her fingers as well.

Criterion: The child spreads soft materials on a piece of paper and maintains interaction with the materials for at least 15 seconds.

AREA: **19.   Fine Motor Skills: Tactile Integration**
BEHAVIOR: 19j.   Spreads firmer materials with hands

Materials: Paste or thick glue, thinned-down clay, paper towels and water for cleanup, paper or other material on which to spread substances.

Procedures:

Place firmer materials on a piece of paper in front of the child. Allow him or her to touch the different materials, getting some on his or her fingers and hands. If the child shows no interest in touching the material, gently prompt him or her to do so by taking his or her hand in yours and guiding it to touch the material. Show the child how to spread the material on the paper. If the child, again, does not respond to your modeling, prompt him or her in the same manner as before.

Vary the texture of the materials with flour, sand, salt, sugar, and so forth.

(continued)

Use in Daily Routines:

At snack time, have the child spread peanut butter on wafers with his or her fingers.

A fun art project that could help teach this item would be to have the child spread a water-based glue on a piece of paper, then sprinkle fine materials over the glue (e.g., glitter, seeds, small noodles).

Adaptations:

Visually Impaired: See the Visually Impaired Adaptations section of item 19i.

Motor Impaired: See the Motor Impaired Adaptations section of item 19i.

Criterion: The child spreads firmer materials on a piece of paper and maintains interaction with the materials for at least 30 seconds.

AREA: **19.   Fine Motor Skills: Tactile Integration**
BEHAVIOR: 19k.   Pokes or plays with clay

Materials: Salt-dough, starch dough, Play-Doh, clay

Procedures:

Hand the child a piece of clay or dough. Take a piece yourself and show the child that you can roll it, pat it flat, stretch it, and so forth. Give the child positive descriptions of the material (e.g., "This feels good," "It's fun to squeeze this").

If the child merely holds the clay, physically assist him or her to poke, pat, and stretch it. Reinforce all attempts to do something purposeful with the clay.

Note: Be sure that the clay is soft enough for small hands to manipulate.

Use in Daily Routines:

Have the child help make the dough with which you are going to play. Have him or her assist you in mixing together the ingredients with his or her hands. Vary the colors of the clay by mixing in tempera paints or food coloring. Vary the textures of clay, as well, by adding sand, flour, water, oil, soap, and so on.

Have the child make imprints in the dough with his or her fingers, hand, foot, or small objects (footprints/handprints can be saved and later painted).

For a child who imitates well, try modeling several activities with the clay, such as patting flat, rolling into a ball, or making a dough snake.

Adaptations:

Visually Impaired: See the Visually Impaired Adaptations section of item 19i.

Motor Impaired: See the Motor Impaired Adaptations section of item 19i.

Criterion: The child independently pokes at or plays with clay or dough for at least 30 seconds.

20.

Fine Motor Skills: Reaching, Grasping, and Releasing

THE FINE MOTOR skills represented in this sequence are those that are involved in the development of accurate reaching, grasping, and releasing of objects. Although it is important to facilitate the development of good reaching and grasping patterns in both hands, it may be advisable to work though the sequence at a different rate for each hand when clearly asymmetric development is evident. Always record which hand is being used for a particular activity and devise a means of getting the child to use the nonpreferred hand for some activities.

Although reaching and grasping skills are facilitated and motivated by the presentation of visual stimuli, they can adequately develop, although very slowly, even with the absence of vision. In order for children with visual impairments to avoid a major delay in acquiring these skills, it is important to be creative both in selecting and presenting toys. Some points to remember are: noisy toys that cease to make noise before the child reaches them may cognitively cease to exist for the child unless he or she has achieved "object permanence," a concept that generally develops later in children with visual impairments, and although most objects are presented at the midline for children with no visual impairments in order to maximize their use of vision in reaching, the midline is the most difficult place to localize a sound. Thus, it is extremely important to be aware of a child's auditory localization skills in order to know the optimum placement for an object, so that it will be found by the child.

20. Fine Motor Skills: Reaching, Grasping, and Releasing

a. Actively moves arm when he or she sees or hears an object
b. Bats at object at chest level
c. Grasps object that is placed in his or her hand (i.e., not reflexive grasp)
d. Reaches out and grasps objects near body
e. Displays extended reach and grasp
f. Rakes and scoops small objects (i.e., fingers against palm)
g. Releases one object to take another
h. Grasps an object, using thumb against index and middle fingers

i. Uses inferior pincer grasp (i.e., thumb against side of index finger)

j. Uses index finger to poke

k. Uses neat pincer grasp (i.e., thumb against tip of index finger)

l. Releases four objects into a container

m. Imitates building a 2-block tower

n. Imitates building 3–4-block tower

o. Releases many objects into a container

p. Grasps two small objects with one hand

q. Imitates building 6–8-block tower

r. Puts a small object through a small hole in a container

s. Puts one pellet into a bottle

AREA: **20. Fine Motor Skills: Reaching, Grasping, and Release**
BEHAVIOR: 20a. Actively moves arm when he or she sees or hears an object

Materials: Any attractive toys or objects (e.g., bright, shiny, colorful) including some that make noise

---

Procedures:

Place the child on his or her back or in an infant seat, so that arms are free to move. Hold up a toy near the child, shaking it slightly, if needed, to catch his or her attention. As the child moves his or her arms, move the object closer, so that the child can touch it.

If the child looks at the object, but does not initiate any arm or hand movement, provide occasional physical prompts. Try different objects to find those that might be interesting. Select toys that also make an interesting sound, to help attract the child's attention.

Use in Daily Routines:

Place a mobile in the child's crib. Make sure that the items on the mobile are hung so that they are interesting to the child who is viewing them from below. Change the items on the mobile periodically. Mobiles should be removed when the child begins to sit independently.

A free-standing frame that could be set in front of the child in an infant seat, from which to suspend a variety of interesting objects, can be very helpful.

Adaptations:

Visually Impaired: Use toys that make an interesting sound with a child with a visual impairment. If the child has some vision, toys that are shiny and larger may be useful and should be presented in that child's optimal visual range.

Motor Impaired: Side-lying may be the most effective position for child with motor impairments that prevent him or her from using his or her arms, freely, against gravity.

Criterion: The child moves either or both hands upon presentation of an object, on several different occasions.

AREA: **20. Fine Motor Skills: Reaching, Grasping, and Release**
BEHAVIOR: 20b. Bats at object at chest level

Materials: Any attractive toys or objects (e.g., bright, shiny, colorful), including some that make noise

---

Procedures:

Hold objects in front of the child at chest level and within his or her arm's reach. If necessary, shake or move an object to attract his or her attention. If the child does not bat at the object, move it closer, so that it touches one or both of the child's hands, and any movement will make the object move. Gradually move the object farther away to promote more active movement on the part of the child.

(continued)

Use in Daily Routines:

Place a mobile in the child's crib. Make sure that the items on the mobile are hung so that they are interesting to the child who is viewing it from below. Change the items on the mobile periodically. Mobiles should be removed when the child begins to sit independently.

A free-standing frame that could be set in front of the child in an infant seat, from which to suspend a variety of interesting objects, can be very helpful.

Adaptations:

Visually Impaired: Use toys that make an interesting sound (e.g., when wound) with a child with a visual impairment. Place the toy so that it is touching or nearby the child's hand or arm. If the child has some vision, toys that are shiny and larger may be useful and should be presented in that child's optimal visual range.

Motor Impaired: Side-lying may be the most effective position for children with motor impairments that prevent him or her from using his or her arms, freely, against gravity.

Criterion: The child bats his or her arms at toys on several different occasions.

AREA: 20. Fine Motor Skills: Reaching, Grasping, and Release
BEHAVIOR: 20c. Grasps object that is placed in his or her hand (i.e., not reflexive grasp)

Materials: A variety of small, interesting toys (e.g., rattles, jar rings, cubes)

Procedures:

Place an object in the child's hand and observe his or her reactions. If the child immediately drops it, give it back to him or her or try another toy of a different size, shape, weight, and so forth. Look for the child's fingers to curve around the object and to hold it 10 seconds or more.

If the child does not respond, try placing your hand over his or her hand, assisting him or her in holding the object. Gradually reduce your assistance and watch for the child to continue independently holding the object. Varying the properties of the objects given and the way in which the object is placed in the child's hand may also be useful in promoting independent grasping.

Notes: Objects should not be smaller than 1½" × 1½", to avoid accidental swallowing.

Do not credit a purely reflexive grasp (i.e., the automatic closing of the hand around any object that touches the palm of the hand). If you get this response, try giving the child toys that are large in diameter or are of a different shape. Make sure that the child is as relaxed as possible.

Use in Daily Routines:

During routine care activities (e.g., diapering, eating, bathing, dressing), hand the child various objects to hold.

Adaptations:

Visually Impaired: Try to use toys that make a sound and/or have an interesting texture with a child with a visual impairment.

(continued)

Motor Impaired: For a child with motor impairments who has marked difficulty grasping, the occupational therapist may suggest a strap with which to attach the toy to the child's hand for brief play periods.

Criterion: The child grasps an object that is placed in his or her hand for 10 seconds or more on several different occasions.

AREA: 20.   Fine Motor Skills: Reaching, Grasping, and Release
BEHAVIOR: 20d.   Reaches out and grasps objects near body

Materials: A variety of interesting toys or objects

Procedures:

Place an interesting object within the child's easy reach and observe his or her attempts to pick it up. If the child does not pick up the object, place it in his or her hand for a few seconds to attract his or her attention to it and then take it and place it within reach again.

If there is still no attempt to pick up the toy, physically assist the child to reach toward and touch the toy. The grasp at this point is usually "palmar" (i.e., fingers against the palm of the hand). Be sure to vary the toys so that the child will remain interested in the task.

Use in Daily Routines:

Place various objects near the child at different times of the day. A free-standing frame that could be set in front of the child in an infant seat, from which to suspend a variety of interesting objects, can be very helpful.

Adaptations:

Visually Impaired: Before the young child with a visual impairment develops a sense of object permanence, it is difficult for him or her to connect the sound of an object with the concept of a physical object. It will probably be necessary to touch the object to the child's hand so that he or she will know to reach for the object. Also, try to place toys in consistent places, so that the child will gradually learn that a particular movement will result in finding a toy.

Motor Impaired: Some children with motor impairments may never be able to grasp with coordination. Let a child work at picking up objects, consulting with an occupational therapist for adaptations that may be needed.

Criterion: The child reaches out and grasps objects in a coordinated fashion on several different occasions.

AREA: 20.   Fine Motor Skills: Reaching, Grasping, and Release
BEHAVIOR: 20e.   Displays extended reach and grasp

Materials: A variety of interesting toys or objects

(continued)

Procedures:

Place a toy at a distance, requiring the child to straighten his or her arm and/or lean forward to reach it. If the child does not reach and pick up the toy, move it a little closer until he or she does reach for it. Gradually present the item further back until extended reach is obtained.

Use in Daily Routines:

Have different objects or toys available to the child throughout the day. Present the items at varying distances from the child's body and while the child is in different positions (e.g., prone, supine, supported sitting).

Adaptations:

Visually Impaired: See the Visually Impaired Adaptations section of item 20d.

Motor Impaired: Supported positioning may be needed to help the child with motor impairments to obtain extended reaching. For the child with stiff muscles, using slow movement and rocking to relax him or her may be useful in facilitating extended reach.

Criterion: The child reaches for and picks up an object at arm's length on several different occasions.

AREA: **20.   Fine Motor Skills: Reaching, Grasping, and Release**
BEHAVIOR: 20f.   Rakes and scoops small objects (i.e., fingers against palm)

Materials: A variety of small objects (when you begin to work with very small objects, it is a good idea to use edible items, since there will be less danger when the child puts them in his or her mouth)

Procedures:

Place small pieces of cereal, such as Cheerios or Honeycomb, on a table or tray in front of the child. Encourage him or her to pick up the food and eat it.

If the child does not spontaneously pick up the cereal:

Place one in the child's hand and guide it to his or her mouth (or simply feed the child one) and try again.
Vary the size and shape of the items (e.g., larger ones will be easier to pick up).
Reduce the size of items when the child masters picking up the larger size.

Use in Daily Routines:

This activity is readily incorporated into meal and snack time. As the child demonstrates success, begin offering him or her a wider variety of finger foods that are easy to munch and swallow.

Adaptations:

Visually Impaired: It may be hard for a child with a visual impairment to become interested in small objects. Focus on edible items and finger feeding. Give the child a taste of what you are presenting and then help the child feel for the food on his or her tray with an open hand.

Motor Impaired: Good supported positioning in a seated position may help the child with motor impairments to achieve this goal.

Criterion: The child picks up several small objects.

AREA: **20. Fine Motor Skills: Reaching, Grasping, and Release**
BEHAVIOR: 20g. Releases one object to take another

Materials: A variety of interesting toys and objects

Procedures:

Give the child a toy. Allow the child a moment to explore and play with that toy, then offer a second toy and encourage him or her to take the second toy as well. If the child does not take the second toy, place it in his or her hand. It may be helpful to reserve a favorite toy to offer as the second choice.

> *Note:* In the normal developmental sequence, when a child first learns to reach for a second object, he or she usually drops the first. It is a more mature response for the child to continue holding both objects.

Use in Daily Routines:

Observe the child at various times throughout the day. When the child is holding a toy, try offering a second toy and note his or her response.

Adaptations:

> *Visually Impaired:* Touch the child with a visual impairment with a second object and talk about the object to encourage him or her to reach for it. An object that makes a continuous sound, such as a wind-up music box, may be helpful.

> *Motor Impaired:* The child with motor impairments may have difficulty releasing the first object. Be sure to allow plenty of time for the child to respond. A larger object may be easier to release than a small one. For the child with stiff muscles, use of slow movement and rocking to relax him or her may be needed.

Criterion: The child releases one object to take or pick up another on several different occasions.

AREA: **20. Fine Motor Skills: Reaching, Grasping, and Release**
BEHAVIOR: 20h. Grasps an object, using thumb against index and middle finger

Materials: Several 1″ blocks; gradually decreasing sizes of objects (edible items are good for this activity)

Procedures:

Present small objects near the thumb side of the child's hand. Encourage the child to use his or her thumb and fingers to pick up the objects. If the child continues to pick up the objects using his or her fingers against the palm, try holding an object between your thumb and index finger so that the child cannot take it from you without using a thumb-against-fingers grasp.

If the child is not successful, do not frustrate him or her—let the child continue to pick up the items with his or her fingers against the palm for several more weeks and then try this activity again.

> *Note:* This grasp may also be referred to as the radial-digital grasp or the three-jaw chuck.

(continued)

Use in Daily Routines:

Offer the child frequent opportunities to finger feed him- or herself various sizes and shapes of food, which will encourage development of more mature grasp patterns.

Adaptations:

Visually Impaired: Encourage the child with visual impairments to "search" for objects with an open hand, but, if necessary, physically guide the hand so that the object rests against the child's index and middle fingers. Encourage the child to pick the object up. Also, work on the child's taking something that you are holding between your thumb and fingers. Using food is often helpful.

Motor Impaired: A child with significant motor impairments may never develop mature grasping patterns. If the child is having significant difficulty, consult an occupational therapist to determine the appropriateness of your goals and adaptations, if needed.

Criterion: The child spontaneously picks up small objects using his or her thumb and forefingers on several different occasions.

AREA: **20.   Fine Motor Skills: Reaching, Grasping, and Release**
BEHAVIOR: 20i.   Uses inferior pincer grasp (i.e., thumb against side of index finger)

Materials: A variety of small objects or finger foods

Procedures:

Provide the child with small objects and observe how he or she picks them up. Using very small edible items is often the best way to encourage the development of this grasp pattern.

Note: As a child develops better skills with his or her hands, he or she will vary use of a variety of different grasps. Within the course of one meal or playtime, it is normal to see a child pick up objects by raking his or her fingers against the palm, by using thumb and forefingers, and by using thumb against index finger.

Use in Daily Routines:

Offer the child frequent opportunities to finger feed various sizes and shapes of food, which will encourage development of more mature grasp patterns.

Adaptations:

See Adaptations section of item 20h.

Criterion: The child picks up small objects with his or her thumb against the side of the index finger, on several different occasions.

AREA: **20.   Fine Motor Skills: Reaching, Grasping, and Release**
BEHAVIOR: 20j.   Uses index finger to poke

Materials: An empty pegboard with ¼" holes, busy box toy, telephone

---

(continued)

Procedures:

Present an empty pegboard to the child and demonstrate how to poke your finger into the holes and pull it out. Guide the child to try this activity with his or her own index finger.

Cut a hole in a piece of wood or cardboard that is big enough for you to stick your finger through. Stick your finger through it and "wave" it at the child, making a game of it. The child will probably reach for your finger. If so, withdraw it gradually, enticing the child to come after it with his or her finger. If the child gets his or her finger through the hole, turn the board slightly so that child can see his or her finger wiggle.

Note: The point of this item is to get good separation of the index finger from the rest of the fingers. Watch for other activities where the child spontaneously does this (e.g., pushing food or toys around with his or her index finger).

Use in Daily Routines:

Provide a busy box-type toy for the child to play with at various times throughout the day. Demonstrate for the child how to push a button to get a buzzing noise or "pop-up" reaction with the toy.

Adaptations:

Visually Impaired: Help the child with visual impairments explore the holes in an empty pegboard with his or her finger. Interesting textures or sticky foods in the hole will reinforce the activity. Easy to push buttons that produce a sound are also useful.

Criterion: The child spontaneously pokes or places his or her index finger into openings in an empty pegboard on several different occasions.

AREA: **20.   Fine Motor Skills: Reaching, Grasping, and Release**
BEHAVIOR: 20k.   Uses neat pincer grasp (i.e., thumb against tip of index finger)

Materials: A variety of small objects or finger foods

Procedures:

Give the child a lot of practice picking up small objects, particularly small pieces of food at mealtime. Observe the grasp patterns that the child uses. If the child persists in using a raking motion (i.e., fingers against palm) when other patterns would be more efficient, try handing the items to the child. Hold them between your thumb and index finger in such a way that the child cannot get them with a raking movement. Also, continue to encourage pounding activities or punching objects with the index finger to increase the separation of that finger from the others.

Use in Daily Routines:

Make small pieces of finger foods available at meal and snack time.

Adaptations:

See the Adaptations section of item 20h.

Criterion: The child spontaneously picks up a small object between his or her thumb and the tip of the index finger on several different occasions.

(continued)

AREA: **20.   Fine Motor Skills: Reaching, Grasping, and Release**
BEHAVIOR: 20l.   Releases four objects into a container

Materials: A variety of small, easy to grasp objects; a container with a wide opening

Procedures:

Place a container in front of the child. Demonstrate how to drop objects into the container. Then dump the objects back out and encourage the child to drop them into the container again. If the child does not attempt the activity, place one object into the child's hand and tell him or her to "put it in."

If the child does not respond, help him or her by holding his or her hand over the container. Tell the child to put the object in the container. If he or she still does not, tap the top of the child's hand until he or she lets go of the object. If that does not work, gently press on the back of the child's hand, bending it forward until he or she releases the object. Praise his or her release!

Using a metal container that makes a loud sound when an object is dropped in may be motivating for some children. Also, experiment with various objects to find some that the child may be interested in dropping in.

Use in Daily Routines:

Encourage the child to clean up his or her toys at the end of a play session by picking them up and dropping them into a container.

Adaptations:

Visually Impaired: Physically assist the child with a visual impairment several times. Use objects and containers that will result in a noise when objects are dropped in. Encourage the child to drop in one object and retrieve it several times before working with several items.

Criterion: The child will drop four objects into a container on several different occasions.

AREA: **20.   Fine Motor Skills: Reaching, Grasping, and Release**
BEHAVIOR: 20m.   Imitates building a 2-block tower

Materials: Several 1"–1½" blocks of identical size

Procedures:

Let the child play with the blocks for several minutes. Tell the child that you are going to build a tower. Build a 3–4-block tower. Knock it down, start to build another, and ask the child to build a tower like yours. Begin with 2 or 3 blocks. If the child does not respond, you may need to physically assist him or her in putting one block on top of another. Express a lot of praise for the child's attempts.

Use in Daily Routines:

Children often enjoy stacking household items such as small cans or boxes. Let him or her have fun doing so through the day.

(continued)

Adaptations:

> *Visually Impaired:* Help the child with a visual impairment feel the blocks that are stacked on top of each other. It may be helpful to have the child hold the bottom block with one hand and place the top block on with the other hand.

> *Motor Impaired:* Experiment with blocks of different sizes and weights if the child with motor impairments is having difficulty. It may be easier for the child to start with magnetic or velcro blocks at first.

Criterion: The child imitates building a two-block tower on several different occasions.

AREA: **20.   Fine Motor Skills: Reaching, Grasping, and Release**
> BEHAVIOR: 20n.   Imitates building 3–4-block tower

Materials: Eight 1″–1½″ blocks of identical size

Procedures:

> See the Procedures section of item 20m.

Use in Daily Routines:

> See the Use in Daily Routines section of item 20m.

Adaptations:

> See the Adaptations section of item 20m.

Criterion: The child imitates building a three- to four-block tower on several different occasions.

AREA: **20.   Fine Motor Skills: Reaching, Grasping, and Release**
> BEHAVIOR: 20o.   Releases many objects into a container

Materials: A variety of small objects (e.g., 1″ blocks, clothespins, bells), a container with a wide opening (e.g., kettle, cookie jar, oatmeal box)

Procedures:

> Give the child six or more small objects (cubes, clothespins, bells). Demonstrate how to drop the objects into a container one at a time. Spill the objects out and then ask the child to put them in again. Give physical prompts as needed. If the child loses interest quickly, try handing him or her another object as soon as he drops one in.

> Make "dumping out and putting in" a game. Vary the task with different sizes of objects and containers. Challenge the child's motor skill (e.g., if the child easily puts clothespins into a big container, try a container with a smaller opening, like a milk jug).

Use in Daily Routines:

> Involve the child in cleaning up after playtime by putting toys into a container.

> During bathtime, the child can retrieve floating objects and drop them into a basket.

(continued)

Adaptations:

> See the Adaptations section of item 201.

Criterion: The child puts many objects into a container on several different occasions.

AREA: **20. Fine Motor Skills: Reaching, Grasping, and Release**
> BEHAVIOR: 20p. Grasps two small objects with one hand

Materials: Several 1″ blocks or other small objects

Procedures:

> Place two blocks or other small toys on a table, next to each other, and ask the child to get the blocks. If needed, demonstrate how to pick up both of the blocks with one hand. Provide physical prompts, placing the child's hands on top of both blocks. It may be helpful to give the child something to hold in the other hand, so that he or she will need to pick up both blocks with only one hand.

Use in Daily Routines:

> The child may spontaneously pick up two pieces of cookie or other finger food in one hand.

Adaptations:

> *Visually Impaired:* Provide physical prompts for the child with a visual impairment. Try placing both objects in the child's hand and asking him or her to hold them. Then place the blocks on a table and guide the child's hand to the blocks. Tell him or her to get the blocks.

> *Motor Impaired:* A child with significant hand involvement may not be able to accomplish this item.

Criterion: The child picks up two small objects with one hand on several different occasions.

AREA: **20. Fine Motor Skills: Reaching, Grasping, and Release**
> BEHAVIOR: 20q. Imitates building 6–8-block tower

Materials: Twelve to sixteen 1″–1½″ blocks of identical size

Procedures:

> See the Procedures section of item 20m.

Use in Daily Routines:

> See the Use in Daily Routines section of item 20m.

Adaptations:

> See the Adaptations section of item 20m.

Criterion: The child imitates building a six- to eight-block tower on several different occasions.

AREA: **20.   Fine Motor Skills: Reaching, Grasping, and Release**
BEHAVIOR: 20r.   Puts a small object through a small hole in a container

Materials: A shoe box with a slot and poker chips; coins and a bank; blocks and a shape box with a single opening; bottle and clothespins

---

Procedures:

Demonstrate to the child how to put a small object through a hole or slot into a container, such as poker chips through a slot. If needed, physically guide the child through the motions. If he or she lacks the accurate control, start with a slightly larger opening, then reduce the size as more skill is gained.

Use in Daily Routines:

This is often a favorite play activity for young children; however, they should be supervised carefully if small objects are being used.

Adaptations:

Visually Impaired: Help the child with visual impairments to explore a hole or opening with his or her finger. Then provide physical assistance, guiding the child's hand to place the object in the hole or slot. Help the child to feel the hole with one hand, while at the same time using the other hand to place the object in it. Provide extra sensory cues, such as dropping small bells into a tall metal cylinder.

Criterion: The child will place a small object in or through a small hole on several different occasions.

AREA: **20.   Fine Motor Skills: Reaching, Grasping, and Release**
BEHAVIOR: 20s.   Puts one pellet into a bottle

Materials: Several small pellets (or small edible items such as raisins), a bottle with a 1″ neck opening

---

Procedures and Use in Daily Routines:

Demonstrate to the child how to drop several pellets into a bottle one at a time. Then pour some pellets out and ask the child to put one pellet into the bottle. If needed, try handing the child one pellet and prompting him or her to place it in the bottle. If the child has difficulty with this process, try practicing the activity with a container that has a larger opening. If the child mouths objects frequently, use edibles for this routine.

Adaptations:

Visually Impaired: Help the child with a visual impairment to feel the bottle and its opening. Then have the child hold the bottle around the neck with his or her thumb and index finger, using the other hand to place the pellet in the bottle.

Motor Impaired: The control required for this activity may be too great for the child with a significant motor impairment. For a child with stiff muscles, relaxation prior to activity may be helpful.

Criterion: The child will place one pellet into a bottle on several different occasions.

21.

Fine Motor Skills: Manipulation

T HE ITEMS IN this sequence represent the child's ability to integrate the skills that were developed in sequence 20, Fine Motor Skills: Reaching, Grasping, and Releasing (pp. 285–297), in order to manipulate objects. The early items tend to be highly dependent on vision, and it is important to encourage children with any degree of vision to use that ability in coordination with their hand skills. Unfortunately some children, particularly those with motor impairments, learn to do some manipulative tasks without looking, and then have significant difficulty moving to a higher level of skills that require the integration of vision and motor abilities (e.g., visual-motor skills).

The later items in this sequence are not as strongly dependent upon vision. Children with severe visual impairments can learn to do these tasks through the use of tactile cues. As soon as the child with a visual impairment is able to pick up and release items efficiently, efforts should be made to involve him or her with these later items (beginning with item 21j.). Of course, decisions will always have to be made as to which activities are most appropriate by considering each child's tactile skills and motor sophistication.

21.   Fine Motor Skills: Manipulation

a.   Looks to one side at a hand or a toy
b.   Looks at or manipulates a toy that is placed in the hands at midline
c.   Brings a toy and the hand into visual field and looks at them when the toy is placed in the hand (i.e., may move head or hand, or moves a toy to the mouth at midline (if the child has a visual impairment)
d.   Watches hands at midline—actively moves and watches results
e.   Plays with own feet or toes
f.   Glances from one toy to another when a

toy is placed in each hand, or alternately plays with the toys
g.   Reaches out for toys and picks them up when toys and hand are in the visual field (modify for a child with a visual impairment)
h.   Reaches out for toys and gets them when the toys (not the child's hands) are in the visual field (modify for a child with a visual impairment)
i.   Looks toward an object and visually directs the reach, or adjusts the reach to

get a noisy object (if has no functional vision)

j. Manipulates objects with hands and fingers

k. Removes rings from a post

l. Removes small round pegs from holes

m. Puts one large round peg in a hole

n. Puts one small round peg in a hole

o. Puts 5–6 small round pegs in holes (i.e., completes task)

p. Unwraps an edible item or other small object

q. Turns pages one at a time

r. Turns a doorknob with forearm rotation

AREA: 21. Fine Motor Skills: Manipulation
BEHAVIOR: 21a. Looks to one side at a hand or a toy

Materials: Brightly colored ribbon; small bells on elastic bands or on loops of yarn or string

Procedures:

Tie various, brightly colored ribbons to the child's wrists and encourage him or her to look at them. Add a few bells to the ribbons and give the child's hands a little shake, so that the bells jingle. Sometimes just stroking or tapping the child's hands will help to draw his or her attention to them.

You may want to do this activity several times in succession, making sure that there is a definite break between presentations (e.g., 5 or 6 seconds). Be sure to look at the child for signs of recognition or excitement when you return the ribbon, bell, or yarn to the child's hand or when you gently shake the toy.

Look for the child to make eye contact with the object. Any affective change (e.g., a smile) when the object is placed in the hand or shaken may indicate that the child is looking at his or her hand (or the toy).

Use in Daily Routines:

This is an easy activity to do for brief periods of time throughout the day.

Adaptations:

Visually Impaired: To better assist the child with a visual impairment make sure that there is ample lighting in the room where you are doing this activity, and use brightly colored or shiny objects that also make noise. Movement of the object may also help catch the attention of the child with limited vision.

Criterion: The child turns his or her head to look at his or her hand (or a toy) on several different occasions.

AREA: 21. Fine Motor Skills: Manipulation
BEHAVIOR: 21b. Looks at or manipulates a toy that is placed in the hands at midline

Materials: Bright, shiny objects that will gain the child's attention (toys that will also emit a noise if shaken or squeezed are recommended)

Procedures:

Hold a toy within the child's reach and try to gain his or her attention by shaking, rattling, or squeezing the toy. With your other hand, bring the child's hand to midline, to the toy. Once the child's hand is on the toy, shake or rattle it for him or her.

Try to let the child hold the toy, independently. Rather than holding the toy for the child, merely try supporting it lightly with 1 or 2 fingers to facilitate the child's holding it.

Use in Daily Routines:

Take regular opportunities throughout the day to present different toys to the child. You may alternate placing items in the child's hands by attaching brightly colored ribbons and bells to his or her hands or wrists to encourage him or her to bring the hands to midline to look at them.

(continued)

Adaptations:

> *Visually Impaired:*   See the Visually Impaired Adaptations section of item 21a.

> *Motor Impaired:*   If the child with motor impairments has difficulty maintaining his or her head at midline or bringing his or her hands to midline, try this activity in a side-lying position.

Criterion: The child looks at or manipulates a toy that is placed in his or her hands at midline for 5 or more seconds on several different occasions.

AREA: **21.   Fine Motor Skills: Manipulation**
BEHAVIOR: 21c.   Brings a toy and the hand into visual field and looks at them when the toy is placed in the hand (i.e., may move head or hand), or moves a toy to the mouth at midline (if the child has a visual impairment)

Materials: Toys or materials that are brightly colored and/or that make a noise when manipulated

Procedures:

> Hold the toy in the visual field of the child. Manipulate it in a manner that will gain the child's attention. Place the toy in or on the child's hand, allowing him or her to bring it back into his or her visual field by him- or herself.

> If the child does not bring the toy into his or her visual field, move his or her hand with the toy to midline or gently turn the child's head toward the hand with the toy. Then manipulate the toy to gain the child's attention.

Use in Daily Routines:

> Incorporate activity during feeding and diaper changing.

Adaptations:

> *Visually Impaired:*   Choose noisy toys to conduct this activity with a child with a visual impairment. Place one toy in the child's hand and help him or her make the noise. Wait to see if the child will then do it on his or her own.

> *Motor Impaired:*   See the Motor Impaired Adaptations section of item 21b.

Criterion: The child brings a toy into his or her visual field or turns toward it when it is placed in his or her hand on several different occasions.

AREA: **21.   Fine Motor Skills: Manipulation**
BEHAVIOR: 21d.   Watches hands at midline—actively moves and watches results

Materials: None required or, if necessary, brightly colored ribbons or mittens with bells

Procedures and Use in Daily Routines:

> Observe the child at various times throughout the day. If the child does not play with his or her hands, place a mitten or bright ribbon or elastic to which bells are attached

(continued)

to the child's hands or wrists. Help the child to bring his or her hand into the midline and shake the child's hand to draw attention to it (repeat this action several times).

Note: Be sure to allow the child to work with both hands.

Adaptations:

See the Adaptations section of item 21b.

Criterion: The child is observed watching his or her hands on several different occasions.

AREA: **21. Fine Motor Skills: Manipulation**
BEHAVIOR: 21e. Plays with own feet or toes

Materials: Ribbons, bells, or booties with bright colors or patterns

---

Procedures:

Place ribbons, bells, or brightly colored booties on child's feet or shoes.

If the child does not play with his or her feet, gently shake them to gain his or her attention. Call attention to the bells, ribbons, or "pretty shoes." Shake the child's foot gently, saying, "Look at the ribbons, hear the bells!" If the child does not reach for his or her feet, try lifting the child's buttocks slightly, with legs in flexion, bringing the feet nearer to the child's hands.

Use in Daily Routines:

Play "This little piggy went to market . . ." while dressing the child. Wait to see if the child then plays with his or her feet.

Adaptations:

Visually Impaired: Use bells or ribbons on the shoes of a child with a visual impairment. Help the child bring his or her hands to his or her feet and to explore them. Describe what is happening.

Motor Impaired: If the child with motor impairments has difficulty reaching his or her feet, position him or her in a flexion and/or side-lying position and help the child bring his or her feet nearer to the hands.

Criterion: The child is observed spontaneously playing with his or her feet or toes on several different occasions.

AREA: **21. Fine Motor Skills: Manipulation**
BEHAVIOR: 21f. Glances from one toy to another when a toy is placed in each hand, or alternately plays with the toys

Materials: 1″ cubes, squeaky toys, rattles

Procedures:

Place a toy in one of the child's hands. Get the child to look at it and then place another toy in the child's other hand. Encourage him or her to look at the other toy. You can

(continued)

tap or squeak the toy or do whatever will attract the child's attention to it. Be sure to allow the child time to look at the first toy before adding the second toy.

Sometimes the child will drop the first toy as soon as a second one is placed in the other hand. Try placing objects in both hands several times and, perhaps, gently holding the child's hands with the toys in them for a few seconds to encourage looking back and forth. Do not frustrate the child, however, if he or she clearly wants to attend to one toy and to ignore the other. If this happens, go on to the next item in the sequence.

Use in Daily Routines:

Offer small toys during bathing, feeding, and/or diaper changing.

Adaptations:

Visually Impaired: Help the child with a visual impairment alternately play with the toys, using ones that make interesting sounds.

Criterion: The child glances from one hand to the other when an object is placed in each hand (or alternately plays with toys) on several different occasions.

AREA: **21. Fine Motor Skills: Manipulation**
BEHAVIOR: 21g. Reaches out for toys and picks them up when toys and hand are in the visual field (modify for a child with a visual impairment)

Materials: Any preferred toys that are easy to pick up

Procedures:

Place a toy within the child's easy reach, near one of his or her hands. Draw the child's attention to the toy by moving it, making it produce noise, and so forth.

If the child does not grasp the toy, touch the back of his or her hand with the toy and then place it so that it is almost touching his or her fingers.

Use in Daily Routines:

Make toys available to the child throughout the day, varying what is offered. It is better to offer just a few toys at a time, rather than overwhelming the child with a large selection.

Adaptations:

Visually Impaired: Give a toy to the child with a visual impairment to play with for a minute. Then remove the toy and lay it next to his or her hand, telling him or her to "get the toy." Touch the toy to the back of the child's hand. A toy that makes a continuous noise may be useful.

Motor Impaired: Very soft rubber, squeaky toys may be helpful for a child with motor impairments who has difficulty opening and closing his or her hands. If the child has difficulty opening his or her hand, it may help to stroke the back of the hand several times to facilitate its opening, so that the toy can be picked up.

Criterion: The child picks up a toy on several different occasions.

AREA: **21.   Fine Motor Skills: Manipulation**

BEHAVIOR: 21h.   Reaches out for toys and gets them when the toys (not the child's hands) are in the visual field (modify for a child with visual impairment)

Materials: Any preferred toys that are easy to pick up

Procedures:

Place a toy within the child's easy reach, but *not* near the child's hand. The toy should be placed where the child cannot see his or her hand and the toy at the same time, and so that the child must move his or her hand to find the toy. For example, place the toy on the table while the child's hands are on his or her lap.

If the child does not pick up the toy, gently move his or her hand into his or her visual field (preferably by moving the arm from the shoulder or elbow). Wait to see if the child then moves to pick up the toy. If not, facilitate further by moving the child's hand closer to the toy. On subsequent trials, try to increase the distance that the child must move on his or her own.

Use in Daily Routines:

Have several toys available to the child when placed on floor.

Adaptations:

Visually Impaired: Choose noisy toys to conduct this activity with a child with a visual impairment. Allow the child to feel a toy for a minute, then move it 6"–8" away from the child's hand. Make a noise with the toy until the child locates and touches it.

Motor Impaired: A child with motor impairments may best conduct this activity in a side-lying position.

Criterion: The child picks up a toy when his or her hands have been out of visual range on several different occasions.

AREA: **21.   Fine Motor Skills: Manipulation**

BEHAVIOR: 21i.   Looks toward an object and visually directs the reach, or adjusts the reach to get a noisy object (if has no functional vision)

Materials: Toys, bottle, food

Procedures:

When offering toys, a bottle, or food to the child, present them at midline and within easy reach. If the child looks at the toy and directly reaches for it, begin presenting items slightly away from his or her midline in various positions.

If the child reaches without looking at what he or she is doing, try to draw his or her attention to the object by tapping it, moving it up to eye level, and so forth.

Use in Daily Routines:

Incorporate this activity into meal or snack time, when offering the child a bottle or finger foods.

(continued)

Adaptations:

> *Visually Impaired:*   See the Visually Impaired Adaptation section of item 21h. Gradually move the object farther from the child, requiring him or her to make some adjustments in his or her reach or position in order to get the object.

> *Motor Impaired:*   Often, a child with motor impairments, but who has functional vision, will learn to grasp and pick up objects without looking at them. This behavior will interfere with the child's development of more advanced skills that require adequate coordination of visual and motor behaviors. Encourage the child's visual attention to hand activities by carefully placing objects in his or her visual field, by holding objects where they can be easily seen, and not allowing the child to obtain them until he or she looks at them, and so forth.

Criterion: The child looks at objects before reaching for them on several different occasions.

AREA: **21.   Fine Motor Skills: Manipulation**
BEHAVIOR: 21j.   Manipulates objects with hands and fingers

Materials: Paper, squeaky toy, busy box

Procedures:

> Place a piece of paper in front of the child. Take a second piece of paper and crumple it up. Tell the child to "get the paper." If he or she does not respond, place paper in his or her hands. Try the same activity with cellophane paper, which makes an interesting crackling sound when manipulated.

> As an alternative, show the child how to squeeze a soft squeaky toy. Demonstrate the functions on a busy box and help the child to manipulate the various activities.

Use in Daily Routines:

> Hand the child a piece of paper while changing diaper.

Adaptations:

> *Visually Impaired:*   Use of cellophane paper with its interesting noise may be useful with a child with a visual impairment. Guide the child's hands at first, showing him or her how to squeeze and crumple the paper.

> *Motor Impaired:*   With a child with motor impairments, use very soft squeeze toys that require little movement in order to produce a sound. Repeated opening and closing of the hand may be quite difficult for some children. Allow the child plenty of time to manipulate paper or toys. Use relaxation techniques prior to each activity to assist in loosening a child's stiff muscles.

Criterion: The child uses his or her fingers and hands to manipulate an object on several different occasions.

AREA: **21. Fine Motor Skills: Manipulation**
BEHAVIOR: 21k. Removes rings from a post

Materials: A post with several rings

Procedures and Use in Daily Routines:

Place a toy post with several rings on it in front of the child. Demonstrate how to remove the rings one at a time. Then replace the rings and ask the child to take one ring off. If the child does not respond, guide his or her hand to a ring. If needed, assist the child in removing several rings. Gradually fade your assistance.

Adaptations:

Visually Impaired: Help the child with a visual impairment to feel the post and rings. Try a game of putting bracelets on and off the child's arms to help convey the concept of pulling a ring off something.

Motor Impaired: A child with motor impairments who has difficulty removing large rings from a post may have more success with small plastic bracelets. If the child is having difficulty pulling the ring up over the post, try tipping the post slightly toward him or her.

Criterion: The child removes one ring from a post on several different occasions.

AREA: **21. Fine Motor Skills: Manipulation**
BEHAVIOR: 21l. Removes small round pegs from holes

Materials: Small round pegs (approximately ⅜″), a pegboard

Procedures and Use in Daily Routines:

Present the child with a pegboard that contains several small pegs. Space them far enough apart so that they are easy to grasp. Ask the child to take out the pegs. If the child removes a peg, praise him or her and encourage him or her to remove others.

If the child does not remove a peg or has much difficulty with the activity, demonstrate how to remove the pegs and then put them back in. Give the child physical assistance, as needed. Use larger or loose fitting pegs if difficulty persists.

Adaptations:

Visually Impaired: Help the child with a visual impairment to feel the holes with his or her finger when the pegs are out. The child should maintain one hand on or near the hole while using the other hand to place the peg.

Criterion: The child removes 3 or more small round pegs from a pegboard on several different occasions.

AREA: **21. Fine Motor Skills: Manipulation**
BEHAVIOR: 21m. Puts one large round peg in a hole

Materials: Large round peg (approximately 1″), a pegboard

(continued)

Procedures and Use in Daily Routines:

Present a pegboard filled with large pegs to the child. Remove the pegs (or let the child do that), then ask the child to put the pegs back into the holes. If the child does not put the pegs in the holes or has difficulty with the activity, demonstrate how to place the pegs in the holes, and then repeat the instructions. Physically assist the child, if necessary, to put one peg in a hole. Then fade your assistance to just holding the child's wrist and then just his or her elbow, and so on, until the child is independently doing the activity.

Adaptations:

Visually Impaired: Help the child with a visual impairment to feel the hole in the pegboard with one hand and to place a peg in a hole with the other. Montessori cylinders that drop completely into their holes may provide useful practice.

Motor Impaired: A child with motor impairments, who is still using immature gross motor grasp patterns, may have more success with knob pegs, which are held in an overhand grasp hold. Start with dropping the knob pegs into a bottle, if the child has difficulty placing them in a board.

Criterion: The child puts one large peg in a hole on several different occasions.

AREA: **21.   Fine Motor Skills: Manipulation**
BEHAVIOR: 21n.   Puts one small round peg in a hole

Materials: Small round pegs (approximately ⅜″), a pegboard

Procedures and Use in Daily Routines:

Present a pegboard with small round holes to the child. Ask the child to put the pegs in the holes. If the child does not put the pegs in the holes or has difficulty with the activity, demonstrate how to place them in correctly, then repeat the instructions and let the child try again. Provide physical assistance, if necessary.

Adaptations:

See the Adaptations section of item 21m.

Criterion: The child puts one small peg in a hole on several different occasions.

AREA: **21.   Fine Motor Skills: Manipulation**
BEHAVIOR: 21o.   Puts 5–6 small round pegs in holes (i.e., completes task)

Materials: Six small (approximately ⅜″) round pegs, a pegboard

---

Procedures and Use in Daily Routines:

Present a pegboard with the pegs in place to the child. Remove the pegs (or ask the child to). Then, ask the child to put all of the pegs back into the pegboard. If the child has difficulty with this activity, demonstrate how to do it, then repeat the command. If the child fails to put all of the pegs into the pegboard, encourage him or her to finish. If necessary, physically assist the child in putting all the pegs in the holes.

(continued)

If the child rapidly loses interest, it may be helpful to give him or her the pegboard with some of the pegs already in it and encourage him or her to finish the activity or to take turns with you until the pegs are in place. Gradually decrease the amount of help that you provide.

Adaptations:

Visually Impaired: Place pegs in a small container next to the pegboard so that the child with a visual impairment can readily find them.

Criterion: The child puts 5–6 small round pegs into the holes.

AREA: **21.   Fine Motor Skills: Manipulation**
BEHAVIOR: 21p.   Unwraps an edible item or other small object

Materials: A small piece of fruit, a piece of candy, or a small toy, wrapped in wax paper or similar wrapping

---

Procedures:

Give the child a small edible item or other object that is wrapped up and ask him or her to open it. If the child does not respond, demonstrate how to unwrap the item and then re-wrap it in front of him or her. Return it to the child and tell him or her to open the candy. Use of a favorite edible item will increase the likelihood of success.

Use in Daily Routines:

Give the child a snack that is wrapped in wax paper.

Adaptations:

Visually Impaired: Use edible items with a child with a visual impairment that have a pleasant aroma. Try giving the child a small taste and then wrapping the remainder up for him or her to open.

Criterion: The child will unwrap an edible item or other small object on several different occasions.

AREA: **21.   Fine Motor Skills: Manipulation**
BEHAVIOR: 21q.   Turns pages one at a time

Materials: Children's book with thick pages

Procedures:

Look at a book with the child, turning the pages and pointing out pictures on each page. Then ask the child to turn the page for you. If needed, lift up one page part way and then ask the child to turn the page. If he or she does not respond, give physical assistance to turn the page.

Use in Daily Routines:

Plan a daily reading time with the child. At this time, encourage him or her to turn the pages of the book for you. Also, have sturdy books readily available for the child, should he or she be interested in looking at them alone.

(*continued*)

Adaptations:

> *Visually Impaired:* Use books with interesting textures, such as *Pat the Bunny,* for a child with a visual impairment.

> *Motor Impaired:* Experiment with different types of pages with a child with motor impairments to find those that are easiest for him or her to manage.

Criterion: Thc child turns the pages of a book, one at a time, on several different occasions.

AREA: **21.   Fine Motor Skills: Manipulation**
BEHAVIOR: 21r.   Turns a doorknob with forearm rotation

Materials: A classroom door with an easy-to-turn handle

Procedures:

> When entering or leaving a room, ask the child to open the door for you. If the child has difficulty with this task, give him or her verbal cues, such as "turn" (physically prompting in the correct direction), then "push" (or "pull"). It is usually easier to open a door that needs to be pushed.

> If the child is unsuccessful, practice with other activities that involve turning (e.g., nested barrels, Kitty in the Keg, plastic nuts and bolts, unscrewing loosely fastened lids from various jars). Incorporating supination (i.e., palm up) patterns into activities may also be helpful (e.g., using one hand to drop small objects into the other hand [palm up] to see how many objects the child can hold before dropping any).

Use in Daily Routines:

> Allow the child opportunities to open doors without assistance.

Adaptations:

> *Motor Impaired:*   Be sure to allow the child with limited mobility opportunities to open a door by holding/supporting him or her in position before the door.

Criterion: The child opens a doorknob using a forearm rotation.

22.

Fine Motor Skills: Bilateral Skills

THE ACTIVITIES IN this sequence were separated from the other fine motor activities because they all involve the use of two hands. They begin with activities in which both hands do essentially the same movements and progress to activities in which each hand performs a different function to accomplish a single task (e.g., one hand holds a bead while the other pushes a string through it). The activities also progress from rather unrefined movements to those requiring considerable coordination.

During the first 2 years of life, children generally do not demonstrate a clear hand preference. If a child is demonstrating a strong preference for one hand before the age of one year, evaluation by an occupational or physical therapist is indicated to rule out any possible difficulties that the child may have in using the nonpreferred hand.

It is extremely important for curriculum users to recognize that not all activities are appropriate for all children. For example, the child with athetoid cerebral palsy might be able, with a great deal of effort, to put beads on a string (item 22m.), but such an activity would never be functional for him or her. The activity would teach the child more about frustration tolerance than about a useful fine motor skill, even though the latter is the item's intent. The more severe the child's handicap, the more important it is to seek the advice of a physical and/or occupational therapist in choosing those activities that will be functional and enjoyable for him or her.

22. Fine Motor Skills: Bilateral Skills

a. Raises both hands when object is presented—hands partially open
b. Brings hands together at midline
c. Places both hands on a toy at midline
d. Transfers objects from hand to hand
e. Claps hands
f. Uses both hands to perform the same action
g. Plays with toys at midline; one hand holds the toy and the other manipulates it
h. Pulls apart pop beads

i. Holds a dowel in one hand and places a ring over it
j. Puts a pencil through a hole in a piece of cardboard
k. Unscrews small lids
l. Puts loose pop beads together
m. Strings 3 large beads

AREA: 22.   Fine Motor Skills: Bilateral Skills
BEHAVIOR: 22a.   Raises both hands when object is presented—hands partially open

Materials: Any attractive toys or objects that the child favors

___

Procedures:

Hold or dangle an object at chest level and observe the child's reactions. If the child does not reach up with his or her hands, try lowering the toy until it briefly touches one of his or her hands, then raise it slightly, finally returning it to midline.

Use in Daily Routines:

Suspend toys in front of the child using a freestanding frame.

Adaptations:

Visually Impaired: Use toys that make a sound with a child with a visual impairment. Try touching the toy to the child's hands, then immediately present it at midline with noise. Assist the child, if needed, to reach toward the toy.

Motor Impaired: If the child with motor impairments is unable to raise his or her arms while on his or her back, place the child on his or her side and try to encourage reaching movements with both hands. Encourage reaching and batting movements, even if the child's hands remain fisted.

___

Criterion: The child spontaneously raises or reaches with both hands toward an object with his or her hands partially open on several different occasions.

AREA: 22.   Fine Motor Skills: Bilateral Skills
BEHAVIOR: 22b.   Brings hands together at midline

Materials: None required, but, if needed, stick-on bows

___

Procedures:

If this behavior is not observed in general free play, put something colorful and easy to remove on one of the child's hands or wrists (e.g., a stick-on bow). Observe to see if the child brings the other hand over to touch it. If the child does not, physically guide his or her two hands to the midline (by gently pushing shoulders and upper arms).

Use in Daily Routines:

When holding a child on your lap, encourage the child to find his or her own hands by gently guiding the hands together. Play the pat-a-cake game with the child, taking him or her through the motions.

Adaptations:

Visually Impaired: Assist the child with visual impairments in bringing his or her hands together. Help the child to rub his or her hands together, exploring both sides of his or her hands.

Motor Impaired: Side-lying is a good position for children with significant motor impairments.

___

Criterion: The child brings his or her hands together at midline on several different occasions.

AREA: **22.   Fine Motor Skills: Bilateral Skills**
BEHAVIOR: 22c.   Places both hands on a toy at midline

Materials: Any attractive toys (e.g., rattles and other toys that make noise)

Procedures:

Hold a toy at midline within the child's reach. Shake or move the toy in order to gain the child's attention. If he or she does not reach for the toy, place his or her hands on the toy. Repeat this activity with various toys at different times.

Use in Daily Routines:

Have toys available to offer the child during bath and diaper changing.

Adaptations:

Visually Impaired: Hold noisy, textured toys at the midline for the child with visual impairments, physically guiding his or her hands to the toy.

Motor Impaired: See the Motor Impaired Adaptations section of item 22b.

Criterion: The child spontaneously places both hands on a toy at midline.

AREA: **22.   Fine Motor Skills: Bilateral Skills**
BEHAVIOR: 22d.   Transfers objects from hand to hand

Materials: Easy to grasp toys that are likely to promote transfer (e.g., plastic bracelet, large yarn pompom, lightweight toys with several "handles")

Procedures and Use in Daily Routines:

Place a toy in the child's hand. As the child plays with it, see if he or she will take hold of both sides of the toy, let go with one hand, and then transfer it back to the original hand. If the child does not transfer, try placing a sticky bow or "circle" of tape with sticky side out on one hand. Encourage the child to pull it off with his or her other hand. Provide physical prompts as needed.

Adaptations:

Visually Impaired: For a child with visual impairments, it may be necessary to provide much more physical assistance (i.e., guiding the child's hands to the object to facilitate transfer). Look for or make toys with interesting textures (e.g., cover a small embroidery hoop with pieces of fabric or yarn, making some smooth and some rough places).

Motor Impaired: If the child with motor impairments has difficulty bringing his or her hands together, try doing this activity in a side-lying position.

If the child has one side that is more affected than the other, begin by placing a toy in the hand that is more affected, as it will be easier for the child to transfer to the less affected side. Later it may be appropriate to encourage the child to transfer the other way.

Criterion: The child transfers an object from one hand to the other on several different occasions.

AREA: **22.   Fine Motor Skills: Bilateral Skills**
BEHAVIOR: 22e.   Claps hands

Materials: None required

Procedures and Use in Daily Routines:

Play clapping games (e.g., Pat-a-cake) with the child. Sing clapping songs in which the child can observe you clapping and in which you can physically guide his or her hands to clap. Gradually reduce the amount of physical assistance provided.

Adaptations:

Motor Impaired: If a child with motor impairments has hands that tend to be fisted, try relaxing him or her by gently rocking and stroking the back of the hand to help open the fisted hands before attempting to play clapping games.

Criterion: The child claps his or her hands without assistance.

AREA: **22.   Fine Motor Skills: Bilateral Skills**
BEHAVIOR: 22f.   Uses both hands to perform the same action

Materials: Large ball, xylophone, or drum and two sticks

Procedures and Use in Daily Routines:

Sit across from the child (e.g., 6' away). Push a ball to the child. Ask the child to roll it back to you. If the child does not respond, provide physical assistance. This activity is easiest to do with two adults, one helping the child and the other receiving and returning the ball.

Show the child how to hit a xylophone or drum, using two sticks at the same time. Play the Pat-a-cake game with the child. The object of this activity is for the child to use both of his or her hands at the same time. If you are unable to elicit a behavior with one activity, try a different one.

Adaptations:

Visually Impaired: Try using a drum or toy piano with a child with a visual impairment. Help the child hit the instrument with both hands at the same time. Gradually fade your assistance.

Motor Impaired: If the child does not sit well independently, try sitting him or her in a corner chair that provides support and helps to bring his or her arms forward. Hitting a drum or toy piano may be easiest, since precise hand control is not required.

Criterion: The child uses both of his or her hands to perform the same action.

AREA: **22. Fine Motor Skills: Bilateral Skills**
BEHAVIOR: 22g. Plays with toys at midline; one hand holds the toy and the other manipulates it

Materials: Interesting toys, particularly those with moving parts

---

Procedures:

Observe the child as he or she holds a toy at midline. Watch to see if the child holds the toy with one hand and pats, feels, pulls, and so forth, with the other. The point is that both hands are being used, but each hand is doing something different.

You may stimulate the child's play by demonstrating what can be done with the toy, but it is more likely that the characteristics of the toys themselves will stimulate the activity.

Use in Daily Routines:

Have a tub of appropriate toys to give to the child when you are talking on the telephone or when you are busy with some other activity. Periodically observe the child to see if he or she is holding a toy with one hand and manipulating it with the other hand.

Adaptations:

Visually Impaired: Use toys with interesting textures that will produce a noise when one part is manipulated.

Motor Impaired: If the child has difficulty maintaining hands together, try doing this activity in a side-lying position. A corner chair may also be useful in promoting hands to midline.

Criterion: The child plays with toys at midline, with one hand holding a toy and the other hand manipulating it.

AREA: **22. Fine Motor Skills: Bilateral Skills**
BEHAVIOR: 22h. Pulls apart pop beads

Materials: Large pop beads (e.g., approximately 1½"–2") that are easy to pull apart

---

Procedures:

Show the child a string of 4 or 5 pop beads. Pull them apart and put them back together. Give them to the child and ask him or her to pull them apart. If needed, give physical assistance.

Note: Different brands of pop beads require differing degrees of strength to pull apart. Select beads that are appropriate for the child. Gradually increase their difficulty as the child gets stronger.

Use in Daily Routines:

Have other toys that involve pulling sections apart and putting pieces together available to the child during playtime.

(continued)

Adaptations:

> *Motor Impaired:* If the child with motor impairments has limited strength, try using balls with Velcro strips on them. Attach the balls together and ask the child to pull them apart.

Criterion: The child pulls apart pop beads in one place.

AREA: **22.   Fine Motor Skills: Bilateral Skills**
BEHAVIOR: 22i.   Holds a dowel in one hand and places a ring over it

Materials: Several ½″ dowels, 5″–10″ long; wooden or plastic rings or "donuts"

Procedures and Use in Daily Routines:

> Sit down with the child and a container of dowels and rings. Let the child explore the materials on his or her own for several minutes, and comment on what he or she does. If the child makes no attempt to put a ring on a dowel, show him or her how to do it. If the child has difficulty, try plastic bracelets, which will be easier to place over the dowel. Provide physical assistance as needed. As the child becomes more adept, reduce your assistance and introduce the rings with smaller holes again.

Adaptations:

> *Visually Impaired:* Help the child with visual impairments feel the hole in the ring. Physically take the child through the activity several times.

> *Motor Impaired:* If one side of the child with motor impairments is more affected, have him or her hold the dowel in that hand.

Criterion: The child places a close-fitting ring over a dowel while holding the dowel in one hand and using the other hand to place the ring.

AREA: **22.   Fine Motor Skills: Bilateral Skills**
BEHAVIOR: 22j.   Puts a pencil through a hole in a piece of cardboard

Materials: Pencils (unsharpened), Tinker Toys, or dowels that are the size of a pencil; 4″ by 4″ squares of cardboard with various size holes in them

Procedures and Use in Daily Routines:

> Give the "materials" to the child and let him or her explore them. Have some of the holes in the cardboard squares large enough so that you could put the child's finger through them, others small enough so that there is just room for the pencil. Play with the child and show him or her how you can stick your finger through the hole, put the pencil through, and so forth.

> If the child makes no effort to do the task spontaneously or imitate it, physically assist him or her to do it.

(continued)

Adaptations:

> *Visually Impaired:*   Help the child with visual impairments to feel the holes in the cardboard and put his or her finger through them. Assist the child in sliding the pencil slowly back and forth across the board until it goes into the hole.

Criterion: The child puts a pencil or ⅜″ dowel through a small hole in a piece of cardboard.

AREA: 22.   Fine Motor Skills: Bilateral Skills
BEHAVIOR: 22k.   Unscrews small lids

Materials: Various small jars with "easy to screw on" lids (e.g., Select jars to fit the size of the child's hands. Baby food jars are appropriate for many children, but may be too large in diameter for very small hands.); small toys or edibles

---

Procedures:

> Present the child with several jars, each of which has an interesting item inside. Ask the child to open the jars or to get the object inside. If the child makes no attempt to unscrew the lids, show him or her how it can be done. Remove the object from the jar, return it, and replace the lid very loosely (i.e., so that one-quarter to one-half turn will get it off). Give the jar to the child to try the task again. Physical assistance may be used but will probably be less effective than making the task easier and letting the child master the unscrewing on his or her own.

Use in Daily Routines:

> Try offering snacks in one or two small jars for the child to open.

Adaptations:

> *Visually Impaired:*   Present an empty jar for the child with a visual impairment to explore. Talk about it and then place a noisy toy or food inside and put the lid on. Tell the child what you are doing. Give the jar to the child. Physically assist the child to remove the lid and get the contents. Then repeat the task. Frequently use the terms "unscrew," "screw," "turn," and so forth.

Criterion: The child unscrews lids from several small jars.

AREA: 22.   Fine Motor Skills: Bilateral Skills
BEHAVIOR: 22l.   Puts loose pop beads together

Materials: Loose-fitting pop beads, (i.e., adjust size and looseness to motor capabilities of the child)

Procedures and Use in Daily Routines:

> Give the child a box of pop beads that are not connected to one another. Allow the child to explore them. If the child makes no effort to put them together, show him or her how to do it; begin making your "necklace" and encourage the child to make one. Physically assist the child, if necessary. Praise his or her efforts as well as successes.

(continued)

Adaptations:

Visually Impaired: Help the child with visual impairments to feel the hole end and the knob end of the pop bead. Working as a team, push the beads together and then pull them apart several times. Gradually fade your assistance.

Motor Impaired: Select pop beads that are very easy to push together or use small blocks with Velcro attached.

Criterion: The child puts loose pop beads together.

AREA: **22.   Fine Motor Skills: Bilateral Skills**
BEHAVIOR: 22m.   Strings 3 large beads

Materials: Large kindergarten beads of various shapes and colors; lace with stiff tip at one end and knot at the other end

Procedures:

Present the child with a container of beads and the lace. With a second lace show the child how to make a necklace, stringing slowly so that the child can observe the process of putting the tip of the lace through the bead and then pulling it from the other side. Provide physical assistance or verbal instruction, as necessary, to help the child accomplish the task. If the child has difficulty, try using a stiff object, such as aquarium tubing or a swizzle stick, for the child to place beads onto at first.

Use in Daily Routines:

Have the child make a necklace to wear for the day.

Adaptations:

Visually Impaired: Use beads with large openings with the child with visual impairments, preferably ones that the child can stick his or her finger through to explore. It will also be easier to start with a stiff lace, such as tubing.

Motor Impaired: A child with motor impairments may do best with a stiff lace or a dowel (e.g., approximately 6″ long) to which the lace is attached.

Criterion: The child is able to string 3 large beads.

23.

Visual-Motor Skills: Pencil Control and Copying

VISUAL-MOTOR REFERS TO the development of drawing skills (and, at a later age, cutting and writing skills). The emergence of visual-motor skills requires integration of visual-perceptual and fine motor skills. As a result, these skills are only just beginning to be demonstrated in this curriculum and are expanded more fully in *The Carolina Curriculum for Preschoolers with Special Needs* (Johnson-Martin, Attermeier & Hacker, 1990). Note, also, that there is considerable normal variability in visual-motor skills development, with girls often demonstrating the developmental advantage.

Children with severe visual or motor impairments may have considerable difficulty with these items. It is important to consult an occupational therapist to determine if it is appropriate to include these items in the child's program and, if so, what adaptations will be necessary.

REFERENCE

Johnson-Martin, N.M. Attermeier, S.M., & Hacker, B. (1990). *The Carolina curriculum for preschoolers with special needs*. Baltimore: Paul H. Brookes Publishing Co.

3. Visual-Motor Skills: Pencil Control and Copying

a. Marks paper with writing implement
b. Scribbles spontaneously
c. Makes single vertical stroke, in imitation

d. Shifts from scribble to stroke and back, in imitation

AREA: **23.   Visual-Motor Skills: Pencil Control and Copying**
BEHAVIOR: 23a.   Marks paper with writing implement

Materials: Large crayon, pencil, or marker; several pieces of paper

---

Procedures and Use in Daily Routines:

Place a piece of paper in front of the child. Pick up a crayon and make several slow strokes on the paper, drawing the child's attention to what you are doing. Ask the child to "write" or "draw" on the paper, like you are doing. If needed, place the crayon in the child's hand. If he or she does not mark on the paper, physically assist him or her in marking the paper. Watch for the child to continue, after you stop providing assistance.

As an alternative, have the child try making strokes in finger paint, using his or her hands or fingers.

Adaptations:

Visually Impaired: Use contrasting colors, such as bright yellow paper and black markers, for a child who has low vision. Also, try making marks in thick finger paint or shaving cream with finger.

Motor Impaired: If the child is unable to hold a crayon or marker, focus initially on doing activities with his or her hand or finger in finger paint. The child may need some type of adaptation in order to hold a crayon. Consult an occupational therapist regarding possibilities. A child with severe motor impairments may never be able to do these activities independently.

Criterion: The child makes several marks on a piece of paper with a writing implement.

AREA: **23.   Visual-Motor Skills: Pencil Control and Copying**
BEHAVIOR: 23b.   Scribbles spontaneously

Materials: Two crayons, pencil, or marker; several pieces of paper

---

Procedures and Use in Daily Routines:

Give the child many opportunities to play with a crayon (or other writing implements) and a piece of paper. Show the child how to scribble on the paper, physically assist him or her if necessary.

After the child begins to readily scribble what you have demonstrated, begin a play session with just giving the child the crayon and paper and observing what he or she does. If the child does not spontaneously scribble, ask him or her to "draw" or "write." Demonstrate, if needed.

Adaptations:

See Visually and Motor Impaired Adaptations section of item 23a.

Criterion: The child spontaneously scribbles.

AREA: **23.   Visual-Motor Skills: Pencil Control and Copying**
BEHAVIOR: 23c.   Makes single vertical stroke, in imitation

Materials: Large crayon, pencil or marker; several pieces of paper

---

Procedures and Use in Daily Routines:

> Place a piece of paper in front of the child and demonstrate how to make vertical strokes. While doing so, say to the child, "Watch me. I am making lines that go up and down." Try adding a sound as you make each line (e.g., "Zip!"). Then ask the child to make a line like you did. If he or she does not, take his or her hand and help him or her make several vertical lines. Then ask the child to make one by him- or herself. If the child is having a lot of difficulty, make a cardboard guide to help him or her (cut a slot in the cardboard about ½ × 8″). Place the cardboard over the paper and guide the child's hand in making the lines using the slot. Then, see if the child can independently do this. After the child is successful a number of times, try the activity again, without the guide.

Adaptations:

> *Visually Impaired:*   Physically assist the child with a visual impairment a number of times in making lines. Make a line in a flat piece of Play Doh for the child to trace with his or her finger. If he or she is resistant, stop and try again a few weeks later. If the child has no functional vision, this type of activity may have to wait until he or she is older.

> *Motor Impaired:*   See the Motor Impaired Adaptations section of item 23a.

Criterion: The child makes a single vertical line in imitation on several different occasions.

AREA: **23.   Visual-Motor Skills: Pencil Control and Copying**
BEHAVIOR: 23d.   Shifts from scribble to stroke and back, in imitation

Materials: Large crayon, pencil, or marker; several pieces of paper

---

Procedures and Use in Daily Routines:

> When the child is marking on a piece of paper, say "Watch me," and make a quick vertical stroke on your paper. Then say, "Can you do it?" If the child imitates the stroke, say "Good, now do this," and scribble for the child. If he or she then imitates the scribble, shift back again to the stroke. Make a game of it!

> If the child does not shift from scribble to stroke, in imitation, physically assist him or her, but keep it fun.

Adaptations:

> *Visually Impaired:*   Physically guide the hand of a child with a visual impairment, while performing the actions described above. Describe what you are doing. Use materials that provide sharp contrasts in colors for the child with low vision.

> *Motor impaired:*   See the Motor Impaired Adaptations section of item 23a.

Criterion: The child shifts from scribble to stroke and back again, in imitation.

24.

Gross Motor Skills: Prone (On Stomach)

IN THE PROCESS of physical development, the abilities that children develop as they lie on their stomachs and extend their bodies against gravity are important for adequate motor function in the upright positions of sitting, standing, and walking. Generally speaking, they begin by lifting their head, then trunk, arms, and legs. The arms, and then the legs, are used to bear weight and move forward. It is important to recognize the difference between normal motor patterns and incomplete or abnormal ones. Watch normal infants as they play in a prone position, demonstrating the patterns found on the Motor Milestones in Infant Development chart (Figure 2, pp. 36–37).

As you work your way through this sequence, strive for symmetry in the back muscles and equal abilities in the right and left limbs. This symmetry is critically important for children with severe motor impairments, since they are at great risk for scoliosis and contractures, both of which should be prevented as much as possible.

Many children with developmental problems object to lying in the prone position, since it is difficult for them to raise their heads against gravity. Children with visual impairments also tend to dislike the prone position, since it cuts down on the amount of visual input they can use. Methods of dealing with the dislike of this position are described with the items of this sequence.

There are many ways in which a child with developmental problems can deviate from normal. If you cannot easily obtain the motor performance described in the items, consult a physical or occupational therapist.

24. Gross Motor Skills: Prone (On Stomach)

a. Lifts head, freeing nose; arms and legs flexed

b. Lifts head to 45° angle; arms and legs partially flexed

c. Extends head, arms, trunk, and legs in prone position

d. Bears weight on elbows in prone position

e. Rolls from stomach to back

f. Reaches while supported on one elbow

g. Supports self on hands with arms extended and head at 90°

h. Pivots in prone position
i. Pulls forward in prone position
j. Pulls self to hands and knees
k. Rocks forward and backward while on hands and knees
l. Plays with toys in an asymmetrical half-sitting position
m. Moves forward (creeps) while on hands and knees
n. Raises one hand high while on hands and knees
o. Creeps up stairs
p. Creeps down stairs, backwards

AREA: **24.   Gross Motor Skills: Prone**
BEHAVIOR: 24a.   Lifts head, freeing nose; arms and legs flexed

Materials: Brightly colored or shiny toys; noisemaking toys

Procedures:

Place the child on his or her stomach and encourage headlifting by placing toys on the floor in front of his or her face. Shake or otherwise activate the toy when the child's head is lifted, to provide motivation. The muscles at the base of the skull and in between the shoulder blades can be stimulated with your fingers, using firm, not light, strokes.

Use in Daily Routines:

Place the child on your chest as you are lying on your back with your head raised. Talk to him or her. Raising the elevation of your shoulders (i.e., making the child more upright) will make head-raising easier. As the child gets stronger, lie flatter so that the effect is the same as being on a flat surface.

Adaptations:

Visually Impaired: Introduce the prone position as quickly as possible; this is not a preferred position for children with visual impairments, so you will have to use interesting sounds or movement games to maintain the child's position. For the child with total blindness, place interesting textures under the hands and face. For the child with low-vision, use colored lights, fluorescent toys, or black and white patterns with sound added.

Motor Impaired: If the child with motor impairments has tight muscles, use relaxation techniques before and during this activity. Gently move the child's shoulder blades and rotate his or her hips. If the arms are extremely tight, place a bolster or towel roll under the shoulders to bring the arms forward. If the legs are thrusting out straight, relax and bend them. A child with weak, floppy muscles (hypotonia) may hold his or her legs in a "frog" position; correct this by holding the legs together. Positioning a child over a wedge can also make headlifting easier.

Criterion: The child lifts his or her head and holds it up, with arms and legs flexed, for several seconds at a time, and consistently does this over a period of several days.

AREA: **24.   Gross Motor Skills: Prone**
BEHAVIOR: 24b.   Lifts head to 45° angle; arms and legs partially flexed

Materials: Dangling toys

Procedures:

When the child is able to lift his or her head independently, place toys in front of his or her face and lift them to obtain head-raising to a 45° angle. Place the child's elbows in the correct position if necessary. The muscles in back of the neck and between the shoulder blades can be stimulated with your fingers, using firm, not light, strokes.

Use in Daily Routines:

Place the child on the floor for several play sessions throughout the day. Use a variety of toys for visual interest. A quilt with Velcro or strings to attach different toys is helpful.

(continued)

Adaptations:

> *Visually Impaired:*   See the Visually Impaired Adaptations section of item 24a.

> *Motor Impaired:*   See the Motor Impaired Adaptations section of 24a.

Criterion: The child lifts his or her head to a 45° angle, keeping his or her arms and legs partially flexed, for 20–30 seconds at a time, and consistently does this over a period of several days.

AREA: **24.   Gross Motor Skills: Prone**
BEHAVIOR: 24c.   Extends head, arms, trunk, and legs in prone position

Materials: Favorite toys, therapy ball, towel roll

Procedures:

> With the child lying on his or her stomach on the floor, your lap, or a therapy ball, gently pull the child's shoulders up, and wait for lifting of the head, arms, trunk, and legs. Release your hold when the child stays up alone, and resume it when the child loses control. Use visually interesting or noisemaking toys to provide motivation. Practice this item and item 24d. together, alternating between them.

> > *Note:*   Children with developmental problems often need work on this item even after they have achieved functional skills at a higher level. Children with tight or stiff muscles will tend to pull their shoulders up and forward, tip their heads back too far, not flatten their upper spine, and thrust their legs stiffly. Children with weak or floppy muscles (hypotonia) will have similar tendencies in the upper body, but will keep their legs spread out. If you cannot easily correct these tendencies, consult a physical therapist.

Use in Daily Routines:

> This is an extremely important item for building postural stability, and should be practiced often throughout the day. See also item 24a. Carrying children over your hip, facing away from you, is a good way of exercising their neck, back, and hip muscles.

Adaptations:

> *Visually Impaired:*   With children with visual impairments, pay special attention to getting lifting of the upper trunk. See the Visually Impaired Adaptations section of item 24a.

> *Motor Impaired:*   See the Motor Impaired Adaptations section of item 24a. Also, holding and swinging the child upside down can help activate extensor muscles.

Criterion: The child lifts his or her head, arms, trunk, and legs off the supporting surface for at least 20 seconds at a time, and consistently does this over a period of several days.

AREA: **24.   Gross Motor Skills: Prone**
BEHAVIOR: 24d.   Bears weight on elbows in prone position

Materials: Favorite toys, mirror, music

(continued)

Procedures:

Place the child on the floor into a position in which he or she is taking weight on his or her elbows. Use toys that encourage the child to lift his or her head. At first, the child's hands may be closed, but work toward open hands, with palms in contact with the floor. Practice this activity in alternation with item 24c.

Use in Daily Routines:

Place the child on the floor for several play periods throughout the day. Since children at this stage are not yet mobile, be prepared to change toys or stimuli often enough to prevent boredom.

Adaptations:

Visually Impaired: See the Visually Impaired Adaptations section of item 24a.

Motor Impaired: See the Motor Impaired Adaptations section of item 24a. Pay special attention to children with tight shoulder muscles, as the on-elbows position can potentially increase problems with range of motion and strength, even though it is a good position for function. For these children, as well as children with weak shoulder muscles, you can place a small towel roll under the shoulders to help keep the position. If necessary to prevent the arms from pulling underneath the body, bring the elbows forward on the floor.

Criterion: The child lifts his or her head and upper trunk into a position in which he or she is taking weight on his or her forearms, with hands open on the floor, and can stay there for at least 30 seconds, then repeats this activity several times a day for several days.

AREA: **24. Gross Motor Skills: Prone**
BEHAVIOR: 24e.   Rolls from stomach to back

Materials: Favorite toys, blanket

Procedures:

Encourage the child to roll by dangling a toy in front of the child's face, then moving it to the side and behind the line of sight. If this does not promote rolling, physically assist the child at the shoulders or hips, start him or her in side-lying position, or place him or her on a blanket and lift one edge. Try for a pattern in which the head and shoulders lead the movement and the hips follow.

Use in Daily Routines:

Use this procedure whenever lifting or turning the child out of a stomach-lying position. Give the child enough time to participate in the movement.

Adaptations:

Visually Impaired: Use auditory or tactile stimuli with child with visual impairments in order to promote rolling from stomach to the back.

Motor Impaired: If the child with motor impairments has stiff muscles, use relaxation procedures before the movement. Make sure that the bottom arm is bent and tucked into the side to avoid shoulder dislocation.

Criterion: The child is able to roll independently from stomach to back, and spontaneously and independently does this several times for a number of days in a row.

AREA: **24.   Gross Motor Skills: Prone**
BEHAVIOR: 24f.   Reaches while supported on one elbow

Materials: Toys that produce interesting displays when touched or batted, but that cannot be grasped (e.g., mobiles, suspended balloons, busy box)

Procedures:

Start this activity by requiring the child to reach straight out to activate a toy, then reposition the toy gradually so that it is above shoulder level and a little out to the side. Do this activity with each arm, and note any asymmetries. Initially, you may need to shift the child's weight to the nonreaching side by placing your hand on the child's buttocks.

Use in Daily Routines:

Provide opportunities for the child to reach out with one arm with the child either on the floor or being carried in the "face out" position.

Adaptations:

Visually Impaired: Use noisemaking toys (e.g., a variety of shiny, brightly colored toys, use high-contrast color) for children with visual impairments. For a child with total blindness or very low-vision, allow him or her to grasp and mouth the toy briefly, then take the toy and hold it 1″–3″ from the child's hand. Sound the toy and intermittently touch it to the child's hand. As the child reaches, allow a brief touch, then reposition it 1″–3″ further away. This task may be delayed in the child with total blindness until the concept of auditory object permanence is well established.

Motor Impaired: Precede this activity with relaxation, if necessary. Also, if the child cannot lift his or her arm, provide physical assistance in lifting, and hold the arm while the child does the batting movement.

Criterion: The child independently and spontaneously reaches up and out to bat at a toy, without collapse of the supporting arm, several times, for a number of days in a row.

AREA: **24.   Gross Motor Skills: Prone**
BEHAVIOR: 24g.   Supports self on hands with arms extended and head at 90°

Materials: Favorite toys, large ball, bolster

Procedures:

Place an interesting toy in front of the child's face, then raise it, encouraging him or her to push up with straight arms. Initially the child's hands may be closed, but work toward open hands with the child's palms in contact with the floor.

Use in Daily Routines:

Make use of floor play time to practice this item.

Adaptations:

Motor Impaired: Practice with the child with motor impairments being positioned over a bolster or ball. Upside-down wheelbarrow-walking is also a good strengthening activity for the arms; if you do this make sure the arms are completely extended overhead.

(*continued*)

Criterion: While lying in prone position, the child independently and spontaneously pushes up to a fully extended arm position, supporting on open hands, with head upright, and can stay there for at least 10 seconds several times, on a number of days in a row.

AREA: **24. Gross Motor Skills: Prone**
BEHAVIOR: 24h. Pivots in prone position

Materials: Favorite toys, bottle

Procedures:

Imagine a circle drawn around the child. Place a toy on the circle to the right or left of the child's head. After the child obtains the toy, move it farther around the circle. It is best not to have other toys in sight; furthermore, sometimes the bottle works best as a lure. Have the child pivot both clockwise and counterclockwise.

Use in Daily Routines:

As the child is playing on the floor or in a crib, periodically move toys to different locations to encourage pivoting.

Adaptations:

Visually Impaired: See the Visually Impaired Adaptations section of item 24f.

Motor Impaired: This activity can be made easier or harder for a child with motor impairments by varying the surface on which it is performed. It will be easier to move on a hard, smooth surface, and more difficult on a carpet. It is also easier to move with clothing on, than it is with bare skin.

Criterion: The child independently pivots 360° in each direction, and demonstrates this several days in a row.

AREA: **24. Gross Motor Skills: Prone**
BEHAVIOR: 24i. Pulls forward in prone position

Materials: Favorite toys

Procedures:

Place a favorite toy just out of the child's reach, and encourage him or her to pull forward to obtain the toy. Initially, you can provide physical assistance in weight-shifting, reaching, and pulling.

Note: It is common for children to push themselves backward at first, when they really want to move forward. They will soon learn to change the pattern.

Use in Daily Routines:

Make a point of placing toys just outside the child's reach throughout the day. Do not immediately respond if the child fusses for the toy; if he or she does not go after the toy, give him or her physical assistance in pulling forward.

(continued)

Adaptations:

> *Visually Impaired:*   See the Visually Impaired Adaptations section of item 24f. for materials. Establish a routine of placing the child with visual impairments in prone position, surrounded by a circle of favorite toys within easy reach. Leave each toy in the same position. As the child learns to obtain the toys, very gradually move them farther away. Let the child hold and mouth the object after obtaining it.

> *Motor Impaired:*   For a child with severe motor impairments, consult a physical therapist for guidance; a mobility device may be useful. If the child has stiff arm muscles, this activity can promote shoulder tightness, and extra range of motion excercises may be necessary. For a child with spina bifida, well-padded clothing is necessary to prevent skin damage.

Criterion: The child pulls forward in prone position on the floor, using his or her arms and legs, establishing this as a means of locomotion.

AREA: **24.   Gross Motor Skills: Prone**
BEHAVIOR: 24j.   Pulls self to hands and knees

Materials: Favorite toys to elicit movement, low obstacles such as pillows or bolsters

Procedures:

> While the child is pushing up onto extended arms, place your hands under the pelvis and lift up and back, waiting for the child to participate by pulling his or her knees under the hips.

> *Note:*   The child who is beginning to do "bottom lifting" in prone position is ready to start this activity. The child who is not yet ready will protest vigorously if you impose this pattern. Presenting low obstacles over which to crawl will promote the necessary leg movements.

Use in Daily Routines:

> Practice this several times a day while the child is playing on the floor. Incorporate the movement into the process of bringing the child from prone to sitting or standing. Give the child plenty of time to participate.

Adaptations:

> *Motor Impaired:*   For children with motor impairments, use physical assistance to keep the alignment of arms, trunk, and legs as close to normal as possible. For children with stiff muscles, avoid excessive bending and pulling in of the legs. If the back sags, give gentle pressure at shoulders and hips, alternating right and left sides.

Criterion: The child independently and spontaneously pulls to hands and knees and can stay there for several seconds. The child does this for several days in a row.

AREA: **24.   Gross Motor Skills: Prone**
BEHAVIOR: 24k.   Rocks forward and backward while on hands and knees

Materials: Music

(continued)

Procedures:

> While the child is on hands and knees, place your hand on the abdomen and gently start a forward-backward rocking movement. Pause and wait for the child to start the movement. Children will often rock to a favorite kind of music.

> *Note:* This is a very important activity, since it involves the middle ranges of leg movement. Immediately after rocking, the child is ready to either creep or move into a sitting position by rotating the buttocks to the floor.

Use in Daily Routines:

> Once the child has begun to assume the hands-and-knees position, carry out the rocking activity several times a day during floor play.

Adaptations:

> *Motor Impaired:* Use physical assistance with a child with motor impairments to keep his or her legs well positioned under the body. You can sit on the floor and place the child over one of your extended legs, using your other leg to keep the child's legs bent.

Criterion: The child independently and spontaneously rocks back and forth several times in a row, for a number of days in a row.

AREA: **24. Gross Motor Skills: Prone**
BEHAVIOR: 241. Plays with toys in an asymmetrical half-sitting position

Materials: Favorite toys, pillows

Procedures:

> Place toys on the floor next to the child at the level of the lower part of his or her ribcage. Physically guide the child into the position shown in Figure 2 (pp. 36–37). Gradually release your hold as the child stays in this position. Do this activity to both sides.

> *Note:* This is a very good position for building head, trunk, and shoulder control, as well as rotational patterns. The weight-bearing side develops stability, and the non-weight bearing side develops more skilled movement. It is also a good transition position for teaching a child how to move to a sitting or standing position.

Use in Daily Routines:

> For children who are not yet safe in a sitting position, use this as one play position several times throughout the day. Use of pillows for positioning helps some children stay up longer.

Adaptations:

> *Visually Impaired:* This may not be a favorite position for children with visual impairments, but it is very important for developing transitional and rotational patterns. Use very motivating visual and auditory toys, providing the child an opportunity to mouth and handle the toy just before the activity.

> *Motor Impaired:* Use your body to control the posture and movements of a child with motor impairments. Make sure the child's foot on the non-weight bearing side is flat on the floor.

Criterion: The child maintains a half-sitting position without support for about 30 seconds on each side, and demonstrates this ability several days in a row.

AREA: **24.   Gross Motor Skills: Prone**
BEHAVIOR: 24m.   Moves forward (creeps) while on hands and knees

Materials: Favorite toys

Procedures:

With the child on his or her hands and knees, place a favorite toy beyond arms' reach. If necessary, place your hand on the child's abdomen to encourage creeping rather than returning to a prone position.

Use in Daily Routines:

The child who is actively rocking on his or her hands and knees is ready to have creeping encouraged several times a day during floor play. Some children creep more readily on a carpet or on grass than on a smooth floor.

Adaptations:

Visually Impaired: See the Visually Impaired Adaptations section of 24i. For children with visual impairments, provide play spaces with toys in predictable locations, by using a playpen, a blanket with a border of toys, or a corner of the room.

Motor Impaired: Give physical assistance to a child with motor impairments, as necessary. If you see a child "bunny hopping" (i.e., moving both arms and legs forward at the same time), consult a physical therapist.

Criterion: The child creeps briskly, and uses this as a form of mobility.

AREA: **24.   Gross Motor Skills: Prone**
BEHAVIOR: 24n.   Raises one hand high while on hands and knees

Materials: Favorite toys, mirror

Procedures:

While the child is on hands and knees, position a desired toy so that the child has to reach out to obtain it. You can also place the child in front of a mirror to prompt arm reaching. Start by requiring the child to reach straight in front of his or her shoulder, and gradually move the toy so that it is above the child's shoulder level and a little out to the side. Do this activity with each arm and note any asymmetric movements.

Use in Daily Routines:

See the Use in Daily Routines section of item 24f.

Adaptations:

Visually Impaired: See the Visually Impaired Adaptations section of item 24f.

Motor Impaired: See the Motor Impaired Adaptations section of item 24f.

Criterion: The child independently reaches up high for an object with his or her supporting arm not collapsing and the upper trunk rotating against the hips. The child demonstrates this ability for several days in a row.

AREA: 24. Gross Motor Skills: Prone
BEHAVIOR: 24o. Creeps up stairs

Materials: Set of 6–10 stairs, about 6″ high and 6″–8″ deep; favorite toys

Procedures:

Place a desired object on a stair, initially just 1 or 2 stairs above the child. If necessary, give physical assistance with arm and leg placement. Gradually withdraw assistance and increase the number of stairs that you wish the child to climb.

Note: Once a child is interested in stairs, safety gates are needed to prevent falls.

Use in Daily Routines:

Encourage the child to creep up stairs when time allows. Provide other low obstacles, such as sofa cushions on the floor, for the child to practice climbing on.

Adaptations:

Visually Impaired: The child with a visual impairment may require a longer period of physical guidance. Help the child explore the contours of the stairs.

Criterion: The child safely and independently creeps up 6–10 stairs, and demonstrates this ability several days in a row.

AREA: 24. Gross Motor Skills: Prone
BEHAVIOR: 24p. Creeps down stairs, backward

Materials: Set of 6–10 stairs, about 6″ high and 6″–8″ deep; favorite toys

Procedures:

Place the child on the stairs, initially just one or two stairs from the bottom. Entice the child to creep down to obtain a toy. Give physical assistance, as necessary, with arm and leg placement. Gradually withdraw assistance and increase the number of stairs that you wish the child to descend.

Note: Once a child is interested in stairs, safety gates are needed to prevent falls. Some children prefer to go down stairs by sitting, facing forward, and lowering themselves to the next stair. The most important considerations are safety and independence.

Use in Daily Routines:

See the Use in Daily Routines section of item 24o.

Adaptations:

Visually Impaired: See the Visually Impaired Adaptations section of item 24o.

Criterion: The child safely and independently creeps down 6–10 stairs, and demonstrates this ability several days in a row.

25.

Gross Motor Skills: Supine (On Back)

THE ITEMS IN this sequence help the child to develop stabilizing functions using the front of the neck, trunk, shoulders, and hips. This stability allows the child to lift his or her arms and legs, bringing them into his or her visual field and using them for play. Items 25a. through 25e. help the child to develop the basic capabilities for self-feeding, so it is appropriate to work on these skills at mealtimes.

For a child with an abnormal motor system, a completely supine position is frequently inappropriate for either exercise or general positioning. A child with weak, floppy muscles (hypotonia) cannot act against gravity; he or she can only lie on the back with arms and legs passively on the floor. Naturally, the child prefers this position over being on his or her stomach, since it allows him or her to observe the environment more readily. However, it is the least preferred position for muscular development. A child with stiff muscles (hypertonia) will often become stiffer when lying on his or her back and this will interfere with the development of more functional patterns.

In order to establish the stabilizing functions that should be acquired with the help of this sequence, the use of side-lying and semi-reclined positions are frequently more appropriate. A child may progress to performing the functions on his or her back or he or she may never achieve this function. A good rule to go by is to always position the child for maximum function, while still providing some neuromuscular challenges. A physical or occupational therapist can provide guidance regarding the best position for a particular child.

25. Gross Motor Skills: Supine (On Back)

a. Turns head from side to side in response to auditory or visual stimuli
b. Bends and straightens arms and legs
c. Brings hands to mouth
d. Maintains head in midline position while supine
e. Reaches out with arm while in a supine position
f. Holds feet in air for play
g. Rolls from stomach to back

AREA: **25. Gross Motor Skills: Supine**

BEHAVIOR: 25a.   Turns head from side to side in response to auditory or visual stimuli

Materials: Any visual and/or auditory stimuli that hold the child's attention

---

Procedures:

Position the child comfortably with his or her head in midline. Move your face to one side so that the child will turn his or her head to see you. You can also talk to the child from the side to encourage him or her to turn to the right and left. It may help to touch the child's cheek on the side toward which you wish the child to turn.

Note: This item is similar to items 3c. and 6a. The aim here, however, is simply to get the child to turn his or her head, regardless of the stimulus.

Use in Daily Routines:

Do this activity often throughout the day, while holding the child. Set up the changing table with a visually attractive object on the wall; alternate the way the child is positioned on the table, so that turning to the right and left will be encouraged.

Adaptations:

Visually Impaired: Pair auditory stimuli with brightly colored, shiny, or high contrast visual stimuli with a child with a visual impairment. Experiment to find his or her preferred stimuli. Help the child touch and mouth the object; touch it to the child's face to help get the turning movement.

Hearing Impaired: Experiment with different types and intensities of sounds to find preferred stimuli for the child with a hearing impairment.

Motor Impaired: A child with motor impairments who has stiff muscles may become stiffer when lying on his or her back, making all movements more difficult. Try a semi-reclining position with this child. If head-turning is followed by arm-straightening on the "face" side and arm bending on the "skull" side, make sure the chin is tucked down, keep the stimuli slow and quiet, and hold the child's arms across his or her chest.

Criterion: The child independently turns his or her head completely from side to side in response to auditory or visual stimuli, and demonstrates this ability several days in a row.

AREA: **25. Gross Motor Skills: Supine**

BEHAVIOR: 25b.   Bends and straightens arms and legs

Materials: Noisemakers on wrist/ankle bands

Procedures:

Move the child's arms and legs rhythmically, then pause and wait for the child to do the movements. Try different starting positions. Stroking the skin on the limbs or stomach may help stimulate movement. Attach wrist/ankle bands with noisemakers that will be activated with movement.

Use in Daily Routines:

Work on this activity several times a day while holding the child. While the child is in the crib, use the noisemakers or attach the wrist/ankle bands with ribbons to an overhead mobile.

(continued)

Adaptations:

> *Visually Impaired:*   See the Visually Impaired Adaptations section of 25a.

> *Hearing Impaired:*   See the Hearing Impaired Adaptations section of item 25a.

> *Motor Impaired:*   If the child with motor impairments has stiff muscles, use relaxation techniques before working on this item. Children with very stiff muscles can work on this activity in a side-lying position. Make the movements as relaxed as possible.

Criterion: The child spontaneously bends and straightens his or her arms and legs, and demonstrates this ability several days in a row.

> AREA: **25.   Gross Motor Skills: Supine**
> BEHAVIOR: 25c.   Brings hands to mouth

Materials: Soft foods, bracelets or mittens, bottle

Procedures:

> Put a small amount of food on the child's thumb and hold it close to his or her mouth. Let the child see and smell the food, and help him or her lick the food off the thumb. A few light finger strokes to the child's mouth may help elicit the movements.

> Place colorful mittens or bracelets on the child's hands to encourage visual inspection of the hands.

> During bottle feeding, place the child's hands on the bottle. From time to time, withdraw the bottle and wait for the child to pull it back.

Use in Daily Routines:

> Incorporate these activities into feeding time.

Adaptations:

> *Visually Impaired:*   See the Visually Impaired Adaptations section of item 25a.

> *Motor Impaired:*   See the Motor Impaired Adaptations section of item 25b.

Criterion: The child spontaneously brings each hand to his or her mouth, demonstrating this ability several days in a row.

> AREA: **25.   Gross Motor Skills: Supine**
> BEHAVIOR: 25d.   Maintains head in midline position while supine

Materials: Any visual and/or auditory stimuli that hold the child's attention, small pillow

---

Procedures:

> Engage the child's attention with his or head in a midline position, and maintain that position. Whether you are using a toy, your face, or a sound, keep the stimulus in the midline. If the child is having difficulty, give assistance in holding the position, then withdraw your assistance as the child takes over. You can also start by placing a small pillow under the child's head.

(continued)

Use in Daily Routines:

       During play sessions, when the child is back-lying, position toys just above the midline of the face. Also, use a pillow for routine positioning if necessary.

Adaptations:

       Visually Impaired: See the Visually Impaired Adaptations section of item 25a.

       Motor Impaired: If the muscles of a child with motor impairments become stiffer when back-lying, change to a semi-reclining position. Children who become very stiff or arch their backs when back-lying should be kept out of that position as much as possible. A side-lying or semi-reclining position is preferred for these children.

Criterion: The child maintains his or her head in a midline position while lying on the back for at least 30 seconds, and demonstrates this ability several days in a row.

AREA: **25. Gross Motor Skills: Supine**
BEHAVIOR: 25e. Reaches out with arm while in a supine position

Materials: Any visual and/or auditory stimuli that hold the child's attention

---

Procedures:

       Hold an interesting toy in front of and above the child's face and attract his or her attention. If the child does not reach out, briefly touch it to his or her hand, then raise it again.

Use in Daily Routines:

       Suspend a mobile above the child's head. Check the mobile from the child's perspective; some of the commercial ones look interesting only from above. During other play and caregiving routines, look for opportunities to ask for reaching. As soon as the child is ready to make choices, reaching can be used to indicated desired objects.

Adaptations:

       Visually Impaired: See the Visually Impaired Adaptations section of item 25a. Also, let the child with a visual impairment mouth and handle the toy. Remove it, sound the toy, then ask the child to reach for it. This skill may be significantly delayed in a child with total blindness.

       Motor Impaired: With a child with motor impairments start by holding the toy close to his or her chest, then gradually raise it. See positioning note in the Motor Impaired Adaptations section of item 25d.

Criterion: The child independently reaches up for an object that is held at arm's length above his or her face, and demonstrates this ability several times over a number of days.

AREA: **25. Gross Motor Skills: Supine**
BEHAVIOR: 25f. Holds feet in air for play

Materials: Brightly colored booties, bells, or bracelets

(continued)

Procedures:

Place visually and auditorily interesting objects on the child's feet. Lift the child's feet to his or her hands, helping him or her to hold on to the feet, if necessary. Place your hand under the child's bottom to help lift the legs. Invent a game or song using this action and play it several times a day.

Use in Daily Routines:

Practice this activity during clothing or diaper changes.

Adaptations:

Motor Impaired: See the Motor Impaired Adaptations section of item 25d. If the child with motor impairments has stiff muscles, precede this activity with relaxation techniques. A child with weak, floppy muscles (hypotonia) will tend to do this activity by only moving his or her leg joints and not lifting the buttocks from the surface. Help him or her by lifting the buttocks, then releasing your hold.

Criterion: The child independently and spontaneously lifts his or her buttocks off the floor and places his or her feet in his or her hands for play. This ability is demonstrated several times, a number of days in a row.

AREA: **25.   Gross Motor Skills: Supine**
BEHAVIOR: 25g.   Rolls from stomach to back

Materials: Blanket, interesting toys

Procedures:

Entice the child to roll from his or her stomach to back by placing a favorite toy to his or her side, out of arm's reach. Assist, if necessary, by bringing one leg up and over the chest, then waiting for the child to complete the roll. Try starting the child from a side-lying position, then moving the starting position farther back. You can also place the child on a blanket and lift one edge to assist him or her in rolling.

Use in Daily Routines:

When the child needs to be in a prone position, use the rolling procedures rather than just placing him or her in prone. Give plenty of time for the child to organize a response.

Adaptations:

Visually Impaired: See the Visually Impaired Adaptations section of item 25a.

Motor Impaired: If the child with motor impairments is very stiff and uses an arching pattern to roll, precede this activity with a relaxation period, and help the child move slowly, in the correct pattern.

Criterion: The child independently rolls onto his or her stomach from the back by first turning his or her head, then bringing one or both legs across the body, using a rotation of the trunk. The child demonstrates this ability several times, a number of days in a row.

26.

Gross Motor Skills: Upright

EFFICIENT FUNCTIONING IN the upright position is the ultimate goal of motor programming and is based on the strength gained in the prone (on stomach) and supine (on back) positions. For overall program planning, however, it is important to distinguish between the use of upright positioning for motor development and the usefulness of this position to promote cognitive and social development, although these purposes often overlap.

Sitting, for example, is a motor skill that involves strength and balance. The motor activities achieved in the prone position strengthen the muscles, and those done in the sitting position are used to increase balance and control. Sitting is also, however, an important position for promoting cognitive and social development; it provides children with a wider view of the world around them, different experiences with object manipulation, and greater opportunity for social interaction. Sitting will only serve these functions, though, if the head can move freely and the hands are free for play, not used for support. A child who must use his or her hands for support should be placed in the appropriate supportive seating devices for cognitive and social activities.

Many children will never achieve independence in standing or walking, but they will need experiences in fully upright positions. A physical or occupational therapist can provide advice on the use of prone standers or other types of equipment that allow children to be as upright as possible, while providing sufficient support to make the position functional for school or play activities.

Sequences 26–I. through 26–IV. contain the same items found in the Gross Motor Activities: Upright sequences in the original curriculum (Johnson-Martin, Jens, Attermeier, 1986); however, the sequences in this edition have been rearranged to correspond with *The Carolina Curriculum for Preschoolers with Special Needs* (Johnson-Martin, Attermeier, & Hacker, 1990).

REFERENCES

Johnson-Martin, N.M., Attermeier, S.M., & Hacker, B. (1990). *The Carolina curriculum for preschoolers with special needs*. Baltimore: Paul H. Brookes Publishing Co.
Johnson-Martin, N., Jens, K.G., & Attermeier, S.M. (1986). *The Carolina curriculum for handicapped infants and infants at risk*. Baltimore: Paul H. Brookes Publishing Co.

26.   Gross Motor Skills: Upright

a.   Holds head steady when held
b.   Holds trunk steady when held at hips
c.   Moves to a sitting position from stomach or all-fours position
d.   Sits alone
e.   Pulls self to standing position
f.   Steps sideways holding a support

g.   Stoops to pick up a toy while holding a support
h.   Removes hands from support and stands independently
i.   Takes independent steps
j.   Moves from hands and knees, to hands and feet, to standing

AREA: **26.   Gross Motor Skills: Upright**
BEHAVIOR: 26a.   Holds head steady when held

Materials: Any visual stimuli that hold the child's attention

Procedures:

Hold the child with his or her head unsupported. If necessary, keep your hand near the base of the child's skull, ready to hold the head in position. Present interesting visual stimuli, such as bright pictures, toys, or masks. Strive for a symmetrical midline position as well as for the child to have the ability to turn to the right and left.

Note: The importance of work on this item cannot be over-emphasized. Head control is the basis of further postural development as well as visual-motor co-ordination.

Use in Daily Routines:

Use this procedure as much as possible throughout the day, whenever holding or carrying the child. Carrying the child in the "face out" position is a good way to promote head control.

Adaptations:

Visually Impaired: Pay particular attention to the position of the upper trunk with a child with visual impairments. Try to prevent the child from letting his or her head and shoulders slope forward.

Motor Impaired: A child with motor impairments will often prefer to cuddle into an adult's shoulder, rather than lift his or her head. For this child, it is particularly important to emphasize independent head control. He or she will also need special positioning for activities requiring visual attention or arm use.

Criterion: The child holds his or her head erect and steady while in an upright position for at least 2 minutes, and can turn to the right and left. The child is able to do this consistently over a period of several days.

AREA: **26.   Gross Motor Skills: Upright**
BEHAVIOR: 26b.   Holds trunk steady when held at hips

Materials: None required

Procedures:

Carry the child with support at the hips. Provide support to the trunk with your hand, and withdraw assistance whenever you can. At first, your hand will be higher on the child's trunk; but as the child gains strength, you can move your control down until it is at the child's hips. The "face out" carrying position is also a good way of promoting trunk control. During carrying, encourage the child to turn to his or her right and left.

Use in Daily Routines:

Use the "face out" carrying position routinely throughout the day. Once a child is fairly steady with his or her trunk control, riding on an adult's shoulders could be fun for him or her and beneficial.

(continued)

Adaptations:

> *Motor Impaired:*   See the Motor Impaired Adaptations section of item 26a.

Criterion: The child holds his or her trunk erect and steady for at least 2 minutes, and can turn to the right and left. The child consistently demonstrates this ability, several days in a row.

AREA: **26.   Gross Motor Skills: Upright**
BEHAVIOR: 26c.   Moves to a sitting position from prone or all-fours position

Materials: None required

Procedures:

> If starting from a stomach-lying position, lift the child's hips, wait for him or her to bend the knees under his or her chest, then rotate the child over one hip into a sitting position. If starting from a hands-and-knees position, rotate the child back and over one hip into a sitting position. Give the child plenty of time to participate in the movement.
>
> *Note:*   The child who is rocking on hands and knees is ready to learn to assume a sitting position.

Use in Daily Routines:

> Incorporate this activity into position changes when they occur naturally throughout play or caregiving.

Adaptations:

> *Motor Impaired:*   Extra time and physical assistance may be necessary with a child with motor impairments. A child with severe motor impairments may never achieve independence in assuming a sitting position, however, he or she should still be given the opportunity to control whatever parts of the movement he or she can.

Criterion: The child independently moves from either a prone or a hands-and-knees position to a sitting position, and demonstrates this ability several days in a row.

AREA: **26.   Gross Motor Skills: Upright**
BEHAVIOR: 26d.   Sits alone

Materials: A variety of toys (e.g., some large, some small), low bench

---

Procedures:

> Move the child into a sitting position as in item 26c. Give him or her support either at the hips or slightly above. Provide toys that are small enough to be picked up, or have a mobile at eye level so it can be activated by reaching out.
>
> You can also place a large toy, such as a busy box, on a low bench and position the child in front of it. This will encourage the child to lift his or her arms while keeping a straight back.
>
> Once the child is fairly stable in a sitting position, start placing toys to elicit reaching to the side and rotating to the right and left.

(continued)

If the child's back is rounded, rock the pelvis forward to create a small arch in the child's lower back.

Note: If the child is not progressing in a sitting position, more strengthening of the trunk and hip muscles may be necessary. Supportive chairs should be used for children who need to be sitting for play and social interaction. Such chairs are prescribed by physical and occupational therapists.

Use in Daily Routines:

Use sitting as a play position throughout the day. If necessary, place pillows around the child for light support. Look at other daily activities, such as feeding time, to see if sitting can be used as a functional position. As much as possible, ensure that the child assumes a variety of sitting positions (e.g., cross-legged, both legs to one side, both legs in front, sitting on a low chair).

Adaptations:

Motor Impaired: A child with motor impairments who wants to sit, but lacks adequate postural control, will use various strategies to remain stable. Some children will W-sit (i.e., sit with heels next to hips). If the child has stiff muscles, this position should be discouraged by praising the child for sitting with his or her feet to the front, and by providing a supported seating alternative. If W-sitting is the only sitting option for a child with stiff muscles, make sure that he or she is being regularly checked by an orthopedist, since that position can promote hip dislocation as well as knee and ankle problems. For the child with weak, floppy muscles (hypotonia), W-sitting is not a great orthopedic concern, but usually indicates need for specific strengthening.

A child who sits with his or her back rounded, the head tipped back, and the legs stiffly extended should have his or her posture corrected.

Criterion: The child can sit with his or her trunk erect, with hands free for play, and can rotate from side to side without losing balance. The child can play in this manner for at least 3 minutes, and demonstrates this ability several days in a row.

AREA: **26.   Gross Motor Skills: Upright**
BEHAVIOR: 26e.   Pulls self to standing position

Materials: Favorite toys, low table or couch

Procedures:

Place toys on a low table or couch. Use a variety of starting positions for the child (e.g., sitting, prone, hands-and-knees, kneeling). Show the child where the toys are, and assist him or her, if necessary, in moving up to a standing position. Most children will start by simultaneously straightening both legs. The more mature pattern consists of first kneeling, then placing one foot flat on the floor, and finally, pulling into a standing position.

Use in Daily Routines:

Make a point of placing toys on elevated surfaces. If there is a heavy chest of drawers, place the toys in a partially pulled out drawer. Always make sure that the items being used to pull up on are very stable.

(continued)

Adaptations:

> *Visually Impaired:* For a child with a visual impairment, pair auditory stimuli with brightly colored, shiny, or high contrast visual stimuli. Use toys that make a continuous sound. Physically guide the child through the movement.

> *Motor Impaired:* Observe the leg and foot positioning of the child with motor impairments while doing this activity. If the child only stands on tiptoes or always keeps his or her knees pulled together, correct the position with your hands and consult a therapist. Some tiptoe standing is normal, and all children should be able to rise up on their toes. If the child has stiff muscles, make sure that he or she follows the tiptoe position with a flat-foot position.

Criterion: The child can independently pull to a standing position by first placing one foot on the floor, and demonstrates this ability several times a day for a number of days.

AREA: 26. Gross Motor Skills: Upright
BEHAVIOR: 26f. Steps sideways holding a support

Materials: Favorite toys, low table or couch

Procedures:

> With the child standing at a support, place toys several inches out of his or her reach, so that he or she will take sideways steps to get to them. Do this to both sides, gradually increasing the distance at which toys are placed. At first, the child will lean against the support, then will stand upright, using only hand contact. Once the child is able to easily step sideways, position the toys to elicit stepping around the corner of the support.

Use in Daily Routines:

> See the Use in Daily Routines section of item 26e.

Adaptations:

> *Visually Impaired:* Move the toys only a few inches at a time with a child with a visual impairment. Make sure that the child actually obtains the toy each time. Repeat this routine many times, with the toys in the same location and the child in the same starting position.

> *Motor Impaired:* See the Motor Impaired Adaptations section of item 26e.

Criterion: The child can step freely along a support and around corners, using light hand support, for several minutes at a time, over a number of days.

AREA: 26. Gross Motor Skills: Upright
BEHAVIOR: 26g. Stoops to pick up a toy while holding a support

Materials: Favorite toys, low table or couch

(continued)

Procedures:

While the child is playing in a standing position at a support, take a toy and place it on the floor. Give light assistance, if necessary, to help the child retrieve the toy and return to upright position. If the child cannot reach down all the way to the floor, place the toy on a low stool at first. Make sure that the child bends at the knees, not at the waist, and that he or she keeps the feet flat on the floor while holding onto the support with one hand. Place the toys to the right and left.

Use in Daily Routines:

This activity can be incorporated into many fine motor, cognitive, and language activities, such as stacking blocks, sorting, matching, and naming objects.

Adaptations:

Visually Impaired: For a child with a visual impairment, pair auditory stimuli with brightly colored, shiny, or high contrast visual stimuli. Use toys that make a continuous sound, and physically guide the child through the movement. It is critical to keep all toys in their same predictable location for many repetitions.

Motor Impaired: Strive for performance like that illustrated in Figure 2 (pp. 36–37) for the child with motor impairments. Give the child physical assistance to obtain correct body position. Alternate between a squatting position and rising onto the toes.

Criterion: The child can independently pick up a toy from the floor and return to a standing position while maintaining support with one hand. The child can do this several times in a row, over a number of days.

AREA: 26.   Gross Motor Skills: Upright
BEHAVIOR: 26h.   Removes hands from support and stands independently

Materials: Small toys, low table or couch

Procedures:

While the child is standing at a support, offer a toy that must be grasped with both hands, or play two-handed games with the child. Offer light hand support, if necessary, then gradually withdraw it. It is usually best to speak quietly and not call attention to the fact that the child is standing. You can also kneel in front of the child, away from any furniture, and use the above procedures.

Use in Daily Routines:

Place the child in a standing position for dressing and eating snacks. Keep the child's attention on the functional activity, rather than the act of standing.

Adaptations:

Motor Impaired: Try to assist the child with motor impairments to stand as straight as possible, with both feet flat on the floor, and his or her ankles in a normal position. Children with severe motor impairments may never achieve independent standing. In this case, provide these children with alternatives, such as a prone stander. Consult a physical therapist for advice.

(*continued*)

Criterion: The child can stand alone for at least 30 seconds, and demonstrates this several times, for a number of days in a row.

AREA: **26. Gross Motor Skills: Upright**
BEHAVIOR: 26i. Takes independent steps

Materials: None required

Procedures:

Place the child in a standing position, either between two adults or against a wall. Encourage the child to take steps by holding your arms out—at first, just a few feet away. Gradually increase the distance between you and the child.

You can also hold one of the child's hands while walking, then gradually loosen your grip.

Use in Daily Routines:

Set up play spaces so that favorite objects are on tables or shelves a few feet apart.

Adaptations:

Visually Impaired: Walking alone is often delayed in children with visual impairments. This activity will require more perseverance on your part. Practice repeatedly in a familiar, predictable play space. Consider using a playpen or corner of a room. Try standing the child on your feet and walking together to convey the idea.

Motor Impaired: The nature of the child's motor impairment will determine whether independent walking is possible. Consult a physical therapist about each child's potential and adaptive aids that may assist a child to walk.

Criterion: The child can walk alone for 5–10 feet, and consistently does this several days in a row.

AREA: **26. Gross Motor Skills: Upright**
BEHAVIOR: 26j. Moves from hands and knees, to hands and feet, to standing

Materials: None required, but favorite toys may be helpful

Procedures:

Move to a clear space on the floor and entice the child to stand by offering your hands or a toy. Give physical assistance, if necessary, by standing behind the child and helping him or her with limb movements.

Use in Daily Routines:

When feasible, take time to use this procedure rather than picking the child up into a standing position.

Adaptations:

Motor Impaired: Take care to guide the child with motor impairments through the movement, with his or her weight being balanced over the feet. This activity should be done

(*continued*)

even with a child with a serious impairment, in order to train him or her to assist in position changes.

Criterion: The child independently moves from a hands-and-knees position to a standing position and remains steadily standing for at least several seconds. The child routinely uses this as a method of attaining a standing position, rather than creeping over to a support and pulling him- or herself up.

Gross Motor Skills: Upright
Posture and locomotion

26. Gross Motor Skills: Upright
I. Posture and locomotion

a. Walks sideways
b. Walks backward
c. Squats in play

d. Runs stiffly
e. Runs well

AREA: **26–I.   Gross Motor Skills: Upright   Posture and locomotion**
BEHAVIOR: 26–Ia.   Walks sideways

Materials: Table, small toys, pulltoys

Procedures:

Have the child push small toys along a table, an activity that will require him or her to step sideways. Hold the child's hands and walk sideways with him or her. Or, set up a narrow path to a desired toy through which the child must walk sideways. Or, hold one of the child's hands and place a pulltoy rope in the other one. Guide the child as he or she walks sideways pulling the toy.

Use in Daily Routines:

Incorporate walking sideways into songs and games throughout the day.

Adaptations:

Visually Impaired: Provide an auditory or bright visual goal for the child with a visual impairment. Introduce "trailing" for short distances by having the child place both hands on the wall, taking sideways steps to a nearby location.

Criterion: The child independently takes several sideways steps while playing, using this ability several times a day, for a number of days in a row.

AREA: **26–I.   Gross Motor Skills: Upright   Posture and locomotion**
BEHAVIOR: 26–Ib.   Walks backward

Materials: Pulltoys

Procedures:

Show the child how to pull a toy while walking backward, giving only necessary physical guidance. You can also stand in front of the child and encourage him or her to take backward steps with gentle touches on his or her chest.

Use in Daily Routines:

Incorporate the above activities several times throughout the day.

Adaptations:

Visually Impaired: Make sure that the pulltoy that is used in this activity produces an interesting sound for the child with a visual impairment.

Criterion: The child independently takes several steps backward while playing, and does this several times a day, for a number of days in a row.

AREA: **26–I. Gross Motor Skills: Upright Posture and locomotion**
BEHAVIOR: 26–Ic. Squats in play

Materials: Small and medium sized toys, cause-and-effect toys

---

Procedures:

Place toys out in the middle of the floor and have the child squat to pick them up. Or, place a cause-and-effect toy, such as a xylophone or busy box, on the floor and guide the child into a squatting position for play. Another way to get the child to squat would be to play a game in which the child walks under tables or through tunnels in the squatting position. Make sure that the child's feet are flat on the floor, his or her knees are bent to about 90° and well separated from each other, and the trunk is horizontal.

Use in Daily Routines:

Look for opportunities throughout the day to have the child pick up objects from the floor for you.

Adaptations:

Visually Impaired: For a child with total blindness, use toys that produce a constant sound cue. For the child with a minimal visual impairment, use brightly colored toys on a floor of a different color. Teach the child to tactilely or visually search for toys while in a squatting position.

Motor Impaired: Give physical assistance to a child with motor impairments as necessary to achieve the squatting position. This is a good activity to do with children who are at risk for developing tightness in leg muscles.

Criterion: The child spontaneously squats down and remains in that position for 5–10 seconds while playing and uses this as a play position several days in a row.

AREA: **26–I. Gross Motor Skills: Upright Posture and locomotion**
BEHAVIOR: 26–Id. Runs stiffly

Materials: Ball, small wheeled toys

Procedures:

Roll a ball or push a small wheeled toy across the floor and demonstrate how to run after it. Encourage the child to imitate you.

Use in Daily Routines:

Repeat this activity several times throughout the day in different settings.

Adaptations:

Visually Impaired: When attempting this activity with a child with a visual impairment, go to a large open area that has an even floor surface. Establish a game of running while holding each other's hands from one landmark to another. Progess to having the child start at one landmark and run alone, following a sound such as your voice or a familiar toy.

Criterion: The child spontaneously runs 3–5 feet with legs stiffly held and feet widely spaced. Arms may be held up and out to the side. The child easily demonstrates this ability, several days in a row.

AREA: **26–I.   Gross Motor Skills: Upright   Posture and locomotion**
BEHAVIOR: 26–Ie.   Runs well

Materials: Ball, small wheeled toys

Procedures:

See Procedures section of item 26–Id.

Note: The running pattern will naturally mature as the child practices with a variety of activities. If you see excessive falling, consult a physical therapist. Note whether the child protects him- or herself against hitting his or her head when falling (children who hit their heads need to wear protective helmets).

Use in Daily Routines:

See Use in Daily Routines section of item 26–Id.

Adaptations:

Visually Impaired: This behavior may be delayed or achieved only minimally by a child with total blindness.

Criterion: The child spontaneously runs 5–10 feet without falling, landing on flat feet, keeping trunk upright, and moving the arms only a little. He or she easily demonstrates this ability, several days in a row.

26–II.

Gross Motor Skills: Upright
Stairs

26. Gross Motor Skills: Upright
II. Stairs

a. Walks up stairs with railing, same-step foot placement

b. Walks down stairs with railing, same-step foot placement

c. Walks up stairs without railing, same-step foot placement

d. Walks down stairs without railing, same-step foot placement

AREA: 26–II. Gross Motor Skills: Upright Stairs
BEHAVIOR: 26–IIa. Walks up stairs with railing, same-step foot placement

Materials: A set of at least three steps that are 6″ high, and about 6″ deep, and have a railing

---

Procedures:

Position yourself close to the child at first, before he or she begins to walk up the stairs. Start the climb by having the child face the railing, holding on with both hands. As the child gains confidence, he or she will let go of the railing with one hand and face forward, up the steps.

Use in Daily Routines:

When time permits, use the above procedure rather than carrying the child up stairs.

Adaptations:

Motor Impaired: If the child with motor impairments has one leg that is stronger than the other, the stronger leg will be placed on the first step when going up the stairs. From time to time, assist the child in reversing this pattern. If the child's motor impairment prevents him or her from walking up stairs, consult a physical therapist for an alternate strategy.

Criterion: The child uses one hand on the railing while walking up at least three stairs, using same-step foot placement. He or she spontaneously does this activity over a period of several days.

AREA: 26–II. Gross Motor Skills: Upright Stairs
BEHAVIOR: 26–IIb. Walks down stairs with railing, same-step foot placement

Materials: A set of at least three stairs that are 6″ high, about 6″ deep, and have a railing

---

Procedures

Position yourself close to the child at first, before you begin to walk down the stairs. Start the descent by having the child face the railing, holding on with both hands. As the child gains confidence, he or she will let go of the railing with one hand and face forward, down the steps.

If the child is fearful, start by using the bottom step only, then gradually adding steps.

Use in Daily Routines:

When time permits, use the above procedure rather than carrying the child down stairs.

Adaptations:

Motor Impaired: If the child with motor impairments has one leg that is stronger than the other, the weak leg will be placed on the first step when going down the stairs. From time to time assist the child in reversing this pattern. If the child's motor impairment prevents him or her from walking down stairs, consult a physical therapist for an alternate strategy.

Criterion: The child uses one hand on the railing while walking down at least three stairs, using same-step foot placement. He or she spontaneously does this activity over a period of several days.

AREA: **26–II. Gross Motor Skills: Upright   Stairs**
BEHAVIOR: 26–IIc.   Walks up stairs without railing, same-step foot placement

Materials: A set of at least three stairs that are 6″ high, about 6″ deep, and have no railing

Procedures:

> Position the child on the stairs. Stand behind him or her and offer light support at the hips. Gradually withdraw support as the child gains confidence.

> Look for varying heights of stairs in the environment on which the child can practice. If he or she is having difficulty with balance, use lower and fewer stairs at first. You can also place books on the floor onto which the child can step up.

Use in Daily Routines:

> Practice this activity as described above in naturally occurring situations, indoors and out. Let the child step up onto curbs and other low surfaces.

Adaptations:

> *Visually Impaired:*   Use stairs with which the child with a visual impairment has become very familiar by crawling. Use the Sighted Guide technique: the child grasps an adult's finger as the adult ascends one step ahead of the child.

> *Motor Impaired:*   See the Motor Impaired Adaptations of item 26–IIa.

Criterion: The child walks up at least three stairs, without using a railing, using same-step foot placement. He or she spontaneously does this activity over a period of several days.

AREA: **26–II. Gross Motor Skills: Upright   Stairs**
BEHAVIOR: 26–IId.   Walks down stairs without railing, same-step foot placement

Materials: A set of at least three stairs that are 6″ high, about 6″ deep, and have no railing

Procedures:

> Position the child on the stairs and give him or her light support at the hips. Gradually withdraw support as the child gains confidence. If the child is fearful, start with just the bottom stair, then gradually add stairs.

Use in Daily Routines:

> Practice this activity as described above in naturally occurring situations, indoors and out. Let the child step down from curbs and other low surfaces.

Adaptations:

> *Visually Impaired:*   Use stairs with which the child with a visual impairment is very familiar. Depending on the amount of vision that the child has, this item may need to be adapted. Consider using the Sighted Guide technique that was described in the Visually Impaired Adaptations section of item 26–IIc. A child with total blindness or very low vision may not be independent in this task until he or she acquires skills with a protected device, such as a long cane.

> *Motor Impaired:*   See the Motor Impaired Adaptations section of item 26–IIb.

Criterion: The child walks down at least three stairs, without a railing, using same-step foot placement. He or she spontaneously does this activity over a period of several days.

26–III.

Gross Motor Skills: Upright
Jumping

26. Gross Motor Skills: Upright
III. Jumping

a. Jumps off floor with both feet

b. Jumps off step with both feet

AREA: **26–III.   Gross Motor Skills: Upright   Jumping**
BEHAVIOR: 26–IIIa.   Jumps off floor with both feet

Materials: Trampoline, bed, rope

Procedures:

Demonstrate how to jump up off the floor. While holding the child's hands let him or her try the activity. Starting on a bouncy surface such as a bed or trampoline will give the child a chance to practice the timing and to build up some strength and endurance. You can also place a rope or other marking on the floor and ask the child to jump over it.

Use in Daily Routines:

Practice this item during active times of the day, incorporating it into games or songs.

Adaptations:

Visually Impaired: Stand behind the child with a visual impairment and jump along with him or her, so he or she can feel the movement.

Motor Impaired: If the child with motor impairments has stiff muscles, follow the jumping movements with squatting (i.e., with heels on the floor) and then rising slowing onto tiptoes.

Criterion: The child is able to jump 1–2 times with both feet off the floor at the same time, demonstrating this ability several days in a row.

AREA: **26–III.   Gross Motor Skills: Upright   Jumping**
BEHAVIOR: 26–IIIb.   Jumps off step with both feet

Materials: Step that is 6″ high, boards or books of varying thickness

---

Procedures:

Start this item by having the child jump off a board or book that is about 1″ thick, holding one or two hands as necessary. When the child can jump down alone, add another inch of height, working up to 6 inches. Help the child organize the movement by saying, "1–2–3–jump down." Expect that the child will do this activity first by leading with one leg, and later learn to jump with both feet together.

Use in Daily Routines:

Set up various jumping opportunities in the active play area, and incorporate jumping into other gross motor sequences.

Adaptations:

Visually Impaired: Encourage the child with a visual impairment to explore the step by crawling up and down before jumping. Always ask him or her to step up and down the stair 1–3 times, immediately before jumping. Teach the child to feel for the edge of the step with both feet before jumping. Consider doing this task barefoot.

Motor Impaired: See the Motor Impaired Adaptations section of item 26–IIIa.

Criterion: The child independently jumps down from a 6″ step with both feet together, demonstrating this ability several days in a row.

26–IV.

Gross Motor Skills: Upright
Balance

26. Gross Motor Skills: Upright
IV. Balance

a. Stands on one foot while hands are held
b. Walks with one foot on the walking board and one foot on the floor

c. Stands on one foot without help
d. Walks on line, following general direction

AREA: **26–IV.   Gross Motor Skills: Upright   Balance**
BEHAVIOR: 26–IVa.   Stands on one foot while hands are held

Materials: Music, shoes, socks, pants, ball

Procedures:

Hold the child's hands as you encourage him or her to lift a leg to music or to kick a
ball. Try to get him or her to lift each leg. When the child can confidently lift both legs,
demonstrate standing on one leg. Encourage the child to imitate you.

Use in Daily Routines:

During dressing and undressing, have the child hold on to you and lift a foot to put
on his or her pants, pajamas, shoes, and socks.

Adaptations:

Visually Impaired: For the child with low vision, provide an easily seen target for foot
placement (e.g., a mylar balloon, fluorescent pattern, bright light). This task may be quite
delayed in a child with total blindness.

Motor Impairment: Make sure that the child with motor impairments maintains proper
foot contact with the floor (i.e., heels should stay down, and the foot should not roll
inward).

Criterion: With hands held, the child is able to raise one foot off the floor and hold it up for 2–3
seconds, demonstrating this ability several days in a row. (Record right and left feet separately.)

AREA: **26–IV.   Gross Motor Skills: Upright   Balance**
BEHAVIOR: 26–IVb.   Walks with one foot on the walking board and one foot on the floor

Materials: Walking board that is 6' long, 2½" wide, 4" high; books

---

Procedures:

Demonstrate walking with one foot on the walking board and one foot on the floor.
Let the child try the activity and, if necessary, give physical assistance. If the child is
having difficulty balancing, remove the supporting blocks that are under the board and
place the board on the floor. Books of various thickness can also be placed on the floor to
practice this skill. The child should practice this activity with the right leg on the board, as
well as the left leg.

Use in Daily Routines:

Use environmental structures such as curbs or other low surfaces to practice this
skill throughout the day.

Adaptations:

Visually Impaired: Try having the child with a visual impairment do this task barefooted
to enhance his or her tactile information. Provide a permanent landmark at each end of the
board to assist the child and add a meaningful sound cue, such as a musical toy, as the
goal.

(continued)

Motor Impaired: More control is demanded of the "board" leg than the "floor" leg, so this activity may be difficult for a child with motor impairments if he or she does not have equal control of both legs. Work for a smooth ascent and descent of the board leg.

Criterion: The child walks the full length of a walking board with one foot on the board and one on the floor, and demonstrates this ability several days in a row. (Record right and left leg separately.)

AREA: **26–IV. Gross Motor Skills: Upright   Balance**
BEHAVIOR: 26–IVc.   Stands on one foot without help

Materials: Music, shoes, socks, pants, stairs

Procedures:

Use the activities that are listed under item 26–IVa., but withdraw hand support and require gradually longer periods of balance.

Use in Daily Routines:

See the Use in Daily Routines section of item 26–IVa. Also, practice walking up and down stairs without a railing.

Adaptations:

Visually Impaired: See the Visually Impaired Adaptations section of item 26–IVa.

Motor Impaired: See the Motor Impaired Adaptations section of 26–IVa.

Criterion: The child is able to lift one foot off the floor and hold it for 1–2 seconds, demonstrating this ability several days in a row. (Record right and left legs separately.)

AREA: **26–IV. Gross Motor Skills: Upright   Balance**
BEHAVIOR: 26–IVd.   Walks on line, following general direction

Materials: 10' line painted or taped on floor, two 6' long boards, footprints or other designs on floor

---

Procedures:

Demonstrate walking along a straight path, either on floor markings or between two boards that are placed on the floor. If the child is having problems balancing, start with boards that are placed 12"–14" apart, and move them closer together as the child gains control.

Note: This item relates only to balance and motor control, not to following specific directions or responding to particular materials. If necessary, you can pass the child by simple observation of gait pattern; consult a physical therapist for guidance.

Use in Daily Routines:

Incorporate this activity into games using imagery of going over a bridge, imitating animals, or similar activities.

(continued)

Adaptations:

> *Visually Impaired:*   For the child with sufficient functional vision, use bright or fluorescent floor markings. For the child with total blindness, observe him or her pushing a cart along a clear quiet hallway toward a meaningful auditory goal.
>
> *Motor Impaired:*   Make sure that the child with motor impairments has a safe means of falling before working on balance activities. The most important consideration is for the child to not hit his or her head on the floor.

Criterion: The child independently walks along a 10′ line, generally keeping the feet on either side of the line, and 4″–6″ apart, and demonstrates this ability several days in a row.

appendix

Object Boards as Aids for Teaching Children with Severe Motor Impairments

S OME CHILDREN WITH severe motor impairments may be unable to indicate their needs or to demonstrate their knowledge through reaching, pointing, or vocalizing in the ways that infants and toddlers normally do. For months, or even years, eye gaze may be their primary means of communication. They may be able to answer the questions "Where's Mama?" or "Where's your shoe?" by looking at the correct location, or respond to the question "What do you want?" by looking at either the glass of juice or the piece of bread held up in front of them.

The usefulness of eye gaze as a communication signal is dependent on the ability of another person to "read" the gaze. This becomes increasingly difficult as the number of choices is expanded. Teaching a child with severe motor impairments to gaze in a precise manner so that others can readily determine where the gaze is directed is an important aspect of intervention.

Object boards are an effective way to teach a child precision in eye gaze while also teaching other information. A piece of Plexiglas, approximately 25" × 30" with a 4" × 6" window cut out of the center, makes a useful board. Pieces of Velcro can be attached to the board and to objects so that the objects can be mounted on the board and changed easily. Common arrangements that facilitate "reading" up to four choices are pictured below. The adult positions him- or herself behind the board, looking at the child through the center window. He or she encourages the child to look at all the things on the board and then says, "Look at me." When the child looks at the adult, he or she asks a question (e.g., "Where is the ball?") and observes where the child looks.

In the case of teaching items i., j., and l. in sequence 1 (each involves looking at the correct place for an object after seeing it covered in 1 of 3 places), a handkerchief can be attached to the top of each of three Velcro strips on the board and the object hidden as described in the item. It is left under one cover by attaching it to the remainder of the Velcro under the handkerchief.

The object board can also be used for sorting tasks. For example, a red box and a green box can be attached to two of the Velcro strips. After demonstrating that red forms go in the red box and green forms in the green box, the adult holds up a red form and asks, "Where does this one go?" Shapes can be sorted the same way, having a sample shape drawn on the side of each box.

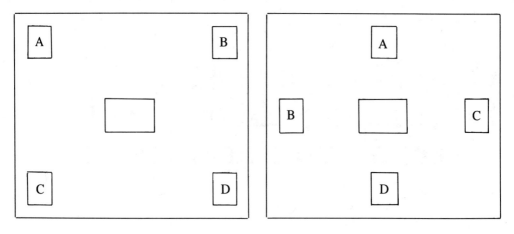

Index